ILLUSIONS OF POWER
NIGERIA IN TRANSITION

JULIUS O. IHONVBERE & TIMOTHY M. SHAW

Africa World Press, Inc.

P.O. Box 1892
Trenton, NJ 08607

P.O. Box 48
Asmara, ERITREA

Africa World Press, Inc.

P.O. Box 1892
Trenton, NJ 08607

P.O. Box 48
Asmara, ERITREA

Copyright © 1998 Julius O. Ihonvbere & Timothy M. Shaw

First Printing 1998

Cover Design: Jonathan Gullery
Book Design: Wanjiku Ngugi

Library of Congress Cataloging-in-Publication

Illusions of power : Nigeria in transition / edited by Julius O.
Ihonvbere & Timothy M. Shaw.
  p.   cm.
Includes bibiliographical references and index.
ISBN 0-86543-641-X. -- ISBN 0-86543-642-8 (pbk.)
1. Political culture--Nigeria. 2. Nigeria--Economic
conditions -- 1960- 3. Nigeria--Politics and government--1960-.
I. Ihonvbere, Julius Omozuanvbo. II. Shaw, Timothy M.
JQ3O96. I58 1998
32-.9669--dc21   97-36556
                                                            CIP

DEDICATION

To the Memory of
Claude Ake (1939-1996)
colleague, comrade and friend

Contents

Nigeria: Key Facts and Figures

Official title:	Federal Republic of Nigeria
Head of State:	General Sani Abacha
Constitution:	a federal republic, comprising a Federal Capital Territory and 36 states, each with a State Governor
Capital:	Abuja (old Federal Capital: Lagos)
Independence:	1 October 1960
Official language:	English (Pidgin, Hausa, Yoruba and Ibo widely spoken. Many other local languages)
Literacy rate:	43%
Surface area:	923,770 km2
Population:	88.5 million (1992) of which: 30% urban, 49% of working age
Growth rate:	3.5% p.a.
per doctor:	9,591
per hospital bed:	1,251
Life expectancy:	51
Human development index:	0.322 (Japan - 0.995; Niger - 0.116)
Infant mortality:	174/1000
Average no. of children:	6.9
School enrolment:	66%
Currency:	Naira $1 = N85 (1997)
GDP:	$100 billion (1980) $21 billion (1990)
Real growth rate:	(1973-85) 0.3%; 6% (1989); 4% (1990)
GNP/capita:	$370 (1987), $200 (1989)
GNP growth rate:	-4.8 (1980-87)
Inflation:	+14% (1986); +20% (1987 estimate)
Investment:	(average 1980-85) -18%
Imports:	$5,755m (1989); $6,215m (1990)
Exports:	$8,285m (1989); $11,070m (1990)
Trade balance:	-$2,060m (1989); -$255m (1990)
Total ODA:	$32 million per annum (1985); $69 million (1987)
Total debt:	$35 billion (1990)
Debt payments:	$6,000m (1990)
Ratio of debt/GNP:	4% (1980); 110% (1987)

**Ratio of debt servicing/
export revenues:** 7.8% (1980); 11.7% (1987)
Principal exports: petroleum (97%) (28% of
GDP), cocoa, gas

Source: *The Courier* (ACP-EC) 106, November-December
1987, 19.
UNDP, *Human Development Report 1990* and *Financial
Times*,"Nigeria Survey", 12 March, 1991.

Acronyms

ABU	Ahmadu Bello University (Zaria)
AFRC	Armed Forces Ruling Council
AP	African Petroleum
ASUU	Academic Staff Union of Universities
BHN	Basic Human Needs
CAFA	Committee for Academic Freedom in Africa
CBN	Central Bank of Nigeria
CD	Campaign for Democracy
CDC	Constitution Drafting Committee
CDHR	Committee for Defense of Human Rights
CDS	Centre for Democratic Studies
CLO	Civil Liberties Organization
CRP	Constitutional Rights Project
DIFRRI	Directorate for Food, Roads and Rural Infrastructure
ECOWAS	Economic Community of West African States
ECOMOG	Economic Community of West African States Monitoring Group
FCT	Federal Capital Territory (Abuja)
FEC	Federal Executive Council
FEDECO	Federal Electoral Commission
FEM	Foreign Exchange Market
FMG	Federal Military Government
GNPP	Great Nigeria People's Party
IBRD	International Bank of Reconstruction and Development (World Bank)
IMF	International Monetary Fund
ING	Interim National Government
IOT	International Observer Team
ISI	Import-Substitution Industrialization
MAMSER	Mass Mobilization for Self-Reliance, Social Justice and Economic Recovery
MOSOP	Movement for the Survival of Ogoni People
MAN	Manufacturers' Association of Nigeria
MOSOP	Movement for the Survival of Ogoni People
NADECO	National Democratic Coalition
NADL	National Association of Democratic Lawyers
NANS	National Association of Nigerian Students
NAP	Nigerian Action Party
NBA	Nigeria Bar Association

NCNC	National Council of Nigeria and the Cameroons
NEC	National Electoral Commission
NEPA	National Electric Power Authority
NGO	Non-Governmental Organization
NIIA	Nigerian Institute for International Affairs
NIC	Newly Industrializing Country
NIC	Newly Influential Country
NISER	Nigerian Institute for Social and Economic Research
NITEL	Nigerian Telecommunications Limited
NLC	Nigerian Labour Congress
NNA	Nigerian National Alliance
NNDP	Nigerian National Democratic Party
NNOC	Nigerian National Oil Corporation
NNPC	Nigerian National Petroleum Corporation
NPA	Nigerian Ports Authority
NNSL	Nigerian National Shipping Line
NPN	National Party of Nigeria
NRC	National Republican Convention
NSO	Nigerian Security Organization
NTV	Nigerian Television
NUJ	Nigeria Union of Journalists
NUPENG	National Union of Petroleum and Natural Gas Workers
NPC	Northern People's Congress
NPP	Nigerian People's Party
NYCOP	National Youth Council of Ogoni People
NYM	Nigerian Youth Movement
NYSC	National Youth Service Council
OIC	Organization of Islamic Countries
OAU	Organization of African Unity
OAU	Obafemi Awolowo University (Ile-Ife)
ODA	Official Development Assistance
ONA	Organization of Nigerians in the Americas
ONN	Organization of Nigerian Nationals
OPEC	Organization of Petroleum Exporting Countries
PEMG	Presidential Election Monitoring Group
PRP	People's Redemption Party
PSP	Peoples Solidarity Party
SAP	Structural Adjustment Program
SDP	Social Democratic Party

SMC	Supreme Military Council
SSS	State Security Service
UNPO	Unrepresented Nations and Peoples Organizations
UN	United Nations
UPGA	United Progressive Grand Alliance
UPN	Unity Party of Nigeria
WAI	War Against Indiscipline
WIN	Women in Nigeria

LIST OF TABLES

ACKNOWLEDGEMENTS

The origin of this book dates back to 1987. Ihonvbere was then at the University of Port Harcourt in Nigeria and Tim Shaw was at Dalhousie. The original chapters have been rewritten several times and new chapters have been added. The ten year delay has been to the benefit of the entire project. Given how rapidly events change in Nigeria, we have had the advantage of updating our materials and information. Our lives have changed significantly since 1987 but our ideas and beliefs have remained almost constant. Nigeria of course has gone through novel policies, contradictions, regimes, and conflicts. Scores of new political movements have emerged in civil society and Nigeria's status as an African power has undergone changes if not modifications. This volume has tried to be as up-to-date as possible.

As we were putting finishing touches to this work, we lost a very dear colleague: Professor Claude Ake. He was one of the 147 passengers and crew killed on November 7, 1996 when a Boeing 727 belonging to the Aviation Development Company (ADC) of Nigeria crashed near Lagos. It is difficult to recount the numerous accomplishments of this great African scholar who left his mark on the content and direction of social science discourse. His death represents a very sad blow to Nigeria's struggle for justice, democracy and stability. It is our hope that his colleagues, friends, and former students will continue to utilize his ideas and extend the boundaries of his academic and political contributions to the growth and development of Nigeria and Africa. We dedicate this work to his memory.

Some of the chapters in this volume have been subjected to academic scrutiny through publication in journals and presentations at learned meetings. We would, in particular like to thank *The Journal of Modern African Studies*. We would also like to thank our numerous friends in Nigeria-journalists, scholars, trade unionists, students, prodemocracy and human rights activists for the continuing faith in the future of Nigeria and for their support for our work over the years. Several of our colleagues and friends have read some of the chapters. We thank them for their comments and suggestions. Ms. Susan Gee of The Governance and Civil Society Unit of The Ford Foundation in New York prepared the camera-ready version of the manuscript. We are indebted to her. Finally, we thank the publisher for doing a great job as usual.

Julius O. Ihonvbere,
Austin, Texas, USA.

Timothy M. Shaw
Dalhousie, Halifax, Canada.

PS: *As we were correcting the copy-edited version of this work, irrepresible Nigerian Afro-beat King, Fela Anikulapo-Kuti (1938-97) died. Fela was undoubtedly the best chronicler of Nigeria's political history, a strong pan-Africanist, social critic, and fearless advocate of social justice and democracy. We would like to dedicate the chapter on "Popular Culture and Civil Society" to his memory.*

INTRODUCTION:
ILLUSIONS OF POWER

a) Preamble: Nigeria as a masquerade

> Nigeria is a complex society, a veritable bundle of
> many potentialities. It is difficult not to think of
> its problems and prospects in superlatives. To live
> and work in Nigeria can easily be an overwhelm-
> ing experience. Trying to understand it can be ex-
> asperating. It becomes obvious how woefully tra-
> ditional concepts of analysis have failed to illumi-
> nate our quest to understand Nigeria when it is
> realized that, despite decades of their use, we seem
> no nearer to achieving our goal (Ekekwe 1986:v)

Nigeria's contemporary history is characterized by illusion:
a populous country where no reliable census had been made
between independence and 1991, a semi-industrialized
economy in which basic infrastructure is unreliable, and a
foreign policy of big claims but minimal performance. In
short, Nigeria has a very distinctive political culture and
political economy unlike that of any other African state
whether in West, Eastern or Southern Africa: great promise
and massive expenditure but disproportionately slim deliv-
ery and reliability. Nigeria is larger than life but smaller
than self-image.

Perhaps the analogy which best captures the country's
illusions is that of the masquerade: a traditional yet "mod-
ernized" public celebration involving disguised dancers and
noisy musicians which frequently becomes coercive. This
traditional form of entertainment and excision - Nigeria's
halloween - has been popularized and vulgarized yet no one
can see the dancers-cum-thieves. Likewise in the political

culture/economy as a whole: the apparent "masquerade" of development, democracy, and direction is a facade hiding real stagnation with consumerism, corporatism and arbitrariness: dreams rather than plans.

The traditional structure of Nigeria, like its dance, has been fundamentally modified since independence without any widespread or sustained agreement on basic values and goals, despite years of military rule and then adjustment and reform. Therefore, development is undirected, sporadic and uneven. The masquerade has to be orchestrated if it is to be transcended and superceded, giving way to a less disorganized and more directed political economy in the twenty-first century. Nigeria cannot become a Newly Influential or Industrializing Country (NIC) unless its national resources are well-managed, -augmented, and -distributed (i.e. minimal corruption, smuggling or aggrandizement). No country has become a NIC without a determined and disinterested state: can the Nigerian bourgeoisie, with its several warring factions, mobilize and manage a social revolution? Structural adjustment adopted in mid-1986 may be a start, but it has to entail political and social as well as economic redirection and renovation. Already UNDP's *Human Development Report 1990* (42) categorizes Nigeria as a country of "mixed opportunities for human development".

Despite all the difficulties and disappointments, however, Nigeria remains a fascinating and friendly place, full of debates and disagreements yet sufficiently well-established and self-absorbed to avoid xenophobic sentiments. Whilst its political culture may at times appear to be chaotic and its political economy anarchic, its history and society remain vibrant and vivid, from the remarkable artists of Oshogbo to the literacy circles of Nsukka and the classic craftsmen of Kano; underneath the appearance of disorder there is a sense of place.

b) Political economy of illusion

In its first 30 years of independence, the political economy of Nigeria has come full-circle, having experienced political change as well as continuity, and economic expansion as well as contraction. By the end of the 1980s the fruits of independence had been tasted by only a few and the lessons of independence learned by even fewer. The high hopes that Africa's largest democracy would be an example for the rest of the continent were dashed in its first decade by political *coups d'etat* and civil war and in its second by economic boom and bust. Hence the uncharacteristic restraint of Nigeria's silver jubilee celebration in 1985 and continued apprehensiveness about the projected return to civilian rule again in 1998 as promised by the rather repressive and unpopular Sani Abacha regime.

This interrelated sequence of political then economic disappointment generated a continuing crisis of political economy in the 1980s ending both the second "democratic" experiment and the "petro-naira" era. The erstwhile parliamentary model and presidential system were both followed by military regimes while the international and industrial ambitions of Africa's aspiring great power were succeeded by a new modesty of achievement and ambition. In short, after endless declarations and debates, following more than 30 years of political and economic proclamations and aspirations, Nigeria in the early 1990s is back to a more modest and realistic set of expectations. With real oil prices down to or even below the levels of the pre-OPEC period, and having experienced a series of unsatisfactory regimes, optimism and idealism had become scarce emotions by the fifth anniversary of President Babangida's accession to power in August 1985. Notwithstanding the rise in oil prices and revenues in 1990, his regime survived its most serious coup attempt in April 1990, only to be forced out of power by popular groups led by the Campaign for Democracy (CD) in August 1993 following the annulment of the June 1993 presidential election.

However, it would be a mistake to conclude that nothing has changed or improved in Africa's most populous and visible state since independence. In Nigeria's first quarter-century, regimes did begin to lay the basis for a more modern and developed political economy by the extension, albeit in a rather hasty and haphazard manner, of roads, ports, airports, communications, education, health and other facilities throughout the federation. To be sure, the costs of these infrastructures and services were highly inflated and their maintenance at best only occasional. Yet the physical if not psychological destruction of the late-1960s civil war (see Table One) was soon repaired and the expansion of the infrastructure accelerated as the oil boom of the early 1970s continued into the very early 1980s. But the high costs and expectations of the first half of the 1970s could not be sus-

tained, especially as the expensive tastes of the Shagari administration were unsupportable no matter how high the
price of oil. The second period of democratic experimenta-
tion, from 1979 to the last day of 1983, was hardly sustainable given the excessive level of personal aggrandizement
and political irresponsibility. The presidential system could
no better discipline itself than its parliamentary predecessor: corruption and accumulation reached new peaks under
Shagari. Hence the massiveness of the expenditures and
the modesty of the results as revealed in military-instigated
investigations. Hence a national boom in personal accumulation rather than collective goods.

Thus, although the return of the officers on New Year's
Eve 1983 may appear to be a replay of the Ironsi-Gowon
succession to Balewa in 1966 (see Table One), in fact the socio-
economic context and culture was quite transformed: an aristocratic society has now become more bourgeois. The after-
shocks of civil war were still reverberating, while today the
gap between incomes and expectations has grown out of
proportion. In short, the general African crisis of the "lost
decade" of the 1980s had particular if postponed manifestations in Nigeria: the civil war was followed by droughts and
the oil bonanza was succeeded by "forex" shortages. The
considerable challenge facing the successive Buhari and
Babangida military regimes from the mid-1980s was how to
resolve and reduce such contrasts and contradictions: structural adjustment with or without a human face? To date,
their record, like that of the lengthy Gowon period (Elaigwu
1986), has been mixed at best. Lackluster economic indicators have hardly been helpful for political reorganization;
hence the delay in the return to civilian rule from 1990 to
1992, and the early 1990 coup attempt.

Much of the analysis of Nigeria has been both orthodox
and imported, just like so much of its culture and consumption. This has been so in terms of economics and politics
alike and within both established "modernization" and "materialist" approaches. Just as palm oil has been succeeded by fuel oil as the primary source of Nigerian dependence so imported modernization perspectives have been
followed by unmodified materialist analyses. Moreover, the
traditional separation of economics from politics found in
both modes - economic determinism in the latter, political
domination in the former - is unhelpful given the intrinsic
interrelationship between the two, particularly over the last

decade. Thus, officially-sponsored and continuing economic and political debates in contemporary Nigeria have a certain static quality to them: the artificial dichotomies of economics and politics on the one hand and of modernization and materialism on the other. The pervasive "cargo cult" extends to analysis as well as to artifacts: "capitalism" and "socialism" do not exhaust the range of possibilities in Nigeria in the 1990s and beyond.

Table 1.1 - Political Regimes in Nigeria

1861 - 1900	*Lagos Colony* proclaimed followed by Delta, Niger(1885) and Oil Rivers (1887) Protectorates under Royal Niger Company rule
1900 - 1914	*Protectorates of Southern and Northern Nigeria*
1914 - 1947	*Merger into Colony and Protectorate of Nigeria*
1922	*Clifford Constitution*
1947 - 1951	*Richards Constitution* with one legislature and three regional councils
1951 - 1954	*Macpherson Constitution* based on consultancies with Nigerians and with a strong central legislature and ministerial government
1954 - 1957	*Robertson Constitution* allowed limited self-government in the Eastern and Western regions.
1957 - 1959	*Self-government* in Eastern and Western Nigeria and then Northern Nigeria
1960 - 1966	*First independent federal government* under Tafawa Balewa with three regional legislatures and premiers. 1963 Nigeria becomes *federal republic* with non-executive president.
1966	*First military regime* under Aguiyi-Ironsi

.....Table 1.1 continued

1966 - 1975	*Second military regime* under Yakubu Gowon, including 1967-70 civil war, with Supreme Military and Federal Executive Councils
1975 - 1976	*Third military regime* under Murtala Mohammed with SMC, FEC and National Council of States
1976 - 1979	*Fourth military regime* under Olusegun Obasanjo
1979 - 1983	*Second civilian republic* under Shehu Shagari as first executive president
1984 - 1985	*Fifth military regime* under Muhammadu Buhari with Supreme Military Council
1985-1993	*Sixth military regime* under Ibrahim Babangida with Armed Forces Ruling Council, Council of Ministers and National Council of States
1993	Interim Government under Chief Ernest Shonekan
1993	*Seventh Military regime* under Sani Abacha with Provisional Ruling Council, Federal Executive Council, and Council of State.

If there are any lessons to be learned from post-independence Nigeria it is that such artificial dichotomies cannot be sustained in analysis, policies or praxis; the political "superstructure" *is* in a dialectical (i.e. two-, not one-, way) relationship to the economic "substructure" and political relations are integrally connected to economic production. Thus simplistic notions of capitalism or socialism, or of democracy and authoritarianism, let alone civilian versus military rule, cannot be sustained, particularly in Nigeria, for its vibrancy and diversity confound *any* monocausal explanation. Moreover, any approach which excluded notions of culture, ecology and gender (WIN 1986) excludes crucial variables: the rich tapestry of Nigerian life, its distinctive environmental zones and the continued resilience of Nigerian women.

In short, any case study of Nigeria presents challenges to a variety of assumptions and assertions. Particulars of the country's future are thus quite unpredictable although past actions and experiences impose their own general imprint. It is symptomatic of Nigeria's status and aura that it challenges and confounds so many approaches and scenarios, almost all of which have been official policies or palavers at one time or another. Africa's self-proclaimed "great power" will remain controversial whether it realizes its ambitions or not; it can hardly be less than *primus inter pares*. Hence the timeliness and distinctiveness of this book: a reflective overview of political economy as both analysis and praxis which incorporates novel elements such as gender, ecology and the so-called "informal sector" and which reflects on the continuous cycles of economics and politics. As Nigeria once again contemplates and debates a return to civilian rule, however circumscribed by both military and economy, so its citizens and friends need historical and contextual insights.

c) **Perspective**

Reflective of Nigeria's distinctive position in Africa is the extensive literature on its political economy and political culture by Nigerians and foreigners alike. Again, unlike some African studies, this field is by no means a monopoly of expatriates; rather, endless debates among Nigerians themselves on a variety of issues are indicative of a vibrant intellectual and cultural milieu with its lengthy genesis in pre- as well as post-colonial times. In general, the early generations of Nigerian scholars were quite orthodox in disposition as was their country and the field as a whole. But as post-independence African problems and disappointments have intensified so more progressive and radical indigenous analysts have followed expatriates' leads or charted their autonomous directions. Yet, as indicated already, some of such progressive perspectives have their limits largely because they typically and uncritically adopt global or comparative frameworks for the specific Nigerian formation. And, despite some appearances to the contrary, the majority of Nigerian scholars do have a conservative disposition even if it is masked by energetic and nationalistic articulation: an irrepressible media and populace.

Although Nigeria is located at the global periphery its particular social structure is not a given: no simplistic product of *dependencia*. Rather, it is the product of history, geography, and technology, of peoples, resources and relations. And in such a complex and dynamic context, analysis is always problematic, in danger of being overtaken by events. Yet structural continuities are as important as superficial changes despite periodization being based typically on political rather than economic cycles.

There are indeed some continuities as well as changes in Nigeria's contemporary situation: preoccupations with economic growth, especially oil, with ethnic balances, particularly regional and religious, and with social development, notably education and communication. On the one hand, political changes will tend to occur more frequently than socio-economic, and personal ambitions will remain constrained by current decrees for only brief periods. On the other hand, there is a continual attempt to redefine the parameters of the national political economy to make it more responsive and responsible: creeping institutionalization sometimes juxtaposed with deregulation. Nigeria may continue to experience economic shocks and political upsets but the civil war is unlikely to be repeated. Indeed, class rather than ethnic inequalities are more likely to be the catalysts of change in the future if not in the past. Despite difficulties in organization and articulation, the urban un- and under-employed along with workers, students, women and other organized groups sometimes come together in a tenuous populist coalition against the *nouveaux riches*, traditional aristocrats and political elites.

Nigeria's version of patriarchal power is symbolized by the ubiquitous "Kaduna mafia" (Takaya & Tyoden [eds] 1987), which resists, even rejects, the claims of "civil society." Successive post-independence state policies have been designed to head-off such a confrontation which economic contraction renders more plausible: "defensive radicalism" or populism (Ake 1978 and 1981b). Buhari and Babangida imposed the fiscal medicine which Shagari's anarchic polity prescribed but failed to administer. The Structural Adjustment Program (SAP) as defined by the World Bank (IBRD) but on Nigeria's terms - i.e. without International Monetary Fund (IMF) finance - was agreed and formally commenced in mid-1986. The record of an uncoordinated implementation of SAP conditionalities have been painful, unhappy and unstable (Adeotun 1989 and 1990). Without safety nets, non-bourgeois forces have borne the brunt while speculators, smugglers, drug traffickers, bureaucrats, importers, and military officers have reaped the gains.

The sequence has not only generated a considerable literature and debate, it has also exposed deficiencies in established perspectives and policies. Any satisfying explanation of people's survival let alone collective development must fully appreciate and incorporate a range of old and new elements. Attention to workers should not be at the expense of peasants; analysis of men cannot exclude that of women; and approaches to production, distribution and accumulation must not overlook the vulnerability of the ecology. In short, a more holistic perspective on this as other case studies is an imperative if continuities are to be identified along with changes.

To be sure, Nigeria is a society in a hurry - such impatience is palpable whenever one ventures out onto the terrifying road system - and yet the short sequences of political and economic shifts take place in a society which is also acutely conscious and respectful of tradition and history. The dialectic of change and continuity is thus central and dynamic, leading to new syntheses and connections. Each period is distinguished by a novel yet inherited pattern of social relations, from the conservative aristocracy of the Balewa administration to the orthodox technocracy of the Babangida dispensation, with the "Kaduna Mafia" being less influential under Shagari and Buhari than the latter (Takaya & Tyoden [eds] 1987) but never really out of power. Yet, the Abacha regime has introduced new debates, new pressures, new challenges and contradictions which are bound to culminate in a drastic restructuring of power, politics, and production relations. In general, shifts of emphasis and influence have been contained within established adaptive institutions. Acronyms may change, but substance continues.

Thus each regime and period is distinctive yet comparable - from the caution of Balewa and the corruption of Gowon through the reformism of Mohammed/Obasanjo and the rapaciousness of the Second Republic, to the repression and arrogant insensitivity of Babangida and Abacha. The authoritarianism of Buhari/Babangida/Abacha marked a return to earlier military motifs with austerity and modesty being the economic correlates. Yet despite "oil gloom" rather than boom, Nigeria's political economy continues to attract external attentions; and student, worker, gender, regional and religious interests within civil society continue to demand internal actions. Some contradictions are contained or resolved - e.g. the call under Shagari for the proliferation of states died an early death (Ekekwe 1986) and yet resulted not only in Babangida's pair - Katsina and Akwa-Ibom - but in a final 30 in late-1991- and in another five in 1996-as the value of the naira given its roller-coaster exchange rate with the dollar and other major currencies has continued to impose severe constraints on state expenditure.

The series of supposedly popular "debates" initiated by the state - economic strategy, housing policy, foreign policy and political future - reveal considerable continuity as well as change among both advocates and issues. The inconclusive austerity drives of the previous Shagari and Buhari regimes - from "Green" and "Ethical" Revolutions to "War against Indiscipline" (WAI) and "Mass Mobilization for Self-Reliance, Social Justice and Economic Recovery" (MAMSER) and War Against Indiscipline and Corruption (WAI-C)- led to Nigeria's version of complex debt renegotiations and incremental naira devaluations. The collective logic and class appeal of structural adjustment - the familiar set of reforms, including deregulation, privatization, devaluation, desubsidization etc. (Carnpbell & Loxley 1989) - was opposed because of resistance to external dependence and reluctance among elite elements (Ihonvbere 1988, 1994). The redefinition of foreign policy has been advanced to reflect internal interests as well as external conditions.

Table 1.2 - Regions in Nigeria

1900	Two protectorates and one colony
1906	Two protectorates
1914	Colony and protectorate of Nigeria
1947	Three regions with 24 states
1963	Four regions, with creation of Mid-West
1967	Twelve states
1976	Nineteen states plus Federal Capital Territory at Abuja
1987	Twenty-one states plus Federal Capital Territory
1991	Thirty states plus Federal Capital Territory
1996	Thirty six states plus Federal Capital Territory

And political debates, official and unofficial, revived notions of confederalism, consociationalism and dyarchy as well as of socialism and capitalism. Yet whatever the ultimate outcome in any of these national "debates" - rejection of IMF loan terms, reevaluation of foreign policy, and reconceptualization of political structures, respectively - the results in practice will be very "Nigerian": continuous individual and collective revisions of economic and foreign policy as well as political preferences and policies.

For if there is one prevailing and endearing characteristic of the Nigerian political culture it is that of *resilience*. Despite hard times, informal networks and survival strategies still serve to overcome cutbacks and constraints. Just as "capitalism" in Nigeria has its own distinctive character - from ubiquitous marketplaces to the limits of indigenization - so any moves towards "socialism" would have a Nigerian flavor. Effective governmental regulation of exchange, environment and society has been quite limited in Nigeria in both colonial and independence periods: customs and interests always subvert rules and procedures, with private gains taking precedence over collective goods. Thus any realistic scenario of future political economy will have to be "mixed": private and state enterprises along with democratic and centralized decision-making. Structures can be neither wholly "privatized" nor "socialized" given the coexistence of individualism and communalism.

The real issue is how effective can any regime be in this irrepressible environment given established expectations and anticipated constraints? It is somewhat ironic that in such a pluralistic and individualistic society there should be so much discussion about "government," which has always been quite ineffective given Nigerians' abilities to subvert or avoid official regulations: every constraint has been endlessly redefined before and after its promulgation. Hence the imperative of attention to informal sectors and relations with particular focus on food, women, smuggling and other unofficial exchanges. Given the dialectic of rules and "corruption," any analysis of Nigeria which stops at decisions and decrees is quite misleading; in this uncontrollable country, few laws or policies let alone leaders and structures are effective let alone authoritative for long. As "society" has long determined "state," structural adjustment comes relatively easy in Nigeria: the belated recognition of substructure despite superficial preoccupation with superstructure.

d) Retrospective

Appropriate attention to these and other distinctive features of Nigeria's political economy help explain survival as well as decline; the combination of peasant production and informal distribution incorporates most people even if their roles and incomes are marginal. Focus on them also advances comparative analysis with other heavily-populated oil-exporting states such as Indonesia and Mexico. Even if national oil and gas reserves are depleted by the early twenty-first century, Nigeria will remain *primus inter pares* in Black, especially West, Africa because of its "traditional" agricultural, mineral, infrastructural and population resources. These may not readily translate into external power and influence, such as that realized momentarily at the apex of the Mohammed/Obasanjo period, but they do prevent Nigeria from slipping into international oblivion. They also constitute the basic capabilities through which economic self-reliance, if not diplomatic or strategic dominance, could be attained in the mid-term future. The only serious contender in Sub-Saharan Africa for economic, diplomatic and strategic influence is post-apartheid South Africa (Ihonvbere 1991).

A more introverted mood and direction - the psychological and philosophical correlates of structural adjustment - has accompanied the precipitous decline of oil revenues in the 1980s with considerable promise for sustainable economic and political renewal. Import-substitution industrialization (ISI) is not a panacea for all states in the Third World but in the case of a large and diversified market like Nigeria it still holds considerable potential. And once economies of scale are generated internally then the regional market can be penetrated in exchange for the continued importation of labor. Nigeria can then become a regional power for reasons of production and communication rather than diplomacy, security and smuggling.

The "petro-naira" period of oil boom and the devastation of the civil war together have diverted and perverted Nigeria's political economy, worsening unhelpful traits such as aggrandizement and regionalisms, respectively. The successive shocks in the early 1980s of petroleum decline and military return in 1993 has failed to provide a therapeutic break in the medium-term compelling a new modesty of expectation, ambition and consumption. Under Abacha, coalitions, contradictions, suspicions, and conflicts have been exacerbated, to dangerous proportions in some instances. This new socio-economic and political environment may yet constitute the foundation for sustained development into the next century, especially if local foods replace imported ones and population expansion is moderated, and if serious lessons are drawn from current experiences so that Nigeria appreciates the opportunities and challenges of the 'new' globalization. Nigeria is, after all, still a petroleum producer, not importer, and if its considerable gas reserves can be productively harnessed for both fuels, feed stocks and fertilizers it remains a political economy with export potential rather than the reverse. Local petroleum consumption may now be some 30% of reduced production - an indication of increased communication on an improved national infrastructure - but at least such energy does not have to be imported. And although the expanse and diversity of the country may constitute a political problem in terms of national integration, and so be one cause of accelerated petroleum consumption, at the level of agricultural and mineral production it is an advantage: a series of environmental zones and hence food and other crops as well as chemical deposits for industrial inputs. Undoubtedly, Nigeria could become a more self-sufficient manufacturing country if it harnessed its own commodity and mineral production more effectively, as well as controlled its own borders and exchange rates; this is the promise of IBRD/IMF-designed and -promoted "policy reforms" which have so-far failed to make much of a difference given the distinctive character of state and class.

In addition to political and petroleum cycles, Nigeria has progressed from pre- to post-colonial rule and from palm to fuel oil dependence. Before the arrival of British traders, soldiers, missionaries and administrators along the coast, the present territory of "Nigeria" (so named by Flora Shaw, later Lady Lugard) was a patchwork of kingdoms with a history of alternate conflictual and cooperative relationships. Such regional links along with Portuguese forts and slaving raids served to sap the vitality of these kingdoms with their trans-Sahara as well as coastal connections. Furthermore their established iron, brass, terracotta and cloth technologies, often related to sophisticated mediums of exchange, were no match for Portuguese and then British guns. The consuls, once established on the coast, first at Calabar and only later at Lagos, soon transformed traditional kingdoms into organized tributaries, with palm oil becoming the commodity which rationalized continued colonization and taxation. The Anglo-French rivalry, which survives today in terms of national market penetration and regional influence, provided a further reason for British persistence. It is symptomatic of Nigeria's extroverted political economy that the initial primary commodity - palm oil exports for British industrialization - should go into a precipitous decline as the second and much more lucrative commodity - sweet Bonny Light - came into prominence. Although urbanization proceeded apace throughout the century and country, the most dramatic shift in the locus of the economy was the traversing of the Cross River: from Calabar's palm oil to Port Harcourt's fuel oil exportation by cargo ship and then super-tanker. But changes in the global political economy are unending as well as unpredictable: just as the price and demand for palm oil peaked in the 1940s so those for petroleum reached their zenith at the end of the 1970s. By then, Nigeria had to import palm oil. Now, in reduced circumstances, it is reviving the original commodity industries -cocoa, cotton, groundnuts, rubber, timber etc.- in a belated attempt to balance its economy and payments; the ignored peasantry is being rediscovered and revived as oil rents and employment continue to shrink.

If Nigeria can reduce its oil dependence and revive alternative primary industries it may yet lay the foundation for greater self-reliance and -sustainment (Ihonvbere and Falola eds. 1991; Forrest 1996). If the new modesty and maturity prove hollow then the specter of debt renegotiations and economic insecurities will continue. The windfall profits from petroleum corrupted value-systems and polluted the environment. Their demise may yet concentrate minds and reduce expectations. But memories of both civil war and petro-naira will fade slowly and legacies of social inequalities - class, spatial and gender - will remain ubiquitous, while the means to overcome or contain them are much reduced.

In such constrained circumstances, effective, not necessarily interventive, government will prove as problematic as it is imperative, while old differences will be resolved only slowly if at all. Civil society is being revised along with the redefinition of constitutional state, but authoritarian tendencies are rarely far below the surface even under so-called civilian administrations. Whether Nigerian impatience will tolerate such an extended period of retrenchment and restraint, let alone redistribution and redirection, remains questionable, although the strictures of military rule combined with the constraints of recession may yet result in a new beginning. Nigeria's 36th anniversary of independence in late-1996 was appropriately modest - hardly an occasion for celebration. The 1997 celebration was rather pretentious given internal conflicts, the unpopularity of the junta, international isolation, and uncertainty about the future. Whether its condition by the end of this century will be improved is a function of history, geography, personality, ideology ... and fate, the latter being an integral aspect of Nigerian culture.

For Nigeria has always been mask- as well as Januslike: a modern facade behind which established interests and institutions continue to operate. Like inoperable telephones or abandoned machines and isolated regimes, the reality of the country is less transformed than it might at first appear. Apparently modern skyscrapers lack internal structure or purpose; they are out of rhythm with the style and pace of life of most people in Abuja, Lagos, Ibadan, Kano or Port Harcourt. As the need for outward symbols declines, so perhaps will the gap between aspiration and realization. Established forms of communication work perfectly well when inappropriate modern systems are "quenched." Just as British notions of town planning seem to have had minimal impact, at least in Southern Nigeria, so the new system of expressways and airports does not replace but rather supplements established personal networks: ebullience occurs in new contexts rather than being restrained by "modern" institutions. Hence the appeal and challenge of this text: how to capture and convey the diversities and dynamics of political culture and political economy in contemporary Nigeria. We conclude this introduction by identifying salient elements in this pair of central relationships: from political culture to political economy, from neotraditional masquerade to structural adjustment.

e) Political Culture

The distinctive "democratic" inclinations of the Nigerian populace generates a tension in "political culture". On the one hand, no regime has been able to contain for long the irrepressible media, interest groups and commentators who continually demand basic rights and needs within civil society. On the other hand, the factionalism inherent in Nigerian politics makes effective organization and negotiation problematic. Thus one salient element in the mid-1985 Babangida coup was "human rights": opposition to political detention and harassment practiced increasingly under Buhari by the National Security Organization (NSO) (now State Security Service (SSS)), a new state security apparatus to contain both anarchistic and antagonistic inclinations. Yet the Babangida regime itself slipped into such practices in response to student, faculty and worker demands after the Ahmadu Bello University (ABU) shootings of May 1986, the petroleum subsidy removal disturbances of April 1988, and the April 1990 coup attempt, which led to multiple executions and the numerous religious riots and massacres in the Northern states. The Abacha junta has embarked on an even more repressive path exemplified in the unpopular execution of nine environmentalists including Nobel Prize nominee Ken Saro-Wiwa in November 1995.

The dialectic of opposition versus order, or change versus continuity is, then, a continuous one with arbitrary arrest and even occasional elimination of media leaders, university professors, trade unionists, and student organizers tending to recur under each regime after successive "honeymoons." The imperatives of power are likely to lead to repetitions of such regulation of Nigeria's anarchistic inclinations no matter whether the government is socialist or capitalist, civilian or military, minimal or inclusive, despite idealistic claims to the contrary. This is particularly so given the resilience and self-consciousness of major social formations and institutions - classes, gender, intelligentsia especially artists and media - which are the focus of this section.

Although traditional social forces, from aristocrats to peasants, remain important in post-colonial social formations like that in Nigeria, new fractions have emerged in response to political and economic changes. Here, for both historical and theoretical reasons, we focus on the indigenous bourgeoisie and on the peasantry, on women, and on popular culture. First, in the Balewa and Gowon periods, administrative, military and technocratic bourgeois fractions became established in addition to comprador, political and intellectual elites: the major beneficiaries of any "fruits" of independence. Demands for new states or even a new country (Biafra) were responses from excluded lumpen-bourgeois interests. The economic expansions and illusions induced by independence, war and then oil led to a dramatic growth in the number of workers as well as city-dwellers, and in new regional centers like Benin, Calabar, Jos, Kaduna, and Port Harcourt as well as in established cities like Ibadan, Kano and Lagos. But perhaps the crucial and continuing transformation, at least in terms of politics and policies, occurred after the mid-1960s and particularly through the 1970s: the formation if not crystallization of a *national bourgeoisie* (Lubeck (ed) 1986). This result of a series of "indigenization degrees" (Biersteker 1978 and 1987) and opportunities for multi-million naira contracts injected a national capitalist element into transnational and state-centric fractions. Institutionally reflected in Chambers of Commerce, Manufacturers' Associations and Service Clubs, the embryonic national, international and state fractions of the bourgeoisie cannot be readily dismissed. It has grown powerful and profitable in response to post-Gowon opportunities - the proliferation of states, universities, breweries, banks, manufacturers, printed media, agribusiness (particularly flour mills), and bottling plants and is central to any future political and economic debates and structures (Smith 1986). In general, its conservative, capitalist orientation leads it to favor devaluation and privatization - the IMF prescription - providing sufficient foreign exchange is available for necessary imported inputs. The national fraction draws strength from technocratic and military elements who have weathered adjustment contractions and conditions. It also seeks political order and a strong state through which to advance production and contracts; hence its intermediary position between aristocratic and modern political elites on the one hand and between transnational and technocratic bourgeois fractions on the other, as reflected in the composition and role of the "Kaduna mafia" (Ekwe-Ekwe 1985).

One further related social change has been the emergence of a new "landed aristocracy" which controls large tracts of land. In response to food shortages, population growth, indigenization policies, and land legislation, a fraction of "gentlemen farmers" has emerged in association with "agribusiness" and big peasants. Many of them were retired officers who reinvested their commissions into such agricultural enterprises- the "farmer generals"; others were indigenous entrepreneurs with a concern for industrial inputs. They clearly identified with notions of "Green Revolution" and the national bourgeoisie and have established backwards and forwards linkages into finance, technology, fertilizers, transportation, processing (particularly fish or chicken freezing and flour milling) etc. Although sometimes associated with transnational interests, the landed aristocracy along with national and technocratic fractions has become a central element in any strategy of economic renewal and redirection; it along with the big peasantry is a major beneficiary of IMF-style "reform."

One final element in terms of the indigenous bourgeoisie, important in both political and economic spheres, is the rise since Obasanjo's hand-over to Shagari of a generation of "retired" officers. Reinforcing national bourgeois elements, these ex-generals have become active and visible in the "new" Nigeria of political and economic debates, of industrial and financial directorships, and of land alienation and indigenized corporations. Their distinctive position became particularly apparent as the several parallel national debates proceeded in mid-1980s, with General Obasanjo being one of the Commonwealth's Group of "Eminent Persons," Joe Garba recalled for duty at the UN, Danjuma chairing a new bank and the National Revenue Mobilization Committee, and Haruna, Jemibewon *et al* presenting papers at various conferences on Nigeria's future structures: the early advocates of some praetorian form of pluralism. Yet, some of them (Alani Akinrinade, Dan Suleiman, Yar Adua, Olusegun Obasanjo, for example) have found themselves, on the opposite sides of the contemporary political divides: standing up for political liberalization and opposing the Abacha junta. This has created a division within the ranks of this otherwise very powerful constituency.

One related set of social changes, a correlate of economic difficulties, has been a) the decline of the proletariat as manufacturing activity has decreased and b) the revival of the peasantry with some impact on increased food and cash crop production. The rapid evaporation of the petro-naira "bubble" in the early-1980s led to a variety of austerity measures, particularly a reduction in imported inputs for manufacturing. Although the market for local products expanded as consumer imports were restricted and smuggling reduced through the mid-1980s 18-month "closure" of land borders, the ability of local manufacturers to respond was limited by the "forex" constraints given their import-dependent orientation. Workers were laid-off as production declined well below 50% of capacity. The imperative of local sourcing was once again recognized but such inputs of chemicals, grains, minerals, metals and parts cannot be instantly available. Hopefully, prior policies such as the "Green Revolution" will yet constitute a basis for such local resources, but forwards and backwards linkages are hard to sustain in a disarticulated let alone disorganized economy. This would however require an inclusive administration with a sense of mission able to inspire not just local and foreign investors but also local consumers.

However, if Nigeria is to survive the decline in oil price and demand - a structural rather than cyclical condition? - then local manufacturing and export diversification are essential. And such directions impact upon class formations and gender relations over time.

The role of women in Nigeria's political culture and economy has always been significant whatever the period. While politically ignored or excluded, Nigerian women have remained economically essential. The classic "marketwomen" of the South continue to dominate informal trade and women constitute the majority in gender-specific professions and agricultural sectors, yet they are less well-recognized; on the other hand women's status in Northern, Islamic communities is more problematic. Nevertheless, characteristic of Nigeria's close connections with European and North American societies, an intellectual fraction of the female bourgeoisie has applied a feminist but not separatist critique to Nigerian patriarchy. The "Women in Nigeria" (1986) caucus has organized national conferences since 1982 and is distinguished by a concern for gender as well as class.

f) Political Economy

If Nigeria's political culture has evolved significantly since independence, with indigenous bourgeois interests becoming well-established, its political economy has been transformed even more dramatically. Although the primary cause of this transformation has been the oil industry, secondary factors have included increased consumption and communication as well as expanded manufactured and reduced agricultural outputs. Along with the petroleum boom went increased foreign investments and imports, which led dialectically to indigenization decrees and large-scale smuggling. The oil bonanza financed massive infrastructural improvements from expressways, airports and docks to urbanization and industrialization. But it also resulted in even greater personal accumulation as successive ruling classes transferred corrupt gains overseas into hard currencies, exacerbating the current debt crisis. Despite dreams to the contrary, the "petro-naira" never trickled down to most Nigerians, where relative and absolute poverty have intensified.

Nigeria may have changed from an agricultural to hydrocarbon exporter since independence but it has remained an essentially *capitalist economy*. In both colonial and post-colonial times it has had significant state involvement, particularly in the oil and other "modern" sectors, at least until the current period of SAP deregulation and privatization. Even then the interventionist role of the state remains rather firm in spite of commercialization and the sale of some government corporations. And foreign investment not only increased dramatically, it also shifted from commodity exports and consumer imports to oil exports, local manufacturing and capital good imports. While the differences between labor and capital have intensified, the primary social dynamic has been the non-antagonistic tension within various bourgeois fractions.

Secondary contradictions have appeared between genders and between unemployed and employed but these have yet to disturb established relations, except at the level of occasional rhetoric.

Although formally a mixed economy with distinctive capitalist elements, after the civil war Nigeria moved towards increased state intervention, until the mid-1980s debt and devaluation shocks. Indeed, until SAP, the degree of state ownership grew consistently and continuously since independence despite alternative strategies such as indigenization. At the federal level, aside from the particular cases of BP/AP (BP was finally let back into Nigeria in 1991 having been banned for trading with South Africa in 1977) and Barclays/Union Bank, the trend towards state control was a function of the expansion and identification of strategic and basic industries and services: oil, electricity, steel, communications and finance. And at the state level, it was a function of the proliferation and industrialization of states: banking, breweries, housing, investment, manufacturing, services, etc. However, given the cost such facilities imposed on declining budgets, let alone inefficiencies and nepotism, the presumed desirability of such state involvement had long been under attack from internal as well as external agencies even before the imperative of structural adjustment. Notwithstanding the legacy of indigenization or Africanization, "privatization" is an increasingly acceptable and popular notion to reduce the role and expense of government despite fears of unemployment. But the pace, price and scope of state disinvestment have yet to be agreed upon and implemented despite a continual series of debt-negotiations, currency devaluations and institutional contractions: the new foreign policy of endless debt negotiations.

Nigeria's distinctive political economy has generated a particular vocabulary of its own. Some of these terms are quite straightforward - counter-trade, discipline, federal character, mixed economy - while others tend towards mystification or diversion - contracts, diarchy, settlement, donations, mobilization grants, zoning, etc. Most of these notions relate to distinctive features of contemporary history, notably to military or presidential periods, to the ubiquitous petro-naira syndrome of mega-projects and massive kick-backs, and to continuing ethnic, regional and religious differences. Thus the concept "contract" carries with it implications of inducement, corruption and incompleteness which permit conspicuous "donations" by practitioners of such contracting to noble causes such as political parties, new states, charities, mosques or churches or national appeals. Likewise, "zoning" represented an attempt during the Second Republic to balance ethnic tensions and encourage national rather than regional parties while "diarchy" is an attempt to incorporate the military into government in a continuous manner. "Settlement" on the other hand refers to the trend under the Babangida and Abacha regimes to bribe, domesticate and thus incorporate established and emerging opposition elements. Political culture and economy thus become interwoven through such distinctive concepts and connections.

In addition to the three "official" debates which characterized the post-1985 period, there has also been a set of related, unrecognized but no less important national issues, the first two concerned with aspects of political economy, the final one with political culture: deregulation and privatization. The first of these - deregulation - has been acted on decisively in advance of sustained debate: the government decided in April 1986 to dismantle all the seven commodity marketing boards, the most important being for cocoa, cotton, grains, roots, rubber and palm. These 40-year-old boards had attempted to regulate price, demand and quality of Nigeria's cash crops since World War II and so to finance colonial then post-colonial government and development (Derrick 1986). But they never achieved the degree of control in Nigeria that they realized in some other African states and oil revenues displaced their political importance. Tentative official efforts to revive agriculture following the introduction of SAP involved the dismantling of one layer of bureaucracy, having previously made the boards regional and then national again. Symptomatic of the imminent decline of king cocoa was the "torching" of Ibadan's landmark "Cocoa House" in 1983, ironically just before the revival of commodity prices and so production in several regions of the country, along with the demise of the Cocoa Marketing Board.

Likewise, the privatization debate has tended to succeed rather than precede decision-making as several parastatals are being identified for either dismantling, commercializing or privatizing. Such parallel issues to devaluation and desubsidization have received insufficient attention and so implications have been inadequately considered. In the mid-1980's, however, many months after the Ayida Committee on devaluation and Onosode Commission on parastatals, discussion was joined as federal and state governments alike considered which companies to either close or sell. Professor Akinade Sanda's June 1986 inaugural lecture at the University of Ife (now Obafemi Awolowo University) was addressed to the question of minimum government and criteria for privatization. Likewise, Ladipo Adamolekun (1986) has called for informed discussion which goes beyond the "rhetorics" of inefficiencies and inequalities as well as beyond the "technicalities" of profitability and technology. Nigeria's state sector has become too central to be cavalierly dismantled in the name of cost-effective government; likewise, national institutions and bourgeois factions may not yet be able to afford all possible sell-offs. Ironically, the privatization process has been bogged down by corruption, confusion, and petty-politics. In early 1997, the Chairman of the official Economic Intelligence Monitoring Committee, Professor Sam Aluko, in contradiction to official policies stated that privatization was an "unpatriotic" act.

The state has had 100% control of airports, airways, electricity, minting, petroleum, posts, railways, shipping, telecommunications, and television corporations along with Durbar and Nigeria Hotels, Ajaokuta, Delta and other steel companies, fertilizer producers, investment companies and defence industries. In addition, the federal government has had partnerships in assorted brewing, car assembly, cement, flour, manufacturing, sugar, transportation and wood industries. In 1984 the total of original loans and investments amounted to N16 billion (about $16 billion), divided almost equally between loans and investments, with the same amounts still outstanding after repayments and increases. By 1997 official foreign debt stood at about $34 billion. Moreover, most of these bodies were clearly unable to pay interest on the loans, and could not make profits, let alone pay dividends on the shares, despite proposals for more autonomy and efficiency made by the Onosode Commission. Thus there will be problems in finding buyers for the unprofitable "white elephants" such as the steel mills, the subject of the Dafinone Committee's inquiry. In other cases, divestment could provide opportunities for national institutions, investment companies and consortia. Clearly the private community favors maximum private rather than collective ownership; ie. concentration rather than decentralization (Uma Eleazu (1986).

The rest of this book is, then, an attempt to develop these themes of change and continuity, reality, and mystery, diversity and homogeneity and, above all, of political economy and political culture: materialism and masquerade. Nigeria's and Nigerians' post-independence resilience is demonstrated in their overcoming of civil war and oil cycles as well as regime changes and external challenges, and now adjustment conditions and contractions.

The remainder of this decade will be a fascinating period during which to observe and analyze Africa's erstwhile great power: will a workable democratic form of politics finally be achieved? Will a sustainable national economy emerge out of structural adjustment? Will it narrow the gap between production and illusion? Or will Nigeria's distinctive energies continue to circumvent and subvert any conceivable structures of political economy and culture? Hopefully, our analysis will at least provide some background and context for informed observation and projection of what is, unquestionably, Africa's most incorrigible state. We turn first to Nigeria's mixed pre-independence inheritance.

CHAPTER ONE

INHERITANCE:
HISTORICAL ORIGINS AND LEGACIES TO 1960

a) Pre-Colonial State System

The territory comprising contemporary Nigeria was made up of several city states, kingdoms and empires before the advent of colonialism: indigenous social and political structures were equally as diverse as the many contemporary ethnic balances — language, genealogy, religious beliefs or modes of survival. This diversity, however, was underlined by a common belief in the strength of the family, which was usually defined as a man, his wife (or wives), children, and members of the extended family. Family in the historical Nigerian context connoted much more than contemporary European or American usage: it played an ambiguous role in the development of society. On the one hand, each extended family taxed the income and resources of its head, thus making it difficult to raise standards of living. On the other hand, family provided a sort of social security as it catered for the weak, old and sick — the "vulnerable groups" the state is usually unable to cater for. The family helped to make living less difficult through collective production, distribution and accumulation.

Contemporary Nigeria was, then, historically composed of city states, empires and kingdoms. We look first at some of its primary characteristics before turning to the slave trade and colonial rule. In what is now Northern Nigeria, the most important of these pre-colonial units was Kanem-Bornu which in fact rivalled the great Western Sudanese empires of Mali, Songhai and Ghana. Kano, Katsina and Nupe were other equally powerful states. In the forest region, the Oyo and Benin empires were dominant while the Igbos had their own clans but without the monarchical structures of the large empires.

In terms of current understanding, four major features on the pre-colonial state system need emphasis in this chapter: first, the political structures of the respective states; second, the intricate trade network, within and between these states and its implications for accumulation; third, political conflicts evidenced in inter- and intra-state wars and elite power struggles; and fourth, the bases of social reproduction especially as embodied in myths, beliefs, values and norms. Of course, we hasten to add that it is impossible to generalize about Nigeria; conditions which encouraged the rise, conditioned the survival, and even determined the demise of these state systems differed significantly (Anene 1960; Arikpo 1967; Ayandele 1966; Hatch 1971).

As already indicated, one of the most prominent and indisputably powerful Sudanese states was Kanem Bornu, which had become well-established by the end of the first millennium. This kingdom thrived on commerce and, before the conversion of the first Mai (King) to Islam, its political and social systems as well as extensive commercial networks had been properly established. The *Mai's* authority was rooted in myth. He was then able to dominate the kingdom's politics and life: the personification of life and power, the central authority whose word was unquestionable. The court, made up of counsellors and members of the aristocracy performed a purely advisory role. The *Mai* ruled through a council of twelve. Its functions became more crucial with the gradual extension of Kanem's boundaries and the establishment of diplomatic and trade relations, particularly with North Africa, and its eventual control of the Sahara trade route to the Mediterranean seaboard. This council, became so powerful that it gradually took control of public policy. Its composition comprised free and slave-born members. The *Yerima* and *Galadima* were the two most powerful of the four provincial governors, all of whom had royal roots.

Though the *Mai* was seen as divine, the Queen mother (*Magira*) exercised enormous political power. The first wife of the *Mai* (Gumsu) also exercised some influence over public policy. The important role of women in Kanem's politics can only be understood in the context of a possible "compromise between Moslem requirements and the dictates of earlier practices... undoubtedly a legacy of the matriarchal system of the original nomadic rulers" (Crowther 1973:41).

Kanem maintained an extensive, well-equipped and - trained standing army under the command of the *Kaigama*. Of course, the provincial governors were important military chieftains; their royal roots and military strength often encouraged them to rebel against the *Mai*. Kanem's control of the Sahara trade routes promoted an expansion of trade relations, especially in slaves which were its primary export: "the wealth of Kanem depended on slaves which it obtained from the countries to the South either in exchange for salt or by raids, to the markets of the North African littoral" (Crowther 1973:40). Pilgrimages were made to Mecca from about 1097 AD, students were sent to other countries, and important religious leaders from Egypt, Tunis, and Mali among others visited the court of *Mai*.

However, by the beginning of the thirteenth century, the kingdom of Kanem was already in turmoil. Dynastic disputes, attacks from neighboring states, especially by the Tuaregs and the Bulalas, and over-extension of its boundaries plagued it. By 1393, Mai Umar Ibn Idris abandoned Kanem and it took over a century for the Saifawa dynasty to reestablish its hegemony and resolve some of the crises which had caused the rapid decline of the empire. Mai Ali Gaji (1473-1501) finally resolved the dynastic disputes, occupied the lands of Bornu and built a new capital at Nagazargamu. This period of transformation, consolidation and regeneration also witnessed the rise of the Hausa states of Biram, Daura, Gobir, Kano, Rano and Zaria.

Like other Sudanese states, the origin of these states is strongly rooted in the mythology of Bayajidda, son of Abddulahi, King of Baghdad. Extensive and reliable accounts of the history of the Hausa states exist (Burns 1955; English 1959; Geary 1965; Morel 1968; Orr 1965). What we wish to highlight here are their political and economic relations and legacies. Each of them had a specific function which it performed on behalf of the others. There was a regional division of labor. For instance, though Kano and Katsina stood out as the most prominent, Zaria to the south was the main source of slaves and it specialized more or less in slave raiding. Gobir's main function was the defence of the northern outpost against external invaders especially the Tuaregs, while Kano and Katsina were mainly centers of trade. Daura was the spiritual center and Rano an industrial base.

Relations among the Hausa states, from the eighth century AD, were also characterized by intense competition and wars. Though Islam trickled down from Bornu until after the Jihads of the 19th century it did not serve as a source of unity. At various points in time, Kano, Katsina and Zaria emerged as melting pots. Under Queen Amina, for example, Zaria's power and influence over the trade routes and over the other states rose considerably. The wars of conquest led by Amina herself promoted the slave trade with North African markets, especially Tunis and Morocco. This slave trading, it should be noted, was mainly for domestic and military purposes but it did enjoy the full backing of Islam, which declared that Muslims had every right to enslave non-believers. The spread of Islam promoted trade, diplomatic and religious contacts, it introduced Islamic systems of law, government and education, and it brought about a more systematic process of documenting the histories of the Hausa states. By the late fifteenth century, the latter had extensive contacts with the states of the Central and Western Sudan. The reemergence of Bornu in the 16th century, especially under the later rule of Mai Idris Katakarmabe (1507-29), led to its overlordship of Bornu in the Hausa states. This was consolidated by Mai Idris Alooma in his numerous wars of unification.

The fortunes of the Hausa states, including Bornu and even the Jukun, fluctuated with shifts in patterns of trade, effectiveness of leadership, and changes in the direction and importance of the trans-Saharan trade routes. In spite of geographical location and economic interests, mainly directed towards North Africa, the Hausa states and Kanem Bornu maintained extensive economic contacts north of the Southern states. In fact, in the days of the Jihad, religious, social and political interests were to spread to the west, Ilorin in particular, and the mid-west; i.e Auchi and its environs. Thus, there was always a link between the North and the South in "Nigeria." In Southern Nigeria the kingdoms of the forest, especially the Oyo and Benin empires as well as the Igbo city states were going through periods of consolidation. Though there are alternative versions of history which suggest that the genesis of the former can be traced to developments in the North, the most widely accepted version of the origins of the Yoruba is again rooted in mythology: how Olorun, the supreme being sent his son, Oduduwa, to the world which was full of water with a handful of earth, a cockerel and a palm nut. Oduduwa scattered the earth on the water which became land, the cockerel scratched it, and he planted the palm nut whose sixteen branches represented the sixteen crowned heads of Yorubaland (Crowther 1973; Johnson 1921).

This original act of Oduduwa took place at a location called Ile-Ife, which the Yorubas of Western Nigeria today revere as their original home, a kind of spiritual center. There are other versions of how Ife was created by an Eastern Prince whose sons founded Benin, Illa, Ketu, Owu, Oyo and Popo. A connection is established in this version between the Yorubas and the Binis. Oranminyan, the grandson of Oduduwa, was supposed to have been sent to rule over the Binis without success because of their quarrelsomeness. He abandoned this kingdom which he called "Ile-Ibinu" (Benin) and on his way founded a new kingdom of Oyo (Egharevba 1936). Images of the early histories of Oyo and Benin are today mostly embodied in their art works, carvings and bronze castings which demonstrate "evidence of great technical accomplishments and the elaborate regalia of the Oni or Kings of Ife, whom many of the bronzes portray, indicating a complex society" (Crowther 1973: 55).

At the height of its power, in the early 19th century, the Oyo empire was bounded in the East by Benin, South by the lagoons and mangrove swamps, North by the River Niger, and West by the boundaries with contemporary Togo. The supreme ruler or king was known as *Alafin*. The provinces of the Oyo empire were ruled by provincial kings with the *Onikoyi* of Ikoyi as the most powerful. Proximity to the capital appears to have determined the level of autonomy enjoyed by the provinces. Hence, the Ekiti in the East, the Egbas to the South-West, and the Ijebu's to the South enjoyed relative independence from Oyo proper, including Ife-Ife, which was under the direct influence of the supreme monarch. The rule of primogeniture, which had been employed in the early periods, was abandoned for a selection process by the *Oyo Mesi* from members of the royal houses as Oyo's political structure became more developed. The Oyo kingdom had ward heads led by the Prime Minister (*Basorun*), seven principal counsellors whose number changed from time to time, and the first son of the *Alafin* who was appointed the Crown Prince (*Aremo*). The latter was required to commit suicide on the death of each Alafin from the early 18th century onwards as a way of checking the possibility of an ambitious *Aremo* plotting the overthrow or death of his father. The Crown Prince was in charge of some vassal kingdoms and the royal children.

Though the *Alafin* was considered divine, the embodiment of life and owner of the land and people, his power was not absolute. He ruled through three eunuchs. The eunuch of the Left (*Osi Efa*) was in charge of political matters; he, like the Aremo, had to die on the death of the Alafin. The eunuch of the middle (*Ona Efa*) who was in charge of judicial affairs and the eunuch of the Right (*Otun Efa*) was in charge of religious affairs. The *Oyo Mesi* could cause the death of an *Alafin* by divining a conflict between him and his "spiritual double" and thus compel him to commit suicide by presenting him with an empty calabash or parrot's egg. To ensure that this power was not abused, tradition required the *Oyo Mesi* to die with the *Alafin*. In addition, the Ogboni society was superior to the *Oyo Mesi*. Made up of the *Oyo Mesi* and heads of important families and religious cults, its decisions were final and binding irrespective of dissensions. The head of the standing army was the *Are Ona Kakanfo* who was directly responsible to the *Alafin*, though the army was raised by the *Oyo Mesi* in their position as ward heads. The *Kakanfo* was expected to commit suicide if he lost a battle. This acted as a spur to his generals.

The Benin kingdom developed a complex administrative structure which in several ways mirrored that of the Oyo. But not much reliable information existed before the advent of Oranmiyan. The Kingdom reached its zenith in the 15th century under Ewuare the Great who extended its frontiers. His rule was harsh and this led to the migration of citizens to lands outside his control. This is the source of the connection between Binis and the other ethnic groups like Ijaws, Ishans and Urhobos. Carvings, art work and bronze castings were the hallmarks of the cultural sophistication of the kingdom. Though bronze casting was supposed to have been introduced by Oranmiyan, today the culture is more developed and preserved in Benin.

Though the kingdom's *Oba* was supposed to be divine and was the high point of political and religious life, his power was checked by the *Uzama* (hereditary kingmakers) and the chiefs, led by the *Iyase*, the former's chief advisor. The provinces were governed on behalf of the *Oba* by chiefs who controlled several villages scattered around the kingdom, a check on rebellion against the Oba by ambitious chiefs. The kingdom maintained extensive trade relations with the Hausa states to the North and the Europeans at the coast who visited Benin in the 15th century. Trade in ivory, carvings, pepper and kolanuts, and later in slaves, flourished along the Benin coast with the Portuguese in particular. Religious and diplomatic contacts were also established with the latter. It is exactly this contact with Europeans at the coast that was to alter the socio-economic and political fortunes and futures of the undeveloped formations that are today collectively called Nigeria.

b) The Slave Trade

The first European to visit Benin was Ruy de Sequiers, in 1472. Joon Alfonso d'Aveiro reached Benin in 1486. This early, seemingly innocent, encounter marked a major turning point in the history of the coastal and interior states. Regional trade between the former and the latter was to be severed and attention directed to external trade with Europeans at the coast.

Whatever the several rationalizations expressed in the literature as to why the Europeans visited the coast of West Africa - political, strategic, religious and/or exploration - the major motive was economic. The need to obtain a direct route to the source of gold from the Maghreb without going through Arab middlemen, plus the frantic search for a sea route to India which would enable the Europeans to by-pass Arab rulers, were the main reasons for the voyages of "discovery." By 1480, the Portuguese had completed their exploration of the coast and a flourishing trade in pepper, fruits, and art works had been established from an offshore trading outpost at Sao Tome. Since the latter lacked any large indigenous population, the Portuguese encouraged Benin to export slaves to it, a trade which was found by both parties to be lucrative. When colonization of the island started in the late-15th century, the demand for slaves increased. The slave trade, though largely the product of the development of capitalist relations in Europe, was to drastically alter the population structure of Africa and the negro race in general. Even as the twentieth century draws to a close, its mpact on the development of Africa remains quite evident.

The Portuguese established a mainland trading station at Gwato, a port in Benin, to promote trade in pepper and slaves. The *Oba* of Benin exchanged ambassadors with Portugal and trading agents, missionaries and presents were sent by the King of Portugal. By 1510, the Kingdom of Benin had become the exclusive source of slaves. In fact, by the mid 1440s, slaves were already being sold in Lisbon. It so remained until palm oil became the main commodity of legitimate trade 350 years later. In addition to making some rudimentary contributions to the development of productive forces and advancing the methods and instruments of warfare, contact with the Portuguese promoted education and the use of pidgin English in the kingdom. Slaves were often captured through war, which at times was instigated exclusively for the purposes of acquiring them for sale at the coast. As well, children were sold by their parents into slavery for a variety of reasons. Debtors, vagrants, strangers, criminals and other social misfits were also so sold.

The period of the slave trade, as we have noted, was one of unprecedented economic and social disaster for the West Coast in general and Nigeria in particular. Over 24 million slaves were removed from West Africa and Angola, but this figure does not take into account the millions that died in the numerous slave raids in this part of Africa. Of this total, it is estimated that only 15 million survived the voyage across the Atlantic. About 22,000 were shipped annually from Nigerian ports, with Benin and its colony of Lagos alone supplying about 4,000. The ports of Bonny, and new and old Calabar were also major slave exporters, supplying an average of 18,000 slaves annually. Even with the abolition of the slave trade in the 19th century, over 4 million slaves still went across the Atlantic from Yorubaland as a precipitate of the Yoruba civil wars of the late 19th and early 20th centuries.

Several causes or reasons for the slave trade have been identified. As Crowther (1973: 72-73) argues, the trade received so much impetus because there was "not enough labor available or willing to leave Europe and live in (the) new lands, so that when it was found that Africans survived well in the climate, and moreover were adaptable both to working in mines and on plantations, the slave trade that had been carried on in a desultory way at the beginning or the sixteenth century received tremendous new impetus. The settlement of North America and the West Indies in the early seventeenth century by Britain and France led to further demands for slaves, especially with the development of sugarcane plantations in the mid-century...." To be sure, slaves were procured through the active collaboration of local elites and were exchanged for cloth, linen, iron bars, bracelets, glass beads, coral, mirrors, gun-powder and exotic wines and perfumes. By the time the abolitionists began to make some inroads into the system of slavery, the trade had completely devastated the West Coast. Local crafts, towns and able-bodied people had been destroyed. Art works were looted and families were separated. The abolition of the slave trade after 1807, initially by Britain and eventually by other slave-dealing nations, had far-reaching socio-economic and political implications for the territory which is today Nigeria as it largely established the basis of Britan's economic relations in the entire West African region.

The pressures behind the abolitionist movement are not our concern here. Suffice it to note that it became necessary to replace the slave trade with so-called legitimate trade. Slavery had to be attacked at the source of supply and at the market-place. This very condition generated tensions between slave raiders, sellers, buyers and abolitionists. In addition, it "forced" the British government, with the active support of the "new" legitimate traders, missionaries and other adventurers to challenge the power not only of Nigerian middlemen but also of its rulers. This development generated a new pattern of trade and economic relationship based on West African economic products rather than slaves. Nevertheless, the former organizations employed in the abolition of the slave trade were easily modified to promote the new legitimate trade in palm oil. New employment, as porters and guards, was created for those who would have become victims of the slave trade.

Commitment to the introduction of legitimate trade (a recurrent phenomenon in Nigerian political economy) therefore generated a steady change in the attitude of government officials and businessmen towards the local rulers, whose autonomy had been accorded high respect by slave dealers in the past (Jones 1963; Ford and Scott 1964). The numerous battles, beginning in 1851 (when King Kosoko of Lagos was forced off his throne by the British on account of his slave trading activities), between indigenous forces on the one hand and British traders and officials on the other - the deportations, executions and imprisonments — were for the most part excuses by the British to penetrate the hinter-land, take control of the source of raw materials for their new industries and ensure a market for their products. Thus, the imperial navy and army began to be employed more frequently in the subjugation and pacification of the interior of Nigeria. The British government had no reservations about hijacking the responsibilities and authority of local coastal chiefs in order to consolidate its economic interests and protect the sources of raw materials for its emerging industries.

c) Indirect And Direct British Rule

As the slave trade was being suppressed through treaties and forms of gun-boat diplomacy, British interests were being established and concretized in the country. The mid-19th century marked the end of the period of "informal empire," and instead the beginning of Nigeria's peripheralization and incorporation into the world capital-ist system and the concrete introduction of capitalist rela-tions of production and exchange. Betwen 1820 and 1984 the number of British merchants in the Bights of Bafra and Benin hd increased from 38 to 134. Trade in oil had more than doubled in about the same period. Without doubt, to the British, this area was a lucrative market.

The suppression of the slave trade was directly accom-panied by the need for markets for the products of the new industries in Britain. Trade which had been conducted through middlemen was now seen as ineffective and un-profitable. British merchants in their search for profits and hegemony over the source of raw materials and markets be-gan agitating for direct control. This in itself created a con-tradiction between the middle-men and the merchants. Nine-teenth century Nigerian history was widely characterized by the resistance activities of middlemen, chiefs and kings to the efforts by European traders to penetrate the interior.

To be sure, the early activities of missionaries and ex-plorers facilitated the eventual penetration of the interior and the defeat of the local forces of resistance. Hence, in dis-cussing the establishment of colonial rule in Nigeria, the in-tricate relationship between Christian missionaries and the early explorers must not be overlooked. This is because the latter actually did the spade work, obtained the relevant treaties through mostly fraudulent means, and identified points of strength and/or weakness in the indigenous systems. The pioneer explorers - Mungo Park, Clapperton, Bath, Baikie and the Lander brothers - were mainly interested in discovering an inland way for trade into West Africa. The African Association, which was in fact a major sponsor of some of the explorations, never hid its commercial goals from the world; its primary concern was with the opening-up of Africa to "legitimate trade."

Like the explorers, the early missionaries used religion mainly to gain access to the interior, loot African art and bronze works after condemning them as evil, and ally with the explorers and military forces of the British to unseat "recalcitrant" African rulers and impose "converts" on the respective states. Their main purpose was, therefore, to facilitate trade between African and European interests and to convert the former to their own religion. In addition, they introduced Western education, language and culture. And, as well as promoting trade, they committed themselves to the protection of British interests in Nigeria (Falola ed. 1986). For instance, it was the Christian missionaries who organized the deposition of King Kosoko of Lagos in 1851.

From the 1800s, the British began to use force on indigenous leaders to impose their hegemony over the various state systems: early "indirect rule." For instance, in 1854, a Court of Equity was established to deal with problems of local trade and Consuls used force to impose British interests on Africans. The appointment of John Beecroft as Consul in 1849 marked a major turning point in British-Nigerian relations. He was responsible for the deposition of King William Dappa Pepple of Bonny and King Kosoko of Lagos. As Kenneth Dike (1956: 14) notes, Beecroft "laid the foundations of British power in Nigeria and initiated the politics which were to characterize the consular period of Nigerian history." The preparedness to use force increased with increased investments in and numerical presence at the Coast. By 1856, there were over 200 firms engaging in various business activities in the Delta.

The road to direct political control was opened with the inability of the Consuls to subjugate the local people completely or to enforce the sanctions imposed on persons who interfered with "free trade." Indigenous rulers obeyed regulations only when the gun-boats were around. As soon as these sailed away, the Consuls found it impossible to collect fines and ensure unrestricted trade between local rulers and traders. Thus it became quite obvious to the Consuls that only the formal establishment of a protectorate in the coastal areas could guarantee British authority and the regulation, if not control of trade. So, in 1857, a combination of governmental, commercial and Christian interests sponsored an expedition led by Baikie on the Dayspring to further imperial interests in the interior of Nigeria. By 1861, when King Decemo ceded Lagos to Acting Consul McKoscry, British interests had been concretely established. Lagos, like the rest of Nigeria subsequently, came under <u>direct</u> British influence as part of the overall strategy of containing, penetrating, dominating and exploiting the interior.

The granting of the Royal Charter to the Niger Company in 1886 was only an attempt to delegate political power to the Company so that it could rationalize its presence and realize its economic goals. The Charter granted the Company authority over all territories with which its agents had treaties. Those territories under the "protection" of the Consul became known as the "Oil Rivers Protectorates." Though the Company was enjoined to abolish slavery, respect the authority of local chiefs and not encourage monopoly in trade, it was obvious that these were not serious injunctions. By granting a company that was after profit and market control "political authority" over all territories with which its agents had signed treaties, mostly in very dubious ways, the Royal Charter could not have expected a rational or peaceful relationship between it and native authorities. The Company set up its headquarters at Asaba near the River Niger and created a constabulary and a court of justice as well as the required administration to further its commercial interests. While its territory in the South was marked by the Oil Rivers Protectorate, there were no boundaries in the North (Crowther 1973: 189-191).

The monopoly of trade by the Company in the hinterland was only the beginning of its influence and political activities. George Goldie Taubman, who is usually referred to as "the founder of modern Nigeria," had, in fact, by 1879 united all the major trading companies in the Niger into the United Africa Company (UAC) so that it could effectively monopolize trade throughout the Niger basin. As well, it was under Goldie that the Royal Niger Company extended its frontiers to the northern part of Nigeria following its defeat of the Emirs of Nupe and Ilorin. This move generated fierce competition between the British and the French who had ambitions to occupy Bornu. This competition led to the creation of a military force under the command of Frederick Lugard in 1898. The West African Frontier Force (WAFF) was later to be expanded and exploited on behalf of Britain's interest in and outside Nigeria.

It is important to note that this alliance between the Company and the Consuls, or rather between the companies and the British government—which encouraged the steady erosion of the power of local chiefs, facilitated foreign monopoly of trade and advanced political hegemony over indigenous states—did not go unchallenged. Nigeria's history is full of battles between British interests and agents on the one hand and African forces on the other. The exploits of King Jaja of Opobo, King Nana of Itsekiri, the Brass Warriors and Oba Ovonramen of Benin are but the well-documented examples of resistance to colonial domination (Crowther 1973; Falola ed. 1986; Dike 1956).

To be sure, superior British arms and, perhaps, better organization enabled the companies and Consuls to triumph: King Jaja was deported to the West Indies on a pension of 800 pounds a year and was said to have died on his way home in 1891; King Nana was deported to the Gold Coast; the Brass Warriors were ruthlessly suppressed; and Oba Ovonramen was deported to Calabar. Each act of defeat strengthened the hands of the companies and the Consuls. For instance, following the deposition and deportation of Jaja of Opobo, the Acting Consul was convinced that this would mark the beginning of the breakdown in the organization and power of indigenous middlemen who had violated British attempts to penetrate the hinterland (Egharevba 1973).

With the containment of Jaja, Nana and the Brass Warriors, the only trading post outside direct British and company hegemony was Benin. Colonial control was completed in 1897 with the Benin Massacre and the trial and deportation of Oba Ovonramen: "The fall of Benin was the last major act in the British occupation of Southern Nigeria and marked the end of one of the greatest and most colorful West African kingdoms "(Crowther 1973: 203).

Up North, the extension of British interests was ostensibly to contain French ambitions, especially as the latter had occupied Brass in 1897. The Royal Charter earlier granted to the Niger Company was withdrawn in June 1897 so that

Britain could on its own pacify the North, especially as a military force had been created in 1897. Full compensation was paid to the Company and the British government took direct control of the whole of Nigeria on 1 January 1900. With this change, the territory was reorganized into three administrative areas under the control of the Colonial Office: the Protectorate of Southern Nigeria, the Colony of Lagos and the Protectorate of Northern Nigeria. The Amalgamation of these two Protectorates in 1914 led to the birth of the nation today called Nigeria (see maps).

From 1900 until 1914, the history of Nigeria witnessed a series of military expeditions against rulers in the so-called Northern Protectorate. The Jihad of Uthman Dan Fodio had welded the North together, imposed Islam as the state religion with Sokoto serving as the "Control and Spiritual Center" and established an efficient and effective legal, administrative, military and educational system all based on Islamic injunctions. Of course, the Northern rulers considered the British, as they considered all non-Moslems, to be infidels who they were bound to resist: Attahiru Ahmadu was deposed in 1902; dubious treaties were signed with the Sultan of Sokoto and Emir of Gwandu which were to be used as excuses to establish political control over both states; the British flag was hoisted in 1900 in Lokoja; Borgu and Kabba were also incorporated; in 1903 it was Kano's turn and, by 1906, the last resistance in Sokoto led by the Chief of Satiru was broken. After Sokoto's fall, the next task was the administration of colonial Nigeria.

It is at this stage that the now infamous policy of indirect rule which had already been employed by Britain in India and Fiji was initiated as a philosophy of governance for colonial Nigeria. For one thing, it was the only option left to Lord Lugard because he had insufficient staff: the inherited administrative structure of the Royal Niger Company was very rudimentary and his budget was small - only 135,000 pounds. Thus, political officers were called Residents. Essentially, the system of indirect rule involved the incorporation and use of local rulers and chiefs as the colonial government's representatives in the respective communities, with the Residents acting as diplomats as opposed to their traditional role of administrators. In the Eastern portion of the Southern Protectorate, where neither an Emirate nor an extensive monarchial system did not exist, the colonial government created the unpopular "warrant chiefs".

Under indirect rule, Nigerians came to witness dramatic changes in social structure: the introduction of the English language, new forms of government, new rules, regulations and forms of justice, class differentiation, intensified urbanization, and spatial inequities and new patterns and modes of accumulation. Given Britain's economic interests in Nigeria, the primary goal of indirect rule was the destruction of traditional society and the promotion of export oriented trade.

It is essential to stress the point, however, that indirect rule was only "indirect" in conception. In, reality, its operation was quite *direct*. If we see this colonial mode of production, domination, control and exploitation in the colonial period in its totality, then the colonial officials and their indigenous representatives can be seen as representing the same interests. In fact, most of the traditional rulers and local representatives such as the Warrant Chiefs in Eastern Nigeria were very much committed to the colonial *status quo* and enjoyed the power delegated to them by the colonial state. Thus, whenever they exercised delegated power - e.g. in tax collection, the conscription of youths for the colonial army, the use of forced labor on behalf of the colonial government and the use of military expeditions against "recalcitrant" chiefs - the British were actually exercising *direct* colonial power. The status, wealth, accumulative base and power of these Nigerians drew support from and depended upon the preservation and continuation of the colonial system. Thus, there was nothing really indirect, for the peoples of the colonized territories saw the chiefs as colonial officials. To them, the presence of the colonial state was real and direct. Moreover, the system of indirect rule ran into problems particularly in the Western and Eastern parts of Nigeria even if it was comparably successful in the North. As a consequence of the World Wars, the impact of Western education, racial discrimination and the belief of the British in the strength of "indirect" economic control, by 1914 the struggle for equality, justice and even self-rule in the colony was already underway: the road to Nigeria's political independence was being mapped out.

d) Nationalism And Political Independence

The amalgamation of Nigeria in 1914 created the initial basis of the struggle for self-rule as it brought the protectorates together and thus created a new political unit. This enabled some Nigerians and non-Nigerians to identify with this new "national" unit rather than the old ethnic or community loyalties. The colonial system, deliberately and otherwise, created a new class of Nigerians - court clerks and messengers, teachers, priests, doctors, journalists, administrators, lawyers etc. Ironically, these were to constitute the first base of indigenous resistance to the colonial status quo.

It is instructive to note that included in the very first generation of those who agitated for Nigeria's independence (or at least for equality) were non-Nigerians. Edward Blyden was from the West Indies and J. P. Jack who edited the *Lagos Weekly Record* was a Liberian. People like Herbert Macaulay and Bishop Crowther, whose activities spanned the whole West Coast, distinguished themselves by organizing effective mass protests: "After amalgamation in 1914, what the nationalists fought was the exclusiveness and racial basis of the Crown Colony system of government. At the beginning, the fight was not so much for self-government, but for a measure of participation in the existing government" (Crowther, 1973: 254).

The recalcitrant attitude of the colonial state and its failure to improve the living conditions of the mass of Nigerians naturally forced the early nationalists to fight for more than equality - they began to demand self-rule through independence. The formation of the National Congress of British West Africa in 1920 was mainly to promote the increased participation of African peoples in the administration of their own countries. Its inaugural meeting in the Gold Coast, which was attended by representatives from Nigeria, ended-up by sending a delegation to the Secretary of State for the Colonies to demand:

i.   a legislative council for each territory with half of the members consisting of elected Africans;

ii.   control of taxation by African members of the legislative council;

iii.   the appointment and deposition of chiefs
         by their own people;

iv.   abolition of racial discrimination; and

v.   establishment of a university in West
         Africa (Sklar 1963; Post and Vickers 1973).

Of course, the delegation was not treated with respect by the Colonial Secretary, Lord Milner and it returned home with no promises or achievements. But the broad basis for specific agitations and struggles had been laid. The importance of collective struggles to win concessions from the colonial state had also been made obvious. In fact, the angry response of the Colonial Governor in Nigeria, Sir Clifford, to the demands of the Congress further demonstrated to its Nigerian members the need to expand and deepen their modes of protest. The Governor derided not only the aspirations of the Congress but also the idea of a Nigerian nation. It is interesting that Sir Clifford, who had so fervently argued against the idea of a Nigerian nation, was to author the country's first constitution in 1922, which made provisions for elected African members on the Legislative Council.

The so-called Clifford Constitution provided for a Legislative Council of 46 members, made up of 27 officials and 19 unofficial, of which three members were to be elected by all adult males in Lagos and one in Calabar. To qualify as a voter, an individual had to reside in a location for at least 12 months and must have a gross income of 100 pounds per annum. Though the latter provisions dis-enfranchised a substantial proportion of the residents of Lagos and Calabar, the Clifford Constitution did open the way for overt organizations to win power at whatever level was possible. Thus several political parties were formed in Lagos to contest for the three seats on the Council. Newspapers were established to promote the ideas and interests of these parties and in the 1923 election the National Democratic Party led by Herbert Macaulay won all three seats. It repeated this feat in the elections of 1928 and 1933. However, until this time, political activities were limited to Lagos and, to some extent, Calabar; towns without legislative seats were left out of the politicking. The *Lagos Daily News* continuously carried hard-hitting attacks against the colonial system and served to educate and mobilize others in support of the movement for independence. In the late-1930's a new generation of Nigerians entered the burgeoning nationalist movement. Their horizons went far beyond Lagos and the outbreak of war in 1939 was to mark a turning point in the effectiveness of this new Pan-Nigerian nationalist movement. The West African Student's Union (WASU) had been formed in 1925 in London for the promotion of African culture by Ladipo Solanke, a Nigerian. As well, new waves of educated Nigerians were beginning to enter into the public service where they were discriminated against in spite of their qualifications.

Those who travelled abroad came home to discover a discongruence between British policies at home and in the colony. Nnamdi Azikiwe returned from America in 1937 as an ardent critic of the colonial administration. Earlier, in 1936, Samuel Akinsanya, H. O. Davis, Ernest Ikoli and J. C. Vaughn had formed the Nigerian Youth Movement (NYM), an off-shoot of the Lagos Youth Movement. The change in its name reflected the new Pan-Nigerian outlook and content of the nationalists. One of the early members of the NYM was Obafemi Awolowo who, like Azikiwe, was later to play a leading role in Nigeria's political life. Zik returned to Nigeria and joined the NYM and, with his zeal and connections to traditional rulers all over the country as well as the effective use of his journalistic skills through his *West African Pilot*, the NYM became much more militant in its attack against limited participation of indigenes and against colonialism in general.

The Italian invasion of Ethiopia led to be the formation of an Abyssinian Association in Lagos in 1935 which did more than criticize the aggression; it also waged a successful attack against the Cocoa Pool introduced by the colonial government as a way of strengthening the latter's control over cocoa production, prices and marketing. The outbreak of World War II served to demystify any remaining illusions still held by Nigerians about Europeans; those who travelled abroad saw poor and honest whites and fought side-by-side with British soldiers. Many of the post-war nationalists were thus exposed to the outside world. What was more, in spite of the agitation and growing opposition to colonial rule and discrimination, the British officials continued to maintain an arrogant distance from the emerging elites, excluding them from government and recreation centers and harassing them at the slightest opportunity. The colonial officers did not attempt to mask their dislike for the new Nigerian elite.

In 1943, the first Nigerians were appointed into the Governor's executive council, though he ensured that those appointed were not prominent members of the nationalist movement. In addition, changing world-wide attitudes to colonial rule, the clause in the Atlantic Charter which emphasized the rights of people to self-determination, and pressure from the Labor Party in Britain were all major contributory factors to the strengthening of the nationalist movement.

Unfortunately, the NYM could not capitalise on these developments: rivalry between Ernest Ikoli, editor of the *Daily Service*, and Nnamdi Azikiwe, editor of the *West African Pilot*, for the vacant Legislative Council seat in 1941 led to the disintegration of the movement. This rivalry marked the introduction of "ethnic" competition into Nigerian politics, reflective of pre-and post-colonial diversions. This was given political expression in August 1944 when Azikiwe formed the National Council of Nigeria and the Cameroons (NCNC) with himself as Secretary and Herbert Macaulay as President. The NCNC's main goal was the attainment of self-rule in Nigeria.

With the formation of the NCNC and the assumption of duty as Governor by Sir Arthur Richards, a new political chapter was opened in Nigeria's history. The Richards Constitution which came into effect in January 1947 was aimed at promoting Nigerian unity, greater local participation in government and increased deliberation on issues affecting Nigerians. The Legislative Council was expanded to 44 members with a majority of the members - 28 - now unofficial. A new development was the inclusion, for the first time, of the North in the central legislature. Regional Councils were also created in the North, East and West. Whatever its merits, the regionalization of politics as a result of the Richards constitution, founded on Nigeria's pre-colonial divisions, laid the basis of subsequent ethnic and regional politics, oppression of minorities and strengthening of the regions at the expense of the central government. In response, the nationalist movement, which had hitherto operated with a Pan-Nigerian outlook, disintegrated into regional parties and movements. The 1947 Constitution thus marked a watershed in Nigeria's constitutional development. Prior to it, "the keynote in Nigerian politics was unification towards a centralized state and the realization of a common nationality...But with the Richards Constitution this tendency towards unification was on the whole arrested" (Crowther 1973: 273).

The initial post-war Constitution was severely criticized not just for the regionalization of politics but also for the unilateral way in which its proposals were conceived and introduced. Even Bernard Bourdillon, who had preceded Richards as Governor, criticized it. The several strikes that were called by the Nigerian Trade Union Congress (NTUC) in 1947, as a result of the inflationary legacy of the war and the failure of the colonial government to amend the wages of Nigerian workers accordingly, were linked with the NCNC, which had been the most consistent critic of the Richards Constitution. The *Pilot* and *Comet*, both of them Azikiwe's papers, were banned during the strike. But the Constitution was also accompanied by a 55 million pound (about US$80 million) ten-year Colonial Development Plan for Nigeria to be subsidized by the Colonial Development and Welfare Fund to the tune of 23 million pounds (about US$30 million).

However, the controversial Richards Constitution did not last for long. In 1948, John Macpherson was appointed the new Governor. Unlike Richards, he decided to consult the people before introducing another Constitution. Taking heed of criticisms by the nationalists, he encouraged nationwide discussion and negotiation over the form of his proposed Constitution, a forerunner of subsequent post-colonial national "palavers." Macpherson democratized local government in the East, and appointed four Africans to his Executive Council; another ex-officio member, Dr. S.L.O. Manuwa, was appointed Director of Medical Services. In fact, Macpherson set up a Commission of six Nigerians to study and make recommendations on the recruitment and training of Africans for the senior service in 1948. This Commission, which included Azikiwe, made its recommendation in the same year, emphasizing that where a Nigerian was available no expatriate should be employed - an early expression of Africanization. The debate at least in part initiated by Macpherson reached the grass-roots and a grand conference was organized at Ibadan in 1948 with representatives from regional councils through to village and divisional councils.

Since this Ibadan Conference, ethnicity has become the bane of Nigerian politics, having its roots in the politicking that broke up the NYM in 1941. The emergence of ethnic-based unions and associations from the mid-1940's onwards did not help matters. For example, in 1944 the Ibibio State Union and the Pan-Ibo Federal Union were formed. Azikiwe, who was then becoming a politician who thrived on ethnic loyalty, became the President of the latter in 1948. Yoruba students in London formed the Egbe Omo Oduduwa or Society for the Descendants of Oduduwa which, though it was branded a "cultural organization," had clear political goals. It was supposed to counter the Pan-Ibo Union whose leader had declared that God had created the Ibos to lead the children of Africa from bondage. The Egbe declared that the Yorubas would not be relegated to the background of Nigerian politics and committed itself to creating and fostering "the idea of a single nationalism throughout Yorubaland" and to the unity of all Nigerians and Nigeria. Yet, the base of this commitment to national unity was to ethnic solidarity.

By this time, the North, which had historically been isolated from Nigerian politics, gradually became drawn into them. Some Northerners had received Western education and were beginning to take some interest in the emerging pattern of politics in the South. The Bauchi Improvement Association was formed in 1943 by a group of Western-educated Northerners, including Aminu Kano, Tafawa Balewa and Sa'ad Zungur. In 1949, the Northern People's Congress (NPC), a cultural response to the Egbe Omo Oduduwa, was formed by Aminu Kano and Tafawa Balewa among others. With the promulgation of the Macpherson Constitution, the Egbe became the Action Group (AG), dominating politics in the West just like the NPC dominated them in the North and the NCNC in the East. It is instructive to note that, throughout the period from the late 1940's to 1950, when the movement was banned, the only truly Pan-Nigerian grouping was the Zikist Movement (ZM) which was "violently anti-colonial" in outlook and employed numerous resistance measures, in spite of harassment, against the colonial state. In the main, the ZM stood against ethnic politics in all its forms and advocated social and economic programs for post-independence Nigeria, with particular emphasis on equity, indigenous control and public participation. Its membership was drawn from all parts of Nigeria.

The Macpherson Constitution, unlike its predecessor, proposed a federal system of government with a strong central legislature and executive. It also recommended that the regions be given "considerable powers." The central executive or Council of State was to have six official and twelve unofficial members who were to be Ministers. The House was to be composed of twenty-two representatives, respectively, from the East and West and thirty from the North, which was larger than any of the other two regions. When the new Constitution eventually came into operation in 1952, however, the central legislature was made up of 148 members, half of them from the North. The Executive Council was made up of 18 members. In the three regions Executive Councils had majority African membership and assemblies had legislative and financial powers. Revenue allocation was based on need and provisions were not made for either premiers in the regions or prime minister at the center.

The 1951-52 election to the regional assemblies was largely fought along ethnic lines, particularly by the AG and NPC. As was to be expected and as has continued to be the tradition in Nigerian politics, the ethnically-based parties swept the seats in their respective regions. Even in the West, where some of the seats were won by NCNC members, they quickly "crossed carpet" to join the AG. However, in spite of its comparatively liberal outlook, the Macpherson Constitution did not resolve the contradictions which colonialism had introduced. The long isolation of the North from Western education and from contact with the South had generated deep-rooted suspicions. In addition, while the NCNC believed in a unitary Nigeria and wanted more powers from the central government, the AG and NPC believed and wanted otherwise. The vagueness of the constitution on several critical isues, and its claim to be a tentative document, set the ground for bitter and opportunistic competititions within and between the parties.

Inter- and intra-party feuds affected the functioning of the Macpherson Constitution. Matters were not helped when on 1 April 1952, Chief Enahoro of the AG in a Private Member's Bill called for self-government in 1956. This did not go down well with the NPC which preferred independence "as soon as practicable;" for many reasons, it still viewed the "quarrelsome" Southern politicians with a lot of suspicion. This sharp difference led to public criticism of the NPC members who were constantly booed in public. To make matters worse, Obafemi Awolowo of the AG who had, during the debate, called the NPC members "British stooges," decided on a tour of Kano City. Riots broke out in mid-May, leading to at least 36 deaths with hundreds injured -- the first case of contemporary ethnic violence. The Northern House of Chiefs and the House of Assembly called for a dissolution of the Federation in an 8-point resolution.

These dangerous precedents or omens were to be partly resolved in the constitutional conference called in London in 1953. The AG and NCNC which were in a temporary alliance went to the conference determined to ask for the creation of a Southern Federation in 1956 should the North stick to its "as soon as practicable" policy. As was to be expected, the NPC was against self-government in 1956 but favored the creation of a powerful federal government and the dissolution of the regions into states. In the end, the 1953 Conference was successful in spite of the antagonisms which had preceded it. The issue of self-government in 1956 was sidetracked and it was agreed that regions which were prepared for self-rule in that year could have it. The three parties agreed to a federal constitution with residual powers transferred to the regions. The powers of the central government were thus limited and revenue allocation was to be based on derivation and the needs of both federal and regional governments, all issues which continue to divide and animate Nigerian leaders. It was decided, against the wishes of the AG, that Lagos should become a Federal territory as the capital of Nigeria.

Another constitutional conference called in London in January 1954 saw the AG demanding a clause on the right of regions to secession, a call which was rejected by the colonial secretary. However, marketing boards, the civil service and the judiciary were all regionalized. A national legislature of 184 members (half of them from the North) to be elected every five years was agreed upon. Ministers to the central government were to be appointed by the leader of the party which won the majority of seats in all the regions. Elections in the regions were not to be conducted simultaneously and the systems differed from region to region. The Constitution which came out of the 1954 conference laid down the basic pattern of government for an independent Nigeria. Between 1954 and 1 October 1960 when <u>political</u>

independence was achieved a further series of constitutional conferences were held.

However, since 1945, the colonial state had ensured that, through administrative and legal manipulations, foreign capital gained a dominant position and role in the Nigerian economy (Falola 1986; Nnoli 1981; Akeredolu-Ale 1975; Osoba 1972 and 1978). Multinational capital itself, following the increased tempo of the nationalist movements after World War II, initiated a grand strategy of incorporating the emerging elites as share-holders, partners, major distributors and even legal and political consultants (Onimode 1982).

Throughout the initial postwar period, the country's main source of foreign exchange earnings remained the exportation of agricultural raw materials to feed Western industries. Science and technology were backward; education was available to only a few; development projects depended on foreign technical and financial aid; and the emerging power elite had absorbed a world view and political and economic orientation that favored dependence on foreign capital and the Western world in general (Ihonvbere 1989; Ihonvbere and Shaw 1988b). It was within this general condition of "underdevelopment," dependence and deep-rooted suspicions, antagonisms and contradictions that the last phase of pre-independence political alignments and realignments took place, in the late-1950's.

Following the introduction of the 1954 Constitution, then, the regions gradually became self-governing as Nigerians came to take-over the direct administration of services, except in the North where the expatriate presence was still strong. In the Federal elections of that year, the NPC won 84 of the 90 seats in the North; in the West, the NCNC won 23 seats; while the AG won 18, the former having capitalised on ethnic affiliation with a part of the mid-west and also taking advantage of the growing demand for a Mid-West region. The NCNC also won the majority of the seats in its traditional base - the East. The NPC thus held the largest member of seats in the Federal House but the NCNC, having won a majority of seats in the East and West, had the right to choose six ministers. Both parties decided to work together in the new federal government. In March 1957, eight months after Queen Elizabeth had paid a visit to Nigeria, the Federal House of Representatives passed a motion demanding independence in 1959.

The 1957 Conference in London agreed that self-government would be granted to the Eastern and Western regions whenever they demanded it; the Federal House was to be enlarged to 320 members elected directly in a nation-wide election, although suffrage was still denied women in the North on religious grounds; and a Prime Minister with a cabinet derived from the House of Representatives or Senate was to be appointed. The minority question, a sensitive and explosive problem in Nigeria since the creation of the regions, was tackled through the 1957 Sir Henry Willink Commission. This Commission toured the entire country. Minorities, especially in the Middle Belt, the Mid-West and South-Eastern parts of the country took the opportunity to express their grievances against discrimination and domination by majority ethnic groups. New states were demanded as well as special provisions to protect minorities. In its report, the Commission recommended against state creation even while admitting that the fears of minorities were genuine. It also recommended a plebiscite to determine whether the people of Ilorin and Kabba wanted to remain with the North or join the Western Region. Finally, the Commission recommended that the Police remain national, human rights provisions were to be included in the Constitution and amendments to it should have nation-wide support. Yet, though this report was adopted in 1958, it did not resolve either the minority question or the clamor for new states.

The 1959 election was the last before political independence. The NPC and its allies won a total of 143 seats, the NCNC-NEPU alliance 89 seats, the AG 73 and independents won 7 seats. Since no party had a clear majority to secure federal power, the NPC and NCNC once again agreed to form a coalition government. Thus Alhaji Abubakar Tafawa Balewa became Nigeria's first post-colonial Prime Minister and Dr. Nnamdi Azikiwe took the "dignified but in itself politically uninfluential post of President of the newly-formed Senate" (Crowther 1973: 299). Independence was formally granted on 1 October 1960 and on 16 November, Azikiwe became Governor-General of Nigeria.

e) Socio-Economic Development From The Pre-Colonial To The Colonial Periods

Production and exchange in the pre-colonial period were "primitive" and for subsistence; there was minimal accumulation. Infrastructure and transport were very rudimentary and meant to serve the needs of small villages and clans. The family was largely the unit of production. Revenues were collected, mainly in-kind such as food-stuffs and work in the king's court. Manillas, cowrie shells, iron bars, bracelets and other items at various times served as currency and in some societies enabled slaves and the poor to pay taxes to the nobility. In the North, following the adoption of Islam by most of the Hausa states, heavy taxes were imposed on non-Muslims, partly as a way of raising revenues to run the complex and extensive mode of administration and partly to encourage non-Muslims to convert to Islam.

The bulk of the population in pre-colonial Nigeria, as now, was involved in agriculture. Even artisans engaged in a little farming to subsidize their income. Land belonged to the royalty who then allocated it directly or through chiefs to farmers, who were required to pay tributes, mostly in kind. Shifting cultivation was the most commonly practiced system of agriculture and, other than large farms in the forests, small gardens for meeting immediate needs were often developed inside or on the outskirts of the villages. Farm implements included locally-made hoes, cutlasses and knives. In the North, some simple forms of irrigation were practiced. The major food items grown included maize, corn, cassava, yams and pepper. Cotton was grown to provide raw materials for the weaving and cloth industries.

Other small scale-industries developed according to the dictates of the climatic and resource conditions in several parts of the country - and so encouraged intra-regional exchange - brass works and bronze casting in the West and Mid-West among the Yorubas and Edos; canoe industry in the Delta among the Urhobos, Ijaws and Itsekiri; cotton-spinning in the North; iron-mining in the Middle Belt, parts of the East and West; glass manufacturing in Bida and parts of Ile-Ife; bead manufacturing in the North; and alluvial tin mining in the Plateau district. In most of these crafts, the producers formed themselves into craft guilds or associations and developed an apprenticeship system.

Not much foreign as opposed to regional trade took place in Nigeria before the coming of the Europeans though there were some trade relations between the Hausa states and North Africa. With the coming of the Europeans, however, trade in pepper, ivory, hides and skins, sugar cane, slaves and palm oil developed with an intricate network of middlemen. For instance, between 1831 and 1850, the volume of palm oil shipped to Britain from West Africa rose from 163,288 lbs to 434,450 lbs. The Northern part of Nigeria specialized in the production of groundnut, cotton, and hides and skins.

The advent of colonialism changed socio-economic conditions in Nigeria dramatically. The hitherto <u>un</u>developed (but not static) social formation began to experience changes in political structures, economic relations, patterns of production, and so on. To facilitate the penetration of the interior and the evacuation of cash crops to the coast, the colonial state embarked on the development of roads and railways. By 1889, about 250 miles of laterite roads had been constructed around Lagos. In late-1895 the construction of a railway line linking Lagos and Otta was authorized though work did not begin until 1898. The reasons for the construction of the railway were as much economic as they were strategic and military. It would, for one, enhance the penetration and control of the country and, second, it would promote commerce, direct contact with producers and facilitate the evacuation of produce (Ekundare 1973: 74).

The construction of roads and railways attracted semi- and un-skilled labor from the rural areas with traditional rulers and warrant chiefs being required to provide forced labor. These changes deepened contradictions between the colonized and the colonizers and, within indigenous communities, between the rulers and their subjects.

To finance infrastructure and administration, the colonial state became preoccupied with the efficient production of cash crops, mainly cocoa, groundnut, rubber, palm produce and cotton. While, unlike the case of settler states in Southern and Eastern Africa, production was left in the hands of peasants, administrative manipulations came to be employed to compel peasants to produce cash as against food crops and to sell to the marketing boards. Taxation and levies were the main means of incorporation. Since people needed the new currencies to participate in the modern economy and to pay taxes, they had to either work for wages or produce cash crops that could be sold for hard cash. Thus, between 1865 and 1889, total production of palm oil increased from 10,552 to 31,580 tons; exports of palm oil rose from 5,288 to 8,718 tons; and exports of palm kernels trebled from 11,871 to 38,528 tons.

In sum, by 1900 the British had effectively laid the basis for capitalist growth without development in Nigeria. Precolonial relations and forces of production and exchange were substantially but not completely transformed (Ekundare 1973). As well, the colonial state had, by 1900, laid an effective foundation for the domination of the Nigerian economy by foreign, especially British, capital (Ihonvbere and Falola 1991; Nnoli 1981; Ake ed. 1985). Impediments were placed in the way of indigenous investors, the old trading houses in the Delta were dismantled and the government declared a policy of state protection for foreign capital. Nonetheless, the country's foreign trade remained largely in the hands of expatriate merchants who could afford the necessary capital to finance imports and exports. Ocean shipping, on which foreign trade depended, was also managed almost exclusively by foreign firms (See Helleiner, 1966 and Akeredolu-Ale, 1985).

In the 60 years between 1900 and 1960, when political independence was achieved, the initial mechanisms and patterns of incorporation of Nigeria into the world capitalist system as a periphery were strengthened. The two world wars, world-wide economic depression, and the multilateralization of imperialism had significant consequences for the determination of Britain to extract surpluses from Nigeria and solidify its domination of the political economy. The expansion of peasant agriculture, increased proletarianization of rural producers, the underdevelopment of indigenous entrepreneurs, accelerating urbanization, the development of infrastructure, introduction of a modern money economy and the careful nurturing of an elite whose world-view was largely rooted in British ideals and culture, are among the indicators of this incorporation, peripheralization and underdevelopment (Nnoli 1981; Williams 1980; Onimode 1982; Olatunbosun 1979).

The country's population increased from 16.8 million in 1900 to 27.4 million in 1945. Within the same period the value of foreign trade rose from 3.9 million pounds to 35.2 million pounds, the value of imports rising from 1.9 million pounds to 15.9 million pounds, the value of exports increasing from 2 million pounds to 19 million pounds (Ekundare 1973: 103). Government revenue rose from 2.7 million pounds to 13.2 million pounds and railway mileage, so crucial to the evacuation of cash crops, jumped from 124 in 1905 to 1,903 in 1945, while that of roads more than doubled from 2,800 in 1925 to 6,225 in 1945.

The colonial state took very limited interest in the welfare of the people. Its expenditures were concentrated on infrastructures, services, communications and other sectors identified as critical to the overall colonial objective of surplus extraction. As Dupe Olatunbosun (1975) has argued, the Colonial Welfare Act was not a coherent plan for development in Nigeria. Rather, it laid the basis for the neglect of the rural majority, spatial inequity and concentration on cash at the expense of food crops. Like contemporary World Bank directives, its focus was almost exclusively on cash crop production for export. It neglected the development of indigenous entrepreneurship and institutions and used resources from the Welfare Act to consolidate the structures it had erected for ensuring increased cash crop production. For instance, between 1912 and 1916 the colonial state established the Moore Plantation at Ibadan; in 1923 agricultural experimental stations like the Moore Planation were set up in Benin, Umuahia and Zaria; and in 1925 a research station was established at Vom in the Middle Belt. In 1927, the School of Agriculture was created in Ibadan and in 1934 the Veterinary School in Kano and the Agricultural Station in Samaru were established. The British made no effort to create a connection between agriculture and industry within Nigeria. Rather, they advanced the externalization of its economy.

In 1946, a "Ten Year Plan for Development and Welfare of Nigeria" was inaugurated. The British government was to contribute 23 million pounds of the estimated 55 million pounds cost, with the balance to be raised through local generation of revenues and loans. It is instructive to note that for the British, the best way for a young nation to develop, especially in view of the growing agitation for independence, was through reliance on foreign and internal loans. The 1946 Development Loan Ordinance No. 3 and the Nigeria (Ten-Year Plan) Local Loan Ordinance No. 10, empowered the Colonial Governor to raise an 8 million pound loan in England and a 1 million pound loan in Nigeria. In spite of these loans and assistance from the British government, as well as the future extension of the Plan in 1955 for 5 years -

ie. to 1960 - and in spite of the recommendations of a World Bank mission to Nigeria in that period, the first Plan achieved almost nothing. It did not believe in or promote either the mass mobilization of the people or expenditure on infrastructures and services which could improve their living conditions.

In sum, Nigeria achieved political independence in 1960 severely underdeveloped and dependent. Foreign capital monopolized practically all sectors of the economy. The dominant indigenous class was weak and unproductive. The state was unstable and unhegemonic. Ethnic antagonism and distrust based on pre-colonial divisions of labor were very deep-rooted and the regional balance was inequitable. The North was in all respects larger than the East and West. Issues of power, politics, resource generation and allocation, and relations with external interests were all influenced directly and/or indirectly by contradictions and coalitions of ethnicity, religion and regionalism (Sklar 1963; Nnoli 1981 and 1978; Falola ed. 1986; Ihonvbere 1994); these were to recur in ever more dramatic forms in the post-colonial period.z

CHAPTER TWO

INDEPENDENCE:
FOUNDATION AND EVOLUTION OF THE CONTEMPORARY SYSTEM
1960-1966

Nigeria attained political independence on 1 October 1960 and became a Republic three years later in 1963. Thus, though the First Republic was formally inaugurated in 1963, the term is usually employed to cover the whole period between formal independence and the time of the first military coup in January 1966. At independence, high hopes were expressed at home and abroad about how Nigeria was likely to be bastion of democracy (and capitalism) in Africa. The peaceful road to independence, the conservative disposition of the ruling fraction of the bourgeoisie, and the commitment of the commercial bourgeoisie to an unequal but lucrative alliance with foreign capital convinced adherents of liberal politics that the Westminster model was bound to succeed in Nigeria. But such assumptions were essentially misplaced.

a) Political Change, 1960-1966: the collapse of liberal democracy

By independence, the contradictions introduced by the historical experience of contact between pre-colonial and pre-capitalist formations with the forces of Western imperialism had not been resolved. Such contradictions arising from the formation's peripheral location and role in the world capitalist system would not allow rational politicking, effective exploitation and utilization of human and material resources and the promotion of growth and development in the interest of the majority of Nigerians. To the emerging elite, the overdeveloped but unhegemonic character of the state, the dominant role of foreign capital, the poor living conditions of the masses and the deep- rooted ethnic antagonisms were not important enough to influence the content and course of politics and development planning. Democracy was taken to mean the absence of socialism, the existence of more than one political party and periodic elections. Such politics had little or nothing to do with popular mobilization, mass education, rational selection and presentation of candidates for public office and the use of political power to address the problems and contradictions of underdevelopment.

Politics in the First Republic was, as a matter of fact, characterized by (i) widespread manipulation of ethnicity, region and religion; (ii) use of public office for personal accumulation and only occasionally for community progress; (iii) violence, manipulation and a total lack or respect for the ideals of the Western parliamentary model which the politicians purported to be practicing; (iv) domination of politics by personalities who led ethnically-based political parties; (v) lack of tolerance and political principles; (vi) marginalization of the electorate and total neglect of the basic needs of the masses except in very few cases, as in the free education policy (without full employment) of the Western region; and (vii) reliance on foreign sources of funding and sometimes direction in the conduct of political affairs in Nigeria.

In spite of these and other problems, however, the Westminster model of politics was still expected to succeed. In post-colonial Nigeria, "stability was anticipated. Nigeria was expected to justify the basic principles of Britain's decolonization policy. The Nigerians seemed to adopt readily the trappings of the parliamentary system, British legal niceties and the traditions of the civil service. Africa's most populous country, with 50-60 million inhabitants, seemed set fair to become an African `little England'" (Hatch 1974: 39).

These political expectations were further buttressed by related economic assumptions: the mix of democracy with capitalism. In the West, there had been lofty expectations and assumptions about the prospects for capitalist development in Nigeria. These were based more on the country's "commercial and social life than on political realities. The conventional view in the West was that Nigeria could be relied on to welcome and defend foreign investment, that she had a well-established middle class, little trouble from her trade unions and few radical voices" (Hatch 1974: 39).

The propitious economic environment was expected to contribute to the nurturing of a democratic tradition. Such idealistic beliefs over-looked the filth, poverty and alienation which characterized post-colonial Nigeria. The power elites after political independence had preserved intact, or had at most only slightly modified or "Nigerianized" inherited modes and relations of production and accumulation (Williams 1976b and 1980; Nnoli ed. 1981; Falola ed. 1986; Ihonvbere 1994). Politics was, therefore, seen to be only an extension of this process. With corruption in high places, and the basic human needs of the majority unaddressed, the electorates were easy victims in the hands of the opulent and egocentric politicians. Perhaps "the ostentation and high living displayed by Nigerian politicians would have been excused if there had been distinct signs of improvement in the lives of a large section of the inhabitants" (Hatch 1974: 39). This was not the case: agricultural stagnation, rising foreign debt, community riots, unemployment, neglect of social services and bureaucratic inefficiency increased as the politicians got wealthier. Politics was seen to be a profitable short-term investment:

> As poverty remained unrelieved, in some cases deepening, the flaunting of opulence by intemperate politicians became insufferable. The hostility they provoked extended beyond the individuals to the system they had used for their personal gain. The political institutions themselves became identified with the activities of those who had misused them; parliamentary democracy itself became tainted in the eyes of many Nigerians (Hatch 1974: 39-40).

The euphoria of independence and Western democracy gradually dissolved into disillusionment with Nigeria's definition of capitalism and corruption. Given the underdevelopment of the local bourgeoisie, politics seemed the most viable route to wealth and accumulation. The capture of state power also seemed to be the only way to improve the status and power of the local bourgeoisie in relation to foreign capital which had, with the direct support of the colonial state, dominated all sectors of the economy. Finally, politics seemed to be the only way to bring basic facilities to neglected rural communities in the context of scarce resources and urban bias in the pattern of development. Yet, these beliefs, in the roles and opportunities provided by politics, increased the atavistic struggle for state power, thus laying the foundations for deepening coalitions, contradictions, conflicts and crises.

It was within these conditions of illusion and disillusion that party politics was conducted in the First Republic. The 1959 election, the first direct election in the country's history, saw the consolidation of the three powerful ethnically-based regional political parties. The NPC won 134 seats, the NCNC 89 and the AG 73. The remaining 16 seats were captured by independent candidates. Alhaji Abubakar Tafawa Balewa, who had become Prime Minister in 1957, was invited by the Governor-General Sir James Robertson to form a federal government even before the results of the elections were returned. The Governor could have waited for the election results and allowed the parties on their own to form whatever coalitions they thought best for them. However, since no party won a clear majority, the NPC and NCNC formed a coalition government. Coalition overtures by the AG to the other two parties were rejected. By the end of 1960, all the 16 independent members of the house had switched over to the NPC bringing its total number of seats to 150. This gave it a clear majority over the NCNC thus reducing the ability of the latter to blackmail it in their coalition.

There was no doubt that the NCNC was perhaps, like its Eastern successors, the most shrewd of the three big parties. By 1962, following the delicate situation it found itself in with the NPC's 150 seats, the NCNC considered three alternatives open to it: (i) disassociate itself from the coalition; (ii) extend its power base particularly in the West, where it was in opposition, and thus increase its own influence in relation to the NPC; and (iii) hope to alter the bargaining strengths of the major parties by influencing returns on voting during the 1962 elections (Dudley 1984: 63-65; Oyediran ed. 1996). The last option was to involve attempts to inflate the figures to favor the NCNC's Eastern base as a way of demonstrating its power. Each of these alternatives had its own limitations. Under the first alternative, the AG could move from opposition into the coalition. In terms of the second, the NPC was quick to understand the attempts by the NCNC to isolate it on the minority issue, creation of states, and through it gain possible control of the West. And in response to the third alternative, the NPC simply cancelled the highly inflated results of the 1962 elections.

The political situation in the West, which dated back to 1961, actually played into the hands of the NCNC. During a tour of the Western Region in 1961, Dr. Michael Okpara the Premier of the Eastern Region had called on the Federal Government to declare a state of emergency in the West as a result of frequent political violence and general insecurity. The dispute between Chief Obafemi Awolowo, leader of the Federal Opposition, and Chief S.L. Akintola, Premier of the Western Region - both members of the AG - must be seen as going beyond personalities and ideology. Both of them were essentially petty-bourgeois elements albeit with some differences in their political beliefs and methods. For instance, the main cause of the conflict, which was to have far-reaching consequences for Nigeria's political history, was Awolowo's belief and desire to see the AG as a federal party and Akintola's commitment to keeping it a regional Yoruba party. Of course, Akintola was openly opposed to Awolowo's "democratic socialist" ideals and the growing influence of those he described as "revolutionary babes who haven't the political astuteness to gain the party a single vote" (Akintola quoted in Ojiako 1981: 96).

Beyond these particular personality and ideological differences, however, we must understand the substance of political opportunism and its relationship to accumulation in such underdeveloped formations. Given that this elite lacked any serious location in the larger society, support and "popularity" had to be "purchased" through the construction of intricate patron-client relations. On the side of the people and local communities, there was the assumption that there was a representative who cared at or near the seat of power. To the political elites, it was all a game. The only way to actually sustain the support of the people was to keep them wanting and waiting. This required extensive involvement in all sorts of deals, manipulations, lies, diversions, even if these culminated in the subversion of the entire political process. Thus, the battle to accumulate through extraction, win access to the state and its resources, and keep the allegiance of the "clients" - more often than not in the face of scarce resources, emerging alternative "patrons" and fierce competition - degenerated into seemingly personal squabbles. In such circumstances, all sorts of ideological or political explanations and rationalizations were invoked. Awolowo was already at the federal center as leader of opposition. He had seen the value of controlling federal power, especially with the NPC's manipulation of the first post-colonial development plan, 1962-1968, to favor the North. In any case, having given up the Premiership of the Western Region for Lagos, it would have been absurd not to expect him to campaign for the expansion of the AG's interests outside the region. Akintola, on the other hand, was Premier of the West. His "clients" were mostly the Yorubas and as Premier, with his accumulative base largely in the West, it was natural to expect him to argue for the concentration of the party's energies and resources in the region.

The Awolowo-Akintola intra-Yoruba rift first broke into the open at the 1962 Jos Conference of the party when Akintola walked out, accompanied by Chiefs Rosiji, Adigun and Adeyi. In February, with the intervention of the Ooni of Ife, the rift was patched up: "traditional" rulers have impact on "modern" politics. But in May 1962, at a meeting of the Western and Mid-Western Executive Committee, and in spite of a spirited two-hour defence of himself, Chief Akintola was dismissed both from the party and from the Premiership by 81 to 29 votes. Later that month, the meeting of the Federal Executive Committee of the AG decided to remove Akintola as Deputy Party Leader and as Premier of the region. He was accused of maladministration and anti-party activities. Thus began a chain of attacks, counter-attacks and all sorts of allegations and counter-allegations characteristic of Nigeria in periods of "democracy." Both factions also competed fiercely for the support of the citizens of the region, thus popularizing division.

These developments led to fighting and serious disturbances in the Western House of Assembly. As a response, the Federal government was forced to dissolve the House, suspend the Governor of the Region and declare a state of emergency in the West. Chief Majekodunmi was subsequently appointed Administrator. With this development, it became easy for the NCNC, in its original bid to alter the power bases of the parties, to introduce a motion in the Federal House for the creation of the Mid-West Region out of the Western Region. This motion was carried in the legislatures of the East and North and ratified by Chief Majekodunmi, the administrator of the West. In the referendum which followed in the Mid-West, 83% of those who voted supported the creation of the region, which came into being in 1963 as the country's fourth region (See Table 1.2). True to its calculations, the NCNC took control of this new region with Chief Dennis Osadebay as Premier. This mix of personality, ethnicity and accumulation came to animate the issue of state proliferation in successive periods of party rule.

At the end of the six-month period of emergency in the West, Chief Akintola was restored as Premier. He renamed his faction of the AG the United People's Party (UPP), but did not enjoy majority support in the regional Assembly. The UPP therefore went into an alliance with the NCNC; the first in a series of factional divisions and coalitions to occur in years of democracy. By the end of 1963, the dreams of the NCNC were gradually coming true - it controlled the East, Mid-West and the West, the latter in coalition with the UPP.

The NPC was quick to recognize the implications of this development for its own domination of the center and continued ability to manipulate Nigerian politics by taking advantage of divisions within the other parties as well as conflicts between them. The 1963 elections, which the Prime Minister had promised, were in sight and a federal election was due in 1964. The NPC therefore decided to intervene in the delicate and tense power balance in the West: it decided to break the UPP/NCNC coalition. The NPC encouraged Akintola to come into alliance with it, convert the UPP into a new political party, announce the dissolution of the UPP/NCNC alliance, and force the NCNC members of his government to join his new political party - the Nigerian National Democratic Party (NNDP) - or be dismissed from office. Akintola, who had earlier argued against Awolowo for a regionally-based party, was now prepared to work with the NPC which dominated the center. They succeeded in launching the NNDP and getting the NCNC members of his government to join the new party. The influence of the NCNC in the West was thus terminated with the NNDP taking control of majority of seats in the Assembly.

The NPC and NNDP went into a new coalition - the Nigerian National Alliance (NNA) - while the AG and NCNC went into an opposition coalition - the United Progressive Grand Alliance (UPGA) - to contest the 1964 federal elections, foretastes of subsequent alliances in the Second Republic. The labels "national" and "progressive" had strong implications for the images which both coalitions sought to convey to the electorate. While the NNA wanted the word "national" to show it was not a sectional party, the UPGA wanted "progressive" to show that it was not conservative. In any case these epithets did not wipe out the image of NNA as a party for the North and UPGA as the party for the South (Dudley 1973 and 1984; Ojiako 1981).

As events turned out, the 1964 election, like that of two decades later in 1983, was the straw that broke the back of Nigeria's fledgling experiment with liberal democracy. The suspicions, contradictions and conflicts which the politicking between 1957 and 1964 had generated were so deep-rooted that it would have required much more than a federal election to resolve them. It was quite easy, for instance, for the AG to brand the NNDP as "traitors" who had betrayed whatever ideals they stood for. Akintola was painted as an opportunist who was prepared to side with the feudalistic, conservative and "illiterate" northerners to dominate the South. The campaigns were bitter, substantive issues were side-tracked, and personalities and anger came to dominate the scene. Violence broke out as thugs roamed the countryside and towns were harassing innocent people and forcing them to buy party cards and flags. Lives and property were destroyed without regard to the laws of the land and the politicians actually fanned the embers of violence and insecurity by making fiery speeches and promoting ethnic, regional and religious differences.

By October/November 1964, the situation was so confused and tense that the President had to call all the political leaders to a meeting in Lagos to agree to a "Code of Conduct" that would govern behavior in campaigns and the subsequent elections. To be sure, all the party leaders agreed to this common code, but as soon as they left the meeting they continued on their old ways. At the federal and regional levels as well as within the parties, wranglings and plottings continued unabated. The need to seize political office to facilitate accumulation remained as strong as ever and the politicians steadily descended into the abyss of anarchy. Thus, by the time the elections were conducted in December, it had "become accepted practice for party politicians to go about campaigning with the protection of paid personal body guards, usually armed with a variety of offensive weapons. Electoral officers were terrorized into absconding their offices" (Dudley 1984: 68). Campaign teams to other regions were harassed and attacked and some were clamped into jail as a way of removing them from circulation. It was obvious to all that there was no way in which the 1964 elections could have been free and fair. All the principles of democracy had been thrown to the winds, the struggle for power and wealth had become the priorities of the political elites. Nigerian capitalism rather than Nigerian democracy became the post-independence motif.

The December "election" saw 80% of the 174 NPC candidates in the North returned unopposed. In the West about 30 percent of NCNC candidates were returned unopposed. And in the East, the NCNC swept the majority of the seats. Mass rigging of elections and falsification of election results took place in all the regions. The UPGA, which had control of the governmental machinery only in the East decided to boycott the elections, but this was effective only in the East. The Federal Electoral Commission (forerunner of Fedeco in the late- 1970s, NEC and NECOM in the 1980s and 1990s) was in crisis, as some of its members resigned on moral grounds against the conduct of the "elections". In spite of the boycott, the violence, rigging and allegations, the Chairman of the Electoral Commission announced the results, which had the NPC winning 166 of the 174 constituencies in the North and the NNDP winning the majority of seats in the West. This meant that the NNA had a clear majority. Alhaji Tafawa Balewa then requested the President, Nnamdi Azikiwe, to call him (the Prime Minister) to form the next government. Azikiwe refused, not on moral grounds as a protest against the conduct of the elections, but because of his sympathy for and identification with the NCNC or UPGA. Both the President and Prime Minister then engaged in a struggle to win the allegiance of the military in the event of a stalemate.

This single action of opening conflict to military arbitration set Nigeria on the road to experiencing its first military coup. By competing for the allegiance and support of the army, rather than addressing the deepening contradictions in the political economy, Azikiwe and Balewa demonstrated to the soldiers that they had a political role to play in the political equation of Nigeria. Following the intervention of the Chief Justice of the Supreme Court and the Chief Justices of the regional High Courts in the political stalemate between the Prime Minister and the President, the latter agreed to call on the former to form a government on certain conditions:

i. The federal government must be "broad based" to include representatives of the NCNC and AG;

ii. Elections in the Eastern Region must be conducted in March 1965 following which NCNC members would be ap pointed to the federal government; and

iii. Elections must be conducted to the Western Regional Assembly in October 1965.

The NNA agreed to these conditions and the stalemate was temporarily resolved. But the crisis had demonstrated weaknesses in the body of the institutions of the new state and their custodians. All three major actors — President, Judiciary and Prime Minister — suffered a diminution in their status. In particular, the President showed he was incapable of distinguishing between his exalted office and his party sympathies. He should have either called the Prime Minister to form a government since the NNA won a clear majority or resigned if his conscience could not allow him to take such a step. By taking the position he took, he failed in his duties as the "father" of the nation and "privatized the office of the Presidency" (Dudley 1984: 71). The state was seen to have minimal autonomy and so legitimacy. In addition, the Judiciary politicized itself and "showed that they were unprepared to differentiate their social roles as pillars of the law from their roles as ethnic leaders and party political figures" (Dudley 1984:71-72). Their intervention probably prevented some of the politicians from taking recourse to the law and thus put to test the neutrality of the courts. The Prime Minister could have resorted to Court action when the President refused to call on him to form a government. Instead, like the President, he resorted to attempting to win the support of the army, thus "making the armed forces ultra-conscious of the blurred boundary lines separating the 'military' from the 'civil' and the 'legal' from the 'political'" (Dudley 1984: 71).

Such a division of powers makes sense only in a context wherein the political process is rational (where it concerns itself with mass mobilization and education; about meeting the basic needs of the people), and about involving the people in planning the future of the nation. This was hardly the case in Nigeria. As Dudley (1984: 70) has rightly argued, politics in Nigeria has rarely been objective:

> ...for the political elite, power was an end-in- itself and not a means to the realization of some 'good' for the community, and whatever the instr-mentalities employed in the pursuit of power, suchinstrumentalities were legitimate. It follows fromthis that any talk about 'rules of the game' mustbe irrelevant, for to talk about 'rules of the game'is to pre-suppose some end or ends which such rules are intended to serve but there can be no such endssince power has been taken as an end in itself...Theonly possible kind of ethic thus becomes that ofprivatization, the preoccupation of the individualwith his personal rather than his social situation.

Whatever the apparent reconciliation between Azikiwe and Balewa achieved, it did not last long. The Eastern regional elections in March 1965 witnessed the triumph of the NCNC. With the appointment of NCNC members into the government, the Federal Executive Council increased to 80. In October 1965, the elections in the West were organized, primarily to test the legitimacy of the NNDP. This was the last blow to the resilience of the rather novel and vulnerable bourgeois democracy in Nigeria. The UPGA, which had hoped to win most seats in the region to make up for its poor showing in the federal elections, "lost" the October contest to the NNDP. It was obvious, however, that elections as such did not take place. The NNDP leaders had boasted before them that they would win no matter how the electorate voted. The latter knew how they voted and were disaffected by the declared election results. They thus withdrew their support for the NNDP government, refused to pay taxes and engaged in all sorts of covert modes of resistance and protest. The NNDP government, in need of cash even to pay salaries and wages as well as meet contractual obligations, slashed the price paid to cocoa farmers from 110 pounds per ton to 10 pounds. In a situation where the majority of the population were farmers, many depending on cocoa production, this unilateral action sparked off a farmers rebellion - the Agbekoya revolt. In the rural areas, farm workers who had not been paid their wages by the cocoa farmers set the farms on fire. The revolt spread to the towns where alienated workers and the unemployed joined in. Party thugs were simply too well prepared and very willing to join in the spread of destruction and terror. In turn, and as evidence of its own insecurity, the NNDP government responded with violence. This only worsened the situation. The Balewa government practically abandoned its ally and diverted attention to hosting an international Commonwealth Conference. A day after this Conference ended, a group of young majors led by Major Chukwuma Kaduna Nzeogwu struck and brought the First Republic to an end, so opening the pandora's box of direct military involvement in governance.

b) Socio-economic change, 1960-1966: the consolidation of neo-colonialism

Socio-economic changes in post-colonial and pre-military rule Nigeria were significantly influenced by the country's colonial experiences (Ake ed. 1985; Ekekwe 1986; Falola ed. 1986; Onimode 1982). The class and power configurations as well as the institutions, structures and contradictions which this experience had generated continued to determine production and exchange relations; alignments and realignments within and between classes; and the general pattern of social reproduction and struggle. The dominant role of foreign capital, plus the distortion and disarticulation of the political economy all combined to concretize Nigeria's peripheralization in world capitalism. To be sure, certain forces had also been created by this experience, which posed fundamental challenges to the *status quo*: the working class, peasants, the tiny fraction of the bourgeoisie that could be described as *national*, and the under- and un-employed. While it is true that these classes and sub-classes were yet to constitute any alternative power bloc to the hegemonic alliance between the Nigerian bourgeoisie and its international counterparts, the pattern of socio-economic change made the process of class differentiation and antagonism irreversible, no matter how intense the contrary centripetal corporatist tendencies.

The ideological disposition of the Nigerian governing class following political independence was heavily in favor of an initially lucrative but grossly unequal relationship with foreign capital (Ake ed. 1985; Ekekwe 1985; Onimode 1982). Thus state power was used to provide incentives to foreign capital despite alternative domestic claims. The limited control exercised over employment generation, profit repatriation, appropriate technology, use of local inputs, pattern of location and so on, were to contribute significantly to the erosion of the tenuous hegemony of the "new bourgeoisie" and to the increasing instability of the state:

> The state offered subsidies and incentives to foreign capital to undertake...investments. Participation by private Nigerian capital was not seriously considered. Nigerian "entrepreneurship" was instead to be encouraged in various small-scale schemes. Public investment institutions (regional development corporations) reflected this balance of forces. The consolidation of Nigerian control over the state apparatus after independence did not bring about any significant shift in this pattern before the collapse of the First Republic (Beckman 1981: 2-3).

Thus, the industrialization policy of the post-colonial government was, at World Bank urging, anchored on a program of import substitution under the rather misplaced belief that transnational capital will not only import investable funds and technologies but will also assist in conserving foreign exchange. The aims of this policy were clearly spelt out in the *First National Development Plan*, 1962-1968 (later extended to 1970 as a result of the civil war). These were: (i) to stimulate the establishment and growth of industries that contribute both directly and materially to economic growth; and (ii) to enable Nigerians to participate to an ever-increasing extent in the ownership, direction and management of Nigerian industry and trade. However, rivalry between the regions on the one hand and between the regions and the federal government on the other, plus political intolerance, mediocre politics, corruption, waste and squandermania made a mess of the country's early efforts at industrialization. As well, misplaced priorities and the politicization of ethnicity and religion easily mediated the early attempt to use state power for the promotion of a visible form of dependent industrialization. Rather, state power was used to entrench foreign interests as members of the "entrepreneurial" class remained concentrated in the service sector, real estate, transportation and in the service of foreign capital. Only a very tenuous relationship was maintained with productive activities. This situation was so visible that Zana Bukar Dipcharima (quoted in Osoba 1972: 93), the Minister for Commerce and Industry, was compelled to note in the Federal House of Representatives in 1961 that the Nigerian economy "strictly speaking, is not in our hands. Over seventy-five percent of our overseas trade is controlled by forces over which we have no control."

This succinct point was supported by Waziri Ibrahim, Minister for Economic Development, when he noted that "planning" in colonial and post-colonial Nigeria had been tailored to "meet the requirements of the imperialists. There is no doubt about it" (Osoba 1972: 93). In spite of these seemingly nationalistic complaints, the larger transnational or comprador fraction of the bourgeoisie was quite content with the *status quo*. As Michael Okpara, Premier of the Eastern Region and National President of the NCNC, put it in a reply to those advocating nationalization of the commanding heights of the Nigerian economy, "Those who are advocating nationalization are communists and they should have the moral courage to say so...Every member of the NCNC should stop saying or doing anything contrary to our policy of working in association and partnership with foreign capital" (Okpara *Daily Times* November 4, 1960). The net consequence of this political disposition was that, by 1966, "the dominance by foreign business had become a concern not only to the government, but also to most Nigerians" (Ezeife 1981: 165). Gavin Williams (1980: 38) succinctly exposes the implications of this unequal alliance between the local bourgeoisie and foreign capital in the early period of independence when he notes that superior access to the credit, supplies, technology and managerial skills of the expatriate firms, gives them major advantages over local entrepreneurs who are then reduced to "compradors"; i.e. "intermediaries between foreign interests and the indigenous polity and economy." This subsidiary position in turn compels the local bourgeoisie to turn to the "state as a source of both capital and contracts," thus pushing them further away from productive activities.

The *First Plan*, therefore, became the main program for rationalizing, redefining and consolidating the relationship between established and emergent social forces in the immediate post-colonial period (Collins ed. 1980; Falola ed. 1986; Nnoli ed. 1981; Olatunbosun 1975). Launched in June 1962, its main targets were: (i) a growth rate of at least 4% per annum; (ii) an investment of 15% of the GDP estimated to raise per capita consumption by about 1% per annum; and (iii) the development of opportunities in education, health and employment for all citizens. Foreign economic assistance was to provide about half of the projected sum of N1,356.6 million that was to be spent over six years. The creation of the Mid-West Region in 1963 necessitated the preparation of a separate regional plan to enable it to fit into the overall framework and projections of the National Plan.

With the Plan in place, its implementation promoted major socio-economic changes in Nigeria. Unlike latter periods, especially in the 1980's, actual investment in public and private sectors by 1966 had exceeded the estimated annual average of 37%. As well, 85% of total planned investment for the economy was realized. Public investment was N 130 million in 1966. Public projects successfully executed included the first oil refinery, the Niger dam and bridge, several trunk roads, the Nigerian security and minting plant and a paper mill.

However, in terms of the overall development of the political economy, the First Plan actually deepened contradictions while concretizing spatial and other inequalities in Nigeria. Rural-urban inequity and drift were not reduced, spatial inequalities introduced in the colonial period were not addressed and dependence on the exportation of a narrow range of cash crops for foreign exchange earnings continued. Many of the programs included in the Plan were not achieved and the respective regions behaved as if there was no national plan or framework as they pursued independent economic policies of their own. The growth rate of recorded capital formation turned negative by 1967, partly as a result of the civil war. The expected annual average investment of N226 million was never attained. The Plan which had accorded high priority to the industrial sector for the Trade and Industry Program failed to live up to its goal (Ekundare 1973; Collins ed. 1980).

By March 1968, which was officially the end of the life-span of the Plan, less than a third of the proposed amount had been committed. Politicization, plan indiscipline and preferences for prestige projects as well as corruption and waste made nonsense of the goals of the First Plan. As R.S. Bhambri (1971: 184) noted, there was an "extreme shortage of well-prepared projects. The most glamorous project - the Iron and Steel Complex - was quietly shelved as the technical problems were more clearly appreciated and the ... regions could not agree on its location. Informed observers became rather concerned as most of the projects started by governments turned out to be 'white elephants.'" In short, the allocation of resources under this period of early independence as well as the structures and institutions set up to manage the reproduction of the accumulation and power processes were incapable of managing the sort of dangerous politicking which was to culminate in the military coup and civil war (Ihonvbere 1986; Dudley 1973).

The Plan, which had as its fundamental objective "The achievement and maintenance of the highest rate of increase in the standard of living and the creation of the necessary conditions to this end including public support and awareness of both the potentialities that exist and the sacrifices that will be required" (Federal Government of Nigeria 1962: 46), did little in the end to uplift the living conditions of the majority of Nigerians. Soaring unemployment (until the civil war provided employment in the armed forces), rural decay, agricultural stagnation, urban crisis, inflation and lack of basic human needs gradually came to characterize "neo-colonial" Nigeria during the period of the First Republic.

Specifically, Nigeria's population grew from 30.4 million in 1953 to 56 million in 1963 and this led to a natural increase in the labor force which, as we have noted above, especially in the context of the neo-colonial education which divorced school leavers from agriculture, remained largely un- and under-employed. The cost of living index, with a base year of 1960, rose from 106 in 1961 in Lagos, for instance, to 117 in 1965 and 127 in 1966. In Ibadan, it rose from 127 in 1961 to 146 in 1966 and in Kaduna from 115 in

1961 to 131 in 1966. As Ekundare (1973: 399) noted, the general demand in reaction to such rising costs of living was for more wages which thus formed the basis for three wage reviews between 1960 and 1971. However, as "wages were reviewed upwards by each Wages Review Commission the cost of living index continued to rise. In fact, no sooner had wage increases been granted than fresh agitations for more wages began."

It is within these conditions that the working classes began to agitate for improvements in their conditions. Strikes, demonstrations, and other covert and overt modes of protest were employed in the struggle against the state and capital. It is important to point out that the uneven development and circulation of consciousness, vulnerability to ethnic and religious and regional manipulations, personality conflicts, opportunism, and infiltration by politicians and foreign trade unions did not enable the working class to be very effective in these struggles (Cohen 1984; Freund 1981; Ihonvbere 1983a; Smock 1969; Toyo 1975; Waterman 1983). However, a general strike in 1963 did force the government to establish the Morgan Commission. But when government failed to publish or implement this Commission's report, a Joint Action Committee (JAC) was set up by workers and another general strike was called in 1964. This strike, according to Gavin Williams and Terisa Turner, "articulated the class resistance of workers and the popular resentment against politicians" (Williams 1980: 85). A 1981 summation of the socio-economic situation in Nigeria during the First Republic, particularly before the oil boom, by the International Labor Office (1981: 1) captures the conditions of the people of Nigeria prior to the civil war:

> If our mission had been working two decades ago (i.e. 1960) we would have pointed to the widespread social problems evidenced by high mortality and illiteracy...malnutrition and over-crowded, poor-quality housing with scant and education. We would have focused attention particularly on the rural areas, where the roads were poor, electricity supplies almost non-existent, adequate housing very rare, water usually inaccessible and impure, health and education services much wea-

ker than in the towns, and employment opportunities scarce.

The ILO (1981: 2) Report further noted that agriculture, "was failing to meet either the food needs of the rapidly growing population, or the income needs of the farmers." Per capita national income was low and there were "severe structural problems. Exports were dominated by only a few commodities...all of them vulnerable to the cycles in the world economy." On the industrial sector in the same period, the ILO (1981: 2) noted with dismay the high level of profit repatriation and foreign domination:

> Some modern industries existed, but these were located mainly in the cities of the South, aggravating geographical dualism... Moreover, most of the capital was foreign and, since profit margins were high, the outflow (of) profits and interest was heavy. New industries used mainly imported inputs and equipment so that setting them up had not saved much foreign exchange, which was a serious constraint on economic expansion. The problem was compounded by the fact that much of the technology which had been imported was more or less inappropriate to Nigerian conditions, especially in view of the emerging problem of unemployment.

It is within these conditions, largely inherited from the colonial experience and reproduced by the dependent accumulative base of the "new" Nigerian bourgeoisie, that Nigeria began to experience serious political conflicts and disturbances beginning as noted above in 1962. These were directly related to the competition among dominant social forces for foreign partnerships, "rents" and profits derivable from such positions. In pursuit of these objectives and opportunities, the Nigerian power elite violated all the known rules of political competition and/or coexistence: arson, thuggery, election rigging, corruption, politicization of the police and armed forces, the establishment of private armies etc. were all employed in the pursuit of accumulation. But together they provided a pretext for direct military intervention in the political economy.

CHAPTER THREE

INTERREGNUM:
MILITARY CONTROL AND CONFLICT
1966-1979

a) Introduction

The military putsch of January 1966 came to most Nigerians
as a welcome relief from the prevailing conditions of insecurity, uncertainty, violence, bitter politics and deepening socio-
economic crisis. Of course, expectations were high as the
military was expected to provide immediate solutions to the
numerous problems facing the country. The new regime
was well-received by the populace. This good reception did
not mean a preference of military against civilian democratic
rule. Rather, it reflected a total disenchantment with the
uncertainty, violence, corruption and waste that had characterized civilian rule since 1960 (Dudley 1973: 109).

The "Ten Proclamations in the Extra-Ordinary Order of
the Day" by the Supreme Council which organized the coup,
provide insights into the state of the nation and the perceptions of the plotters, a group of Majors led by Nzoegwu.
The proclamations issued very stern warnings that:

> -looting, arson, homosexuality and rape, embezzle-
> ment, bribery and corruption, obstruction of the
> revolution, abotage, false alarm and assistance to
> foreign invaders are all offenses punishable by
> death sentence;

-demonstrations, unauthorized assemblies, non-cooperation with the revolutionary troops are punishable in varying manner up to death;

-assistance to wanted persons attempting to escape justice and failure to report anti-revolution activities are punishable in varying manner up to death;

-refusal or neglect to perform normal duties or tasks that may of necessity be ordered by local military commanders in support of the change will be punishable by any sentence imposed by the local military commander;

-spying, harmful or injurious publications and broadcasts of troop movements or actions will be punishable by any suitable sentence deemed fit by the local commander;

-shouting of slogans, loitering and rowdy behaviour will be rectified by any sentence of incarceration or any more severe punishment deemed fit by the local commander;

-illegal possession or carrying of firearms, smuggling or attempts to escape with documents and valuables, including money or assets vital to the running of any establishment, will be punishable by death sentence;

-doubtful loyalty will be penalized by imprisonment or any more severe sentence;

-wavering or sitting on the fence and failing to declare open loyalty for the revolution will be regarded as an act of hostility punishable by any sentence deemed suitable by the local commander; and

-tearing down an order of the day or occupation proclamation or other authorized notices will be penalized by death (Dudley 1973: 112-113).

There is no doubt that these proclamations were reflective of the desperation of the young officers who had planned the coup. However, the proclamations and subsequent pronouncements demonstrate clearly the populist orientation of the plotters: they were more concerned with the elimination of corruption, nepotism, ethnicity, inefficiency and waste rather than a fundamental socio-economic and political restructuring of the Nigerian social formation. In the words of Ben Gbulie (1981: 72-73), one of the major actors in the January coup, their goals had included the desire to:

> ...break with the past; to end five long years of civil mal-administration; to eradicate tribalism, nepotism, god-atherism, pluralism, retardation of social integration, bribery and corruption, blind leadership, profiteering, political jobbery and graft, to instil into Nigerians a sense of nationalism; to wrench power from the corrupt and inept politicians solely for the promotion of the common good; to create a favourable atmosphere for peace and stability to return to the country; to extirpate election rigging and outlaw carpet-crossing; to lay the ghost of political oppression; to fashion a code of conduct for public accountability; to abrogate the obnoxious and repressive press laws, guarantee press freedom, safeguard civil liberties and restore the right of public protest; to indigenize the economy and win for Nigeria true economic freedom; to break the backbone of feudalism...set the pace for the emancipation of all Africa from both colonialism and neo-colonialism.

To be sure, these lofty and general goals did not include the need for restructuring the patterns and relations of production and exchange.

Of course, the Majors' coup failed in the East (though the majority of the seven core officers who planned it were Ibos), Lagos and the Mid-West and was only partially successful in the West. While prominent politicians including the Sardauna of Sokoto were killed in the North, this did not happen in other regions. Failure in other regions but the North enabled General J.T.U. Aguyi Ironsi, the General Officer Commanding the 2nd Battalion at Ikeja, to 'hijack' the coup process on behalf of senior officers and to put a permanent stop to Nzeogwu's disturbing rhetoric. On seizing power the latter had no idea of what exactly he could do with it: the "mode of his coming to power was such that he could hardly have been expected to have any clear-cut ideas of reform. It is even open to question whether he was capable of conceiving what forms of reforms were needed, a fact which his seven month's tenure of office was to demonstrate" (Dudley 1973: 114).

In his speech—a response to the handing-over broadcast by Senator Nwafor Orizu, President of the Senate who acted as head of state and government —General Ironsi blamed the politicians and the crisis in the Western region for the situation which encouraged the Majors to stage the January coup. He announced decrees suspending the offices of President, Prime Minister and Parliament. It was also decreed that there should be a military government in each of the four regions; this decree thus suspended the offices of Regional Governors, Premiers and Executive Councils. While all local government and native authority police were brought under the control of the Inspector-General of Police, the Judiciary, the Nigeria Police Special Constabulary Force and civil servants were allowed to continue functioning as before.

In another broadcast, on 17 January 1966, General Ironsi outlined the policies and patterns of authority that were going to guide his regime: the Supreme Military Council (SMC) was to exercise the functions of the Federal Military Government (FMG); Federal Permanent Secretaries were to be directly responsible to the FMG; the regions were to be administered by Military Governors, assisted by advisers, and Permanent Secretaries in the regions were to be directly responsible to the military governors; military governors were directly responsible to be Head of the FMG who was also the Supreme Commander of the Armed Forces; and all laws, regulations, orders and official instructions, unless or until modified or abrogated by the FMG, were to remain in force. The next day, 18 January 1966, Ironsi appointed Lt. Col. C.O. Ojukwu as Military Governor of the Eastern Region, Lt. Col. F.A. Fajuyi for the West, Lt. Col. D.A. Ejoor for the Mid-West and Lt. Col. H. Katsina for the North. Thus was established, for the first time, a military government in Nigeria.

b) The road to the civil war, 1966-67

General Ironsi's seven month rule was plagued with crises, indecision, mistakes and contradictions which, predictably, culminated not just in his overthrow in July 1966 but laid an irreversible path to civil war. A major debate still surrounds the issue of how Ironsi and the Generals and Colonels succeeded in outmanoeuvring the January Majors (Dudley 1973: 113-115). His personal capacities for initiative and decisiveness especially in moments of uncertainty have also been questioned. He was confronted, on coming to power, with the problem of suppressing the disturbances in the Western Region; he had to restore confidence in government and ensure the return of law and order. Before his regime was able to settle to business, however, he was faced with Isaac Adaka Boro's revolt in the Delta area of the Eastern Region demanding an independent state. Furthermore, his regime was saddled with the responsibility of dealing with the coup plotters, some of whom had attained a near mythical stature in the perceptions of the public. Other problems included whether to publish the names of officers killed in the January coup; how to contain or manage possible negative or positive reactions; and, finally, how to handle the crisis of the economy, particularly the problems of unemployment, food dependence, urban instability and crime and the lack of confidence in government institutions.

Commenting on how Ironsi responded to these problems, Dudley was rather uncompromising:

> A genial, convivial man, he was never regarded as very intelligent and he owed his position as GOC more to his seniority — and to underlying political considerations — than to any innate ability he may be said to have possessed...Ironsi believed that things left alone would 'right themselves.' Unfortunately for Ironsi, things just do not have a way of sorting themselves out...A great deal of imagination and initiative was demanded which he was incapable of providing... What might have been the 'right' decisions at the 'wrong' time (Dudley 1973: 114).

We are not interested here in joining the debate about Ironsi's personality and comportment. But Dudley's assessment above provides some insight into why the General moved from one mistake to the other until he was finally ousted.

In his broadcast to the nation on 28 January 1967, Ironsi outlined the policies and programs of his administration. Essentially, taken together, the policies demonstrated a commitment to the neo-colonial *status quo* and a belief in the fact that the elimination of superstructural (even superficial) contradictions and sources of conflict would promote law and order, growth and economic development. Though Ironsi had promised an end to "corruption and dishonesty in our public life with ruthless efficiency" and to "restore integrity and self-respect in our public affairs," he also made a fundamental political error when he declared that "All Nigerians want an end to regionalism. Tribal loyalties and activities which promote tribal consciousness and sectional interest must give way to the urgent task of national reconstruction" (Ojiako 1979: 21).

The error arose from the fact that Ironsi interpreted the problems of the social formation as arising from the visible manifestations of historically-determined contradictions. Thus, oppression, violence, exploitation and corruption were not the contradictions of neo-colonial Nigerian society. Rather, these are just manifestations of more fundamental contradictions in the system. In spite of promises to end waste, encourage foreign and indigenous investors, reduce the number of ministries at federal and state levels, cancel overseas tours by public officials, solve the problems of unemployment, scarcity of food and rural decay, review incentives to private investors, provide adequate housing for workers and "re-appraise educational policies to ensure high and uniform standards throughout the country" (Ironsi 1967 in Ojiako 1979: 21), the announcement of Decrees No. 33 and 34 on the Unification of the Civil Services of the Federation on 24 May 1967 set the course to civil war. However, this announcement was preceded by other problematic concrete actions and developments.

In March 1967, the regional military governors were brought into the Supreme Military Council (SMC), the country's highest organ of government under the chairmanship of the head of state. This tended to heighten personality clashes, jealousies and competition within the SMC. More importantly, major contradictions arose between General

Ironsi and the SMC on the one hand and the Federal Executive Council (FEC) on the other. The latter, made up of seasoned bureaucrats who controlled considerable information and were largely well-educated, held conflicting views on numerous issues with the poorly-educated and administratively inexperienced members of the SMC.

This situation forced the head of state to rely on a caucus "composed of trusted friends and aides...made up of men like Mr. Francis Nwokedi, Mr. Gabriel Onyuike and Mr. Pius Okigbo" (Dudley 1973: 119, also Ojiako 1979 and 1981). Nwokedi was appointed by Ironsi as a sole commissioner in charge of putting forward proposals for the unification of the public services in the regions and at the federal level; Onyuike was appointed to replace Dr. T.O. Elias as the country's Attorney-General; while Okigbo, who had been Nigeria's special Ambassador in Belgium, was appointed to two key positions: Permanent Secretary in the Finance Ministry and Economic Advisor to the FMG. In spite of their personal merits, the fact remained that these appointments were seen as an attempt by Ironsi to surround himself with people from his own ethnic group.

Matters were not helped when Ironsi dismissed some air force cadets, who had already completed up to two years of service, on "educational grounds." In April 1966, twenty-one Majors were promoted to the rank of Lt. Colonel of which eighteen were Ibo-speaking. These promotions took place in contravention of the SMC's one-year embargo on promotions in the army. Ironsi also set up three major commissions to address some burning issues confronting his administration viz:

i. The Nwokedi Commission on the Unification of the Public Services;

ii. The Adebo Commission on the Economy;

iii. The Williams Commission on Constitutional Review.

The first Commission recommended the unification of the administrative and executive cadres of the civil service in the regions and federal government; this was accepted by

Ironsi. The second Commission was a total failure to the extent that personality clashes amongst its members not only militated against regular meetings and effective work but also meant that all it could submit was a rather incoherent "Guide-Posts for the New Development Programme" which emphasized so-called "perspective planning". And the third, Constitutional Review Commission headed by Chief F.R.A. Williams, which was required to study and identify constitutional problems in the context of a united Nigeria, was encouraged to work out concrete proposals to be submitted to a Constituent Assembly followed by a Referendum. In his address to the inaugural meeting of this study group on 24 March 1966, Ironsi stated the Commission's terms of reference to be to:

-Identify faults in the suspended constitution which had been unable to promote stability, peace and development;

-Determine the extent to which the constitutional powers of the regional governments contributed to the strengthening of regionalism and the weakening   of the central government; and to determine the extent to which the structure and territorial divisions of the country under the suspended constitution contributed to the weaknesses of the defunct regime;

-Consider the merits of:
   (a) unitary government,
   (b) federal government;

-Suggest possible or desirable territorial divisions for Nigeria;

-Consider the merits or otherwise of:
   (a) one-party system,
   (b) multi-party system;

-Examine the voting system, Electoral Act and revisions of the Voters' Register;

-Determine the extent to which the pattern of party politics promoted tribal consciousness, nepotism and abuse of office;

-Examine the impact of professional politics on the weaknesses of the defunct governments; and

-Determine how party politics and regionalism violated traditional chieftaincies and institutions and advance possible remedies.

These terms of reference again demonstrate, to a large extent, the superstructural and reformist character of Ironsi's program. No deadline was given to the Williams Group to submit its report. And, in spite of the discredited nature of the traditional rulers and chiefs, Ironsi, who saw them as intermediaries between the government and the people, placed a lot of emphasis on their rehabilitation. This Commission never submitted its report before Ironsi's death on 29 July 1966 (Ojiako 1979; Dudley 1973).

Ironsi's major mistake, however, which led to riots and chaos, especially in the North, had to do, as mentioned earlier, with his promulgation of Decrees Nos. 33 and 34 based on the Nwokedi Commission's Report on the unification of the civil service. The proposed reform program was to include:

-The abolition of federalism as a system of government in the country;

-The replacement of the regions with "groups of provinces";

-The immediate banning and proscription of all ethnic associations, about 80 of them;

-The banning and proscription of all political parties;

-The establishment of a national military government;

-The appointment of military prefects; and

-he introduction of a new economic plan.

The broadcast of 24 May 1967 announcing the Promulgation of Decrees 33 and 34, focused mostly on the seventh item, the introduction of a new economic plan. The other more 'radical' pronouncements were thus left for people to interpret in spite of their highly explosive nature given:

-traditional reliance of people, especially urban dwellers, on ethnic associations;

-the fact that politicians, their thugs and supporters were expecting Ironsi to actually hand-over power to a civilian government in three years;

-the traditional hostility and distrust between the North and the South (fanned by bourgeois elements on both sides in their search for spheres of influence);

-the minority question; and

-the undefined roles of the Military Prefects and the unexplained structure of the "groups of provinces" (Dudley 1973; Balogun 1973; Nzimiro 1978; Ojiako 1981).

The immediate consequences were mass demonstrations and riots in the North. These demonstrations were initiated by students in Zaria. The lack of information on such far-reaching pronouncements fuelled rumors and misinformation. It was therefore easy for Northerners to suspect that the policies had been sponsored by "some special interest group surrounding Ironsi." The riots in Zaria degenerated into mass killings of the Ibos, looting and destruction of property. The riots led to a mass exodus of Ibos from the North, especially as they were subjected to constant attacks and harassments as well as their properties looted. Ironsi did little to bring the sponsors and participants in these riots to book. Rather, he intensified his romance with traditional rulers and chiefs. In fact, he was in Ibadan on 28 July 1966 to open a conference of "natural rulers" when he was over-thrown in what is now know as the "July Return Match" - a supposed reaction to the Ibo-sponsored Nzeogwu and Ironsi coups by the Hausa-Fulani.

Dudley (1973: 134-135) suggested that it is perhaps in-appropriate to see the events of 29 July 1966 as either a coup or a mutiny since "the leaders had no intention of replacing those to be removed from authority either with themselves, or with men of their choosing." He believed, rather, that "rebellion" would be a more appropriate description: "a revolt against general or specific state of affairs which have come to be regarded as undesirable and unjustifiable."

While it is true that it is possible to read into the July counter-coup some ethnic dimensions — Hausa-Fulani ver-sus Ibo — it is perhaps more appropriate to see the counter-coup, like those after it, as precipitates of a failure to man-age deepening socio-economic and political contradictions arising not only from the general crisis of neo-colonial capi-talism but also from the country's marginal location and role in the world economy. The military regime of Ironsi did not appear to be capable of initiating policies likely to contain the steady deterioration in the living conditions of the masses. Yet the emphasis on political reforms deepened intra- and inter-class contradictions leaving room for the ma-nipulation of ethnicity, religion and region in the struggle to conserve or retain political privileges and economic oppor-tunities.

With Ironsi's abduction and subsequent death, the most senior military officer was Brigadier Ogundipe who could not exercise much control or influence over the troops. His failure to begin his actions against the coup plotters by re-voking the provocative Decree No. 35 equally cost him the loyalty of the now highly-politicized army. In frustration, he resigned as Head of State on 31 July and left for London to serve as Nigeria's High Commissioner. This situation paved the way for the emergence of Lt. Col. Yakubu Gowon (who was Ironsi's Chief of Staff) as Head of State and Su-preme Commander of the Armed Forces.

In spite of the circumstances which enabled Gowon to emerge as head of state, Lt. Col. Ojukwu, a young Oxford-trained Ibo officer who had been appointed Military Gover-nor of the Eastern Region by Ironsi, was unwilling to recog-nize and accept him as such. The fact that he, Ojukwu, had been promoted Lt. Col. some six months before Gowon was perhaps one strong factor that determined his position. Of course, Ojukwu had his own personal ambitions and was perhaps reacting to the wanton killing of Ibos in the North. He was later to lead the Eastern region in a secession bid in 1967.

In his initial broadcast to the nation, Gowon noted that his new position as head of state had the "consent of the majority of the members of the SMC." He identified an urgent need to "stop the country from drifting away into utter destruction." The most "important" and controversial aspect of Gowon's speech was when he declared:

> As a result of the recent events and the other previous similar ones, I have come to strongly believe that we cannot honestly and sincerely continue in this wise, as the basis for trust and confidence in our unitary system of government has been unable to stand the test of time. I have already remarked on the issue in question. Suffice to say that putting all considerations to test, political, economic as well as social, *the basis for unity is not there,* or is so badly rocked not only once but several times. I therefore feel that we should review the issue of our national standing and see if we can help the country from drifting away into utter destruction...(Federal Military Government n.d.:11)

The phrase, "the basis for unity is not there..." was later to be extracted from the broadcast and used by Biafran propagandists during the civil war to justify Gowon's support for secession. A careful reading would however reveal that Gowon did not support secession. Rather, he was referring to Ironsi's unitary system of government as lacking a basis for Nigerian unity. Gowon then went ahead to revoke Ironsi's Unification Decree No. 34 and released Chief Obafemi Awolowo and other AG detainees as well as Drs. Michael Okpara and K.O. Mbadiwe plus thirteen other members of the NNDP.

On the same day, August 1, when Gowon made this broadcast, Ojukwu also expressed doubts as to whether Nigeria could ever remain one nation; he condemned the "brutal and planned annihilation of officers of Eastern Nigeria origin" and expressed his view that Brigadier Ogundipe rather than Gowon should have assumed office as head of state. These positions showed visible divisions within the army and military hierarchy. As Dudley (1973: 143) has noted, "though Nigeria remained constitutionally a federation of four regions, in practical terms, these formed two units: one, the East, headed by Lieutenant - Colonel Ojukwu, and the other, the rest of the Federation, made up of the West, North, Mid-West and Lagos over which Gowon was in control."

By the time an Ad Hoc Conference was called in Lagos in September 1966 to discuss the political future of the country, influential elements in the East, particularly at the universities of Nigeria (Nsukka) and Ibadan, were already making proposals, conducting feasibility studies and mobilizing people in the East for secession. The killings in the North in reaction against Ironsi's Unification Decree, the continuing harassment of Easterners in the North, the killing of officers of Eastern origin in the July military coup and the "by-passing" of Ojukwu for Gowon - a "Northerner" - in the succession process following Ironsi's death, were some points of agitation for succession. Delegates (mostly politicians) who attended the Lagos Conference were actually in a belligerent mood, behaving like the representatives of "nations" as against regions.

In his address to the National Conference, Gowon urged these delegates to rule out two options:

-the complete break-up of the nation and

-a unitary form of government.

He, however, suggested that they could seriously consider:

-a federal system with a strong center,

-a federal system with a weak center,

-confederation and

-an entirely new arrangement peculiar to Nigeria.

However, the delegates had actually arrived with specific proposals reflecting largely the interests, aspirations and problems of the respective regional elites.

In these fissiparous circumstances, the North opted for confederation. It argued that it was willing to negotiate for a future state but declared the existing situation completely unsatisfactory. The East also opted for confederation. No other option was acceptable to it: each region should be autonomous and should be allowed to issue its own currency. The West, which had teamed up with Lagos to present a "common front," also opted for confederation, while the Mid-West opted for a federation but with more states; it wanted no right to secession. Amongst the four regions, the East was the most rigid in its position. Its proposals were also the most extreme — separate currencies, regionalization of the armed forces, no strong central government, no creation of states, and so on — demands bound to destroy the fragile and uncertain base of the country. As Enahoro, the leader of the Mid-Western delegation also noted: "we believe that the organization of Nigeria on anything less than a federal basis would do violence to our own beliefs and the endeavors of nationalists in this country over the years" (Enahoro quoted in Dudley 1973: 158).

After a brief adjournment, however, the North changed its position: it now opposed any attempt to allow Nigeria to disintegrate and called instead for a strong central government! It also opposed the demand for a right to secession and called for the creation of more states. A second development was that Lagos decided to dissociate itself from the West's position and influence; it denounced confederation and opted for federalism, and the creation of states. Realizing that he was gradually being isolated, Chief Awolowo, who had earlier on chastised Chief Enahoro for opting for federalism, now came to accept it.

These quick changes in positions demonstrate the fluid nature of political interests within the ranks of the Nigerian bourgeoisie beyond region, religion and ethnic locations. Perhaps these changes in positions and proposals can be attributed to a recognition by the respective regional bourgeois fractions of the need for unity within their ranks as well as the advantages of a larger entity within which to execute their economic programs, promote accumulation and expand their respective spheres of influence. Of course, the minorities in the respective regions were in favor of a federal system with more states while the dominant forces in each region also favored a larger political entity which would facilitate a greater generation of surpluses than fragmented entities with different currencies, ideologies, etc.

The delegates adjourned on October 3, for three weeks. Before they convened again on the 24th, the now infamous massacres had taken place in the North. Before they left, Gowon had agreed that some "damage" had been done and sanctioned Ojukwu's call on Easterners to leave the North. When the delegates met on October 24, the East was conspicuously absent; its delegation felt insecure in view of the presence of Northern troops in the West (defined to include Lagos). Once again Chief Awolowo expressed strong views on the presence of such troops in his region, which strengthened the position of the East. Gowon was forced to adjourn the conference.

The September massacre of Easterners in the North led to a total withdrawal of support for the Federal Government by Easterners and prompted a mass exodus of Easterners from the North and West. The East practically ceased to have anything to do with the Federal Government. Ojukwu reemphasized his misgivings about Gowon as head of state and supreme commander of the armed forces and also expelled non-Easterners from the East. In January 1967, the East confiscated 206,000 pound sterling worth of produce, property of the Northern Nigeria Marketing Board (NNMB), impounded property belonging to Nigerian Railways and prevented the supply of crude oil to the North.

The Aburi Meetings of 4-5 January 1967 did not help matters. Arguments over conflicting interpretations of the agreements supposedly reached at Aburi only increased tension and the desire of the elites in the East to secede. As well, the attempt to patch-up issues at a SMC meeting in Benin on 9 and 10 March (with Ojukwu refusing to attend) did not ease tensions in the country. By the end of March 1967, Ojukwu passed an edict which stipulated that "all revenue due from any source whatsoever in Eastern Nigeria collected for or on behalf of the Federal Government shall be paid to the Government of Eastern Nigeria" (Ojiako 1979: 47). The edict also empowered the government of the East to take over all the departments and statutory corporations belonging to the federal government. Reasons advanced for this act included the need for resources to rehabilitate about 1.8 million Easterners who had fled from other parts

of Nigeria, the failure of the Federal Government to implement the Aburi agreements and the delay by the Federal
Government in paying the East its statutory allocation. As
expected, Lagos declared these actions illegal. Postal and
other means of communication between the East and the
rest of Nigeria were cut by April 1967. A Conciliation Committee headed by Chief Justice Adetokunbo Ademola tried
to resolve the impasse between the East and the rest of Nigeria and, by May 1967, as a result of the efforts of this Committee, Gowon lifted all sanctions against the Eastern Region. The Ademola Committee could, however, not get the
regional government to reciprocate.

Meanwhile, in the East, a two-day meeting of a Consultative Assembly met on 27 May at Enugu and passed a seven-
point resolution calling on the military government of the
region to declare "at an early practical date Eastern Nigeria
as a free sovereign and independent state by the name and
title of the Republic of Biafra" (Ojiako 1979: 47 emphasis
added). This prompted an immediate reaction from the Federal Government which on the same day declared a state of
emergency throughout the Federation; passed a decree dividing the four regions into twelve states to "remove the
fear of domination" and promoting a "basis for stability";
and reimposed economic sanctions against the East until the
Ojukwu administration abrogated "its illegal acts." Three
days later, on 30 May 1967, in a morning broadcast in Enugu,
Ojukwu declared the "Independent Republic of Biafra" on
the grounds that the people of Eastern Nigeria could no
longer be protected by any authority outside the new Biafra.
The civil war that followed this proclamation of Biafra was
not to end until January 1970 (Falola and Ihonvbere eds. 1988;
Ihonvbere 1986; Madiebo 1980).

This section has only briefly attempted to highlight the
developments which culminated in the civil war. Of course,
certain landmarks have been left out but the crucial issues
that can be deduced include, first, the fact that most Nigerians were mere victims of the power-play between factions
and fractions of the Nigerian bourgeoisie inside and outside
the military; and second, the inevitable and rapid march to
political breakdown was largely the result of the very deep
contradictions inherited on the attainment of political independence. The fragility of the state and the politicization
(and manipulation) of primordial loyalties by the regional
bourgeoisies were such that it would have been impossible

for all to transfer allegiance to a central authority without a major attempt at resolving the contradictions. This was partially done at the political level — restructuring of authority in the armed forces, creation of states, the defeat of Biafra, etc. But the underlying socio-economic contradictions remained, to be moderated only in the passing period of oil boom.

c) Socio-economic developments, 1966-1979

The 13 year period of military governance and civil war was also one of fundamental changes in the structures of the Nigerian economy. Not only can it be regarded as the highest point of economic nationalism in the country but also the succession of civil war, post-war reconstruction and the advent of oil boom contributed in a paradoxical way to both strengthening and weakening the economy. Nationalistic economic policies, partly engendered by the lessons of the war, contributed significantly to the expansion (even if not empowering) of the bourgeoisie, reinforced foreign capital-local bourgeoisie alliances, strengthened and weakened the state at the same time, and altered the position of the country in the international division of labor, moving it from a position of a classic peripheral state to a relatively semi-peripheral one, at least in the African context and at least for a while (Ekundare 1973; Williams ed. 1976b; Williams 1980; Nnoli ed. 1981; Onimode 1982).

In his broadcast to the nation on 2 January 1966, Ironsi found time to court foreign investors when he declared that:

> The Government realises that a few unscrupulous foreign and Nigerian businessmen and contractors have contributed their own share to the tragic plunders and waste of the past. There will be no place in the new order for such profiteers and adventurers. The Government, however, reassures all honest businessmen and genuine investors who are in the majority and who can contribute to the country's development that they are most welcome" (quoted in Ojiako 1979: 22).

In the same speech, he made it categorically clear that "in the field of economic development, Nigeria will require foreign capital and technical know-how from abroad." While there is nothing fundamentally wrong with these positions the fact remained that at that time there were hardly any systems of regulation, control and evaluation of foreign investments in the country. As well, the local bourgeoisie was only interested in partnerships: opportunities to serve as agents and reap lucrative profits and commissions. In any case, given the nature of the politics of decolonization since 1945, the Nigerian economy was already under the effective control and domination of foreign investors. It is precisely this dominant position that enabled them to play a major role in the civil war and to influence the pattern of post-civil war reconstruction and rehabilitation.

THE WAR ECONOMY

The civil war had far-reaching effects on the political economy of Nigeria. Other than the general dislocation and overall disruption and decline in production and exchange activities, the war also affected the country's geo-politics and external relations in ways which had deep implications for economic relations in the post-civil war period. Thus, twelve states were created out of the pre-war four regions, principally to create divisions within the ranks of the secessionists. Relations with the then-Eastern bloc especially the Soviet Union were established and strengthened. More control was exercised over the oil industry as the drive for revenues to finance the war intensified. The creation of states strengthened the federal government at the expense of the states so, for the first time, it was possible to speak of "one Nigeria" as a basis for national mobilization.

> -The Federal Government in pursuance of its policy of isolating the Biafrans took several measures. These included:
>
> -the imposition of an embargo on merchant shipping and on other sea traffic with the exception of oil tankers,
>
> -the closure of the Onitsha bridge over the River Niger to merchandise traffic,

-a ban on statutory corporations and other agencies from transferring funds to the East,

-the suspension of some constitutional rights and the declaration of a state of emergency,

-the amendment of the Treasury Bills Act to raise the limit of treasury bills as a percentage of estimated federal revenue from 40 to 50 percent,

-the imposition of a ban on the exportation of a number of essential food items,

-the increase of duties payable on goods, and

-the adoption of measures to streamline the country's financial system.

In addition, measures were introduced to ration the use of foreign exchange while a stand-by automatic short-term credit was negotiated with the IMF. Some fringe benefits for public officers were abolished, a companies decree was promulgated requiring foreign-owned companies with businesses in Nigeria incorporated abroad to be incorporated in Nigeria before the end of 1968; and companies earlier granted pioneer status were not required to pay income tax on that part of their profits which exceeded the total amount of capital allowance earlier granted by virtue of their pioneer status.

To be sure, these responses were made to the specific and general dislocations caused by the declaration of Biafra and the outbreak of hostilities. Given the vital role played by petroleum in the calculations of both sides, the oil companies, other foreign companies and banks were direct objects of government war measures. Revenue flow to the Federal Government, especially from the East, declined precipitously. As well, food shortages occurred as the usual supplies from the East were held up in the rebel enclave. Commerce in all parts of the country - an activity in which the Easterners had participated vigorously - was disrupted. In addition, the amount of foreign investment declined as a result of the high risk levels caused by the civil war.

It is appropriate at this point to discuss briefly the development of Nigeria's oil industry. This is because oil played a major part in the calculations of both parties to the conflict and was to be the most important factor in post-civil war economic development and political reconstruction. The history of the Nigerian oil industry dates back to 1908 when the German-owned Nigerian Bitumén Corporation began exploration activities in the area of present-day Lagos. Its activities were halted, however, with the outbreak of World War I. In 1937, the establishment of Shell-D'arcy Exploration Parties, a consortium owned by Royal Dutch Shell and British Petroleum (later to become Shell-BP Petroleum Development Company of Nigeria), resumed exploration activities in the Niger Delta. In 1938 Shell-BP received an Oil Exploration License for all of Nigeria. This was reduced to 40,000 squares miles in 1957. Though World War II disrupted the company's prospecting activities, 1951 saw renewed activity in the Niger Delta and oil was struck in 1958. By 1961, Shell-BP had been joined by other international 'majors' and 'minors' such as Texaco, Gulf, Agip, Safrap, Phillips, and Mobil. These have since dominated the Nigerian oil industry and have integrated Nigeria further into the world capitalist system though their vertical global operations and control of technology, high-level manpower, information and finance (Ihonvbere 1984; Soremekun ed. 1995).

Since being first discovered and exported in 1958, oil production gradually increased from 17,000 in 1960, to 2.1 million barrels per day in 1970. The production figure reached 2.06 million in 1980 and until the glut in the world oil market, when production declined to 0.64 million in August 1981, this figure remained almost constant. The production capacities of the companies have varied with time. For instance, in a typical month, e.g., June 1979, total oil production was 72,371,002 barrels. Of this total, Shell-BP produced 56.6%, Gulf 16.2%, Mobil 11.1%, Agip 10.0%, Elf 3.1%, Texaco 2.2%, Pan Ocean 0.3%, Tenneco 0.2% and the Nigerian National Petroleum Corporation, 0.4%. Also in June 1979, the United States alone bought 42.4% of Nigeria's total oil exports, the Netherlands bought 12.3%, (West) Germany 10.9%, UK 10.3%, Bahamas 4.9%, Italy 4.0%, France 3.9% and Holland 2.8%. These statistics show that international capital dominates both the production and export of Nigerian oil. In terms of exports, the Nigerian oil industry is totally dependent on Western markets.

However, as oil production and exports increased, so did government participation and revenues. In the colonial period, profits accrued to the oil companies while the colonial government collected taxes and royalties from them. Following political independence in 1960, the post-colonial government collected royalties and various taxes based primarily on a 50-50 profit sharing arrangement (less operating costs) which the colonial authority had introduced in the period of decolonization. Through several decrees, government participation in all foreign oil companies increased from 50% to 60% for the ten year period beginning in 1972. Shell-NNPC is the exception - the government owns 80% - a precipitate of the nationalization of British Petroleum in 1979 (which was only lifted in mid-1991). The Nigerian government also created, through Decree No. 18 of 1971, the Nigerian National Oil Corporation (NNOC) which was empowered to engage in prospecting for mining and marketing of oil as well as "in all other activities associated with the petroleum oil industry." The NNOC was changed to the Nigerian National Petroleum Corporation(NNPC) in 1977 and was charged with the "overall control of the oil industry."

Revenues collected from the crude oil exports increased dramatically over the years. In particular, the OPEC oil price increases following the 1973 Middle East crisis further increased revenues accruing to the Nigerian government. Thus, oil revenues rose from NO.2 million in 1953/59, to N2.4 million in 1960/61 and N16 million in 1964/65. By 1973, the government was collecting N1,403.3 million from oil exports. This increased to N6.4 billion in 1977 and, between 1979 and 1983, Nigeria collected N43.6 billion from oil exports. With the glut in the world oil market from the mid-1980s, revenues declined precipitously. They recovered briefly during the Gulf crisis in late-1990/early 1991, but fell again with the liberation of Kuwait.

The Biafran forces, beginning around mid-1969, embarked on a strategy of sabotaging and bombing oil installations in Nigeria. Thus national oil production declined from the usual pre-war 700,000 bpd to below 400,000 in September 1969. Statistics on oil production, export and revenues were consequently placed on the list of restricted information. Revenues from oil exports which stood at N22.5 million in 1966/67 declined to N20.9 million in 1967/68 and to an all-time low of N14.8 million in 1968/69. These declines affected Nigeria's foreign reserves and credit-worthiness.

The decision by the Federal Government to pay for all arms purchases in hard currency further drained foreign reserves. Furthermore, the government's internal debt level increased from 317.8 million pounds in 1968 to 436.9 million pounds in 1969. By the end of 1969, external debt stood at 87.9 million pounds. These developments partly compelled the government to introduce austerity measures.

The social democratic influences of the Federal Commissioner for Finance and Vice-Chairman of the Federal Executive Council, Chief Obafemi Awolowo showed clearly in some of the populist policies adopted by government during the war period. Hence, in a nation-wide broadcast on 1 October 1967, the Minister announced that the Federal Government had decided "to give free financial assistance, not loans, to all secondary school pupils and university students who for good reasons certified by the Authorities concerned to the satisfaction of the Federal Government, are unable to pay their fees. This free financial assistance will be in addition to the usual scholarship awards to deserving pupils and students" (Awolowo 1970). The government also decided to award scholarships "in large numbers, and the grant of free financial assistance, not loans to qualified pupils in the Northern States" in order to bridge the educational gap between the North and the South. Children of federal armed forces personnel, wherever they might be in the country, were to enjoy "free primary education" as were children of members of the armed forces and the police who lost their lives in the war.

It needs to be mentioned that this time hundreds of thousands of children were out of school as a result of the hostilities, the general tensions throughout the country and the massive return of Igbo teachers to the East. Of course, the policies also went to some extent to encourage the troops in the battle-field, "bribe" the students from opposing other government policies, and accede to some long-standing demands of organized labor. But these concessions only paved the way for more austerity measures. In addition to those already highlighted, the government ordered all ministries except Defence and Internal Affairs to make a 1 percent savings in approved estimates of expenditure; a committee was set up to revitalize public corporations with a view to making them profit-yielding; some capital projects were suspended or frozen; the number of foreign missions were reduced; arrears of income tax and duties amounting to about

5 million pounds were recovered; and ill-gotten gains by public officers were recovered (Awolowo 1970). Finally, a Troop's Comfort and Relief Fund was established and One Nigeria Bonds were introduced. Of course, all industrial protests by workers were banned and a state of emergency was declared.

As mentioned earlier, the decision to purchase armaments, food, uniforms, transportation and war equipment in hard currency drained the country's foreign reserves. In the first year of the war, Nigeria spent 33.5 million pounds; this increased to 98 million in 1968 and to 107 million pounds in 1966, declining to 51.05 million pounds in 1967 but rising again to 52.65 million pounds in 1968. Defense expenditure, however, continued to increase from 12.55 million pounds in 1966 to 53.75 million pounds in 1967 and 81.31 million pounds in 1968; in 1969, it was 179.96 million pounds. However, by the end of the civil war, largely due to the careful management of the economy by Chief Awolowo, the reverses caused by the conflict were already being rectified. For instance, sea ports were re-opened, some of the earlier economic measures were relaxed, oil exports revived and the trade surplus, which had declined to N41 million in 1967 and to N35 million in 1968, rose to N167 million in 1969.

What is certain, however, is that the emergency policies adopted during the war were not in any way reflective of an increasing desire to establish national control over the political economy especially through the expansion of the productive base and the displacement of foreign capital. Rather, they were aimed at plugging loopholes, extracting more surpluses from peasants and workers, and defining spheres of interest and operation for local and foreign capital; hence the indigenization decrees of the 1970s. In fact, throughout the war period, the head of state kept emphasizing the fact that Nigerian development could be attained only by "remaining in the system of world capitalism" (Gowon quoted in Solodonikov ed. 1969: 34). This was largely to reassure transnational investors and the Western capitalist countries.

POST-WAR REHABILITATION, RECONSTRUCTION AND CONSOLIDATION OF DEPENDENT CAPITALISM, 1970-1979

The civil war ended in January 1970. Its consequences were far-reaching in all sectors of the political economy. To end the hegemony of the four regions - East, West, North and Mid-West - and strengthen the Federal Government, Yakubu Gowon had created 12 new states in 1967. In the post-civil war period, significant economic activities especially in construction, took off at the various state capitals. The oil sector began to make a significant contribution to foreign exchange earnings and GDP, the nation was able to identify its reliable friends and, perhaps, enemies within and outside the continent as a result of the different postures taken by other countries towards the civil conflict. The war also resolved some of the contradictions within the ranks of the bourgeoisie especially in its quest for accumulation. The emergence of a more powerful Federal Government vis-a-vis the 12 states redirected the focus of class competition and conflicts from their regional and ethnic bases towards the central government, especially as the latter collected and presided over the allocation of growing oil 'rents'.

Thus, the most formidable tasks which confronted the Nigerian state after the civil war were the rehabilitation of the Igbos, especially the "Igbo bourgeoisie", and the reconstruction of war-damaged structures. General Gowon, as head of state, announced a nine-point program which would lead to civilian government on Independence Day (1 October 1976). This 9-point program, in his own words, was supposed to: "lay the foundation of a self-sustaining political system which can stand the test of time in such a manner that a national political crisis does not become a threat to the nation's continued existence as a single entity and which will ensure a smooth and orderly transition from one government to another" (Federal Ministry of Information 1970). The program required:

-the reorganization of the Armed Forces;

-the implementation of the National Development Plan;

-the eradication of corruption in national life;

-the settlement of the questions of the creation of (further) states;
the preparation and adoption of a new constitution;

-the introduction of a new revenue allocation formula;

-the conduct of a national population census;

-the organization of genuinely national political parties; and

-the organization of elections and installation of popularly-elected governments in the states and at the center.

The attainment of these political goals required the strengthening and expansion of the productive base of the economy. It was for the attainment of these objectives, within the framework of post-civil war rehabilitation and reconstruction, that the *Second National Development Plan, 1970 - 1974* was launched. The Second Plan aimed at a capital expenditure of N3.2 billion during its four-year life span. Though the nominal public investment program was N2.2 billion, the effective size of the program was N1.6 billion while the private sector was expected to contribute the other N1.6 billion. Gross Domestic Output was expected to increase from N3 billion in 1969-70 to N4 billion in 1973-74 in real terms. The average annual growth was expected to be about 7 percent.

To a large extent, vigorous attempts were made to implement the projects of the Plan. For instance, most of the abandoned plantations in war-affected zones were rehabilitated. In addition, the federal and state governments intensified their extension services, and supply of fertilizers and other requirements to farmers during the plan period. Over 40,000 tons of fertilizer was distributed to farmers by the government of North-Western State alone. The Marketing Board system was reorganized to enable farmers to receive much higher prices for their produce (Ojiako 1979: 70). The governments went into "direct production" in the agricultural sector and introduced large state farms and plantations; war-damaged industrial facilities were reconstructed, particularly the cement factories at Nkalagu and Calabar; new commercial ventures such as in fish-trawling, paint production, textiles, salt-refining, alcohol production and motor car assembly in Lagos and Kaduna were established. The Second Warri refinery and the single phosphate fertilizer plant at Kaduna were also established under the Plan. In addition, 2,200 miles of roads were reconstructed, the Enugu airport was built and work was initiated on new airports in Kano, Lagos, Jos, Ilorin and Calabar. Two new ships were bought for the Nigerian National Shipping Line (NNSL) in place of expensive hired ones, the port facilities at Calabar and Port Harcourt were rehabilitated, the national airline, Nigeria Airways acquired two Boeing 707, two Boeing 737 and two F-28 aircraft and all state governments equally intensified their efforts in the area of infrastructural development.

Under the Plan, primary school enrolment increased from 3.5 million in 1970 to 4.5 million in 1973; secondary school enrolment increased from 343,300 in 1970/71 to 649,000 in 1973/74; and twenty new Federal Government Secondary Schools, four Colleges of Technology, nine Trade Centers, and three Federal Schools of Arts and Science were established. The Federal Government also took-over the University of Nigeria. In view of the increasing importance of the oil sector in the economy, the government moved to establish its presence through direct participation. In 1971, it not only joined OPEC but also established the Nigerian National Oil Corporation (NNOC). It also acquired majority equity participation in all the major oil companies while favourable production-sharing contracts were signed with service companies.

The country's external trade under the Plan period also showed some improvement over the pre-war level. The increasing contribution of the oil sector to the total volume and value of Nigeria's trade could no longer be overlooked. In the 1973-74, fiscal year, the value of exports was N2.3 billion, much more than the projected value for the Plan period. It is significant to note, however, that the value of primary exports actually declined. Hence, from a base of N375.6 million in 1970-71, primary exports declined to N247.8 million in 1972-73. Given the weak productive base of the economy, the country continued to import practically all required goods and services. Imports maintained an upward movement during the 1970-74 period, with the singular exception of 1972-73 when, in response to the economic slowdown of that year, import values fell from a level of N1.079 billion in the previous year to N990.1 million. One of the important explanatory factors responsible for this decline was the contraction in agriculture income (Ojiako 1979: 73; Ake ed. 1985; Ihonvbere 1994).

In spite of the foregoing achievements, the Plan hardly met any of its five stated primary objectives:

-a united, strong and self-reliant nation;
-a great and dynamic economy;
-a just and egalitarian society;
-a land of bright and full opportunities for all citizens; and
-a free and democratic society.

Specifically on the third point, the document explained that "A just and egalitarian society puts a premium on reducing inequalities in inter-personal incomes and promoting balanced development among the various communities in the different geographical areas in the country. It organizes its economic institutions in such a way that there is no oppression based on class, social status, ethnic group or state."

Just as Gowon failed to implement this nine-point program and was later to declare the promise of a return to civilian rule in 1976 as "unrealistic," so the Plan moved in an opposite direction from these five principles which, since then, have come to constitute the fundamental objectives and directive principles of state policy. The exchange of a monocultural economy induced through the neglect of productive activities especially in agriculture for a concentration on import and distributive activities as well as dependence on a foreign-dominated oil sector were laid in this Plan period (Ihonvbere and Shaw 1988b; Ihonvbere 1984, 1987, 1989, 1994, 1996).

Thus, in spite of the propaganda about self-sufficiency and self-reliance, the rural areas were in fact neglected, agriculture was abandoned, the food-import bill rose significantly while uncoordinated state intervention into the agricultural sector disrupted relations of production and rural harmony (International Labor Office 1981; Williams 1980; Sano 1983).

Mass poverty was actually heightened contrary to the propaganda about the quest for justice, equality, egalitarianism and full opportunities for all citizens. Most of those displaced by the war could not be rehabilitated and some even resorted to prostitution and armed robbery. Unemployment figures rose rapidly as the economy failed to expand in a significant way to accommodate the products of the school system and misplaced priorities, mismanagement, massive corruption, plan indiscipline, excessive concern for prestigious projects and jamborees heightened tensions. In fact, beyond some token gestures made to the Easterners, the Gowon administration concentrated its efforts and resources on (i) sports, cultural jamborees and a directionless foreign policy and (ii) rehabilitation of foreign capital and the consolidation of an unequal alliance between foreign and domestic capitals with the former as the dominant partner.

Of course, the question of freedom and democracy within an authoritarian military framework is rather problematic. The military leaders had no constituency and were not accountable to anyone except to themselves. The Plan period was thus characterized by wanton abuse of the human rights of students; labor leaders, social critics and journalists were detained or jailed; and badly thought-out and badly implemented public policies deepened social contradictions, ethnic and religious antagonisms, industrial unrest and widened the gap between the rich and the poor (Achebe 1982; Ake ed. 1985; Forrest 1982). That the military administration pursued policies of reconstruction, rehabilitation, self-reliance and national control of the economy half-heartedly was, of course, reflective of the class position of the military fraction of the Nigerian bourgeoisie. This is interesting because in spite of its limited expertise and contradictions the military wing, it is still relatively more cohesive and disciplined than its civilian counterparts. Yet, it lacked the capacity to carry through any far-reaching reforms even in the long-term interest of the bourgeoisie. Let us briefly illustrate this with discussion of the indigenization decrees.

INDIGENIZATION AND THE CONSOLIDATION OF DEPENDENT CAPITALISM

The colonial experience had preserved for foreign capital a dominant place in the Nigerian economy (Osoba 1977;

Akeredolu-Ale 1975; Falola ed. 1986). The period of decolonization enabled this capital, through a grand program of incorporation, to absorb the emerging elites as agents, legal advisers, political consultants, shareholders, sole distributors, representatives etc. They thus served as a form of "political insurance" against volatile politicking and possible nationalization without compensation and ensured not only access to the state but also to state patronage. The indigenous elites, on the other hand (who accumulated substantial cash capital with limited risks through this lucrative but unequal alliance), were quite content to reproduce the relationship rather than engage in any serious restructuring. Hence, under the Second Plan the government opted for "indigenization" as against nationalization not to mention "nationalization and socialization."

According to the *Second National Development Plan, 1970 -74*, "political independence without economic independence is but an empty shell." Hence the recognition that a "truly independent nation cannot allow its objectives and priorities to be distorted or frustrated by the manipulations of powerful foreign investors." Thus the government set out to "acquire by law, equity participation in a number of strategic industries." This was to be an on-going process with the sole purpose of ensuring that "the economic destiny of Nigeria is determined by Nigerians themselves" and to "widen and intensify" government participation in industrial development. To achieve these objectives, the government declared its interest in "joint participation with private enterprises (foreign and indigenous)." This form of partnership, the government made it clear, did not preclude "complete government control and exclusive public ownership of very strategic industries" (Second National Development Plan 1970).

It is clear that the first part of the above policy emphasized ownership or participation not control or transformation. As to the second part of the government's position, no industry or sector has, up to the 1990s, been defined as "very strategic." So, the emphasis has been on joint ventures and other forms of partnerships. Such unequal arrangements have not affected the control of foreign investors over technology, information and high level manpower. The marginalization and domination of indigenous investors and the distorted, disarticulated and peripheral character of production and exchange within the social formation continued to militate against the industrialization of the country and the possibility of its emergence as a Newly Industrializing Country (NIC) (Ake, 1978, 1985; Nnoli ed. 1981).

Between 1972 and 1977, the government tried through a series of five Nigerian Enterprises Promotion Decrees, to define the spheres of interest and operation between local and foreign capitals. The goals of these policies had nothing to do with the creation of a viable, self-reliant and productive base for the economy. Rather, they were aimed at reducing areas of tension, expanding the scope of operation of the local bourgeoisie, consolidating foreign domination of lucrative and strategic sectors of the economy and reinforcing Nigeria's dependent path to capitalist development:

> ...the indigenization process was interested less in control than in ownership. The Nigerians who have acquired foreign enterprises have been keen on retaining the foreign management of these enterprises, particularly the management of production. A powerful and vociferous lobby has continued to press with some success for easier expatriate quotas. In the joint ventures, including involving government participation, production continues to be left to foreign shareholders and experts who control the technology of production...Nigerians...hold the honorific position of chairman and the top positions in administration, personnel and public relations, while foreigners...occupy the management positions of the production line (Ake 1985: 21-22).

Thus, indigenization has since the early-1970s not resolved the contradictions between political and economic power: the latter in the hands of foreign capital and the former in the hands of the local bourgeoisie. What is important, however, is the high degree of the subordination of political to economic power in view of the incorporation and domination of local capital by its foreign counterpart (Ake 1978: 48). Without doubt, the series of decrees in the mid-1970s widened the base of the local governing classes through their expanded participation in the economy. The Nigerian Industrial Development Bank (NIDB) and the Nigerian Bank of Commerce and Industry (NBCI) were specifically set up and encouraged to sponsor the desire of the local bourgeois fractions in their bid to buy equity shares in foreign firms.

Of course, changes and revisions have been made to the program since the rather crude and simplistic initial legislation of 1972 which had only two schedules: Schedule I exclusively reserved for Nigerians and Schedule II required to have at least 40 percent indigenous equity participation. The 1977 Decree, for instance, reclassified enterprises into three Schedules. Schedule I was reserved exclusively for Nigerians - advertising and public relations, casinos, and gaming centers, department stores, commercial transportation etc.; Schedule II contained 57 enterprises in which Nigerians were required to own at least 60% equity shares - fertilizer production, cement production, beer brewing, boat building, insurance, mining and quarrying, banking, etc.; and Schedule III contained 30 enterprises in which at least 40 percent indigenous equity participation was required - glass and glass products, tobacco manufacture, drugs and medicines, electrical appliances, watches and clocks, aircraft, textile industries, etc. (Ake ed. 1985; Beckman 1982, 1985; Eleazu 1986; Evans 1979).

In spite of attempts under the 1977 Decree to ensure strict compliance, through stiffer penalties to defaulters and lesser concentration of shares in a few hands, foreigners flouted the laws in several ways. Even before its abandonment under structural adjustment in the late 1980s, they used Nigerians as fronts, bribed government officials to obtain exemptions on various grounds, manipulated and exploited immigration laws to qualify for exemption, automated their production processes in order to qualify for Schedule III status, and distributed shares among many ordinary shareholders thus rendering them powerless over the decision-making process of the enterprises. As Tom Forrest (1982: 339) noted, the "sphere of foreign capital accumulation has not been greatly affected by the growth of the Nigerian bourgeoisie, by indigenization, or by the extension of the state sector. State intervention has greatly favored large-scale foreign enterprise, the indigenization exercise notwithstanding." To be sure, the failure to implement the nine-point program, the arrogance of power, high-scale corruption, mismanagement, a flamboyant, expensive but largely ineffective foreign policy, deepening contradictions and class fractionalization all combined to ensure the fall of the Gowon regime in 1975.

d) The Murtala/Obasanjo Regime: The Consolidation Of Neo-Colonialism And The Transition To Civil Rule

In his 14th independence anniversary nation-wide broadcast on 1 October 1976, General Gowon dismissed plans for civil rule as "unrealistic" - since "it would be utterly irresponsible to leave the nation in the lurch." Furthermore, he argued that civil government would "throw the nation back into confusion," because it was evident that "from the general attitude, utterances and manoeuvres of some individuals and groups and from publications during the past few months, it was clear that those who aspire to lead the nation on the return to civilian rule have not learnt any lesson from the past experiences" (Gowon in Ojiako 1979). Following this broadcast, however, it became clear that his regime would not last to witness any transition to civilian rule. Given the height of prevalent social tensions, contradictions and conflicts it was easy to project that the class factions or fractions which controlled the means of coercion were likely to cash in on the situation and oust Gowon. In fact, this happened on Tuesday 29 July 1975 at 6.00 a.m. when Colonel Joseph Naven Garba, then head of the Brigade of Guards, announced that the Gowon regime had been overthrown in a bloodless <u>coup d'etat</u>. Gowon was then away in Kampala, Uganda attending the 12th summit meeting of the OAU. The coup brought to power Brigadier Murtala Muhammed as Head of State, Brigadiers Olusegun Obasanjo as Chief of Staff Supreme Headquarters and Theophilus Danjuma as Army Chief of Staff, Alhaji M.D. Yusuf became Inspector-General of Police, Commodore Michael Adelanwa, Chief of Naval Staff and Colonel John Yisa Doko, Chief of Air Staff. In rationalizing the coup, Brigadier Muhammed in a nation-wide broadcast on 30 July stated: "After the civil war the affairs of state, hitherto a collective responsibility, became characterized by lack of consultations, indecision, indiscipline and benign neglect. Indeed, the public at large became disillusioned and disappointed by these developments. This trend is clearly incompatible with the philosophy and image of our corrective regime" (Muhammed, reproduced in Ojiako 1979:79-83). Brigadier Muhammed also complained about the neglect of the armed forces, inaccessibility to both public and advisers, insensitivity to public opinion, bad advice from traditional rulers, corruption and chaos.

The new regime restructured the government into three levels: the Supreme Military Council, the National Council of States and the Federal Executive Council. The 1973 census, which had generated so much tension, was cancelled, new governors were appointed for states, protection was guaranteed to foreign nationals and investments, and a firm stand was taken against corruption and graft: "...the task ahead of us calls for sacrifice and self-discipline at all levels of our society. This government will not tolerate indiscipline. This government will not condone abuse of office" (Muhammed quoted in Ojiako 1979: 80).

While swearing-in the new military governors on 31 July, the new head of state explained why those who had served under Gowon were removed from office: "The former Governors were removed because of allegations of graft and misuse of public funds and widespread dissatisfaction with their personal conduct. There were complaints of ostentatious living, flagrant abuse of office and deprivation of people's rights and property. Other allegations were perversion of time-honored government procedures, nepotism and favoritism, desecration of traditional rulers. All these gave the impression that the states were being run as private estates" (Ojiako 1979: 83). The Murtala regime then embarked on a massive "shake-up" and "clean-up" exercise which saw the dismissal, retirement, suspension, demotion etc. of hundreds of thousands of leaders and workers - commissioners, professors, cleaners, judges, soldiers, policemen, clerks, chief executives, in fact all categories of workers - in the public services and parastatals for indolence, indiscipline, corruption, lateness to work, inefficiency, irresponsibility, mismanagement and other crimes. Of course, there was a lot of witch-hunting and many persons who deserved to be terminated, jailed or detained actually presided over the exercise in their respective departments, using the opportunity to settle old scores and eliminate their immediate subordinates.

In October 1975, as a demonstration of its commitment to return the country to civil rule, the regime set up a Constitution Drafting Committee (CDC) to which Brigadier Muhammed recommended an executive presidential system of government in place of the old Westminster model. The CDC was headed by a prominent bourgeois lawyer Chief Rotimi Williams. In February 1976, the government created seven new states bringing the number to 19 and a decision was reached to move the federal capital from Lagos to a more central location in the country, Abuja.

Boundary issues, corruption and the stabilization of the economy occupied the attention of the Muhammed regime. It is instructive to note that, for all the enthusiasm, activity and nationalism demonstrated by the new government, its commitment to the reproduction of Nigeria's dependent capitalist path of "development" remained intact. While Nigerians were being harassed and dismissed by the day, the corrupt foreign-dominated and unproductive private sector did not attract the attention of the new government. In fact, many members of the bourgeoisie affected by the "clean up" exercise were back in the regime as consultants, part-time and full-time board members, contractors and in other capacities even before the assassination of Murtala Muhammed in February 1976 in a bloody coup attempt led by Colonel Suka Buka Dimka.

e) The Dimka Coup And The Obasanjo Regime, 1976-1979

On 13 February 1976, Lt. Col. Suka Buka Dimka attempted to lead a coup d'etat which failed, though he did succeed in assassinating General Muhammed. The reason for the attempted coup by the so-called "young revolutionaries" was that "Murtala Muhammed's hypocrisy had been detected." Dimka also accused the regime of going "communist" (Dimka in Ojiako: 1979). With the coup failed and Murtala assassinated, the next in command, General Olusegun Obasanjo reluctantly, "against his personal wishes and desires," accepted the mantle of leadership.

In a nationwide broadcast, Obasanjo promised that there would "be no change in policy." However, this was not to be: the economy gradually slid into stagnation and decay, inflation rose to 25% (sometimes more), the country became totally dependent on the oil sector for revenues, agriculture was neglected, rural decay set in, armed robbery, smuggling, unemployment and prostitution became national problems, bureaucratic inefficiency, and ineffectiveness, corruption and social violence came to characterize the political economy. Draconian labor decrees were enacted, students and social critics were repressed, Nigeria took a jumbo loan from Euro-American financial institutions, the food import bill rose and the military carefully stage-managed the transition to civil rule to ensure that the interests of capital, foreign and national, were preserved. In the heady days of high-priced OPEC oil and the count-down to civilian rule, the Third Plan and constitutional committees provided a formal context for capitalism and democracy in Nigeria at the end of the 1970s.

f) The Third National Development Plan, 1975-1980

The philosophical framework of the N30 billion Third Plan remained the same as that which informed the Second Plan. This included self-reliance, egalitarianism, justice, equal opportunities, unity, freedom and democracy. However, the level of investment was to be about ten times the level of the Second Plan; in fact, at the time this was the largest development plan the country had ever had, with the private sector expected to contribute N10 billion of the total package.

The size of the new Plan reflected the increasing contribution of the oil industry to the national economy. It was thus easy for the oil state of Nigeria to enjoy relative financial autonomy. It no longer relied on foreign aid, taxes or tariffs in order to keep development projects afloat. It was easy to use oil wealth in the lubrication of the edges of class contradictions, buy-off opposition and sponsor an adventurous and expansive foreign policy (Ihonvbere, 1982a, 1986).

The Plan expected GDP at 1974-75 factor cost to grow by 8.5% in real terms to about N16,756 million to 1976-77. Though this was never really achieved, just as the sectoral projections were not met, the figures do not reveal the depth of the crisis generated within the economy by the Third Plan. Extreme dependence on the oil sector and neglect of the rural areas and agriculture weakened the economy's base and concretized its dependence on external forces and interests. For instance, the value of merchandise exports was projected to reach N8,269 million in 1976/77. Of this, the oil sector was expected to contribute N7,913 million. As Ojiako (1979: 165) commented "like many of other Plan forecasts, actual magnitudes have fallen far below the projected levels. The total value of...exports in the period under review (1976/77) was only N6,743 million, about 81 percent of the plan forecast..."

It is interesting to note that while export figures declined, imports actually increased. The latter were projected to reach N3 billion but actually increased to over N5 billion, an excess of over N2 billion or almost 70 percent, over the projected level. The direct consequence of this was a rise in the national deficit level, with profound medium-term implications. There were, therefore, severe balance of payments problems. For instance, the anticipated balance of merchandise trade of N5,296 million was not realized as only N1,271 million or 24% of the target was achieved. For the current account, a deficit of N220 million was recorded as opposed to the projected surplus of N3,635 million. Total gross national savings declined by 16.7%

Perhaps the great lesson of the Third Plan was that Nigerian leaders and planners learnt that "development" had more to do with people than with money. Huge budgetary allocations did not in any way resolve the contradictions within sectors of the economy. The Plan period was plagued with corruption, waste, indiscipline, mismanagement and drift. Massive reviews did not help the situation as the cost of living shot up and unemployment figures rose. Food, clothing, and other basic needs gradually became luxuries for the poor. In the 1976/77 fiscal year alone, "food items, clothing, other services, tobacco and kolanuts and drinks recorded the highest price increases of 28.2 percent, 25.3 percent, 23.9 percent, 22.4 percent and 18.1 percent respectively." In addition, the "index of food items which went up by 42.1 percent in 1975 rose by 28.2 percent in 1976" (Ojiako 1979: 166). The country's external debt rose from N355 million in 1976 to N380 million in 1977. Over-inflated contracts, corruption, increased import bills for food and capital goods equally depleted foreign exchange earnings. The Head of State had cause to note in his 1976/77 budget speech that: "while government revenue for the 1975-76 fiscal year was N3.9 billion, recurrent and capital expenditures totalled N4.7 billion. Thus a deficit of N0.8 billion was recorded in the first nine months of the fiscal year" (Federal Ministry of Information 1977).

In the same year, according to Obasanjo, Nigeria spent all its foreign exchange earnings and "dipped into accumulated reserves." In his subsequent 1977/78 budget speech, he complained bitterly about "rapidly accelerating price inflation, economically crippling congestion of our ports, widespread shortages of essential commodities, a deficit in Federal Government finances and... deterioration in our balance of payments position" (Federal Ministry of Information 1977). Such complaints were repeated in the 1978/79 fiscal year by Alhaji Shehu Shagari, the country's first executive civilian president in his 1980 budget proposals to the National Assembly (Falola and Ihonvbere 1985). As Shehu Musa (1979: 45), Permanent Secretary in the Ministry of Finance noted in 1979:

> Among the various disequilibria observed in the economy at the close of the last financial year (1978/79), were elusive but galloping inflation, an almost inexorable rise in government spending occasioned largely by development commitments in the wake of dwindling revenue and the tapering-off of foreign earnings, a lopsided dependence on imports, the perennial high consumption propensity, a less-than satisfactory level of foreign investment a disappointing level of non-oil exports, and an unsatisfactory growth in agricultural and industrial output.

It is obvious, therefore, that the *Third National Plan, 1975 - 1980* hardly contributed to strengthening and diversifying the base of the Nigerian economy. As far as its effects on the condition of non-bourgeois forces was concerned, the various May Day speeches by labor leaders during the Plan period show very clearly that poverty, alienation, unemployment, insecurity and fear characterized the daily existence of the average worker.

The cosmetic measures announced in the "State of the Nation" broadcast by General Obasanjo back in June 1976 made little difference in terms of meeting the five fundamental objectives of development planning in Nigeria. Further revisions to the indigenization decree, reform of the Marketing Board system and the creation of eight Commodity Boards, the establishment of rent tribunals to attempt rent control, efforts to control inflation by banning price increases, the introduction of the Operation Feed the Nation (OFN) and so on, all failed woefully on the part of the government to implement them. On a more important note, they failed because the innovations and programs were largely superficial and, in most cases, diversionary. They did not in any way address the structural contradictions and deformities of the Nigerian social formation, particularly the question of ownership and control of the Nigerian economy. It is within the context of this dependent, foreign-dominated, corruption-ridden and crisis-ridden economy and society that the transition to civilian rule was initiated in 1975 and effectively executed on 1 October 1979.

g) The Transition To Civil Rule, 1975-1979

One of the reasons why General Gowon was overthrown in 1975 was that he reneged on his earlier promise to disengage from politics and return the country to civil rule. That singular action earned him the enmity of those professional politicians and fractions of the armed forces that were interested in such disengagement. On coming to power, General Murtala Muhammed promised to return the country to civil rule in 1979. Within a few months, he had announced a five-stage disengagement program:

> -appointment of a Constitution Drafting Committee (CDC), 1975;
> -creation of New States, 1976;
> -elections into a Constituent Assembly, 1977;
> -ratification of the Draft Constitution and lifting of the ban on active politics, 1978; and
> -general elections and military disengagement, 1979.

In speech after speech, even after the assassination of General Muhammed, the military leaders reiterated their promise to disengage (Falola and Ihonvbere 1985; Ihonvbere and Shaw 1988; Ihonvbere 1994). This constant renewal of the pledge bought the support of politicians and other interest groups and encouraged such persons and coalitions to accommodate the economic chaos which accompanied the implementation of the Third Plan. As indicated above, on 4 October 1975 a 50-person committee under the chairmanship of Chief Rotimi Williams was set up to prepare a draft constitution for the country. Chief Obafemi Awolowo declined to serve on the committee on the grounds that he was not a "constitutional draughtsman." The real reason, however, was that participation in the CDC would have interfered with his elaborate plan to form a political party and run for the presidency following the lifting of the ban on politics. When he declined to serve, he was not replaced. The CDC comprised at least two representatives from each of the 12 states and others selected by the government. In his address to the inaugural meeting, General Muhammed advised the CDC to give serious consideration to eight crucial matters:

-ambiguous commitment to federalism;

-elimination of cut-throat political competition based on a system or rule of winner takes all;

-a de-emphasis on institutionalized opposition to government power;

-decentralization of power;

-evolution of a free and fair electoral system to ensure adequate representation at the center;

-depoliticization of the census;

-establishment of an executive presidential system; and

-constitutional restriction on the number of new states.

The CDC, which was largely made up of the representatives of fractions and factions of the Nigerian bourgeoisie, completed its work on schedule making sure that it did not depart fundamentally from General Muhammed's suggestions and that its recommendations did not in any way affect the structure and relations of production and exchange in Nigeria. The only two really radical members of the CDC, Drs. Segun Osoba and Yusuf Bala Usman, two well-known historians, had cause to disagree with the ideological underpinnings of the Draft CDC Report. They, therefore, wrote a Minority Report which was carefully ignored by both government and the media. The official Draft Report was submitted to General Obasanjo on 14 September 1976 and was thrown open for a nation-wide debate on 7 October 1976. Memoranda were to be submitted to the new Constituent Assembly.

The Constituent Assembly was made up of 203 members elected from Local Governments on the basis of five members per Local Government. The balance was then computed on the basis of population. In addition, the government appointed certain persons to represent specific interest groups such as students and women. But these representatives of non-bourgeois forces were effectively harassed and marginalized in the Assembly itself by its Chairman Justice Udo Udoma. The proceedings were seen more as a forum for making connections, forming the nucleus of political parties, and engaging in all sorts of political alignments and realignments, all in preparation for the abrogation of the ban on active politics. Within a few months of its existence, over 20 "Committees," "Associations," "Movements," and "Groups" with criss-crossing memberships and political programs had been formed by the members of the Constituent Assembly. In fact, some of the populist programs of the military such as the National Youth Service Corps(NYSC) and the Land Use Decree were thrown out by the Assembly. The fundamental objectives and directive principles of state policy which had guided Second and Third Development Plans were made non-justiciable.

The delegates performed clean political surgery on the Draft, cleansing it of any populist pretensions. Bala Usman (1979: 131) provided an apt summary of the extent to which petty-bourgeois interests dominated the deliberations of the Constituent Assembly: the Assembly men made provisions to protect private property, to allow private ownership of television and radio stations, and to operate foreign bank accounts while treating the issues of collective ownership of land and land-for-the-user with levity. Their activities showed clearly "that they had no interest in the objectives of government but only in the mechanics of getting power and wielding it."

All the same, the Assembly formally completed its assignment in August 1978. Prior to that General Obasanjo had, on 15 November 1976, inaugurated a 24-man Federal Electoral Commission (FEDECO) under the chairmanship of Chief Michael Ani. The functions of this Commission included the conduct of elections, delimitation of constituencies and registration of political parties. As well, on 14 July 1978, all military governors were redeployed to purely military duties. The states were now to be governed by Military Administrators. It is important to note that the Constituent Assembly hardly paid attention to the suggestions, criticisms and comments of the public. The majority of the members were largely concerned with the entrenchment of policies, programs and institutions that would facilitate accumulation on ethnic, religious, regional, class and other grounds. It is not surprising, therefore, that the military administration, in its "overriding concern...to ensure good government, orderly progress and harmony of the nation..." (Federal Ministry of Information, 1978) had to recommend the use of Hausa, Igbo and Yoruba as official languages in addition to English, which the Assembly had recommended. Also, the decrees relating to the National Youth Service Corps, National Security Organisation, Public Complaints Commission, and Land Use, were integrated into the Constitution. The Assembly had, in its wisdom, eliminated these. Altogether, 17 amendments were made to the Constitution by the departing military government.

On 21 September 1979 the military government promulgated Decree No. 25 and the *Constitution of the Federal Republic of Nigeria, 1979* was born, though it was to take effect from 1 October 1979. As well, the ban on active politics was lifted. Within three months more than 50 political parties were formed. Of these, only 17 applied for registration, following a series of "well- publicized splits, reconciliation and mergers" (Ojiako 1979: 261). On 23 December 1978 FEDECO announced that only five parties - the Great Nigeria People's Party (GNPP); Nigerian Peoples's Party (NPP); National Party of Nigeria (NPN); People's Redemption Party (PRP) and Unity Party of Nigeria (UPN) - would be allowed to contest the 1979 elections.

In spite of superficial differences between these parties and over-publicized conflicts among their leaders, there was not much real difference among them. To be sure, the PRP was somewhat more to the left than the other four; and the UPN had social democratic leanings though all its leaders were petty-bourgeois. But none of the five parties had a scientific, revolutionary program for a fundamental restructuring of the Nigerian social formation. The leaderships were petty-bourgeois and were equally committed to liberal politics played within the dictates of bourgeois law and constitution. In all five parties the masses never had a say in the drafting of manifestos, selection of candidates, finances, campaign strategies and so on. They were merely objects of manipulation in the new political process. None of the political parties had a concrete program for transferring power to the non-bourgeois forces; none was sufficiently anti-imperialist to adopt a program of the nationalization and socialization of the means of production and exchange. All that Nigerians were exposed to were rhetoric, fine speeches, lies, corruption, thuggery, and slogans.

In the elections that followed the campaigns, during which no serious issues were raised, the most conservative of all the parties - the NPN - won the majority of seats, states and the presidency. Senatorial elections were held on 7 July 1979: the NPN won 36 seats from 12 states, the UPN 28 seats from 7 states, the NPP 16 seats from 4 states, and GNPP 8 seats form 3 states and the PRP 7 seats from two 2 states. The Federal House of Representatives elections were conducted a week later on 17 July; again, the NPN won 168 seats, the UPN 111, the NPP 78, the PRP 49 and the GNPP 43. On 21 July elections into the State Assemblies were held; the NPN won 487 seats, the UPN 333, the NPP 226, the GNPP 115 and the PRP 143. Finally, the gubernatorial elections were held on 28 July; the NPN won in 7 states, the UPN in 5, the NPP in 3, the GNPP in 2 and the PRP in 2. In the presidential election, which was the last to be held, on 11 August 1979, Alhaji Shehu Shagari of the NPN polled, 5,798,857 votes, Chief Awolowo of the UPN, 4,916,651, Dr. Nnamdi Azikiwe of the NPP 2,822,523, Alhaji Aminu Kano of the PRP 1,732,113 and Alhaji Waziri Ibrahim of the GNPP polled 1,686,489. So, Alhaji Shehu Shagari was pronounced by FEDECO as having satisfied section 34A sub-section (1) (c) (1) of the Electoral Decree No. 73 of 1977 by scoring the highest votes in the election. As well, he had satisfied sub-section (i) (c) (ii) of the same section by scoring not less than one-quarter of the votes in each of at least two-thirds of all the states in the Federation. Thus, he was declared the President-elect of the Second Federal Republic of Nigeria.

These elections did not and could not change the base and structure of politics in Nigeria for several reasons. First, all the parties were ethnically-based. Second, the three major parties were reincarnations of the old ones which together wrecked the First Republic. Third, the campaign speeches and manifestoes did not provide a fundamental program for transforming neo-colonial dependence in Nigeria; they all revolved around the personalities of old politicians, traditional rulers or a cabal of aristocrats, retired civil servants, retired generals and businessmen. What is more, fourth, the major parties scored their highest votes in their respective ethnic bases - NPP - East, NPN - North and UPN - West. Fifth, the electioneering campaigns were accompanied by bitterness, conflicts, violence and abuse. These in themselves were designed to intimidate weaker parties and politicians as well as to divert the attention of the public from the deliberate neglect of the real issues - national control of the economy, political stability, mobilization, self-reliance, empowerment, human rights, accountability and the provision of Basic Human Needs. And finally, several court cases were instituted against election results at all levels, which undermined their legitimacy further. Other political parties rejected the results of the Presidential elections. Opposition candidates simply refused to believe that they could lose the various elections (Falola and Ihonvbere 1985).

Of course, the judiciary at this point in time was the last place any politician could obtain justice. By then, it had been highly politicized and corrupted. The mass media was no different as they all danced to the political interests or sympathies of their respective owners, chairmen and editors. Many lawyers and journalists saw the period as a golden opportunity to acquire wealth and the courts dismissed serious election petitions on flimsy "technical" grounds. Newspapers wrote editorials welcoming and praising new governors even before the final results were announced.

Generally these "results" were reflective of the specificities of politics in Nigeria's neo-colonial society. However, the tensions, petitions, conflicts, deepening economic crisis and other symptoms of underdevelopment did not prevent the military regime from handing over power to the elected civilians. On 1 October 1979 when Alhaji Shehu Shagari was sworn in as Nigeria's first executive president, General Olusegun Obasanjo retired to a multi-million naira farm in Ogun State. But, as the next chapter indicates, the palpable and predictable limitations of civilian rule did not contain all the contradictions and demands. Thus, soon after the second set of civilian elections, the officers returned to power: the cycle began again on New Year's Eve, 1984.

CHAPTER FOUR

Second Republic:
Presidentialism and Petroleum
1979-1983

The second half of the 1970's was marked by two parallel yet related processes which together seemed to symbolize the transformation of Nigeria's political economy. First, at the level of politics, the run-up to 1979, was as indicated, a period of intense constitutional debate and political manoeuvre, leading to the mid-1979 series of elections. And second, at the level of economics, the period was notable for the sudden, sustained rise in the price of Nigeria's primary export, petroleum. This conjuncture of military withdrawal and oil boom constituted a promising context for the return to civilian government. But at the level of social relations it also transformed expectations and values: corruption escalated in scale and scope along with competitions for office and for contracts.

Thus, the Second Republic, rather than serving as the model for a continual era of civilian rule, as anticipated in the long CDC debate in the mid-1970's, became an unseemly interregnum between reformist military regimes. Shagari's NPN government struggled through its first term and a second round of national elections on the back of a fading petro-naira boom. But, because of its acquisitive inclinations, it could not impose the necessary austerity and honesty required by declining national income and integrity. The return of the officers on New Year's Eve 1983 was, then, an inevitability as well as a relief given the chaos and rapaciousness of the NPN administration, revealed starkly in the second set of elections in mid-1983.

To be sure, previous military as well as civilian regimes had benefitted from access to national resources. But the scale of plunder between 1979 and 1983 was unprecedented (Madunagu 1982, 1984; Falola and Ihonvbere 1985). This distinctive style of unofficial privatization or personalization has been classified as "anarchic" by Mazrui (1986:16): "The state's resources went into private hands partly because there was no effective control. President Shehu Shagari might himself have been personally clean, but he did not check or control the process of privatization." Orthodox analyses of this period still tend to concentrate on constitutional provisions and official decisions. But such a superficial perspective would miss most of the relations and reasons which caused the Buhari coup on New Year's Eve, 1983: the anarchic political economy in which political position could be readily and rapidly translated into personal accumulation because of the continuation of impressive petronaira resources and permissive political culture.

a) Democracy In A State Of Anarchy

The Second Republic was designed by the (majority) Constitution Drafting Committee (CDC) to be a democratic federal system with an executive president and two elected assemblies: Senate and House of Representatives. As noted in the previous chapter, the minority report of Segun Osoba and Bala Usman commented, however, the CDC treated only "superstructural" political issues, declining to recognize the social bases of the Nigerian political economy: its essentially dependent capitalist substructure (Falola & Ihonvbere 1985:24-25 and 36-39). The return to democracy was, therefore, based on a superficial analysis and a belief in the efficacy of constitutionalism.

In reality, two factors were assumed to excuse or explain this idealistic position: petroleum and indigenization. Yet the former has proven unstable and the latter problematic (Ake 1985:21 and 20); hence the demand from CDC's successor, the Political Bureau, for a commitment to a socialist rather than mixed economy. But, we will see in the next chapter, the Political Bureau's efforts to learn from the failures of the CDC, the foresight of the minority report, and the cautionary legacy of the Second Republic did not ensure receptivity by the Babangida regime: politics are still assumed to be separable from economics. In particular, it would appear that the unfortunate record of the Second Republic's Federal Electoral Commission (FEDECO) in failing to contain corruption and manipulation might have demonstrated the need to make certain structural and institutional changes to the process of political competition. It has become clear that the disregard of the distinctive character of capitalism in Nigeria - the oil-dependent "rentier" economy (Ihonvbere & Shaw 1988b) - serves to undermine any well-meaning attempts to craft the ideal polity through constitutional means alone.

The Second Republic represented, then, a flawed attempt to institute a post-British and post-military regime which would capture and contain the intense contradictions of Nigeria following both civil war and oil boom through a directly-elected executive presidency in a federal structure quite unlike the parliamentary system of the First Republic. The bicameral legislature consisted of a House of Representatives with 450 members while the Senate had 95, five from each of the 19 states. These states, whose Governors were also elected directly, had single Houses of Assembly, whilst local authorities were also elected directly. The President, who was not a member of the National Assembly, appointed his own administration as did the 19 Governors. Both President and Governor had to not only win a majority of the federal or state votes but also had to secure at least one-quarter of the votes in two-thirds of either the states or local government areas, respectively; this check constituted an attempt to enforce "federal character" and to avoid minority candidates by requiring ethnic pluralism.

The 1979 constitution enshrined the principle of the separation of powers, both between federation and the states and among executive, legislative and judiciary. Presidential appointments to senior federal positions had to be confirmed by the Senate.

The return to civilian rule was by no means uncontroversial as the election results treated at the end of the previous chapter were quite disputed and inconclusive, particularly in the case of the presidency, which resulted in an unsuccessful appeal by Chief Awolowo against the election of Shehu Shagari. The Second Republic was thus launched in controversy, with the military and NPN working to support each other, particularly against the UPN. In general, as can be seen from the election results, the divisions in the federation remained, once again expressed

95

through party politics; NPN in the north, UPN in Yorubaland, NPP in Iboland, with minority parties like PRP and GNPP being successful only in their leaders' areas, Borno and Kano, respectively (Adamu & Ogunsanwo 1983).

The ruling NPN forged an alliance with the NPP, reminiscent of that in the First Republic, which thereby secured positions and influence. But the pragmatic accord between North and East was never an untroubled one as the NPP was continually concerned about being absorbed while some of its Representatives and Senators declined for particular reasons to accept party discipline. The agreement collapsed in mid-1981 leading to further fragmentation and paralysis. The alternative, so-called "progressive alliance" of UPN, PRP and GNPP was then reinforced with NPP, a formidable challenge to the incumbent NPN in the run-up to 1983. Yet it too, typical of Nigeria's intense idiosyncratic politics, had difficulty in maintaining cohesion or agreeing on a common list of candidates, symbolized by the unwillingness of either of the two grand old men of the UPN and NPP – Awolowo and Azikiwe, respectively – to stand-down for each other. This lack of cohesion was exacerbated by incessant federal-state disagreements and legislative-judiciary misunderstandings.

As the Shagari regime became more politically embattled and economically vulnerable so it escalated both rhetoric and repression, especially, in the run-up to the second set of elections, in which it needed to win an absolute majority of seats and positions to avoid further vulnerability to minority parties in another coalition. As Falola and Ihonvbere (1985:78) lamented: "The accord and alliances were partly symptomatic of the problems of political instability and the inability of the national bourgeoisie to create a viable hegemony. These problems were also reflected in state-federal relations, the inability of the president to command general acceptance and the tendency towards fascism and political repression".

Politics in the Second Republic was, then, intense and bourgeois: intense because considerable resources as well as status were at stake and bourgeois because they were superficial, personal and non-ideological. The 50 months were characterized by endless debates about the spoils of and disinterest in economic production reflecting a highly Nigerian agenda of "federal character," "zoning," coalition-formation and state-creation. Despite its radical rhetoric, the UPN was not really concerned about the social poor or economic bases either; the real opposition to the NPN lay in sections of the media, academe, unions and professions. Status and style were everything as politicians fought for high-rise housing on Victoria Island in Lagos, generous incomes and benefits, and lavish travel allowances: there was every incentive to travel out, especially to the US on so-called "study tours" to see how to implement a federal presidency. The costs of democracy in terms of direct and unseen expenses were enormous. And the urban poor, rural peasants, most of the elderly and children, and many women all suffered as the economy was both neglected and abused.

Although the formal costs of democracy constituted a small proportion of the real costs in terms of diverted and wasted resources, they were not insubstantial. The annual costs of operating the National Assembly totalled some N44 million in addition to another N40-50 million for salaries. Further, Fedeco cost N45 million to run. The total annual bill for the basic operations of Nigeria's peculiar brand of democracy in the Second Republic was some N125-150 million (Falola & Ihonvbere 1985: 109-113). And at election times or party conferences the ostentatious attraction and distribution of funds constituted a further demonstration of the arrogance of power and property.

Explanations for the widely-recognized deficiencies of the Second Republic can be placed on a spectrum from the personality of the President to the political economy of peripheral capitalism; middle-range criticisms include problems of consensus and the constitution. Perhaps the most (in)famous diatribe about the character of Nigerian politics and society at the time was Chinua Achebe's (1982) lament *The* Trouble with Nigeria published just before the chaos of the 1983 elections; while the most authoritative is the International Labour Office's report First Things First (1981) treated below in Section c.

Amongst other trenchant critiques of the political economy are those by Claude Ake (1985), Edwin Madunagu (1982), Okwudiba Nnoli (1978, 1981) and Bade Onimode (1982); this radical materialist perspective is most developed in Falola and Ihonvbere (1985). The middle-level criticisms derive from orthodox lawyers and students of public administration. Amongst the latter is Lapido Adamolekun's (1985) lament for the lack of consensus, constitutional and political, which deprived Nigeria of good government; he attributes this lack largely to ethnic rather than class struggles:

> ...in the actual operation of the 1979 Constitution, practice has departed significantly from theory.The federal character concept which was expected to help ensure unity and stability has become a critical factor in the intense partisan competition among the political actors. Worse still, the consequent preoccupation of the politicians with the maintenance of inter-ethnic, communal and sectional equality has undermined the effective functioning of the key political institutions - the political parties, the executive and the legislatures. Equally significant is the fact that the emphasis on ethnic group equality, which has been essentially an elite affair, has meant a de-emphasis on other forms of inequality which directly involve the majority of the population (Adamolekun 1985:45).

Adamolekun captures widespread disillusion with the masquerade character of public life in Nigeria during the period - forms of collective democracy and ideology covering private preoccupations and accumulation - as well as with the inattention to exponential inequalities. The new political elite flaunted its power and patronage so that respect for authority declined to minimal levels. Politics were widely seen to have become a game in which winning was much more important than strategy or style. The endless series of political manoeuvres and gestures were exposed as mere power plays, superficial attempts to attract allies and create coalitions in the run-up to the second set of elections in mid-1983.

If the 1979 elections were controversial, those of 1983 were much less credible (see Table 4.2): the intervening political decay, disorder and decadence undermined vestigial confidence in the objectivity and efficiency of Fedeco, the judiciary and the police alike. The indecent clamoring for office and access combined with escalating intemperateness and intimidation eroded belief in the electoral process even before the clearly unreliable and unrepresentative results were announced. In any case, despite intimidation and corruption, the dominance of the NPN was hardly credible. The corruption of Nigerian politics in 1983 made a coup inevitable; the only questions were when and whose. As Falola and Ihonvbere (1985:227) assert, "other than the newspapers, by the time Shehu Shagari was sworn in October 1983, the majority of Nigerians knew that in spite of police intimidation...the NPN government could not survive until 1987."

Likewise, given the glaring deficiencies of the first as well as second elections, a coup became an inevitability from the early 1980s onwards: "The rabid corruption of political office-holders, the failure of some state governors to perform, personality clashes, intra-party feuds, conflicts between some state governments and the federal government and closures resulting from efforts to superimpose the political party's constitution and structure over the power and authority of elected officials were bound to impact upon the 1983 elections." Falola & Ihonvbere (1985:207-211) proceed "to identify six major internal contradictions which affected the outcome of the 1983 elections":

-the non-performance and arrogance of power of most of the 19 state governors who ignored the plight of the masses;

-the worsening living standards of the majority, especially following the impositions of austerity measures in 1982;

-intense intra-bourgeois class contradictions leading to political and economic alignments and re-alignments reflected in frequent "decampings" from one to another party and the proliferation of parties to six, including the supposedly radical Nigeria Advance Party (NAP);

-the unpreparedness and biases of Fedeco;

-the partisan and anti-popular role of the police; and

-the non-objective and non-rationality of the Nigerian press.

99

In the event, as the climax of a period of arbitrary rule and economic decline, "no one, except members of the defunct NPN, would argue that the 1983 elections were free and fair" (Falola & Ihonvbere 1985:216). Indeed, it really became apparent that no election had occurred in 1983. Rather, given the new corporatist tendencies of the "Kaduna mafia" a "selection" was carried out through a "strong alliance between the police, Fedeco officials and members of the ruling NPN, with the latter supplying the money" (Falola & Ihonvbere 1985:217). Thus these elections exacerbated rather than contained social divisions and tensions: ethnic, religious and class chauvinism, rampant corruption, economic disinterest and mismanagement, regional claims, widespread violence and rigging. The results were so patently fixed that even to NPN insiders and supporters they were incredulous.

Following the formal month of voting there was an ominous and extended period characterized by a mixture of intense litigation, frequent violence and widespread disillusion in which most people displayed disregard and disbelief of the results; even the victors felt cheated. A majority of the governorship results were contested in the courts with variable results. To be on the safe side, decamping to the NPN accelerated, just in case it declared a one-party state, supported by its corrupted police, especially the mobile units. In such inauspicious circumstances, President Shagari and his new regime ruled for three months, from 1 October to 31 December 1983. On New Year's Eve 1983 the inevitable happened, to the delight of most Nigerians: the Buhari coup terminated the undistinguished and unloved NPN regime. The Second Republic was over: a disappointing and disillusioning 50 months of lackluster and indulgent civilian rule. Rather than oppose military intervention in politics, Nigerians, on New Year's Day, January 1984, exchanged pleasantries with: "Happy New Government"!

b) Economic growth without development

The Second Republic was inaugurated as the oil-boom peaked but its populist and ostentatious leaders declined to treat the visible symptoms of over-dependence on the petroleum mono-commodity or over-reliance on imported foods, parts, skills and technologies. Instead, the trend was away from, not towards, incremental and effective indigenous control of the economy as Nigeria became a Mecca for unscrupulous contractors and entrepreneurs. Election to the National Assembly or appointment to the over-staffed civil service became licenses to extract "dash," much of which was deposited in European banks. Growth was to be achieved through state-financed mega-projects in roads, steel-plants, energy installations, university campuses and hospitals, with "trickle-down" accruing via sub-contracts or corruption. The place of the technocrats and national bourgeoisie - the leading fractions under Gowon, Mohammed and Obasanjo - was taken once again by the politicians and compradors. The political economy came to reflect an extreme level of dependence on exports of oil and imports of foods, luxuries and turn-key plants. By the early 1980s, under civilian rule, Nigeria had become a classic "rentier" state, with the politicians as the rent collectors (Ihonvbere 1982b, 1985, 1988; Ihonvbere and Shaw 1988b).

John Toye (1987:117) has suggested that the "new" "political economy of rent-seeking" represents a useful approach through which to explain growth and accumulation without development. If for him India was a "rent-seeking society" (Toye 1987:122) then Nigeria during the Second Republic would seem to have been, par excellence, another rent-seeking polity; one in which the political class, aided by the bureaucratic bourgeoisie, extracted personal surplus from control over contracts and licenses. This transformation was facilitated, in our case, by a permissive political culture on the one hand, and a generous oil-based exchequer on the other. Rent thus collected could be exported because of the foreign exchange income resulting from the flow of oil exports. Whilst the bonanza lasted - and as the 1980s dawned only a few skeptics in Nigeria doubted that it would last for a long time if not forever - the rural-urban and rich-poor gaps were disregarded; food imports were preferable to the new class to food production as foreign exchange could thereby be accumulated. As Falola & Ihonvbere (1985:94) assert, whilst collapsing several elements including extroversion into one concept:

> The problems and contradictions of a rentier state,
> were, more than ever before, brought into the open
> under the Shagari administration. It is necessary
> to understand the nature of the rentier state in or-

der to comprehend the implications of oil wealth
for an economy which relies on revenues from a
sector over which it has limited control and which
is not integrated with other sectors of the economy

The ambitious long-term plans of the post-war Mohammed/
Obasanjo period to expand both infrastructure and
indigenization were thus subverted by the short-term imperatives of political or bureaucratic office under Shagari.
To be sure there was corruption of both proposals and resources under the military but the overt and unabashed rapaciousness of the NPN regime generated opposition even
within the Kaduna mafia. This was no proto-NIC with a
dirigiste, "developmental state"; rather it was a classic commodity bubble in which personal enrichment was the criteria rather than collective good.

The characteristics of the rentier state in Nigeria were
five-fold: i) concentration on circulation rather than generation of wealth; ii) reliance on one capital-intensive source of
commodity income, namely petroleum; iii) neglect of agriculture, rural areas and food production; iv) disregard of
labor and encouragement of capital, especially foreign; and
v) extroversion of the economy through international trade
and finance, both formal and informal, rather than internal
integration. To be sure, the rhetoric of the *Fourth National
Development Plan, 1981-85*, prepared under Shagari, responded to such a vulnerable and unsustainable condition
but its ideology was so far removed from reality as to be
laughable: self-reliance, agriculture first, small projects,
maintenance, enhanced private sector and social equity.
Despite a belated recognition that petroleum demand and
price might not be sufficient for the massive N82 billion capital investment envisaged over the first five years of the 1980s,
the Plan nevertheless still called for

> ...rapid economic growth and structural change
> with relative stability in   domestic rices...Consc-
> ious effort will, however, be made during the
> Fourth Plan period to promote a more even distri-
> bution of income and thus obviate the long-term
> social disharmony that could result from the
> present trend (Fourth Plan 1981:40).

Neither the economic nor the political preconditions for Plan implementation were present during the 4 1/2 years of the lackluster Shagari administration. If previous plans had suffered from ineffective execution because of administrative diversions and social pressures - the state as private facilitator rather than collective director - then that of the civilian interregnum was doomed or flawed from the start. The political culture and political economy were hardly propitious as individual power and property were the criteria rather than national. Aside from visible and widespread corruption, the cost of growth in Nigeria was exorbitantly high and the degree of appropriateness and maintenance low. Moreover, the direction of the economy was ominous if petro-naira were to stagnate or decline; a dramatic shift from agriculture to energy and a less dramatic change from commodity exports to domestic manufacturing, or at least assembling.

Growth in aggregate terms following the civil war was impressive but its distribution in regional, spatial, and class terms (let alone gender) was highly skewed; the North, cities and bourgeoisie benefitted more than the South, countryside and non-bourgeoisie. Thus while manufacturing and electrical production trebled over the decade of the 1970s, agricultural production either stagnated or declined, even before allowance is taken of rapid increases in demand because of increases in population, income and migration. Likewise, there was a remarkable increase in external trade with a simultaneous shift from a diversified commodity base to a high-level of dependence on petroleum. There was also a parallel change in directions of external trade, away from Britain and towards Europe, Japan and the US.

Not only was the petro-naira bubble unstable because of dependence on oil exports and food imports, it also relied on increasing amounts of internal and external credit. Official and private loans were relatively uncontroversial while the economy was expanding but once it began contracting in the early 1980s debtors became nervous and difficult: the mid-1980s marked the beginning of an official preoccupation with debt negotiations and repayments as well as with a managed devaluation of the naira. By the mid-1980s, Nigeria was effectively a debtor nation, unable to effectively manage or service its debts in spite of huge oil resources.

The rationales for this heavy level of borrowing are threefold: national and private investment and government over-expenditure. But the reasons for such investment are intimately connected to the character of the political economy and culture, specifically, how to sustain and profit from the boom period of the rentier state. Moreover, these figures severely underestimate the foreign exchange "leakage" caused by smuggling on the one hand and "exportation" of ill-gotten gains on the other.

Despite the dependent and vulnerable character of the petro-naira political economy, and despite all the difficulties of communication, inefficiency and corruption, the financial system of Nigeria grew dramatically in the late-1970s and early-1980s. An underbanked economy was transformed because of market forces in the cities and government policies in the countryside so that by the end of 1985 there were almost 1300 bank branches throughout the Federation belonging to some 30 commercial banks, all of which were majority Nigerian-owned and some of which were totally indigenous. The largest commercial (First, Union, African, National and Continental and United) and merchant banks all had international shareholding and connections but were subject to Central Bank of Nigeria (CBN) jurisdiction. The financial sector, including the embryonic but active Lagos Stock Exchange (1-2,000 securities traded each month, mainly government stock, for an average value of N20-30 million monthly) both expanded for and serviced the series of indigenization decrees, providing a balance to rapid state sector growth in the 1970s. They also served to provide a platform for World Bank-driven privatization conditions in the mid-1980s; an essential correlate for national capital accumulation and reproduction.

Despite the series of indigenization decrees over the previous decade, by the early-1980's, the crucial manufacturing sector was particularly volatile because of three interrelated external factors: imported inputs, smuggling and foreign investment. Because of the latter - foreign capital and technology - the first factor has been crucial; i.e. imported parts, chemicals and metals (Ake ed. 1985; Agbese and Ihonvbere 1991; Biersteker 1987). But because of the rentier character of the state, all too little foreign exchange has been available for such costs so the level of assembling has been unstable, as revealed in cycles of industrial production. The second factor, smuggling, has also undermined internal production by undercutting local sources in terms of price and presumed quality: a clear case of comprador factions competing with national and technocratic interests. For example, the CBN <u>Annual Report</u> for 1985 (29) in explaining the cause of a reduction in Nigerian's textile production explained that the "decline was due to a...'silk invasion' of Nigeria's textile market. Smuggled silk, lace and guinea brocades from China, and other countries of South East Asia freely gave unfair competition to locally-produced textile products." Other major sectors - electronics, foods, cigarettes, alcohol - were also seriously undermined by smuggling based on the inflated value for the naira and a permissive rentier state. In short, this distinctive political economy was characterized not only by familiar contradictions between labour and capital or the peasantry and the state but also by tensions within the ranks of the bourgeoisie, both between larger and smaller entrepreneurs, but also between national and technocratic fractions on the one hand and comprador and political fractions on the other. The ambiguities and tensions over the series of indigenization decrees reflect this contradiction as do inter-party and inter-state divisions. In general, the more developed South favored private national capital whereas the less advanced yet politically dominant North preferred state and international capitals at least until it caught up to the South.

Clearly, the oil-dependent rentier economy of Nigeria constituted a classic case of growth without development. Largely a reflection of the tenuous connection between Nigeria's bourgeois class and <u>productive</u> activities, oil seemed to have deepened negative coalitions, community tensions, class contradictions, and general alienation of non-bourgeois constituencies. As the ILO's <u>First Things First</u> (1981:5) laments; "There is little evidence that Nigeria's big expenditure has made much impact on the conditions of the majority of the population. The distortions experienced by the other oil exporters seem to have been repeated in Nigeria." Despite significant aggregate expansion in the post-war period of constitutional debate leading up to the 1979 elections, this growth was neither equitable nor sustainable. The benefits went to a minority within and outside the country while the majority eked out a marginal existence. The infrastructure was improved and expanded but at massive cost while ill-gotten gains were amassed in foreign banks and properties. Despite promises of popular benefits in terms of educational and health facilities, food and water resources, housing and electricity, the realities of life for most

Nigerians improved marginally at best during the civilian interregnum. Democracy did not bring development despite macro-economic expansion.

c) Corruption Of A Political Economy

During the unfortunate Shagari presidency, the visible corruption of the polity and the palpable corruption of the economy together eroded popular values and confidence, which had already been undermined by the shock of the civil war. The petro-naira "dream" was one of get-rich-quick through association with politicians or contractors. Ostentatious births, marriages and burials became the order of the day, with ill-gotten wealth being "sprayed" on supporters and collaborators. In such heady times, the dignity of production, agricultural or industrial, was overlooked. The criteria of success escalated from Mercedes-Benz to personal jets for "big men" and from stereos to VCR's for the middle-class. The consumption ethic fuelled the import boom and smuggling epidemic, which were both based on an overvalued currency. But to maintain popularity, the new political class declined to grasp the nettle: the distinction between collective and personal property, between state and society became very blurred.

Aside from literary and polemical attacks on the state of Nigeria in the early 1980's the most sustained and objective critique is contained in the ILO's report First Things First. Its analysis of the failings of planning in Nigeria is perceptive and prescient, placing constraints and contradictions in comparative perspective, prophetically, even before the evaporation of the oil boom:

> In view of the imbalances already evident in Nigeria before the oil boom, experience elsewhere carried the warning that its transient proceeds could easily be wasted. The challenge was all the greater because Nigeria's oil reserves were relatively small, especially in relation to its population. Moreover, there was much greater poverty than in any of the other major oil exporters (with the possible exception of Indonesia). As the outset, Nigeria needed a strategy that would take advantage of the bonanza of revenue for two main

purposes which were mutually compatible: to alleviate poverty and to create an economic structure that would survive when the purchasing power of oil exports - as before long it will - levelled off and declined (ILO: 5).

Even before the incidence of oil gloom and political change the benefits of an increased GNP had not reached the majority despite rhetoric and planning to the contrary:

> There is still much acute poverty in Nigeria. The most obvious constraint on alleviating this used to be financial - the national income was too low. Then, in the 1970's, this obstacle had apparently been removed by the rapid acceleration in the value of oil exports. The National Development Plans took advantage of the greatly increased revenues of stimulated economic growth with big investment projects, mostly in the cities. The assumption was that, in due course, the increases in income would trickle down to the poor. Since the overall rate of economic growth has apparently been fast in the past two decades, there should be by now signs of substantial improvements in the living conditions of the majority of the Nigerian people. These are not evident. Indeed...large numbers are worse off in numerous respects, especially in the rural areas but also in the big new slums of the cities (ILO: v).

And aggregate growth did not even reinforce prospects for a developmental state of self-reliance, as dependence and consumption both increased, despite the claims and ideology of successive Plans. Again, with uncanny foresight, *First Things First* sounded a note of caution:

> One cannot even say that the Nigerian economy is now fundamentally stronger. Within a few years - perhaps one more decade - the real value of the receipts from oil (i.e. the imports they will buy) will probably level off and start to decline. So Nigeria needs other exports, capable of earning many

> billions of Naira and of bearing an increasing share
> of the cost and technology on which the economy
> has come increasingly to depend (not to speak of
> servicing the growing foreign debt). The country
> also will require a higher degree of self-sufficiency.
> Yet, with every year that passes, the proportion of
> oil in total exports gets closer to 100 per cent, and
> imports, even of food, are increasing rapidly (ILO:
> v)

In short, the ILO team diagnosed the "Nigerian disease"
with considerable insight and nuance; perhaps their only
fault was to be too cautious rather than too critical. And,
like many other students of this ebullient yet incoherent
political economy, they shied away from explanation, possibly because of their intergovernmental status: "...while we
can give a generalized picture of distortions and inequities,
it is much more difficult to find out exactly what has happened in various sectors...The data...almost without exception... are shown to be seriously inadequate. Where they
exist their quality is often dubious..." (ILO: 6).

The ILO, in contrast subsequent IBRD/IMF directives,
advocated greater *self-reliance* rather than extroversion, attention to BHN rather than GDP, or to development rather
than expansion:

> Despite the heavy political emphasis on planning,
> there seems to have been no conscious strategy of
> development in the past. There were, however,
> implicit priorities - on economic rather than social
> development; on urban areas rather than rural; on
> industry rather than agriculture; on new works
> rather than maintaining and improving existing
> services. *To meet the country's basic needs and achieve
> greater self-reliance would have required a very differ-
> ent, indeed the opposite, set of priorities.*
>
> ...the goals of the National Development Plans
> were never more than indicative...underspending
> was chronic in virtually every sector.
>
> The Plans also attached far too much importance
> to economic growth *per se*. Growth does indeed
> seem to have been fast, but the figures have a very
> shaky statistical foundation. Moreover, *overall*

> *growth rates have little meaning, since the basic struc-*
> *tural problems, the inequalities and imbalances, have*
> *apparently increased.* (ILO: 10) (emphasis added)

And these structural and social conditions could not be relieved by constitutional drafts or political changes alone, no
matter how determined Buhari and Babangida were to be
reformist.

If the Buhari coup evoked a mixed response in Nigeria
- the majority were relieved while the minority of politicians,
bureaucrats and contractors who had benefitted from access
to 'loot' were disappointed as well as worried — there was a
similarly ambivalent reaction in the West, which also reveals
the diversity of major external interests in Nigeria (Falola
and Ihonvbere 1986; Ihonvbere 1985). On the one hand,
Northern democratic governments lamented the demise of
the presidential system even though they recognized its
palpable deficiencies. And, on the other hand, foreign capitalist institutions welcomed the greater likelihood of economic stability and debt repayment under the officers. Since
then, significantly, Nigeria's links with the World Bank, International Monetary Fund, and Western companies and
markets have expanded and evolved with the return of the
soldiers which coincided with the imperatives of structural
adjustment.

CHAPTER FIVE

OFFICERS RETURN:
SOLDIERS AND STRUCTURAL ADJUSTMENT
1983-1992

The second experiment with civilian government was terminated on New Year's Eve 1983. Since 1 January 1984, Nigeria has once again been ruled by officers, some of whom were associated with and affected by the Mohammed/Obasanjo period if not the earlier Gowon regime. As with almost all coups, that of Muhammad Buhari was intended to cleanse the body politic: something of an imperative given the palpable corruption and disintegration of the Shagari presidency, particularly during and after the mid-1983 "elections." But the economic times were not propitious for either social reform or diplomatic reassertion; after 20 months of growing repression the lackluster Buhari regime was replaced by Ibrahim Babangida, a self-proclaimed inheritor of Mohammed's mantle - from Supreme Military Council (SMC) to Armed Forces Ruling Council (AFRC), although 13 members of the former included 15 new officers to constitute the latter.

Unlike the euphoria of the brief Mohammed administration in the early 1970s, the interregnum of Buhari in the early 1980s was perhaps the most controversial and unpopular regime yet experienced in Nigeria. Major-General Buhari with his widely hated number two, Tunde Idiagbon, imposed military solutions on the terminally-ill body politic: imprisonments and trials of ex-politicians and detentions of opponents. A series of decrees were enunciated to legalize such repression, notably Decrees Number 2 which facilitated detention without trial and Number 4 which was used to silence many democratic voices. The National Security Organization (NSO) became an independent authority harassing and detaining at will. The democratic spirit of Nigeria was contained but not crushed.

To be sure, under Buhari some of the excesses of the Shagari period were eliminated - rampant corruption of contracts and import licenses- and essential steps were taken to restructure the economy in the context of declining oil revenues and continuing urge for personal accumulation. Efforts to recover ill-gotten gains were initiated and retrenchment in the bloated civil service was pursued with vigor in order to cut the public wage bill and promote bureaucratic responsibility and efficiency. The regime also continued negotiations with the IMF for short-term stabilization assistance.

After the transparent rape of the country under the civilians and with the visible decline of public services and mores, a dose of military discipline was not entirely unwelcome. But military solutions soon got out of hand in a political culture neither familiar with nor tolerant of such excesses. Moreover, it soon became apparent, as Northerners associated with the disgraced NPN were treated more leniently than Southerners from opposition parties, that the Supreme Military Council (SMC) was but the military wing of the "Kaduna mafia" (Ekwe-Ekwe 1987). Babangida stepped in to control the disregard of human rights and extreme deflation of the post-Shagari economic measures:

> In the context of the deepening economic depression and painful but imperative austerity measures, escalating repression not only engendered profound resentment and bitterness among a people who cherished their personal freedom, it also permitted the regime to govern without any effort to forge a popular consensus or to be accountable for its actions. Perhaps most fatally, the regime's arrogance led it to ignore critical opinion and the imperative for some consensus building even within its own senior military ranks. After their downfall, Generals Buhari and Idiagbon were pointedly condemned by their successors for their monopolization of power and their paranoiac in-

tolerance of debate and criticism even within the
military (Diamond 1987b: 202).

To prove his 'human rights' orientation - popular without
formal democracy - Babangida launched a series of great
"debates" notably over the IMF: a nation-wide "palaver"
over debt, devaluation, privatization and reorientation. The
"ethical revolution" of Shagari, and "War Against Indiscipline" of Buhari were succeeded by the "Mass Mobilization
of Self Reliance, Social Justice, and Economic Recovery"
(MAMSER), a euphemism for "structural adjustment with
a human face." Despite an unsuccessful coup attempt in
1987 and student and labor unrest in June 1986, the
Babangida regime implemented a wide-range of structural
reforms in 1986-7 under the guise of an economic emergency:
an "indigenous" package of IMF/IBRD-informed measures
from devaluation to deregulation. The controversy over and
intensity of this adjustment combined with protracted debates over constitutional forms led the government in mid-
1987 to postpone the promised return to civilian rule from
1990 to 1992. It also moved to ban all previous politicians
and bureaucrats from future competition for office, thus ensuring that the proposed Third Republic would not constitute a replay of the chaos and corruption of the Second. As
if to mark the transition from the old guard to a new generation, several prominent first republic politicians including
one of the two "fathers" of federation - Obafemi Awolowo -
died in May 1987; the university he financed and founded -
Ife - was renamed after him.

The two official and one unofficial "debates" which paralleled that over the economy were on political structure,
foreign policy and on religion, respectively. If the first two
national discussions had the regime's seal of approval the
third, on religion, did not. Indeed, its very existence and
extremism have raised fears throughout the country for stability of institutions, relations and values. In a period of
unanticipated and intense economic contraction, one without the safety-valve of party politics, it may not be surprising that religious fundamentalism has come to fill the void
in Nigeria as elsewhere (Mazrui 1988). The catalysts for
unprecedented religious expression and confrontation were
the so-called "Maitatsine" riots in several northern cities in
the first half of the 1980s and the regime's sudden membership in the Organization of Islamic Countries (OIC) in 1985.

These served to release latent apprehensions about north-ern, Moslem dominance of post-Obasanjo governments around the supposedly ubiquitous "Kaduna mafia." The inconclusive OIC Shagaya Commission of Enquiry led the Babangida regime to establish an Advisory Council on Religious Affairs (ACRA). But precisely because this Council includes most religious tendencies it has been less than united, with the Christians boycotting some of its meetings in early 1988. The religious issue has foreign policy as well as domestic implications — how much fanaticism is imported from Libya or Iran amongst Moslems or from the US amongst Christians? — and has replaced or reinforced ethnicity and region as divisive social forces (Clarke 1988). Thus in addi-tion to issues of constitution, economy and external rela-tions a related debate has arisen about the place of religion in Nigeria: a divided or secular society?

a) Political Economy Under Structural Adjustment

Notwithstanding its many detractors and a series of diver-sions - labor unrest, sporadic violence, and cabinet reshuffles - the Babangida administration — as successor to the lack-luster Buhari regime — started out·repeating the reformist role of the Mohammed/Obasanjo period in very different and difficult circumstances: low oil prices, strong pressures for democratization from popular forces, high debt repay-ments and increasing inflation. The mood and style of the country changed dramatically in parallel with the Structural Adjustment Program (SAP) and Foreign Exchange Market (FEM): from over-optimism and inflated expectations to excessive and misplaced pessimism. The heady days of petro-naira yielded to unrelieved gloom about shrinking real incomes and decaying institutions. The middle and work-ing classes have been particularly hard hit — declining sala-ries, benefits and jobs along with involuntary retrenchments and retirements — while the peasants never really benefitted from the boom and the bourgeoisie still has ways to com-pensate for shrinking forex receipts. Thus SAP and FEM constitute an historic conjuncture not only in terms of policy direction but also in terms of political economy: changing internal as well as international terms of trade mean differ-ent social contradictions and coalitions (Lubeck 1986), with female labor and income being more important than ever to both households and nation.

Structural adjustment towards a more "realistic" currency and "self-reliant" economy was inevitable in Nigeria as in many other parts of Africa but the Nigerian case is distinctive because the policy followed from a national debate and was not tied directly to IMF conditions. The goals of Nigeria's SAP, as stated by the Federal Military Government in July 1986 were; i) to restructure and diversify the productive base of the economy in order to reduce dependence on the oil sector and imports; ii) to achieve fiscal and balance of payments viability over the period; iii) to lay the basis for a sustainable non-inflationary or minimal inflationary growth; and iv) to lessen the dominance of unproductive investments in the public sector, improve the sector's efficiency and intensify the growth potential of the private sector (Adeotun 1990; Ihonvbere 1991; Aluko 1987). To achieve these goals, the government was to implement the usual policies of privatization/commercialization, deregulation, desubsidization, devaluation and other demand management policies. To be sure, the state had to restructure the economy to reduce the foreign exchange leakage and to satisfy debtors at both London (private) and Paris (public) "clubs," but the mixture was an indigenous and flexible one, which initially gave the impression of being more responsive to shifting internal pressures and external situations. The Second Foreign Exchange Market (SFEM) was but a one-year interim stage (mid-1986 to mid-1987) in which the (black) "market" value of the naira became the official rate; and monthly auctions of foreign exchange then gave way to continuous applications and negotiations for international currencies.

During the first full year of FEM - 1987 - Nigerian banks disbursed $2.6 bn, mostly through the auction: $995 m for raw materials, $748m for machinery, spare parts and CKDUs, $704m for finished goods, $227m for food imports and $12m for the agricultural sector. In 1988, $3.9 bn was projected for FEM and another $1.7 bn for debt-servicing; in addition $1.2 bn was anticipated in other foreign exchange receipts: loans, aid and investments. All these are very modest figures compared to the extravagant hey-day of the oil-boom and Shagari periods.

The devaluation of the naira to about one-fifth of its established official rate (more against strong European and

Pacific currencies, less against the weak US dollar) was but the most dramatic and visible element of SAP from mid-1986 onwards. It served to transform not only external but also internal terms of trade. Initially, the comprador class lost ground to national fractions, including landed aristocrats and big farmers. Import Substitution Industrialization (ISI) became feasible and attractive again providing smuggling and dumping were contained – one reason for lengthy border closures in the mid-1980's – and external inputs and parts were available. However, as adjustment got under way, the inability to maintain financial discipline, widespread corruption and political opposition to the unequal distribution of the costs of adjustment, reversed this trend: compradors – drug pushers, currency traffickers, importers and exporters, contractors, used car dealers and landlords – came to be the real beneficiaries of SAP (Aluko 1987; Adeotun 1990; Olaniyan and Nwoke eds. 1989; Ihonvbere 1989, 1990).

For a period, traditional "colonial" commodities were revived through a combination of increased foreign markets and reduced naira prices – jumps in production as well as price of cocoa, cotton, groundnuts, palm oil, rubber etc. - and an expanded internal industrial demand. Ironically, deregulation may have produced fewer domestic restraints on trade – from wheat to metals, beer to plastics – in part in response to the pressures of indigenous industrialists (see Table 5.2). Agricultural programs which got bogged down in bureaucracy in the Second Republic were now executed not so much through massive investments in river basins or state farms as through "market forces": agribusiness to produce internal industrial inputs and commodity production to secure higher external prices for cocoa, palm oil, rubber, etc. In the process some industries and interests were drastically affected – e.g. flour-milling and bread-baking, beer brewing and vehicle assembly – but the liberation of market forces in an essentially ebullient and laissez-faire economy like that of Nigeria served to open up new opportunities, particularly industrial innovation and renovation. SAP has transformed established assumptions and relations in Nigeria's political economy: the national bourgeoisie, farmers and internal traders have all been affected in particular ways. It has certainly benefited comprador factions, contractors and external traders. Female production is more essential and extensive than ever. Yet, it has caused misery and disillusionment amongst the majority of the people (*Newswatch* 5 October 1990; *African Concord* 3 September 1990; *Quality* 27 September 1990; *Africa Event* October, 1989).

SAP may have a positive macro impact - from a consumer to a conserver economy — but on the micro level it has created considerable hardship, unemployment, adjustment and uncertainty, leading to determined opposition by an unlikely coalition of Manufacturers of Nigeria (MAN) (fears of deindustrialization) and Nigeria Labor Congress (NLC) (fears of unemployment) (Agbese and Ihonvbere 1997; Ihonvbere and Ekekwe 1988). The former's leaders were appeased somewhat by the reflationary 1988 budget but Congress' cadres were incarcerated in mid-1986 and late-1987 and relieved of their offices in mid-1988 as symbols and centers of resistance to SAP. But if organized labor has suffered retrenchment, the un- and under-employed have endured further marginalization with both forced and voluntary reemigration of workers from ECOWAS. Real unemployment is well over 50% despite this, however, and the ubiquitous informal sector can only advance survival, not accumulation and reinvestment.

It is fortuitous for the regime that there is such a flexible non-formal sector of exchange, repair, small-scale production and black market for there has never been widespread social insurance, and structural adjustment has eroded whatever minimal welfare services existed. But no country can grow through informal trade alone, and formal production and distribution have declined significantly in the 1980s under oil "gloom" — and then officers' "reform": deflation, retrenchment and commercialization. Stores are full because few can buy while basic commodities continue to be inflated; the high prices of education, health, transportation (especially vehicles if not gas) and food mean fewer savings and luxuries. Happily, the new modesty had moderated illusions of endless consumption and corruption and some maintenance is finally taking place, but the indulgent aberration of the oil boom remains the yardstick rather than the more modest regularities of pre- or post-oil periods.

Structural adjustment has, then, already generated social adjustment: strengthening of the national bourgeoisie, of big peasants and of the female-dominated informal sector. But comprador factions have also done very well. The drug business is booming more than ever. Trafficking in foreign currency remains very lucrative in spite of the attempts to curtail its influence through the *Bureaux de Change*. Corruption has equally reached an unprecedented level under structural adjustment; a level which makes the politicians of the Second Republic look like saints (Ihonvbere 1991; *Newbreed* 1 October 1990; *Analyst* January 1987; Okoye in *African Guardian* September 24 1990). However, the middle classes and workers are without doubt worse off with many non-nationals returning to neighboring states under pressure of either the law or the economy.

The shifting internal division of labor back to agriculture for foods and commodities and towards local rather than foreign inputs is to be welcomed: a long-anticipated and overdue corrective. But the distribution of the gains remains problematic; the unequal distribution of the costs and pains of adjustment continue to mediate efforts at national mobilization and integration and to militate against the creation of the prerequisite environment for redevelopment. The social as well as financial coalitions and correlates have to be in a propitious position, and this remains problematic as it is not entirely predictable or manageable.

If Nigeria is comparable yet distinctive in Africa in terms of successive civilian and military regimes as well as the cycle of economic boom and bust, it is now so in terms of structural adjustment (see Martin 1991). For, unlike so many Third World regimes, Nigeria initially rejected any notion of a deal with the IMF — the outcome of the national debate of late-1985 was negative — but proceeded to design its own program, with IBRD policy assistance yet no direct finance. And unlike most African states, Nigeria, negotiated with London as well as Paris Clubs as indicated below. Moreover, except for low quality of commodities and so sub-premium prices - Nigeria's privatization exercise has proceeded slowly, despite lengthy anticipation and debate.

Following a visit to Nigeria in mid-1988 by British Prime Minister Margaret Thatcher, some 13,000 companies from 50 countries accepted less than attractive terms for unsecured debts of US$4.6 billion. However, a disgruntled group of creditors, Confidential Recoveries, continued to oppose the deal as unsatisfactory. They might yet go as far as to insist on Nigeria declaring a default. Under the agreed terms, debts were to be paid off at the rate of 1.25% of principal and accumulated interest until 1990, thence 2% until 2010. These terms do not approach the earlier negotiations with London (private) and Paris (official) Clubs of insured debtors, but then many of the uninsured note-holders engaged in extravagant and corrupt deals during the Shagari era. And they may yet be repaid earlier if higher debt-equity "swaps" are arranged or Nigeria's economy improves (*West Africa* 25 January 1988: 116-117).

Yet, Nigeria's still rising foreign debt profile remains an obstacle to both the adjustment program and negotiations with its creditors. At the end of 1990, the foreign debt stood at $30 billion (*The Punch* 17 October 1990). For most of 1990, the Finance Minister, Alhaji Abubakar Alhaji was busy bargaining with the London Club on a Nigerian proposal to convert commercial bank debts into 30 year bonds at 6.25 per cent interest a year. Following a recent rescheduling agreement with the Paris Club, the United States cancelled $32 million of debt owed to it by Nigeria (*Financial Times* 28 January 1991). Such gestures, while important, make very limited impact on the country's debt profile for, as Richard Synge has noted, "Without a lasting solution, the debt issue could continue to be a destabilizing factor for the economy in the years ahead and deprive Nigeria of the foreign support and investment it sorely needs in the 1990s" (*West Africa* November 26-2 December, 1990).

Privatization and localization have continued to advance in Nigeria encouraged by World Bank preferences and indigenization experiences. Captains of industry have emerged in several regions and sectors and deregulation of airlines, petroleum sales and commodity distribution have encouraged new local investments: Kabo, Okada and GAS airlines (no longer "charter" but recognized "schedule" carriers), General, Soca, and Florie gas stations, and a range of cocoa, palm and rubber exporters. Backwards and forwards linkages and connections are encouraged, with a few major Nigerian companies exporting capital to Western, Eastern and/or Southern Africa. But the major state-owned businesses have yet to be sold — Nigeria Airways, National Electricity Power Authority, communications companies, assorted manufacturing plants, service sectors etc. — although the debate over what parastatals should not be privatized has advanced awareness and decision.

In early 1988, the government issued a five-fold categorization of 78 companies hitherto owned by state or federal governments—full or partial privatization, full or partial commercialization, or public institutions. The more commercial enterprises - breweries, hotels, food producers, insurers etc. — fall into the first category; banks, cement producers, paper and steel mills, oil distributors, vehicle assemblers, newspapers, NNSL, and Nigerian Airways fall into the second; the third category includes NNPC, NITEL, mining and property companies; and the fourth NEPA, NPA, NTA, railways, steel companies, currency and stamp printer and river basin authorities. Only educational and cultural institutions are to fall into the category of public institutions (*West Africa* 25 January 1988: 146-147). This categorization and treatment follows the lines of internal recommendations (Sanda, 1986) and external comparisons, a judicious mixture of Nigerian expertise and African and international experience.

The sequencing of SAP and FEM are nevertheless quite problematic in an ebullient and insistent political economy like that of Nigeria. It will depend on a mixture of supportive external events — no dramatic rise or fall in the value of oil and gas, no general rejection of the terms of debt renegotiations, and no major international conflict which might spill-over to engulf Nigeria, such as a protracted Middle East war - and internal elements - gradual but careful reflation of the economy, orderly return to workable and sustainable civilian administration, and containment of populist, fundamentalist and regionalist pressures.

Despite inevitable yet unorganized public resentment, President Babangida appears to have been quite adroit at managing events and opinions. The "Maradona" of Nigerian politics (as he is often addressed by the media) — distinguished by his unpredictable political actions rather than footwork in soccer — has survived controversial debates over devaluation, constitution, housing and foreign policy and, in association with determined monetarists like Drs. Kalu Kalu, Olu Falae, and Chu Okongwu, has agreed and sustained terms with the World Bank. Whilst the senior technocratic elite may be rather thin and isolated, preoccupied by foreign exchange rates and debt renegotiations, it has thus far been quite masterful and consistent.

While the federal government's level of expenditure continued to grow in the mid-1980s despite soldiers' return and debt negotiations its distribution has evolved dramatically, reflecting the imperative of military's interests and World Bank conditionalities. Expenditure has shifted from social services and infrastructure to security and agriculture. Likewise, the soldiers have been more effective revenue collectors than the politicians and more conservative spenders, at least until the reflationary 1988 budget: more centralized expenditure and a reduced deficit. Nevertheless, the cost of servicing debt continued to grow as interest payments increased and naira values fell: from N1.5b in 1983 to N2.5b in 1985. The total public debt remaining— $11 billion.

Meanwhile, aside from marginal changes in national non-oil production and exportation, the quantity and value of Nigeria's oil sales continue to decline or stagnate compared to the brief oil "bubbles" of the late- 1970s and early-1980s (and momentarily during the Gulf war of late- 1990 and early- 1991). In short, the economic run-up to the 1993 return to civilian rule has not been as positive or supportive as that of the late-1970s. As Barclays Bank of London noted in a recent review of the Nigerian economy, the years of austerity and the unequal distribution of the pains of adjustment "have placed considerable social hardship on the populace" and "could slow-down the adjustment programme and endanger the government's objective of transferring political power to a civilian government in 1992" (*ABECOR Country Report*, July 1990).

The current period of economic planning and constitutional engineering is particularly intricate: how to prepare the financial and political bases for democracy. Despite the set-back of disorganized and disorderly local elections in late-1987, the New Year's budget of 1988 displayed flexibility and realism. Nigerians felt they had already suffered enough in 1987 under a period of "Pay higher now for a better future." In the run-up to the budget they demanded improved incomes and services and no further erosion of subsidies, particularly not of petrol. The NLC and MAN are constrained in their adversarial roles under the military yet popular pressures led to the beginnings of reflation and re-direction. The 1988 budget at N24.3 bn (N13.7 bn for the federal government, N8.2 bn for the states, N2.5 bn for local governments and N0.54 bn for mineral producing areas and ecological problems) reflected the reflationary policies of the regime. But revenue at N15.7 bn left a N8.6 bn deficit to be made up by internal and external loans. In 1987, recurrent expenditure was limited to N10.7 bn, although this was up from N5.6 bn in 1986; in those two years, capital expenditures were but N6.7 and N5.9 bn, respectively.

The 1990 budget estimated a planned revenue of N25 billion at the federal tier of government against a total planned expenditure of N39.8 bn. The performance of the budget showed some improvement in 1989 revenue receipts of N27 bn. However, the deficit component rose from the projected N10.8bn to N22.3bn. This was the highest deficit experienced by the Nigerian economy in the previous seven years. Officially, the economy grew at the rate of 5.2% at 1984 constant prices, the Composite Consumer Price Index dropping from a 50% increase in December 1989 to 31% in the first quarter of 1990, to 22.1% in May and 16% in October. However, as the authoritative UBA has noted, "the effect of the drop in inflation rate was not felt substantially as costs of living and prices of most goods and services continued to soar within the year" (*UBA Monthly Business and Economic Digest* January 1991: 2).

The 1991 budget was announced against the backdrop of certain novel developments in the economy. For the first time in the recent period, the country budgeted a surplus of N0.1bn. It also tried to address itself to some of the pains of adjustment as well as the "socio-economic problems created by previous budget provisions." It also made room for a new revenue-sharing formula designed to allow funds to get to the grassroots. This new formula gives 50% to the Federal Government, 35% to the states and 15% to the local governments. This contrasts with the previous arrangement of 55%, 35% and 10% respectively.

The main objectives of the first budget of the new decade were control of inflation, expansion of the private sector, control of population growth, achievement of a higher GDP growth ratio and the control of liquidity within the system (*UBA: Monthly Business and Economic Digest*, January 1991: 4). In line with the monetarist policies of the adjustment regime, under the 1991 budget, total federal expenditure was held at N38.66bn, a 4.9 decline from the 1990 figure. Recurrent expenditure was estimated at N25.581bn, a 6% decrease from the 1990 figure. Capital expenditure was estimated at N13.085bn, a decrease of 2.7% from the 1990 figure.

As with its predecessors, this budget has to contend with fluctuating fortunes in the oil market and the ability of the regime to maintain financial discipline, check waste and corruption and create the required "enabling environment" for economic recovery. Whichever way the country's political fortunes might shift, the price of oil, on which the economy is still exclusively dependent, will be the single most important factor determining the success or otherwise of the 1991 and successive budgets.

The petroleum price issue as dogma and dialectic is characteristic of politics under SAP: general guidelines from Bank, Fund and creditors which are bent in practice because of continual domestic debate and disagreement in what Watts (1987: 33) claims to be "the most dynamic and volatile economy in Africa." The national bourgeoisie in Nigeria has been concerned about the price and availability of raw materials and spare-parts for years; the 1988 budget did little to allay their concerns as tariffs on completely knocked-down units (CKD's) remained high and prices for parts exorbi-. tant. Moreover, some industries, like breweries, may contract further if bans on certain raw material imports are not lifted.

The contradiction between free, if not cheap, imports and devaluation and deregulation is thus apparent; deindustrialization will continue unless local industry is protected from sustained dumping and smuggling. MAN therefore seeks some import controls as well as priority for spare parts and raw materials. It is also concerned that reflation seems to imply the revival of government expenditures. In short, the Nigerian definition of structural adjustment throws up its own set of contradictions which reflect social history and current conditions, one of tenuous coalition within a military-dominated social order. As Michael Watts (1987: 295) has cautioned, explanation and projection will have to be sensitive to "the changing balance of forces and conditions of struggle that will inevitably emerge from the current Nigerian conjuncture."

b) Political Culture Under Officer's Rule

The political debate of the mid-1980's, which had been centered on the Political Bureau and then Constitution Review Committee (CRC) was subsequently directed by President Babangida's mid-1987 declaration on the timetable for and terms of any return to civilian rule: the Third Republic. The rather idealistic continuing discourse over the merits of one political party, diarchy or triarchy was effectively terminated by the announcement of a four-year schedule of elections to culminate in a national civilian government in 1992. The regime's response to the Political Bureau's rather radical preference expressed in its official "Cookey" Report of April

1987 for a "socialist" state with representation for women and workers was unequivocal: two parties only, no official ideology and no reserved seats; i.e. a continuation of the open "mixed economy."

The Political Bureau's report was never published, with *Newswatch's* attempts to leak it leading to a six-month ban; but the government's white paper ("Towards 1992") indicated that it was quite progressive, within a "political economy" mould (Agbese 1989). Any transition back to civilian rule will, however, be contained by long-standing traditions and short-term interests — limited institutional pluralism with continued democratic pressures - so that less moderate positions — military-dominated diarchy or popular socialist economy — are unlikely to be either considered or implemented as indeed they were not under the CDC in the late-1970s.

When Nigeria marked 27 years of independence in the fall of 1987, it had experienced just 10 years of non-military rule. By 1992 it will have been run by officers for 22 years, so civilian leaders have had considerably less experience in office than the officer corps. Moreover, the Balewa and Shagari periods were hardly glorious or mourned. However, the military legacy is not only problematic in terms of politics; it is also so in terms of economics and defense. First, retired generals have become influential business managers, political actors and owners: a distinct bourgeois fraction that is intolerant of governmental inefficiency and intervention. And second, military leaders have been preoccupied by domestic responsibility rather than external security; except for rearrangement and reorganization under Shagari, the army has suffered benign neglect from several generations of politicized officers. Interestingly, the officers' corps has so far managed to keep the other ranks in line: Nigeria has not witnessed any mutiny in the armed forces.

The mid-1987 white paper "Towards 1992" provided the regime's response to the Political Bureau's preferences then; it included not only a two-party presidential system with a federal structure and series of elections but also part-time rather than professional legislators who would only be reimbursed for their service in the legislature. Not only was the old guard including several generations of retired officers and elements of the Kaduna mafia banned, but the new guard is unlikely to find post-Babangida politics as lucrative as those excesses of the Shagari period. However, the successor to Fedeco, the National Electoral Commission (NEC), had as many problems with the first local government elections in December 1987 as did its predecessor. The 1990 local government elections on the two-party basis did not fare much better either as violence, low turn-out, money and manipulation characterized the exercise (Agbese and Ihonvbere 1997; Ihonvbere 1991e). And the proposed census in 1992 was controversial and problematic as earlier attempts. As Watts (1987:5) indicates "in Nigeria it is difficult to know what is fact and what is fiction because basic statistics are probably close to worthless." After spending hundreds of millions of naira, declaring three work-free days and mobilizing several hundreds of thousands of teachers and military personnel, the population commission announced a figure of 88.5 million, much lower than all previous projections used by the World Bank and the Nigerian government.

Characteristic of the Babangida regime's reservations about popular pressures in Nigeria was the promulgation of a potentially draconian Decree, Number 19, as its response to the Political Bureau was announced. Thus, in addition to postponing elections from 1990 to 1992, banning ex-politicians and officers, and establishing a schedule for a series of elections, culminating in that for president in 1992, Babangida announced in mid-1987 that any opposition to the transition would be treated and tried as sabotage. Fears were expressed that Babangida's Decree No. 19 was the equivalent of Buhari's Decree No. 4 which was widely used to harass opposition and which was a contributory factor in Babangida's own coup in favor of human rights. As Larry Diamond (1987b:224) warns, "the authoritarian impulse did not die with the overthrow of the Buhari-Idiagbon regime."

Finally, one element in the response of the AFRC and the National Council of States to the Political Bureau's report, "Towards 1992," was to create two rather than more states, for a total of 21, plus the Federal Capital Territory of Abuja. Once again, Babangida followed in the footsteps of his mentor Muhammed who, in 1976, added seven to the dozen created by Gowon in 1967 (see Table 2.1). Under the Shagari administration, calls for state creation got quite out of hand - 53 were demanded, largely by excluded elites who expected that such new states, each with a capital, airport, university, bureaucracy, and brewery, would lead to lucrative contracts and patronage (Ekekwe 1986). The Bureau received calls for 13 new states; it recommended 6; AFRC approved just 2. Happily, 21 can be divided by 3, which will simplify calculations of victories in two-thirds of the states essential to the crucial presidential election. At the time, President Babangida cautioned that no further demands for state creation will be entertained during the transition to 1992. Clearly, previous proliferations of states have been expensive propositions which a diminished Nigeria can ill-afford: Akwa Ibom and Katsina States (see map at front) will not be more prosperous as established neighbors like Kano and Imo, respectively. Ironically, they were created at a time when the AFRC was moving to undermine state rather than federal or local power. But, typical of Babangida's pronouncements and policies, nine new states and over 50 local governments were created in 1991, bringing the number os states to 30 and local governments to 500!

Under Babangida there was a power shift towards both centralization and localization, diverting resources and influences from both federal ministries and state governments, as reflected in the National Council of States. At the national level, moves to politicize the appointment of Permanent Secretaries and place the Central Bank directly under the President in early-1988 symbolized such centralization while, at the regional level, local government elections and increased budgets along with the revival of "traditional" rulers is indicative of the erosion of the power of states.

Babangida emerged as the most powerful president Nigeria has ever had, at last until General Sani Abacha entered the political scene in 1993. He was in addition to being head of state, the Minister for Defence. He was chair of the AFRC, Council of States, Council of Ministers, Police Service Commission and the Armed Forces Consultative assembly, set up as a forum for monitoring the "feelings" and complaints of middle-ranking military officers (Ihonvbere 1990d and e).

To transcend established difficulties of inter-regional and ethnic differences and balances, a new emphasis on the local level and its direct links with the center is emerging — as anticipated in the AFRC's white paper "Towards 1992" - compatible with notions of diarchy or triarchy and a novel two-party political system without the older generation of discredited or deceased politicians and previous military rulers. Despite the embarrassing shambles of the late-1987 local government elections under an ineffective NEC, the federal regime continued to rehabilitate the so-called "traditional" rulers through officially-sponsored regional meetings of established "elders" and to throw more money at the three Local Government Studies Centres - OAU, Nsukka and ABU: the revival of "indirect rule" (see Chapter One) for the 1990's? Meanwhile, the technocrats in the Council of Ministers continue to administer the redirected political economy as instructed by the AFRC and IBRD.

The rehabilitation and reinforcement of local government - the primary "electoral college" for the constituent assembly - in association with a review of university centers for their professionalization is symptomatic of the new role of orthodox "policy relevant" political science and public administration in Nigeria under Babangida. There have been series of such social scientists under earlier administrations, particularly Mohammed/Obasanjo, but the Political Bureau had more of them than CDC as do NEC and MAMSER. Notwithstanding the demise of Bolaji Akinyemi as foreign minister in late-1987 or the lackluster performance of Professor Awa at NEC before he was unceremoniously removed and replaced by Humphrey Nwosu, MAMSER was later headed by Jerry Gana and Sam Oyovbaire served as Advisor to the Vice-President and later became Minister for Information. Other professional political scientists served in advisory capacities at the state level as well as several more in the diplomatic service in addition to the group in MAMSER. To be sure, economists have also served a series of regimes, notably Adebayo Adedeji under Gowon, but it is curious to observe the role of political scientists of largely orthodox persuasion working for a relatively authoritarian state. The more radical political economists have equally been attracted to the seat of political power (see chapter on civil society). In the Political Bureau, Eddie Madunagu clearly tried to maintain the radical pressure and tradition of Osoba and Usman (before he was unceremoniously removed for allegedly leaking the decisions and debates of the Bureau to the public) but suggestions for a socialist state with reserved representation for women and workers were rejected unequivocally by the AFRC in "Towards 1992."

Although Second Republic politicians were initially banned from competing for election in the Third Republic - a consensus of Political Bureau and White Paper ("Towards 1992", 1987) - they were less harshly treated under Babangida than under Buhari. In early-1988 Shagari and his vice-president, Ekwueme, were released from house arrest. In late-1987 Gowon's rank of general was restored. He was paid all his allowances and, with his sinecure position as Research Professor at the University of Jos, his rehabilitation was virtually complete. By the end of 1989, he was representing the President at important occasions. Both he and his opponent, Ojukwu, are now "respected" figures in the Nigerian elite once again. In mid-1991, the Babangida regime restored the military ranks of officers probed and dismissed from the armed forces by the Murtala regime in 1976 as part of the on-going process of rehabilitating possible opposition elements and rewarding allies in and outside the military organization. Despite frequent police harassment of press and radicals, in general the Nigerian penchant for reconciliation and coexistence was revived under Babangida from its relative absence in the last days of Shagari and the atypical regime of Buhari.

While the official agenda in Nigeria in conformity with proliferating World Bank conditionalities concentrates on the return to civilian administration and economic prosperity, there are some underlying features of the political economy and culture which are worthy of attention, some of which we treat in the next chapter, not least because they will, over time, come to affect politics as well as economics. Some of these - definitions of state, political economy and development - were raised in the Cookey Report but not accepted in the AFRC White Paper ("Towards 1992" 1987).

First there continued to be a lack of distinction made between state and society in either public or private domains: does civil society have any autonomy? Or does the state pervade the whole community? This issue became especially salient as the state is being re-defined under structural adjustment reforms: does its contraction mean less or more influence? Can a parasitic structure be transformed into a dirigiste entrepreneur? Can Nigeria become a NIC without an activist state? Second, devaluation has generated new forms of informal activity to sustain forex habits; smugglers have become "long-distance traders" and drugs have joined money and electronics as commodities. Third, as reforms have caused worker unemployment, particularly amongst men, so the informal sector and agriculture have become feminized: affluent women have emerged as "cash madams" and women have put together alternative structures for seeds, lands and distribution to replace the marketing boards. And, finally, the distinction between formal and informal sectors, as between state and society, is becoming blurred, in part because of the privatization ethos. Employees in the informal sector are becoming bourgeoisified. In short, the current period is not only one of debates about democratization and deregulation, it is also one of profound social change which will impact upon political economy and political culture no matter how refined the constitution or revived the economy.

CHAPTER SIX

POPULAR CULTURE AND CIVIL SOCIETY

Nigeria's political culture is as distinctive as, plus inseparable from, its political economy, containing both popular
and elite, idiosyncratic and structural elements. As already
indicated, the national social context has always had democratic elements which made successive rulers somewhat accountable to popular responses, no matter what period or
regime. Indeed, as suggested at the start of Chapter One,
civil society had always stretched from family to community, including in particular a rich variety of interest groups
and NGOs. Thus, even if Nigeria has failed as a model of
parliamentary, presidential and federal arrangements, it has
remained an example of ebullient civil society. Given such
irrepressible "informal" participation and organization, it has
already met many of the political conditionalities now attached to adjustment reforms, even before the formal transition back to civilian democracy.

This chapter treats salient elements in Nigeria's civil society from established social structures like population,
ethnicity, religion and education (to which we also return in
the final chapter on scenarios) to contemporary popular culture embodied in the media: newspapers, magazines, television and radio. And we also analyze specific interest, pressure or professional associations such as students, intellectuals, workers, women and the novel range of NGOs, especially human rights and civil liberty groups. Whilst we anticipate and advocate informal and formal forms of participation and accountability, we also recognize the continual

tendencies to corruption and authoritarianism. Indeed, we note contemporary regimes' continued ability to coopt or repress parts of civil society as well as exclude them from or include them in patterns of renewed corporatism. The established dialectic of regime type and social change is likely to extend into the next century no matter what the longevity of the post-1993 government, as indicated in the concluding chapter, because of the resilience and diversity of national civil society.

Nigeria is the most populous as well as distinctive country on the African continent. Its *official* population of 88.5 million (1991 census) is higher than that of all the other West African states put together. This huge population has been both an asset and a constraint in several ways. On the one hand, it makes the problem of personpower less pressing and, on the other hand, it taxes the resources of the country, sometimes, to limits which the state cannot effectively manage. The density of population is over 300 per square mile, over a quarter of which lives in urban centers.

Ethnicity has always been perceived as a major issue in Nigeria. Its major ethnic groups are the Hausas, who make up about 21 per cent of the population, the Yorubas, who make up 20 per cent, the Ibos, who constitute 17 per cent, and the Fulani who constitute 9 per cent, with the rest being the so-called "minorities." The Hausas and the Fulanis as well as the Kanuris originate in and occupy the Northern part of the country; the Tivs and Ibibios, who are considered minorities, occupy the Middle-Belt region; the Ibos occupy the Eastern part of the country; and the Yorubas dominate the West. The Binis, another minority group, along with the Urhobos and Itsekiris predominate in the Mid-West; while the South-Eastern and South-Western parts are occupied by several minority groups—the Efiks, Ikwerres, Kalabaris, Ijaws, and the Ogonis. Altogether, there are over 250 different ethnic groups and over 450 dialects spoken though English is the country's official language.

As regards religion, Christianity and Islam were both introduced from outside - from Western Europe and the Middle East, respectively - but the majority of Nigerians still worship and/or believe in traditional forms of religion - Ogun, Sango, Olokun, and other deities. On the surface, though, it is estimated that 50 percent of the population, mostly in the Northern parts, are Moslems while 40 per cent, mostly in the South, are Christians of various sects and denominations. Relations between these two major formal religious groups have not been particularly harmonious since political independence (see below) (Ibrahim 1991; Williams and Falola 1995; Olukoshi and Agbu 1996).

The Nigerian social formation, with its distinctive ethnic, regional and religious composition, has been plagued by coalitions, contradictions and conflicts, especially since the 1980s. As noted in previous chapters, the state, though unstable, has to a large extent succeeded in creating some harmony of interest between foreign and local capitals, yet its relations to civil society in general and to non-bourgeois forces in particular are still tenuous and full of ambiguity. Indeed, it can be said with a high degree of certainty that the economic and social crisis which followed in the wake of the precipitous decline in oil rents in the early-1980s had some positive effects in crystallizing social relations and positions (Barber 1982; Beckman 1981 and 1982; Iyayi 1986). It also enabled popular forces to strengthen their organizations, sharpen their social perceptions and relate their activities more to the contemporary struggle for empowerment and democracy (Onoge ed. 1993; Ihonvbere 1994). Thus even in advance of World Bank and other democratic conditionalities (devaluation, deregulation, desubsidization, and destatization), the mid-1980s witnessed the blossoming of radical popular culture, the emergence of civil liberty organizations, and the strengthening of students' movements, all dedicated to the call for democracy, social and economic justice, political accountability, and the protection of disadvantaged groups in the midst of deepening economic crisis (Mustapha 1986; Onoge ed. 1993; Soyinka 1996).

The vibrancy of popular culture and the apparent strengthening of civil society served in several ways to compel the military to commit itself to disengagement from politics and, occasionally, to make concessions to non-bourgeois forces. Hence, following every coup d'etat, disengagement from politics has always been part of the package put before Nigerians in regimes' quest for legitimacy (Adekanye ed. 1989; Dudley 1973; Ojiako 1979). In fact, in the case of the November 1993 Abacha coup, the military held "consultations" with critical segments of the Nigerian society before unseating the lame and illegal Interim National Government (ING) headed by Ernest Shonekan. As well, it must be mentioned that the increasing militancy of popular forces served to caution bourgeois elements on the imperative for some degree of unity if they were to survive the challenges posed to bourgeois domination by peasants, workers, students, prodemocracy movements, and civil liberty organizations in the country. In this chapter, we set out the basic developments in this area which show both the vibrancy of popular culture and the directions for popular empowerment in the 1990s and beyond. At its end, we draw specific conclusions on the implications of these for both continued bourgeois power and domination over politics and possible alternative democratic directions in the future.

a) Popular Culture

One aspect of Nigerian society which has remained irrepressible no matter what the character of the regime or the state of the economy is its arts and music. Since political independence these have served as not just a means of entertainment but also as political instruments for information, education, mobilization and for pressuring successive regimes, particularly the military. While the artists can easily be grouped into two broad groups - the traditional and the modern - their goals have differed with their ideological postures and functions (Waterman 1990). True, the functions of influencing politicians and policies cut across these divides, but the traditional artistes, who perform mostly in indigenous languages, have tended to be more conservative and pro-status quo than the modern ones. The popular culture of Nigeria continues, then, even in the context of deepening economic and political crises and widespread uncertainties about the future. To be sure, it seems to thrive more when a civilian government is presiding over a boom, such as Shehu Shagari's first months in power as the country's first executive president after thirteen years of military rule (Falola and Ihonvbere 1985; Ojiako 1979; Joseph 1983).

The country's popular culture is closely associated with its political culture, which is "naturally" democratic, even anarchistic, as well as capitalist or competitive. Despite claims or dreams to the contrary, related to enduring inequalities and some left organizations, the prospects of an early transition to socialism in Nigeria have always been minimal and may be impossible with the end of the Cold War (see below). Social pressures and complaints have grown in the

1980s with the advent of Nigeria's version of commonplace "structural adjustment" policies, yet radical change remains quite unlikely. To be sure, opposition forces in the country are growing in number and strengthening both their organizations and political tactics (see next section). This crystallization of class positions and creation of political networks to facilitate praxis, has yet to reach a level where it can pose a major challenge to the bourgeoisie or the state.

Popular culture in Nigeria as elsewhere, embodies national as well as communal and personal ideals and ideologies, history and experience. Whenever Nigerians meet abroad, no matter how different their values or views, they engage in animated debates about their country. A cursory survey of debates on "Naijanet" on the internet confirms this eternally quarrelsome political nature. These "quarrels" often reflect broader, African, Third World or even global discourses about democracy, development, economics and ideologies. Because Nigeria is so large in terms of people and territory, no Federal regime has ever really imposed its rule completely; certainly the British colonial government never did so. Although Nigeria never really followed the 1970s continental trend towards African socialism or "Afro-Marxism," it is more comfortable and compatible with the 1980s transition towards African democracy or "Afro-capitalism." We discuss its experience with structural adjustment policies elsewhere in this volume. Here we focus on the other primary continental and global trend: towards civil society and formal democracy. Notwithstanding familiarity with military regimes, Nigeria never experienced one-party state rule. Yet its myriad interest groups, professional associations, religious organizations and NGOs have drawn strength from the revival of civil society and democracy in Eastern Europe and elsewhere in the South.

Nigeria has a rich and diversified culture, with different expressions in North and South, city and countryside, rich and poor communities. In this section we focus on music, theater, television and the media, especially magazines and newspapers. These are often interrelated in performers, messages and ownership, with considerable state control but also, especially by African standards, continual pressure for pluralism. Nigeria is very "plugged in" to global communications, yet also displays a distinctive "national" character and flavor. Some of its writers have achieved global acclaim, such as Wole Soyinka (first Nobel Prize for Literature to an African in 1986) and Chinua Achebe, as have its singers - Sade Adu, Fela Anikulapo-Kuti, Olatunji, and King Sunny Ade, for example (Ayu 1986). On a more contemporary plane, we can note the acclaim which SEAL has received world wide, especially in Europe and the United States of America.

As mentioned previously, ideological and political interests, postures and interpretations differ significantly among artists in Nigeria. Thus, first, among the traditional artistes there are musicians like Sunny Ade, Ebenezer Obey, Dele Abiodun, Dan Maraya Jos, Victor Uwaifo, Waziri Oshomah, Prince Adekunle, Oliver de Coque, Oriental Brothers, Warrior, Chief Osadebey, Chief Kollington Ayinla, and Idowu Animashaun, to name a few, concentrating their efforts on praise singing, glorifying the rich, and turning a blind eye to the increasing poverty, unemployment and deprivation which followed both the oil boom and the subsequent economic contractions of the 1980s (Barber 1982, 1984; Kinney 1970; Waterman 1990). Of course, these "traditional" artistes also have works which address social issues. But they are inconsistent and often simplistic in their social and political perceptions and prescriptions. Part of the reason has been the degree of exposure both to Western education and the audience to which they appealed: the rural people and the wealthy. But second, on the other hand we see musicians like Evi Edna Ogholi, Ema Ogosi, Majek Fashek, The Mandators, Andy Shurman, Jide Obi, Christiana Essien-Igbokwe, Felix Liberty, Ras Kimono, Charly Boy Oputa, Chris Hanen, Sunny Okosun and Jonel Cross to name a few, who have dedicated their energies to a completely new form of music. Their messages have been those of change, revolution, mobilization, empowerment, and liberation. They have attacked corruption, injustice, unemployment, underdevelopment, foreign domination, and other manifestations of inequality and oppression in the Nigerian social formation as well as apartheid in South Africa. Their brand of music has been political in content and liberational in philosophy involving prescriptions, not necessarily for a socialist transformation, but for a society of relative equality, justice and accountability.

Fela Anikulapo-Kuti stands out among Nigerian artists, both nationally and internationally. Since the 1960s he has grown to represent the conscience of the nation: irrepressible, militant, anti-corruption, anti-exploitation, anti-injustice and anti-imperialism. His mode of exposition has been that of popular radical political economy, with a clear understanding of the historical origins of Nigerian (and African) underdevelopment. In spite of countless acts of harassment from successive governments, including a five-year jail term under the Buhari/Idiagbon regime, Fela has remained as creative and critical as ever. He has through his numerous works - which include *Unknown Soldier; Suffering and Smiling; Sorrow, Tears and Blood; Colonial Mentality; Everything don Scatter; Teacher don Teach Me Nonsense; ITT: International Thief Thief; Coffin for Head of State; Army Arrangement; Zombie; Why Blackman dey Suffer; Gimme Shit,I Give You Shit; Beast of No Nation; Just Like That; Double Wahala;* and *Overtake don Overtake Overtake* - demonstrated to the Nigerian people that art does not necessarily have to be pro-*status quo* or pro-state to make a meaningful contribution to the struggle against underdevelopment and dependence. Until his death in August 1997, Fela remained the most consistent critic of military dictatorship in Nigeria, refusing to allow changing circumstances to alter is views about his sworn "enemies" like Olusegun Obasanjo and Chief M.K.O. Abiola. Ironically, in spite of the prodigious output, the majority of Nigerians artists remain poor and unacknowledged: a reflection of the nature of an underdeveloped market and unliberated minds too preoccupied with the challenges of survival rather than the pleasures of the arts.

At the level of the theater, Nigeria continues to enjoy a vibrant and widespread culture of artistic creativity and originality with new and contemporary artists incorporating into their sketches the search for solutions to the numerous problems and predicaments of the country. It is interesting that though the state in the late-1970s initiated a process of attempting to incorporate some artists into its program for building hegemony and promoting the interests of the dominant classes, the theater still manages to remain independent in its expression and explanation of national problems which have refused to go away in spite of the 1970s oil boom. Ola Balogun, Eddy Ugbomah and Wole Soyinka continue to produce films which are critical of prevailing social, economic and political relations in the country. There are also, "traditional" film producers like Baba Sala, Ade Love, and Hubert Ogunde. An interesting aspect of the work of these "traditional" film makers is that their messages, though anchored in indigenous cultural relations have, unlike traditional musicians, idioms and ideological postures which are similar to the group of "modern" film makers. Baba Sala's *Mosebolatan* and *Orunmoru*, Ogunde's *Aiye* and *Jaiyesinmi* as well as Ade Love's *Taxi Driver* all celebrate the virtues of hardwork, honesty, and the triumph of disadvantaged groups over the forces of oppression. Soyinka, Ugbomah, and Balogun have also devoted their films to criticizing the prevalent get-rich-quick mentality in the country, the erosion of traditional values by Western education, the dangers of armed robbery, and the problems which the wealthy pose to society when they abuse their power, try to influence government policies and exploit the poor.

Popular theater on television or Nigerian sit-coms has witnessed the works of artistes and programs like Baba Sala, Koko Close, Aluwe-Ojo Ladipo, Masquerade-Chief Zebrudaya Okorigwe Nwogbo Alias 4.30, Inside Out, Hotel de Jordan, Village Headmaster, and Hot Cash (Willie Willie). The essential messages in these indigenous TV productions are all the same - evil is bad and greed is dangerous; it pays to be patriotic, honest, hardworking, incorruptible and dedicated to one's profession and country. There are also, of course, some "soft" "apolitical" shows on television such as *Behind the Clouds* , *Mirror in the Sun* and *Ripples* which have the same ingredients as soap operas in the West: the corruption, profanity, vanity, irresponsibility and intrigues within the ranks of the educated, rich, and famous. They reflect in large measure the chaotic situation within the ranks of Nigeria's new bourgeois classes and are quite popular among non-bourgeois groups in the country.

At the level of the media, the relative freedom, even libelousness, of the Nigerian press is legendary. Military rule has not in any significant way affected the desire for information on, humor about and critical analysis of politics and economics. Though the government has had cause to descend on media houses, such as the bans on *Newbreed Magazine* (1978) and *Newswatch* (1987), more weekly magazines have emerged in Nigeria than in any other African country. More vibrant magazines have taken the lead in frontal attacks against the state and its custodians-*TELL, The News, Tempo, Razor,* and *The Week* to name a few. Their proprietors, editors, writers, and printers have suffered for the publicly displayed courage. Editions have been seized, mysterious fires have destroyed their facilities, and a few have been jailed-Chris Anyanwu, Chris Mbah, and Kunle

Ajibade. Virtually every one of the 21 states has at least two newspapers, usually one government- and the other privately-owned.

It is this unquenchable popular desire for "correct" and "alternative" information that has encouraged strong competition between private and official media, especially amongst the "dailies." Thus federal or state government-owned *newspapers* like *The Daily Times, The New Nigerian, Nigerian Observer, The Tide, The Chronicle, The Pioneer, The Statesman, Nigerian Standard* and *The Sketch* have had to upgrade the quality of their reporting, coverage of events and analysis of issues to compete effectively with the more dynamic and innovative privately-owned media. However, the latter has had its own problems: frequent interference by often politically-ambitious proprietors, government censorship and heavy competition for profits sometimes leading to the sacrifice of news for convenient silence to protect certain even proprietorial interests. Thus newspapers like *The Guardian, The Punch, The Tribune, The Champion, Vanguard, New Democrat, The Triumph* and the *Concord* have contributed immensely to exposing frauds and injustices and to providing information which are usually "overlooked" by the government media. Sunday newspapers are equally popular and circulate widely. Most of the educated elites and urban residents rely on these Sundays for a summary of the previous week's developments. Papers like *Sunday Guardian, Sunday Concord, Sunday Tribune, Sunday Observer*, and *Sunday New Nigerian* are published by their respective dailies.

Beyond the newspapers, as noted already, *magazines* have become the order of the day in contemporary Nigeria. Until the early-1970s, this business was dominated by general interest magazines like *Spear, Drum, Boom, and Woman's World* . By the mid-1970s, political as well as general interest magazines came to dominate the media world. Now magazines like *The President, Newswatch, African Concord, African Guardian, Thisweek, The Sunday Magazine, Newbreed, Nigerian Newsweek, The Nigerian Economist, Development Outlook, The Analyst, Platform,* and *Quality* have become invaluable and reliable sources of current information and critical analysis of developments in the country. At the other end of the spectrum are "soft" and general interest weeklies and magazines which thrive on gossip, jokes and the exposure of corruption and scandal in the society. These include *Prime*

People, Ikebe Super, Lagos Life, Lagos Weekend, Modern Woman, Vintage People, Super Story, Top News, Lulu, and *Hints,* which have, perhaps surprisingly, thrived in a period of economic hardship as sections of the country became bored with or alienated from hard politics and shifted to the mundane and the exotic. Generally though, the printed media has been of invaluable use to raising political groups in the mobilization and dissemination of information.

A very important part of the Nigerian media is the vernacular as well as English periodicals and newspapers. These papers and magazines published in local "ethnic" languages have served as a means of getting information to the grassroots and mobilizing rural people for political action. Such publications include *Abokiyar* published in Hausa, *Aworerin* printed in Yoruba by the Ministry of Education in Ibadan, Oyo State, and the Hausa *Fitila and Gaskiya ta fi Kwabo.* There are also weeklies like *Albishir* and *Yancin Dan Adam*(Hausa) and *Eleti-Ofe, Gboungboun, Irohin Imole,* and *Irohin Yoruba* (Yoruba). Finally, there are a few vernacular dailies like *Imole Owuro* and *Isokan* (Yoruba) and *Amana* (Hausa). It is interesting to note that the majority of the vernacular papers are either in Yoruba (spoken in the West) or in Hausa (spoken in the North). In one sense, this is the result of the traditional historical mode of mobilization in the two regions of the North and the West: through such vernacular newspapers. It is equally a reflection of the fact that these two "ethnic" languages are the most developed and most widely studied in schools in the country. Conversely, the Ibo language, spoken in the East, is increasingly being reduced to writing, and studied at higher institutions in the Eastern part of the country.

The vibrant character of popular culture in the country has directly impacted upon the on-going strengthening of civil society and the increasing move to transcend religion, region, and ethnicity in the analysis and practice of the Nigerian reality. The media, theater, and other aspects of popular culture have in the last decade developed very strong affinities to other political and civil liberty associations which are currently involved in the struggle for democracy and democratization. This is the focus of the next section.

b) Civil Society

Politics has always been a determinant aspect of life in Nigeria. If Nigerians are consistently interested in anything, it is politics - political parties, revenue allocation, political appointments, recruitment, sanctions and so on. This is precisely why virtually every aspect of life and issue in society has become irrevocably and intractably "politicized". Every development is first and foremost viewed and analyzed as a political issue before it is integrated into political discourse. This vibrant political culture has remained irrepressible despite decades of military dictatorship and frequent bans on political activities, restrictions on the power of the judiciary, curtailment of press freedom and the freedom of speech and organization, and the deepening economic and social crisis in the country.

On the contrary, political restrictions and economic difficulties have combined to encourage mass mobilization, political organization and political activism. They have also encouraged the strengthening and the creation of new sociopolitical, civil liberty and general interest organizations which in large measure serve as the focus for articulating popular interests in society. It is also the strength and vibrancy of these organizations that have compelled the state to check its excesses and make frequent if partial and reversible concessions to popular forces. For instance, the pressure on successive military regimes to accept and announce disengagement programs as soon as they seize political power is to a large extent a measure of the strength of civil society in Nigeria. Historically, Nigerians have always seen military rule as "an abnormality" which must not be allowed to become permanent (Dudley 1973, 1982). Pressures and actions to defend and strengthen civil society have come from women, youths, students, peasants, workers, professional cooperatives, intellectuals and their respective organizations.

For example, as far back as the pre-independence period, Nigerian students have been very active participants in the nation's politics; in several instances they, more than labor, have served as the "conscience of the nation." They were involved in the early nationalist movements both inside and outside the country and they took an active part in the organization of nationalist political organizations and parties in the period leading to Nigeria's political independence. As well, the independence era witnessed increasing

141

political consciousness and activism on the part of Nigerian students. As noted in chapter two below, one of their earliest actions was in protesting the Anglo-Nigerian Defence Pact signed by the newly independent state and the British government in 1960. This would have converted Nigeria into a British military base and possibly drawn the country into the then bitter Cold War politics.

However, during the civil war, Nigerian students were divided, their disagreements largely reflecting the geographical division of the country during the war itself: students from the Eastern part supported Biafra while the others supported the federal government. In spite of such divisions, students on both sides of the war maintained a clear and patriotic position, critical of foreign involvement and placing the blame on the bitter factional politics of the older generation Nigerian dominant class. The post-civil war era saw a renewed and reorganized student movement under the national umbrella organization, the National Union of Nigerian Students(NUNS). NUNS served as a clearing house for student unions in higher educational institutions throughout the country advocating strong and critical anti-imperialist positions on several issues. These postures easily brought them into conflict with the government, culminating in the proscription of their union in 1978 following a nation-wide protest against the educational, political and economic policies of the military regime under General Olusegun Obasanjo. Since this proscription, NUNS has changed its name successively from the National Organization of Nigerian Students (NONS) to, now, the National Association of Nigerian Students (NANS). The latter enjoyed a brief period of official recognition under the civilian regime of Shagari but was again proscribed under the military regime of Buhari. Yet, this proscription has not in any way deterred Nigerian students from retaining their loyalties to the national body which now operates underground. As well, in the process, NANS has become ever more radical, more critical and perhaps better organized in its opposition to the state, and in its promotion of popular education and the pursuit of discipline and accountability within higher institutions in the country.

The labor movement has had an equally stormy history. Historically, it has been a major actor in Nigerian politics. The policies of forced labor, low wages, discrimination, brutality, conscription during the World War II, and gener-

ally poor working conditions forced it to organize and become a formidable part of the nationalist movement (Lubeck
1987; Madunagu 1982; Onimode 1982; Shenton 1986).
Though Nigeria has never had a labor party (recent attempts
in this direction were frustrated by the Babangida regime) -
which means that the working class has never really had a
political organization through which to openly compete for
state power — workers have for a long time been engaged in
serious political campaigns aimed at strengthening civil society, empowering non-bourgeois forces and serving as a
check on the abuse of power by the agents of the state.

However, typically yet somewhat ironically, political independence exacerbated the marginalization of the labor
movement as the post-independence leaders quickly moved
to depoliticize the masses in order to create room for the
rationalization and legitimization of inherited unequal relations with foreign capital. Until 1977 the Nigerian labor
movement was deeply engrossed in bitter ideological and
other political divisions and conflicts. The mushrooming of
over 500 trade unions meant that they were in competition
with one another. In the Cold War period, they were dependent on conflicting external ideological sources of funds and
foreign assistance. And they were also easily susceptible to
the prevailing regional, ethnic and other primordial divisions
in the country. Such divisions weakened the labor movement against both the state and capital, politicians and em-
ployers. As well, the overriding influence of foreign trade
unions and political interests made the labor movement
something of a security problem as it readily became vulnerable to penetration by bipolar foreign security agencies.

The conditions of anarchy, corruption and confusion in
the workers' organizations provided a convenient excuse for
the government to proscribe the existing unions in 1977, appoint an administrator and reorganize the labor movement.
Consequently, a central trade union organization - the Nigeria Labor Congress (NLC) - was created and all unions were
reorganized into 42 industrial unions compulsorily affiliated
to the NLC with the payment of check-off dues made com-
pulsory. As well, affiliation to any foreign trade union body,
beyond those sponsored by the Organization of African
Unity (OAU) and the United Nations (UN) were prohibited.

It is ironic that, though the indigenous working class
identifies the Nigerian state to be one of its principal enemies, it is the state that gave it strength, plus a sense of

143

direction and established a basis for its subsequent role as the vanguard of the workers and other oppressed groups in Nigeria. True the national labor movement is still plagued by ethnic, religious and regional divisions, opportunism, poor leadership, lack of ideological clarity, insufficient resources and constant harassment from the security forces, yet it has come a long way from its deplorable condition in the early 1970s. It has forged strong linkages or coalitions with students, intellectuals, popular organizations, progressive professional associations, like the Nigerian Bar Association (NBA) and the Nigerian Medical Association (NMA), and progressive womens' organizations, like Women in Nigeria (WIN). It has devoted substantial resources to the publication of position papers, research reports and the popular *Workers' Charter of Demands* which makes populist claims on the Nigerian state and outlines alternative economic programs for self-reliance and national liberation.

However, though the NLC maintains offices in each of the state capitals, very few of them are effective. And only a handful of the leaders combine experience in the labor movement with the intellectual capacity to understand the specificities of the contradictions and struggles within and between social classes in the country. The NLC tried to organize a Labor Party in 1990 to mobilize the working class, professionals, youths, women and other forces in a popular coalition. But the military government refused to recognize it as one element in its rejection of all independent attempts to form political parties leading towards the Third Republic.

Nigerian intellectuals have, like labor and students, been active participants in the politics of the pre- and post-independence periods. For many of them, participation in national politics has its origins in their role in the various students' organizations of the pre-independence era. From the Association of University Teachers of Nigeria (AUT) they reorganized and redefined their goals in the 1970s and set up the Academic Staff Union of Universities (ASUU). Like the NLC, this academic union has always been at loggerheads with the Nigerian state. Yet, the majority of senior public officials — advisers to governments, consultants and ministers as well as commissioners — have always been drawn from the universities.

However, one tradition which has emerged in Nigeria is that there has always been a distinction between scholars' performances while at the university service and when in government. While in the former, Nigerian intellectuals have been known for their radical politics, and relative forthrightness, honesty and insistence on accountability and justice. As part of its corporatist strategy, however, the government has increasingly picked on militant and vociferous intellectuals and appointed them to important political positions, which is where such qualities previously associated with them evaporate. It is therefore appropriate, in some respects, to place the blame for the crisis of Nigerian society on a section of the intellectual "class." It must be mentioned, however, that, as a group, they have never really been empowered, though there is little reason to believe that the majority of them seek empowerment. The leadership of their organization has, typically, been far ahead of the membership in terms of social consciousness, political commitment and ideological clarity. This situation has been one of the main weaknesses of the intellectual "class" and explains why it has been very vulnerable to internal division and manipulation by university administrators and agents of the state.

A large section of the academic elite is still very conservative, and the crisis of the economy and society, reproduced within the universities in the lack of funds, teaching and research facilities and in oppressive conditions of service, has further marginalized many of the intellectuals from current researches, ideas and discourses in their respective disciplines. It needs be mentioned, however, that ASUU has been in the forefront of the struggle for strengthening civil society through the establishment of inter-organizational linkages, popular education, mass mobilization, development of political programs and the empowerment of popular organizations around universities. Through political positions, research and involvement in the activities of the NLC, as well as active support for students' organizations, ASUU has contributed immensely to disseminating information and strengthening the broad base of opposition to the state and its agents throughout the country.

It is important, then, to isolate the role and political activities of radical intellectuals in Nigeria; in particular, their role in the politicization of discourse and in extending some strength and legitimacy to oppositional groups. Their teachings, publications and political actions have extended well beyond the campus, having significant and far-reaching impacts on the content of school curricula, particularly in the social sciences and the humanities in Nigeria. In the 1960s, while some militant and even radical non-socialist political postures were tolerated, there were no strong, radical, ideologically-inclined groups in the country. At best, there were some Pan-Africanists with broad interpretations of the origins and nature of the country's crisis and with at best populist solutions. In university institutions, academics regarded as being radical or socialist inclined were harassed, ridiculed and discriminated against. Their ideas were conceived to be stupid and utopian and their political prescriptions were seen as impracticable. In fact, in the 1960s during the Cold War it was a crime to travel to socialist countries and to be found with socialist or communist literature. The prevalent ideological postures were those of liberalism and capitalism involving unrepentant subservience to Western culture, tastes and ideological prescriptions.

However, all this changed in the 1970s as the state increasingly failed to provide for the people. Corruption, political intolerance, and the manipulation of ethnic and other primordial interests became widespread and the general inability of the bourgeoisie to constitute itself into a hegemonic class combined with other factors to deepen the nation's crisis and reproduce the conditions of dependence and underdevelopment. The failure of the various development plans to improve the lot of the people, the mismanagement of oil rents, the widening gap between the rich and the poor, and the increasing repression of popular groups all strengthened the analyses, ideological postures and prescriptions of radical intellectuals.

Finally, the persistence of these intellectuals in their politics and their interpretations of reality as well as their strategy of involvement in the struggles of students, peasants and workers gave further legitimacy to radical postures, politics and policy alternatives. Radical intellectuals, albeit with important differences and disagreements - like Claude Ake, Eskor Toyo, Bade Onimode, Ola Oni, Segun Osoba, G. G. Darah, Omotoye Olorode, Omafume Onogie, Yusuf Bala Usman, Laoye Sanda, Okwudiba Nnoli, Iyorchia Ayu, Akin Oyebode, Festus Iyayi, Tunde Fatunde, Princewill Alozie, Eddie Madunagu, Bene Madunagu, Niyi Osundare, Eme Ekekwe, Inya Abam Eteng, Aaron Gana, Jibrin Ibrahim, Adebyo Olukoshi, Rauf Mustapha, and Ayesha Imam (see bibliography) to mention a few — are unanimous in their political positions and prescriptions for a more democratic and socialist society, one in which the power and interest of non-bourgeois forces would determine the pattern and direction of development. Of course, these positions and prescriptions have meant constant confrontations between the security forces and such radical intellectuals. Incidentally, these confrontations only served to strengthen their radical positions and give their prescriptions more credibility. Harassment from security agents also attracted more supporters especially among students and workers to the camp of the radicals. Thus, today, the image of radical positions and politics are no longer those of the 1960s. Their positions are taken seriously, their political capacity to influence the direction of politics is not underestimated, and their prescriptions are not neglected even if they are not often accepted.

On the contrary, the state has tried to adopt a corporatist strategy towards the radical intellectuals by inviting them to take up important positions in government even in the most repressive and conservative regimes. The Babangida administration used this strategy effectively to coopt, even domesticate, opposition from the broad left, and thus dividing the radicals and to some extent eroding their credibility and seriousness in view of their collaboration with the regime in the implementation of unpopular and harsh structural adjustment programs. Given that most of these intellectuals went into the regime on their own personal recognition and in the absence of any strong organization on the ground to check either the conditions of their recruitment or their functioning in office, their participation has neither strengthened the left nor improved its credibility with its traditional constituency — labor and students. The participation of leading leftists (using this in a broad sense) like Ikenna Nzimiro, Eme Ekekwe, Ada Ugah, Alaba Ogunsanwo, Tunji Olagunju, Jonathan Zwingina, Omolara Ogundipe-Leslie, and Godwill Ogbogodor, and of social critics like Wole Soyinka and Tai Solarin in Babangida's military regime, can be said to have negatively affected the place of the left in Nigerian politics. It now appears to have a price: political appointments. However, the participation of such leftists in government has in some way encouraged students and workers to make a distinction between *personalities* and *principles*.

There is a segment of Nigerian intellectuals that is often overlooked: exiles or those based abroad. They have utilized their better salaries and working condition, access to technology and information, as well as opportunities to strike political connections to strengthen their counterparts at home and to empower popular organizations. Scholars like Pita Agbese, Ike Udogu, Femi Vaughn, Gloria Emeagwali, Femi Taiwo, Biodun Jeyifo, Ropo Sekoni, Bolaji Aluko, Kayode Fayemi, Pat Williams, and Kelechi Kalu have, at least, on the intellectual plane articulated holistic alternatives to what they see as a disarticulated and decadent Nigerian predicament.

One relatively recent development in Nigeria which more than any other development demonstrates the growing power of civil society is the increasing number of civil liberty organizations and the expanding interest in human rights issues, world peace, the environment and the status of women and children. Organizations like the Civil Liberties Organization (CLO), National Democratic Coalition (NADECO), African Democratic League (ADL), National Conscience Party (NC), Campaign for Democracy (CD), National Committee of Democratic Lawyers, Committee for Defence of Human Rights (CDHR), Committee for Defence of Justice in Nigeria (CDJN), the Ife Collective, Uhuru House, Bala Mohammed Memorial Committee, Mahmud Tukur Memorial Committee, Massline, Constitutional Rights Project (CRP), Nigerian Environmental Studies Team (NEST) and Movement for Peace and Justice (MPJ) have arisen as a reflection of the growing popularity and legitimacy of such movements in the international system. They also reflect the growing need to defend civil liberties and to put pressure on the state from diverse directions on similar issues. They did succeed, as demonstration of a new found power, to force General Babangida out of power in 1993 and to make the country ungovernable for the ING. This goes against the traditional reliance on trade unions for the defence of disadvantaged groups. Increasing repression by the state, and widespread incidents of human rights violations and other forms of oppression in virtually every aspect of Nigerian society have made the relevance of these organizations critical to the struggle for democratization and the strengthening of civil society.

The Nigerian state has over the last five years found it increasingly difficult to ignore these civil liberty organizations which are mostly led by young professionals, largely lawyers and intellectuals, and which demonstrate boundless energy in their effort to ensure accountability and justice in all sectors of society. These human rights organizations have contributed in several ways to restructuring traditional patterns of challenging state power, fighting oppression without resort to violence, protecting and expanding political space, educating the public about their rights and making Nigeria part of the transnational global movement for the promotion of democracy and development. Moreover, they can take refuge in contemporary adjustment conditionalities which now call for political as well as economic liberalization. This, however, did not stopped the military government of Babangida, and since 1993 that of General Abacha from throwing their leaders into jail without trial, harassing their members and accusing them of all sorts of crimes-no prodemocracy leader in Nigeria has been spared this bitter experience. Again, local prodemocracy and human rights organizations have ben strengthened in their campaigns from support provided by overseas-based prodemocracy movements like the UK-based Nigerian Democratic Movement (NDM), Oduduwa Movement, Movement for National Reformation (MNR), and Solidarity Movement for Southern Minorities; the Canada-based Democratic Alliance of Nigerians in Canada (DANIC), Canadian Association for Democratic Movement in Nigeria (CADMN), and Canadian Organization for Human Rights and Democracy in Nigeria (COHDN); and the US-based Organization of Nigerians in the Americas (ONA), Nigerian Democratic Movement (NDM), Nigerian Democratic Task Force (NDTF), Oduduwa Youth Movement (OYM), Nigerian Democratic Alliance (NDA), and Action Group for Democracy (AGDF).

Women have perhaps always been the most exploited and marginalized group in Nigerian society. In both pre- and post-colonial Nigeria, women have remained oppressed and ignored in both political and economic terms. At best, governmental responses to rectifying this inequity have been cosmetic and token. In government appointments, laws of inheritance, and in access to credit and to education and to other opportunities, women have been treated as secondary citizens. Unfortunately, typically they have not had strong and formal organizations capable of defending their interests and protecting their gender rights. At the grassroots level, women have various cultural associations dedicated to forging unity among them and to protecting their interests. Many of these are cultural organizations restricted in their functions because of traditions and constraints imposed by men. To be sure, a few of these local organizations have become politicized in recent times, taking positions on policy matters in their communities and challenging existing discriminations against women.

In the post-independence era, the wives of top bureaucrats, military officers and senior politicians have come to appropriate the functions of defending the rights of women. These are largely elitist, urban-based and narrowly-composed organizations which in reality are concerned with the interests of city dwellers and the spouses of the already privileged. Two such conservative elitist organizations are the National Council for Women's Societies (NCWS) and the Nigeria Army Officers Wives Association (NAOWA).

By contrast, Women in Nigeria (WIN) has over the last decade or so tried to represent the interests of a broader composition of women in Nigeria. WIN is composed of radical female scholars, professionals and other representatives of popular organizations. It has succeeded in distancing itself from the NCWS and shown a relatively sophisticated and holistic understanding of the problems and conditions of women in Nigeria. It is the only women's organization that has succeeded in admitting men into its fold and succeeded in preventing them from hijacking the organization. More importantly, WIN conceives of its struggles within a framework of the total liberation of all oppressed and exploited forces in society. Unfortunately, however, WIN has not succeeded in penetrating the structures of power and policy making in Nigeria in order to influence public policy and contribute significantly to female liberation in Nigeria (Amadiume 1987; WIN 1984, 1985).

Another important grassroots women's organization worthy of mention is the Country Women Association of Nigeria (COWAN) which operates largely in the rural areas and is dedicated to the empowerment of women. Like WIN, it is still faced with challenges from entrenched rural values, power structures which favor men, and a deficiency of resources to mobilize women for political action. Organizations like COWAN, it must be mentioned, still revolve around their founders and still suffer from opportunism and traditional networking. Other women in Nigeria have also organized themselves along professional lines: Association of Female Journalists, Association of Women Lawyers as well as doctors, accountants and so on. These organizations are, in the first place dedicated to isolating and highlighting the numerous problems and challenges faced by women in a male- dominated semi-Islamic society. The creation of a National Commission on Women initially headed by Professor Bolanle Awe might have led to the popularization of gender issues. Unfortunately, the Commission has been politicized and has not so far worked closely with WIN and COWAN to empower women, their organizations, and programs.

One major problem which has plagued the Nigerian polity and society since political independence has been that of corruption. In addition to ethnic, regional and religious divisions and antagonisms, corruption has reduced the legitimacy of the state, eroded the credibility of political leaders, replaced merit and hard work with strong and complex patron-client relations, accentuated inefficiency, ineffectiveness and general disorder in the bureaucratic apparatuses and led to mismanagement, waste and, ultimately, economic crisis. Corruption has today permeated all aspects of Nigerian society and public affairs; and private business can hardly make progress without indulging in some corrupt practices. In government, the judiciary, the universities and other educational institutions, the police and the army - in fact in all sectors of the polity and economy- corruption has become the main engine of activity. It is so pervasive that it has almost become an accepted practice: politicians buy votes; students bribe their teachers for grades and other favors; customs officials hardly perform any tasks without kickbacks; the judiciary is open to corruption by those with money; and the army and police are as vulnerable to corruption as tax officers, clerks, civil servants and businessmen and women.

Why has corruption become such a major problem in Nigerian society? The main explanations are that the weakness and unproductive nature of the dominant classes make them prone to accumulation largely through unproductive activities. First, in their effort to organize the entry and participation of foreign interests in the economy, facilitate the easy repatriation of surpluses and ensure their prominent participation in such economic arrangements, Nigerian elites have over the years contributed to the direct subversion of promulgated rules and regulations and promoted a pervasive culture of corruption, waste, graft and manipulation. Second, the absence in the country of social insurance schemes of any sort has encouraged those with access to public funds to help themselves by putting aside substantial amounts for their own future. This becomes even more possible given the inability of the state to discipline the dominant classes. The predominant capitalist ideology rationalizes corrupt practices and the rich - irrespective of the source of their wealth — easily become the privileged and the respected even in rural communities where they are made chiefs and spokespersons. Third, the advent of military regimes since the first coup of 1966 has contributed significantly to the spread of corruption and its promotion to unprecedented proportions in the society. Given the dictatorial and command character of the military, its reliance on decrees and its tendency to abuse monopolization of the means of coercion, it has become clear that the best time to loot public resources without any fear of being probed in the future is under military regimes. Succeeding civilian governments are often afraid to probe military regimes for fear of being overthrown by formerly corrupt officers. In any case, the military, more than any other type of government has done more to rehabilitate discredited and disgraced politicians and persons in the country's political history.

Finally, fourth, the absence of clearly enunciated and enforceable rules and regulations specifying the need to declare assets publicly and the sanctions for engaging in corrupt practices, have encouraged public officials and business persons to engage in corruption without fear of recriminations. Thus today one major obstacle to the developmental success of national and regional organizations, governments, federal, state and local public policies and political parties is the problem of corruption. Trade unions, students' unions, universities, the military, political parties and churches have not been spared from the numerous scandals which have been all too common in the country since political independence (Madunagu 1983; Agbese and Ihonvbere 1997).

The non-hegemonic character of the state in terms of its inability to exercise a viable degree of control over social classes and society without resort to and reliance on violence, the limitations of the bourgeoisie, the weak productive base of the economy and the general condition of social and economic decay have all constrained societal development, which in several ways hampers social mobility in Nigeria. Mobility within and between class positions has not generally been based on diligence or performance. While educational qualifications have played a prominent role in determining location in the social hierarchy, particularly in the first years of independence, they have become largely secondary factors, being replaced by status based upon patron-client relations, ethnic and religious considerations, and military rank or status. The advent of military governments has provided new and unequalled opportunities for people with little or no education, expertise or experience to climb the social and political ladder and become prominent and affluent overnight. Given the limitations of Nigerian military officers in terms of their understanding of the complex relations and coalitions which drive society, they have had to rely heavily on formal and informal cabinets through which to govern the country. In this way, intellectuals, politicians, old school mates, and members of similar religious and ethnic groups as well as traditional figures have been elevated to important positions in order to achieve legitimacy for and divert pressure away from the state (Agbese and Ihonvbere 1997; Ekekwe 1986; Madunagu 1982; Onimode 1982).

Over the decades of independence a complex network of connections to military officers has emerged in Nigeria. These have become the mechanism for redistributing public resources through informal channels as senior military men enrich their friends, wives, relatives, town folks and business persons all of whom help them to siphon stolen funds either out of or as investments in the country. As opportunities for formal employment contract in the economy, especially since the economic crisis which followed the precipitous decline in oil rents in the 1980s, the easiest way to gain employment, contracts, admission into either higher institutions or the military academy, and climb the political ladder in the political parties has not been via merit. Rather, state of birth, ethnic origin, religious affiliation and connections to certain prominent figures, especially top business persons, military officers, traditional rulers and bureaucrats, have been the easiest routes to higher positions, greater wealth and social prominence. This is not to say that in some cases laid down rules do not exist, although at best these are used for less than half of professional exercises from recruitment to promotions and retirements. These tendencies have come to be challenged and subjected to serious and rigorous criticisms by popular forces, in particular by student, labor and civil liberty organizations. But such interest groups have achieved very little from the government beyond lame promises to insist on accountability, equity and fair play in the future.

Contemporary Nigeria has moved a long way from its state of development in the 1960s and 1970s. The decline in oil rents, decades of military rule, two failed civilian experiments with Western-type democracy, and several poorly thought out economic policies- such as indigenization, Operation Feed the Nation (OFN), Green Revolution and moral revolutions like the War Against Indiscipline (WAI), the National Orientation Movement (NOM) and the Ethical Revolution- have served to politicize the society and influence the content and direction of politics, alignments and contradictions. Belief in democracy and social justice has tended to promote unity among non-bourgeois forces and strengthen civil society. This has helped to create a grassroots culture transcending ethnic and other primordial loyalties.

High levels of investment in formal education in the 1970s advanced awareness among the people, reduced the degree of superstition, and promoted social mobility within the limits of other constraints arising from the character of state and class. According to the Federal Ministry of Education, adult literacy in 1984 averaged 65 per cent. In 1987 there were 11,276,270 pupils in primary schools and 2,858,373 in secondary schools. There were a total of 24 universities of which 18 were Federal- and 6 were state-owned. By 1989, there were about 300 teacher training institutions with over 450,000 students plus over 30 polytechnics. The urge for higher education has continued to remain very high, notwithstanding the above comments on its limitations because of the important role the certificate is still allowed to play in social mobility. At the same time, increased educational opportunities reinforced by exposure to NANS and ASUU mean more awareness and easier mobilization as well as a steady decline in the strength of ethnic, religious and other primordial considerations in political activities.

Popular organizations from trade unions to student movements have been strengthened in their demands for a more democratic society partly as a result of the failings of various governments to provide for their basic needs and partly as a precipitate of rising consciousness, mobilizational work by political groups and frequent confrontation with the agents of the state. Increasingly, Nigerians are turning to local governments as fora for political participation and putting pressures on higher levels of government for facilities and infrastructures. Essentially, the process of recapturing local initiative, strengthening grassroots participation in politics and redirecting public and political interests away from successive Federal governments to the rural areas has increased the relevance of local government in recent times. Such renewed interest in local political areas as bastions of power has coincided with new political arrangements which require that all political aspirants seek acceptance and approval from their respective local government party branches before qualifying to vie for higher office. While this is a significant development, along with the actual restructuring of local government areas, the problems of gender discrimination, limited resources, low level of political experience and minimal degree of enlightenment still hamper the ability of the rural people to take control of political initiatives and constrain the influence of the rich and powerful.

The role of youth associations, age grades, cooperatives, voluntary organizations and religious associations, many within an NGO or PVO format, has become very important in the struggle to build and sustain civil society in the country. In the rural areas, age grades and development associations are still very relevant in the struggle to promote development, keep up community spirit and develop political awareness. The degree of political commitment and enthusiasm to participate in politics to empower communities and their organizations in rural Nigeria is remarkable. Many of these local groups discuss political issues regularly and try to influence elections at the local government level. In the urban centers, youth associations and voluntary organizations like the Boy Scouts, St. Johns Ambulance Brigade, Boys Brigade, Brownies, Red Cross, Girl Guides and so on, have become very popular with youths who see them more as avenues through which to acquire some power. To be sure, part of this perception comes from the militarization of the people's culture, a precipitate of decades of military rule and exposure of successive generations of youths to the "power of the uniform." At political rallies, independence day celebrations, public functions and sporting competitions, such youth organizations perform para-military functions and acquire a sense of organization, discipline and power which they can bring to bear on their participation in their age grades and community associations.

As well, as already mentioned, since the early 1980s religion has come to take a completely new dimension in the country. Right now it performs a rather paradoxical role of strengthening and weakening civil society at the same time. The North-South divide which more or less equates with the Christian-Moslem divide has been a recurring source of tension, conflict and bloodshed in the country. First, negatively, mutual suspicions between the Christians and the Moslems have affected economic planning, political development, the national census, resource allocation, the promotion of merit and the location of industries and other important facilities. Since 1985 there have been over a dozen major religious riots in the Northern parts of the country. This has promoted general insecurity, ethnic tensions, the repatriation of capital from the North to the South, a reduction in investments and uncertainty. But, secondly at the same time, and positively, religion has served as a source of public education, mobilization and strengthening of civil society. One phenomenon can be conceded to Nigeria's leaders: they respect and fear religious rulers although the record lies more in the desire to give the impression that they are God-fearing. Thus, for many religious leaders, the church and the mosque have become powerful as well as insulated institutions for making political pronouncements and taking visible pro-civil society positions against the state. To be sure, increasing access to educational opportunities has to some extent reduced the power and influence of organized religion as people begin to see beyond the facade of religious leaders, many of whom have become very wealthy "in the name of God." However, reduced access to education because of SAP may revive religious appeal, particularly if it can provide basic needs which the state can no longer satisfy.

In recent times, some young entrepreneurs have invaded the ranks of the Christians and converted religion to nothing more than a business or show business. Televangelism has equally become popular among the Christians. On radio and television, the latter take up Sundays to proselytize while the Moslems take the Fridays. Though Nigeria is supposed to be a secular state, increasingly the government has found it very difficult to stay away from religious matters because of the strong influence the latter have on political matters. State involvement in religion, seen by the Christians as favoring the Moslems because of government involvement in the annual pilgrimage to Mecca, has been a source of tension between both major religions. Yet, many of the so-called religious riots that have taken place in recent times, usually in the North, between Christians and Moslems have had strong political and economic undertones. One possibility for the future is the increasing politicization of religion. Liberation theology is equally becoming popular in the country. With such developments, religion's potential contribution to building and strengthening civil society cannot be overestimated.

Finally, then, in response, political action and intellectual discourse in Nigeria seem to be shifting away from traditional neglect of the relevant role of popular culture and popular organizations in the nation's quest for growth and development. With the opening up of political space because of both democratization processes and SAP conditionalities, along with the very enthusiastic response of the people to such opportunities, it can only be expected that cross-organizational and class linkages will be established, extended and strengthened in the future: a popular coalition to counteract official authoritarianism or corporatism. With such a development, civil society can serve as a credible check on the excesses of the state and its custodians, whether formally or primarily civilian or military. Thus, many of the constraints placed by the post-independence state on mobilization and self-reliance might themselves be limited in the interests of longer-term sustainable and popular development.

CHAPTER SEVEN

THE SEARCH FOR INTERNATIONAL STATUS
1960 - 1991

Nigeria has always been Africa's most populous state. But the external extension of its internal capabilities did not commence with any seriousness or style until the early-1970s when the conjuncture of peace and petroleum - the conclusion of the civil war and the escalation in the price of oil - produced a potential "middle power" in West Africa (Ate 1987; Ihonvbere 1982a; Ogunsanwo 1986). Nigeria had always been primus inter pares; now its agricultural, entrepreneurial and economic resources could serve as the bases of its outward-looking orientation. This potential began to be appreciated and mobilized during the Mohammed/ Obasanjo interregnum when Nigeria took the initiative over Angola (Daddieh & Shaw 1984), Zimbabwe and other African issues. But the return of a civilian administration in 1979, albeit under very different constitutional and economic circumstances than the First Republic, led to the revival of Balewa-style "quiet diplomacy"; and neither of the successive military regimes have regained the visibility or influence of the mid-1970s despite considerable determination and debate (Ihonvbere 1991, 1994; Ogwu 1986).

In retrospect, then, the Mohammed/Obasanjo period has increasingly looked like a "golden age" of Nigerian foreign policy. So Edet Inwang (1982:58) has lamented that "in the years after Angolan independence, lip service rather than respect has been paid to Nigeria's leading role in Africa and the Third World." He cited Nigerian citizens in the jails of West Africa, a falling oil price, and an inability to project power into either the Chadian or Cameroonian conflicts as evidence of a failed foreign policy. To revive Nigeria's status and influence, Inwang and others have called for a reduction of dependence on the West; i.e. for a transformation in the bases of Nigerian diplomacy. And in his inaugural lecture as Professor of International Relations at the University of Ife (now Obafemi Awolowo University) in the early-1980s, the late Olajide Aluko (1981a) called for a return to realistic national interests rather than the problematic quest for grandeur.

In contrast to such positions on the decline in Nigeria's effectiveness or potency, top foreign polity decision-makers view the "new modesty" as a function of two interrelated developments: i) the maturation of Nigeria's political and diplomatic structures and ii) the evolution of the global system in the direction of new complexities (Shaw 1987). President Shagari (1981), for example, recognized increased concern about apparent "set-backs," especially over Chad, border conflicts with Cameroon, the ECOWAS defence protocol and negotiations for Namibian independence. These issues, amongst others, have "aroused deep emotions among Nigerians." However, Shagari explained that "The Federal Government's studied restraint in the face of these apparent challenges and provocations has given rise to feelings of anxiety and doubt about our national resolve. Some would like to have Nigeria mount a military expedition to expel Libyan forces from Chad, while in the case of Cameroon's belligerent provocation, they advocate a primitive military retaliatory raid....Our foreign policy has been meticulously geared towards promoting good neighborliness...adherence to the provisions of international law...precluded any hasty recourse by us to military response in these situations until all diplomatic pressure failed."

Another interpretation of such "new realism" in Nigerian foreign policy is that the Mohammed/Obasanjo period was not really one of significant initiatives but rather an aberration: an unusual period in which individual actions appeared to add up to a new era but may instead have really been random reactions to contemporary events. As Stephen Wright (1981:1685) has suggested, "diplomatic successes in bringing ECOWAS into existence (over French hostility), Angolan independence (over American opposition) and the British petroleum nationalization affair contributing to Zimbabwean independence all served to bolster the image of a dynamic and powerful foreign policy. It may be more accurate, however, to see these events as separate or sporadic successes rather than as linked events in a constant chain of political power. These successes were also partly assisted by favorable external factors..."

Such "revisionist" ideas about the tenuousness of Nigeria's power (Shaw & Aluko eds. 1983) led to a retreat from the middle power thesis and towards a new realism as the difficult decade of the 1980s dawned. This transition was most clearly marked in Olajide Aluko's inaugural lecture referred to above. For, from being a "nationalist" in orientation (see Aluko 1981b and 1987 and section d below) he had become a somewhat skeptical revisionist for three main reasons:

> The first is the lack of purpose and consistency in our foreign policy since the mid-seventies. The second has been the tendency of the Nigerian government and some powerful sections of the public to over-estimate our ability to influence external events, and perhaps shape world events in our own image. An example of this was the recent statement of the Minister of External Affairs, Professor Ishaya Audu, that Nigeria was 'longing to become a world super-power soonest'. The third is the psychological trait among Nigerian leaders and some sections of influential opinion-moulders that we have a great deal of freedom and manoeuvre in the conduct of our external relations (Aluko 1981a: 9-10).

If Aluko represented the new realism then Claude Ake and Stephen Wright amongst others reflected the new radicalism (Shaw & Fasehun 1980; Falola and Ihonvbere eds. 1988). The latter group gave limited room for a relatively autonomous foreign policy given the underdeveloped, foreign dominated and dependent nature of the economy. As well, issues of state, power, politics, production and society are often articulated in support of the position that, at best, Nigeria's foreign policy can only be a reflection of its overall marginalization in the international division of labor, with occasional shows of *influence* rather than *power*. Stephen Wright (1981: 1686) suggests, for example, that "the neo-colonial nature of the Nigerian economy is a major constraint...the economy is open to manipulation by non-Nigerian forces, particularly the multinational companies." This theme was developed further by Ake (1981a: 1163) in his own critique of the character of Nigeria's political economy when he argued that "Our economy is still oriented outwards and locked into dependence on the West....Our ruling class appears to be largely confined to the role of ensuring the existence of the political conditions of accumulation. Many are quite happy riding piggy-back to affluence on Western capital..."

It is essential, therefore, to review Nigeria's record in the area of foreign policy to date for, as one advocate of Nigeria - Andrew Young (1981:654) - has asserted, "Nigeria is in some important respects Africa's most powerful nation." Meanwhile of course, at the turn of the last decade of the twentieth-century, the bi-polar system was transformed with profound implications for the traditional "nonalignment" assumptions of a Third World state like Nigeria, which we treat below.

This debate about realism and radicalism has salience and intensity because of the expansive external aspirations of successive regimes and established interests, notably academe, entrepreneurs, media and sports teams. These all tend to adopt state-centric assumptions — foreign policy as government declarations and actions rather than non-state relations extending to informal exchange of goods and peoples - and to focus on major events: abrogation of the Defense Pact with Britain in 1963, relations with the powers during the civil war, recognition of the MPLA government in Luanda in 1975, pressure on Britain via BP and Barclays Bank over Zimbabwe in the late-1970s, and the ups-and-downs of regional political strategic and economic connections (Olusanya & Akindele eds. 1986a and b). Hence the discourse over power and influence, particularly related to the rise and fall of oil income, and the difficulty of treating debt and devaluation as major aspects of foreign relations.

Despite its general conservatism and occasional chauvinism, there is a foreign policy establishment in Nigeria centered on the Nigerian Institute of International Affairs (NIIA) in Lagos, established right after independence, the National Institute of Policy and Strategic Studies (NIPSS) in Kuru, outside Jos, revived during Murtala/Obasanjo era, the Nigerian Society of International Affairs (NSIA), the *Ni-*

gerian Journal of International Affairs and *Nigerian Journal of International Studies,* and reporters, particularly at *The Guardian* and *New Nigerian* as well as vibrant weekly magazines such as *TELL, Newswatch,* and *The News.* Characteristic of the interconnections amongst these were Bolaji Akinyemi's moves from Ibadan to head the NIIA before becoming foreign minister and those of Ibrahim Gambari from ABU to NIIA and thence minister and back as Ambassador at the UN in New York. Gabriel Olusanya, a Professor of History with a bias for International Relations also moved from the University of Lagos to head the Institute before becoming Nigeria's Ambassador to France in 1991. If such career patterns are quite common amongst the realists they are largely absent among the radicals who remain in academe or media; perhaps the sole exception now being Alaba Ogunsanwo's appointment as Nigeria's Ambassador to Botswana, a position he held until late 1996. But the latter do enliven the series of conferences at NIIA and NIPSS and provide alternative agendas for constitutional commissions and policy planners. And symptomatic of the adjustment era in Africa, several new private or NGO-type research groups have been created by leading Nigerian academics-cum-activists such Adebayo Adedeji's African Centre for Development and Strategic Studies (ACDESS) and Claude Ake's Centre for Advanced Social Studies (CASS). Over foreign and development policy there are defined positions and disagreements related to mode of analysis and roles in society as well as to existential events, notably the rise and fall of petro-naira and of successive regimes.

a) Continuity And Change

While there has been some controversy recently, culminating in the mid-1980s Kuru Conference and NIIA Silver Jubilee discourses, about the degree of success or effectiveness of Nigerian diplomacy there is still a considerable consensus about its continuity, despite the occasional appearance of change. For despite several transitions in regime since 1960 - and a continuing evolution in political economy - the overall orientation has remained quite consistent: the tenor has been cautious, conservative and continentalist. Interestingly, apparent increments in Nigeria's power capabilities did not have a dramatic impact on its foreign policy direction, although this reverted to an unabashedly status quo stance with the return of a civilian administration in the late-1970s and the termination of the Cold War in the late-1980s. Indeed, the only period in which the country did appear to shrug-off some caution was, as we have seen, during the Mohammed/Obasanjo interregnum (Akinyemi 1979), an historically brief period between the characteristic Balewa-Gowon and then Shagari administrations; the subsequent Buhari military government was too preoccupied by regime security and national insolvency to focus on external image and influence (Shaw 1987). Yet, in spite of economic crisis and a precipitous decline in oil rents, Babangida, surprisingly tried to maintain an activist foreign policy within the constraints imposed by structural adjustment and a mounting foreign debt profile as noted below (Ihonvbere 1991a and b, 1994). The present Abacha junta presents a completely new approach and response to foreign policy issues arising largely from the mismanagement of Nigeria's political fortunes (see concluding chapter).

If the first civilian administration failed to mobilize Nigeria's potential in international affairs - the "sleeping giant" - the first military regimes were preoccupied with civil strife and then civil war: Gowon had little time for foreign policy except when it affected the outcome of the national conflict. Nevertheless, while the orientation has been characterized by a high degree of continuity, there has been an increase in activity, befitting an aspiring middle power, particularly given the new challenges and opportunities of the end of bipolarity and the on-going competition with South Africa as well as initiatives in Liberia and Sierra Leone. Indeed, while internal critics may now call for caution and calculation external expectations have continued to increase, economic difficulties notwithstanding.

The sixties were, then, symbolized by passivity. The Balewa government rejected all forms of foreign assistance from the Eastern bloc, banned Nigerians from travelling to socialist countries, opposed all militant anti-colonial moves in the continent, especially those initiated by Kwame Nkrumah of Ghana and Sekou Toure of Guinea, and interpreted the problem of apartheid in purely racial and moral terms. While allowing unfettered freedom for Western diplomats in the country, those of the Soviet Embassy were controlled and monitored; very generous incentives were provided for foreign investors and the Balewa government took sides with the West on virtually every issue at the United

Nations (Aluko 1981b; Akinyemi 1978; Idang 1973; Ihonvbere 1982b and 1991; Shaw and Aluko eds. 1983). The seventies, in contrast to the 1960s, were characterized by relative activity, with the eighties being distinguished by continued involvement without proportionate influence and the nineties have opened with a transformed global context of an end to the Cold War: unipolarity in security issues and multipolarity in economic ones. Internal contradictions, crises, and conflicts also precipitated formidable challenges to Nigeria's external image and relations with sanctions being imposed by western powers and the country earning a suspension from the Commonwealth over the annulment of elections and the execution of nine environmentalists including Ken Saro-Wiwa. Having been somewhat preoccupied since independence with the African condition seeking to end apartheid, Nigeria is now concerned about how to relate to the emerging multi-racial regime in the southern Africa. At the moment, South Africa seems to be taking the initiative, attracting more interest and attention, and providing Africa with an authentic voice especially with Nelson Mandela at the helm of affairs. While Nigeria is being hemmed in and criticized at the Commonwealth, UN, and several international fora, other major nations are capitalizing on its diminished status to expand their interests. An example is the recent election of Kofi Annan as replacement to Egyptian Boutros Boutros-Ghali as Secretary General of the UN, a position Nigerians have longed for over the decades.

The accelerated tempo of Nigeria's external affairs after the rather desultory period of the first decade was the result of an historic conjuncture at the beginning of the new decade of the 1970s: i) the ending of domestic hostilities and internal crises and ii) the beginning of international energy and economic crises. Both of these events enhanced Nigeria's external position in the early seventies and together constituted the backdrop to the exertion of its considerable capabilities and its transition into the second civilian republic. But the demise of civilian rule was accelerated by the decline of oil income and gross mismanagement so the post-Shagari officers lacked the revenues and expectations of the Mohammed/Obasanjo golden age. Though revenues improved somewhat under the Babangida regime, the challenges of demilitarization and human rights abuses did not serve to expand the country's credibility: it more or less lived off its earlier record and goodwill, lucky that its size and resources made it impossible for Nigeria to be ignored.

Despite the continuity in Nigeria's economic orientation - an essentially dependent and capitalist system - its activism in foreign relations coincided with the shift in focus from world to African affairs. Economic alignment did not seem to exclude increasing nonalignment in politics, even if the line separating the two was more ephemeral than real:

> There is an element of continuity in Nigerian foreign policy in that all the various regimes subscribed to 'non-alignment' at the international level and good neighborliness in Africa. What varied was the way successive regimes interpreted these cardinal principles and the extent to which other intra- and extra-Nigerian events shaped the execution of these policies (Ogunbadejo 1980: 763).

However, over the last 30 years the structure of the national political economy has not been static. In spite of deepening political crisis and rapid regime turnover, Nigeria has begun to achieve recognition as part of the semi-periphery in terms of both industry and diplomacy. This process has generated new, more national structures whose interests have demanded shifts in external direction; one being more attention towards Africa, especially towards neighboring consumer markets and labor sources.

Nigeria's Afrocentric activism - which came to affect its attitudes towards and relations with non-African actors - was revealed most dramatically in its recognition of the MPLA regime in Angola (Daddieh & Shaw 1984) and most consistently in its advocacy of regionalism in West Africa (Ojo 1980; Ihonvbere 1983b). These twin strands in its Africa policy - liberation in Southern Africa and integration in West Africa - are likely to continue into the mid-term future providing i) its national leadership does not undergo sudden change in terms of its bourgeois origins and ii) its national income does not go into dangerously precipitous decline. To be sure, with the "liberation" of South Africa and the election of the ANC leadership, Nigeria would certainly continue to strive to maintain a presence in the Southern Africa region. With the demise of apartheid, West Africa, the first in the three concentric circles (the other two being Africa and the World), should begin to reoccupy center-place in the country's foreign policy calculations-peace in Liberia, stability in Sierra Leone, cooperation with Ghana, raproachement with neighbors especially Cameroon, and so on. However, before making a general evaluation of the bases of Nigeria's power and the levels of Nigeria's interactions we look at some contemporary incidents in its foreign relations some of which produced President Shagari's (1981:204) defensive assessment in the middle of his term:

> Nigeria, like most other regional powers, must learn to contend with problems associated with leadership and the attendant responsibility. This is a classic constraint which Nigeria will be called upon to live with. This administration's response to this predicament has been, however, consistent with our national character and African policy. These are some of the considerations for my preference for international arbitration on our border dispute with Cameroon...It is not because we lacked the will or capacity to resolve the problem through other means.

As the 1980s opened, then, the optimism of the 1970s tended to be matched by a new awareness of constraints and contradictions, notwithstanding continuing attempts at local agricultural production and indigenous ownership. Nigeria became more dependent than ever on one product - petroleum - and on capitalist countries and corporations, despite rhetorical attempts to disengage and diversify (Ogwu 1986). Hence the imperative of realism about debt, devaluation and moderation as the officers returned, reinforced in the 1990s by the end of the certainties of the Cold War globally and apartheid continentally.

b) Foreign Policy In The 1980s

If Nigerian foreign policy was able to exploit a favorable conjuncture of forces in the 1970's, particularly its oil resources, it seems to have been constrained by new complexities and challenges in the 1980s. First, at the national level, the revival of democratic forms and then military rule and the instability of petrol revenues inhibited dramatic initiative. Second, at the regional level, ECOWAS was marked by interstate wrangles and by intrastate conflicts. Third, at the continental level, OAU affairs entered a new period of controversy and Southern African liberation did not proceed at the same pace, following the independence of Zimbabwe until the end of the decade. And finally, fourth, at the global level, the Cold War returned under Ronald Reagan's presidency and the global economy failed to expand, symbolized by "Black Monday" in late-1987. In short, at all levels, until the late-1980s, the world of the Shagari and then Buhari administration was more perplexing than that of the Mohammed/Obasanjo regime: North-South relations were now marked by national protectionism rather than global negotiations and East-West relations by super-power antagonism rather than middle-power mediation. And the officers returned to treat the economic crisis rather than political chaos; they were preoccupied by debt, devaluation, deflation and regulation rather than by grandeur.

Although in the early-1980s the new presidential system faced difficulties at national (troublesome democratic processes), continental (protracted diplomacy over Namibia), and global (revival of bipolarity) levels, it was at the regional level that constraints and complexities were most apparent with, of course, implications for the other three levels. Aside from continuous negotiations within ECOWAS, whose creation had been sponsored in 1975 by Nigeria and continues to be sustained by Nigerian financial support, the major issues in Nigeria's backyard were three-fold: coups, civil wars and border disputes. The coups were those in Ghana (the first and second comings of Jerry Rawlings), and then Burkina Faso; the civil wars were in Chad and the Sahara; and the border disputes were with Benin and Cameroon.

In none of these regional crises did Nigeria exert its capabilities with great style or success either before or after the officers returned; rather, the image of initiative created after the MPLA recognition and Zimbabwe liberation was discredited if not shattered as the eighties opened. Hence the new realism or maturity, as reflected initially in President Shagari's foreign policy review and in Professor Aluko's inaugural address and then in the Kuru conference and NIIA anniversary. Wright (1981:1685) commented on Olajide Aluko's new caution in the face of the former's new consternation:

Aluko's attack (on contemporary foreign policy) was more significant in that it showed a marked change of attitude from his previous conception of a strong and powerful Nigeria having a dynamic and forceful role to play in African and global affairs. Aluko's perception now is that Nigeria has in fact over- estimated its power to act within the international system, and its leaders have tried in recent years to achieve things which were never really attainable. Aluko believes that by exaggerating the crusading element in Nigerian foreign policy, the government has tended to ignore and leave undefined the fundamental 'national' interests of the country.

We return to this revisionist-realist-radical debate later in the chapter; here we note the basic features of such contemporary challenges to Nigeria's power.

First, Nigeria responded with caution and criticism to the second Rawling's coup in Ghana having, perhaps, over-reacted to this first political intervention in 1979 and to Master Sergeant Doe's overthrow of the Americo-Liberian dynasty in Liberia the same year. In December 1981 Nigeria was somewhat ambivalent: it opposed the removal of the civilian Limann regime by force of arms but it also sought to prevent a decline into assassinations as happened during Rawling's first incarnation and during the subsequent overthrow of Sankara in Burkina Faso in late-1987. So whilst the Shagari regime was troubled by military interventions in general and by one in a neighboring and analogous country in particular it maintained diplomatic relations and, after a hiatus, even continued the flow of oil despite Ghana's continuing debts. As in Chad, the fear of expanded Libyan involvement was a salient factor in Nigeria's conciliatory decision-making.

So second, notwithstanding the complexities of the situation and getting a "bloody nose" in a short military intervention in 1980, Nigeria was active in preparing for and in the dispatch of an OAU peace-keeping force to Chad in late-1981. This followed the withdrawal of 5000 Libyan soldiers from Njamena and the acceptance of US logistical support. The OAU unit was two-thirds Nigerian and was commanded by a Nigerian. But such a force could not be sustained for long given continued fighting and ambiguity in its mandate; it took French power and persistence to secure Habre in power and the demise of Gaddafi's Saharan adventurism.

The continued struggle of Polisario for the independence of the Sahara was equally perplexing and also involved Libyan and French interests as well as those of Algeria, Morocco and major powers. Like Chad, it also entailed diplomatic manoeuvres; indeed in late-1981 President Shagari attended a joint Chad-Sahara summit in Nairobi. The retreat of Mauritania from control over its part of the Sahara led i) to the establishment of the Saharawi Arab Democratic Republic (SADR) and ii) to the isolation of Morocco, which declined to withdraw to its own extended borders. The desert battle was joined in early 1982 by a diplomatic battle when the OAU Secretary-General let SADR representatives join the Organization; once again, the moderates fought the radicals by undermining the effective operation of the OAU. As in Chad, Nigeria was in the vanguard of attempts to mediate this dispute but African and extra-African interests were persistent and complex, and the desert war sank into the endless dust of a stalemate.

Finally, third, the administration had to deal with a more direct threat to its national integrity with border incursions from Benin and Cameroon in 1979 and 1980 and 1981, respectively. The former disputes were along the border of Sokoto State and were both brief and contained. But the latter one was more visible, violent and threatening as oil revenues were potentially involved. On 16 May 1981, water-borne Cameroonian troops stationed along the Akai Ate River on the Cross River State border opened fire on a Nigerian patrol in five support boats: five Nigerian soldiers, including a commissioned officer, were killed and three others seriously injured.

The incident occurred along an increasingly tense and historically controversial border and despite the President's visit to the Cameroonian capital four months earlier. Following Nigeria's stern protest note, the Cameroon Minister of State for Foreign Affairs visited Lagos a week after the incident to express regret. But the Nigerian Security Council insisted on an unconditional apology and full compensation; the Cameroon Embassy in Lagos was attacked by crowds in late-May. Pressures grew on the Nigerian administration for revenge but in mid-July President Ahidjo agreed to pay full compensation and in January 1982 he visited Nigeria to mark the end of the affair. As in the Benin dispute, a joint boundary commission was revived with Cameroon during Ahidjo's visit. West Africa (27 July 1981: 1683) hailed Nigeria's handling of the latter bilateral conflict as "a triumph for President Shagari's qualities of restraint and humanism. The President was under considerable pressure from the Nigerian Army, some politicians and some elements of the press to respond aggressively to the killings." As it turned out, beyond Ahidjo and Shagari, the border problems with Cameroon, in what has become known as the "Bakassi Affair" continues to condition relations between both countries.

The decline of petro-naira combined with growing social problems such as unemployment and crime led to a mood of xenophobia in the early-1980s, with illegal aliens being identified as the main culprits. Thus, rather than addressing the structural problems of dependence on oil exports and Western imports or the major causes of financial difficulties - overvalued naira, black market and massive accumulation of foreign exchange overseas by the ruling clique - the regime blamed and harassed minor yet visible symptoms: regional workers who had come to Nigeria to labor in menial jobs in the booming economy which Nigerians declined. The expulsion in early 1983 of almost 2 million aliens, at least half of whom were Ghanaians, did not go down well with either ECOWAS neighbors or the foreign policy elite although it was welcomed by the impoverished and chauvinistic population who had been misled by the government into blaming the so-called aliens for their problems (Ogunsanwo 1986:104-5). Despite the spirit as well as intent of ECOWAS, Nigeria closed its overland borders for 18 months from the start of 1983, to reduce smuggling of goods and return flow of workers rather than treat the causes not symptoms of underdeveloped economies and overvalued currencies. As Ogunsanwo (1986:108) comments,

> "...the military government decided that it was a question of security both economic and military and therefore the borders had to remain closed....The problems of the borders, smuggling and economic sabotage...will continue...as long as we run the present system of economy...."

As events were to show, these moves were symptoms of regime desperation in the face of rapid delegitimization, instability, uncertainty, and economic decline arising from gross mismanagement, corruption, and fall in oil revenues.

Given such contemporary coups, civil wars and border disputes, Nigeria and other ECOWAS members have encouraged the development of a strategic component in West African regionalism. The ECOWAS Heads of State agreed to a regional defense pact in June 1981 consisting of a Defense Council (of Heads of State) and a Defense Committee (of Ministers of Defense and Chiefs of Staff). These institutions could call upon the joint defense force of units from ECOWAS armies to deter external aggression against any member, although considerable logistical and political problems remain to be addressed; as indicated in the regional force -ECOMOG- dispatched to Liberia in the aftermath of the anti-Doe civil war.

Aside from this regional response which, like the OAU expeditionary force in Chad, may not always be effective in practice, and notwithstanding continuing discussions about an OAU African High Command, Nigeria augmented its national defense capability in advance of the officers' return by buying sophisticated and expensive equipment for all of the armed services: Alpha jet trainers, Jaguar jet fighters, and Roland ground-to-air missiles for the airforce, frigates and corvettes for the navy, and Leopard tanks and local armored personnel carriers for the army. However, the problems of credibility and effective deterrence remain even under renewed military rule. This gap between policy and performance led to public as well as academic debate at the apparent setbacks of the early 1980s multiplied, especially with the mainly Nigerian ECOMOG force becoming bogged down in Liberia in the early 1990s.

For example, on 2 July 1981 the *New Nigerian*, reflecting widespread public opinion, carried a front-page editorial on "The need to shake-up our foreign policy." After lamenting the declining "effectiveness of our foreign policy since our glorious days over the Angolan crisis," the editorial complained in a manner typical of major or middle powers that despite the commitment of considerable sums to African liberation, especially to Angola and Zimbabwe, "we do not seem to command respect commensurate with the financial commitments we have made to them." The editorial went on to advocate the design of a "well-defined foreign policy framework to guide our actions" and a reduction in the "widening credibility gap between what we say and what we do."

In his partial response to such concerns President Shagari in a 1981 address recognized that "there has been a great deal of public debate on matters such as the situation in Chad Republic, the border incident with Cameroon, the ECOWAS defense protocol, the deadlocked Namibian independence negotiations and the implications for Africa of the change of governments in the USA and France, to mention just a few." But he denied that Nigeria could not respond with appropriate force - "it is not because we lacked the will or capacity to resolve the problem through other means" - insisting that it was Nigeria's very leadership role—not its weakness - which "precluded any hasty recourse by us to military response...until all diplomatic persuasions had failed."

In some ways, then, the civilian administration like the preceding and succeeding military regimes attempted to bring Nigeria's foreign policy into line with changes in both external and internal environments. In the mid-seventies a particularly favorable conjuncture of forces - the "petro-naira" windfall and a benign global system - enabled the soldiers to engage in innovative behavior; by the early-eighties a distinctly unfavorable conjuncture—inadequate external income and a malign global system—forced upon both civilian and soldiers a period of retrenchment. And the pre-occupations of debt re-negotiations and payments plus return to democracy meant that it could hardly respond to the challenges and opportunities of an end to both bipolarity and apartheid in the early 1990s.

c) Definitions And Levels Of Interaction

One method by which to judge the success or otherwise of Nigeria's foreign policy is to examine its own definition of national roles; another is to distinguish between different levels of interaction. Despite changes in regime, in issues and in activism, as well as in global contexts, there has been remarkable continuity in intention if not performance.

First, in terms of national role conceptions, in addition to the President's review of foreign affairs, we may cite from the 1979 Second Federal Constitution (section 19):

> The State shall promote African unity as well as
> total political, economic, social and cultural libera-
> tion of Africa and all other forms of international
> cooperation conducive to the consolidation of uni-
> versal peace and mutual respect and friendship
> among all peoples and state, and shall combat ra-
> cial discrimination in all its manifestations.

If liberation as advocated in the last constitution remains
elusive then self-reliance as espoused by the earlier, mili-
tary-appointed Adedeji Review Committee (cited in Aluko
1981a:13) also remains problematic:

> -The defense of our sovereignty, independence and
> territorial integrity;

> -The creation of the necessary political conditions
> in Africa and the rest of the world would facilitate
> the defense of our sovereignty, independence and
> territorial integrity;

> -The creation of the necessary economic and po-
> litical conditions in Africa and the rest of the world
> which would foster Nigeria's national self-reliance
> and rapid economic development;

> -The achievement of collective self-reliance in Af-
> rica and the rest of the developing world;

> -The promotion and defense of social justice and
> respect for human dignity; and

> -The promotion and defense of world peace.

Clearly no state by itself could ever achieve all such goals
simultaneously in the complex contemporary order; some
ranking of them is necessary. In Nigeria's case its own role
conceptions- e.g. national developer, regional leader, liberation supporter, *status quo* mediator, and global equalizer -
may have shifted between periods, which leads to the related question of different levels of interaction.
     Second, then, Nigeria interacts at several external lev-
els — regional, continental and global — and these, like na-

tional role conceptions, may change in importance over time. Moreover, they are all interrelated so that, say, Southern Africa policy (liberation supporter) had implications for West African (regional leader) and extra-African (global equalizer) roles. Such interrelationships work both ways; i.e. Nigeria can use them itself as a form of pressure but external interests can in turn employ them as leverage on Nigeria. The latter, "dependence" perspective has been expressed by Wright (1981:1685) "...the neo-colonial nature of the Nigerian economy is a major constraint...the economy is open to manipulation by non-Nigerian forces, particularly the multinational companies". And the former, "influential" viewpoint has been articulated by Andrew Young (1981:655):

> Nigeria will endeavor to foster its interest in economic development and stable trade relationships with the West while simultaneously continuing to use its influence with Western nations and corporations in the interest of its political goals on the African continent, especially with regard to South Africa.

The balance between Nigeria's interests and influence and those of other actors change, not only between issues and levels but also over time; hence the apparent decline in Nigeria's foreign policy effectiveness in the eighties and nineties. The reasons for this may be clarified if we examine more closely the roles and goals included in its crucial Africa policy. First, at the continental level, Nigeria's policy of supporting pan-African unity and diplomacy has led it into active involvement in a range of OAU issues. Its role of status quo mediator has occasionally brought it into contact or conflict with leading external actors - e.g. over Chad, Sahara or the Middle East — while its support for the creation of an African Common Market symbolized by the April 1980 Lagos economic summit and declaration (Adedeji & Shaw eds. 1985) and now Abuja 1991 OAU declaration of an African Economic Community which is to come into full effect in 2025 may bring tension with major external corporations or trading blocs like the EC. Conversely, as an aspiring middle power, Nigeria may sometimes act in concert with such extra-continental interests, so reinforcing its claim to a special, intermediate status. The concert of middle powers advocated by Bolaji Akinyemi when foreign minister at a Lagos Conference in 1987 was one such attempt to give practical expression to middle power aspirations and claims: an African middle-power consortium in a post-bipolar world?

Second, at the level of Southern Africa, Nigeria's support for anti-racist African nationalism has put it more directly in opposition to various Western countries and corporations although, once again, shared commercial interests, and conservative values moderate antagonisms between center and semi-periphery. Therefore, notwithstanding Nigeria's aversion to racism, its support of the liberation movements has overall been quite limited; it emerged as a "helpful fixer" between the 5-nation Western "contact group" over Namibia and the 6-nation association of Front Line States, particularly in the late-1970s before the escalation of South African destabilization and repression throughout the 1980s. In general, it supports political rather than economic change, although the military's recognition of the MPLA regime in Angola in the mid-1970s was mistakenly taken to be a move towards a more radical stance. Rather, it was an attempt to regain African cohesion to avoid extracontinental manipulation. It was therefore an aberration when compared to characteristic attempts at mediation over Chad and the Sahara in the early-1980s; as well as opposition to Sankara's experiment in Burkina Faso and continuing suspicion of Libyan intentions. More representative of underlying interests was Nigeria's assistance in the Lancaster House negotiation and agreement over the independence of Zimbabwe. But the internal and external limits on mediation are apparent, as revealed by Akinyemi's removal as Foreign Minister over alleged unauthorized contacts with Israel among other reasons.

Finally, third, at the West African level, Nigeria's advocacy of regional integration, especially free trade in goods and labor (the expulsions of West African, especially Ghanaian, migrant workers in the early-1980s notwithstanding) along with defense cooperation, is reflective of two interrelated concerns-development and stability plus greater control over extra-regional intervention (e.g. from France, Libya or the super-powers). Its national interest lies particularly in industrial expansion and strategic containment, hence its concern not to exclude but simply to regulate foreign, especially European, involvement in both national and regional economies and polities. Without doubt, Nigeria's initiative after the civil war in 1970, to sponsor the creation of the Economic Community of West African States (ECOWAS) was borne out of several factors: the need for security in the sub-region, the search for a larger market, the desire to confirm its leadership aspirations, the need to check growing French presence (which had been used to pressure some Francophone states like Cote d'Ivoire to support the Biafran secessionists during the civil war) and the desire to use the country's new oil wealth to sponsor economic ventures and possibly emerge as the industrial heart of the sub-region (Ojo 1980; Ihonvbere 1982a and b). However, despite widespread recognition of and respect for Nigeria as a middle power, subsequent difficulties in the more complex and less benign world of the eighties - for example, protracted negotiations over Namibia, complications in Chad and Sahara, and Tanzanian and Senegalese involvement in Uganda and Gambia, respectively - renewed fears of Nigeria being either over-committed or under-powered, whether under civilian or military rule.

This new skepticism or realism has been reflected by Wright (1981:1685) even for Nigeria's central Africa policy: "The recent border clashes with Benin and Cameroon, the mistakes and failure to act effectively in Chad, and the refusal to intervene in Equatorial Guinea in the late-1970s, all are issues which have troubled Nigeria and which have not received the appropriate response." Yet, responding to such obviously important developments and challenges might get Nigeria embroiled in affairs quite beyond its capabilities. As Aluko, (1981: 33) has argued "the psychological error made by most Nigerians in and outside government (has been) that because of the size, population, and the agricultural and mineral resources in the country we are destined to lead Africa." So in addition to distinguishing between and ranking of different levels of interaction, as well as disregarding alleged distinctions between civilian and military regimes, two other factors can be used as means to analyze foreign policy continuities and changes, particularly given the new post-bipolar context of 1990 onwards.

First, we can identify and examine the scope of the "national" interest. As Wright (1981:1685) indicates, there has been a continuing debate, particularly between different regimes, "about whether the focus should be egocentric, that is to say purely Nigerian, whether it should serve the West

African region, Africa as a whole, or at its broadest, the interests of the black people throughout the world."

And second, we can delineate and discuss the bases (or lack thereof) of Nigerian "power," especially in its relational or relative aspects; i.e. in relation to other periods and relative to other actors. Although Nigeria's economy has grown rapidly it remains dependent on, and to some extent mortgaged to, external interests, as revealed in the debt negotiations and naira devaluations of the mid-1980s. Moreover, although it has grown at an impressive rate, even under the burden of structural adjustment since the mid-eighties while other African states have only expanded marginally even if not negatively, Nigeria's economy is still relatively small and underdeveloped compared to those of both old and newly industrialized states. The vulnerable and unstable bases of Nigeria's economic power along with its post-civil war dependence on petroleum revenue are revealed in the quite dramatic fluctuations which have occurred in GNP over the last decade. The current deterioration in economic fortunes and in the general conditions of living which have combined with other contradictions to deepen alienation, uncertainty, and violence is clearly a negative in the constriction of grand foreign policy objectives beyond the 1990s (Ihonvbere 1994; Agbese and Ihonvbere 1997).

But this question about the bases of power relates to the general issue of approaches to its foreign policy, dependence being but one possible mode of analysis. We conclude this chapter and anticipate our conclusion by putting Nigerian foreign policy into this general analytic perspective. The late-1990s are also an appropriate occasion to attempt an evaluation given the constraints of adjustment, developments in Eastern Europe and South Africa, the end of the Gulf crisis and the American declaration of a "New World Order" plus the monumental developments within Nigeria itself, not least regime changes, failed transitions, and the unpopular remilitarization of the political landscape.

d) Alternative Explanations And Projections

Given the growth of challenges to the intention and implementation of Nigeria's foreign policy in the 1980s and 1990s, this final section identifies three major positions and projections in the ongoing debate. These alternative views about Nigerian politics, economics and foreign policy - about the bases, effects and limits of Nigeria's political economy in a hierarchical world system - can be categorized into three distinct types, each of which offers a cohesive yet contrasting view about continuities and changes, influence and constraint: the "idealist" versus the "realist" (disagreement over contemporary and future forms) and the "realist" versus the "radical" (disagreement over historical, current and projected structures). We have already mentioned these in passing; here we examine them more directly and extend the logic of their analysis into the mid-term future. We recognize that the majority of analysts of Nigerian foreign policy, indigenous and foreign alike, are "realists," as befits its place of relative "power" at the semi-periphery; only a minority are either "idealists" or "radicals," although the latter group are growing in influence as the constraints on and contradictions of foreign relations increase (Shaw & Fasehun 1980).

Characteristic of the dominant realist position, as well as reflective of differences within this particular "paradigm," is the work of Bolaji Akinyemi (1978) and Olajide Aluko (1981b), at least until Aluko's inaugural lecture (see Aluko 1981a). Both of these leading scholars - it is not coincidental that they were Director-General of the Nigerian Institute of International Affairs and Professor of International Relations at the Universities of Ibadan and of Ife (now Obafemi Awolowo University) respectively - have taken it to be axiomatic that Nigeria is powerful and influential. They may be in disagreement about some of the causes of this power and influence - political direction, bureaucratic style or economic resources - but they exhibited few doubts about the overall character of Nigeria's external stature and status. In this shared assumption - one on which Akinyemi based his diplomatic forays as foreign minister under Babangida until late-1987 - they have reflected the perspective of most Nigerian scholars and statesmen, as well as that of most students of Nigeria: Nigeria is seen to be a Newly <u>Influential</u> Country (NIC), Africa's "great power." If any skepticism is admitted by the realists about Nigeria's standing it is usually about certain aspects of its power base: i) how long will oil (and gas) reserves last, ii) how long will civilians or soldiers control the government, and iii) how long will contemporary confusion continue in the infrastructure? In general, though, such difficulties are taken to be surmountable given Nigeria's financial and entrepreneurial resources. In short, the mood is very optimistic and rather heady, largely predating debt and devaluation. With the full arrival of a democratic South Africa on the political scene, some realists are beginning to moderate their claims and expectations, realizing the overall superiority of South Africa and its clear attractiveness to the West, investors, and even Africans in diaspora!

By contrast to the still dominant realist position (Aluko 1987), the two minority positions are considerably less optimistic and popular. The idealist view is less developed and debated than the radical one and is not identified with the work of any single scholar or school. Rather, there are elements of idealism in the writings of several Nigerians such as Mazi Ray Ofoegbu (1978) and Aluko (1981a): what should be the bases and directions of Nigerian foreign policy? For instance, the latter came to lament deficiencies in Nigeria's economic, strategic and political structures and argued for greater attention being given to the national interest rather than to regional and/or continental affairs: for a careful balancing of means with ends rather than a reckless pursuit of grandeur. Again, idealists are increasingly becoming disillusioned with continuing military intervention, sanctions from abroad over a variety of issues and transgressions, the suffocation of civil society, economic and social decay, fragmentation of the political class, and the fear that Nigeria might just never recover from its underdeveloped and dependent nature.

Despite this commentary on current policy, the realist and idealist positions are not really very far apart. Rather, the latter consists of redefinitions of or revisions to the former; that is, if Nigeria is to be influential in the future then it must reform its political economy and federal bureaucracy to make its goals more realistic and realizable. Moreover, in some ways, the idealist position is preemptive of the radical one; it anticipates future (positive) relations as a way of responding to current (negative) criticisms.

By contrast, the other minority position - that of the radicals - is much less optimistic and idealistic. Instead, it sees Nigeria as a Newly Industrializing Country confronting all sorts of contradictions and constraints such as those suggested above; the future is less clear and less attractive than in either of the other perspectives. Rather, both indigenous and foreign analysts in this genre see Nigeria as an essentially dependent state, albeit one at the semi-periphery rather than at the periphery (Falola and Ihonvbere eds. 1988). Its place in the world system and its emergent class society (with, of course, transnational connections) will constrain both its present and future influence, as indicated in Inwang's (1982:58) critique: "...(the) dangerous dependence on countries hostile to Nigerian's African and Third World interests leads obviously to the...reason why Nigerian's glorious moments in Angola are not about to be repeated in Namibia. This dependence has forced Nigeria to shift its foreign policy strategy, though the objectives remain the same. In Chad and Cameroon, for example, it is obvious that the root of the crises is French imperialism."

So, instead of an assured future, Nigeria's growth and influence are seen to be both unstable an unsustainable; the favorable conjuncture of forces that generated the oil boom may not be repeatable. As a state at the semi-periphery, Nigeria did experience rapid, if uneven growth, in the 1970s; hence widespread assumptions about its power potential. However, the projection of oil-based boom into the future remains problematic because of both internal contradictions and external changes, as symbolized by debt debates and deals.

Such radical analysis clearly remains the minority school of opinion, yet one that is growing in its forcefulness as Nigeria's rapid but unsteady growth generates further uneven development. Moreover, its persuasiveness is reflected in the fact that the major debate now is between realists and radicals (see Shaw & Aluko eds. 1982; Akindele & Ate, 1986; Ihonvbere 1994); the idealist perspective is usually mobilized only in defense of the realist position rather than in its own right. One positive and immediate result of this growing debate is that both realists and radicals have had to reconsider their assumptions and evidence, especially the political and economic bases of foreign policy. These have generated a set of contrasting scenarios for the future, both explicit and implicit.

In this chapter we have focused on the evolution of the national and global situations, as well as on relations at the intermediate regional and continental levels, as the background to both change and continuity, success and failure in foreign policy. Although Nigeria benefitted significantly from the initial stages in the break-up of the post-war Bretton Woods system - the high price of oil - it has not continued to do as the impacts of recession and protection undermine the bases of its potential power. Whilst, then, we would not

want to go as far as Wright (1981:1686) in identifying continuities - "No real distinction has been made between the
Obasanjo and Shagari administrations in the field of foreign
policy because, in broad terms, none exists" - we would suggest that the Mohammed/Obasanjo golden age was historically specific and restricted. The trend back towards more
modest, quiet diplomacy was to be expected given Nigeria's
impressive resources and emerging status in a "new" world
system characterized by strategic unipolarity and economic
multipolarity-US military hegemony and regionalized industrial and financial blocs — as well as the end of apartheid.

Moreover, despite some half-hearted attempts to revive
the aura of the Mohammed/Obasanjo period — boycott of
the 1976 Commonwealth Games in Edmonton and the Concert of Middle Powers Conference in Lagos in 1987 — the
Babangida regime took realist constraints and idealist complaints seriously. Furthermore, though it was to some extent been diverted from effective Afrocentrism by the new
high politics of debt negotiations and naira devaluations, it
continued to make some major achievements in the sphere
of foreign relations. Hence, in spite of the constraints of structural adjustment, Babangida served as ECOWAS chairman
for an unprecedented three terms, Rilwanu Lukman served
as OPEC's president for six terms, Major-General Joe Garba
became the President of the UN General Assembly, Chief
Emeka Anyaoku became the Secretary-General of the Commonwealth, Nigeria initiated the peace talks between the
Angolan rebel forces and the Angolan government, General
Olusegun Obasanjo served as a member of the
Commonwealth's Eminent Persons Group and Babangida
became the Chairman of the OAU in mid-1991.

In mid-1990, at the start of the post-cold war period and
before the Gulf war, Nigeria, against opposition from some
ECOWAS members like Cote d'Ivoire and Burkina Faso,
initiated the creation of an ECOWAS Monitoring Group
(ECOMOG) to intervene in the Liberian crisis and stop the
post-Doe carnage. Nigeria contributed more than half of
the troops, bore the cost of the operations without external
assistance, supplied most of the military equipment and took
in thousands of Liberian refugees. When, towards the end
of 1990, the "peacekeeping" ECOMOG force decided to become a "combat" unit due to the intransigence of the warring Liberian parties, Nigeria's Major-General Joshua
Dongoyaro replaced Ghana's Lt-General Arnold Quainoo

(*The Nigerian Economist* September 3, 1990; *The African Guard-ian* October 29, 1990; *Newswatch* September 17, 1990; *West Africa* 26 November-2 December, 1990). Justifying this uni-lateral intervention, which almost broke up ECOWAS, Presi-dent Babangida was emphatic about the fact that Nigeria could not stand aloof and watch the "massive destruction of property, the massacre of all the parties, of thousands of in-nocent civilians including foreign nationals, women and children ..." (*African Concord* 21 January 1991). The military operation - mounted at about the same time that the United States, which had declined to intervene in its long-standing *de-facto* colony of Liberia, was leading the Allied coalition in Desert Storm in the Gulf- was certainly an attempt to rees-tablish Nigeria's might as well as a demonstration of its re-gional power, structural adjustment notwithstanding (Shaw and Ihonvbere 1996).

In spite of this and other achievements, with debt, eco-nomic and political reform as the new bases and centerpieces of foreign policy, Nigerian leaders have substantially toned down the rhetoric of the 1970s and exhibit more caution in their financial generosity, even to the needy African nations. The novel modesty in government resources and rhetoric has deflated external expectations to more reasonable lev-els: neither Newly Industrializing nor Newly Influential Country (Shaw, 1987). To this extent foreign policy in the 1990s has suffered from fewer not more illusions than in the 1970s. The inflated national image, encouraged by Bolaji Akinyemi as academic advisor, NIIA Director and then for-eign minister has been abandoned in place of more realistic calculations conditioned by deepening internal crises and external pressures. The beginning of this new appreciation could be seen in Ike Nwachukwu's tenure as Minister for External Relations and the policy of "Economic Diplomacy" - using foreign policy to promote national economic inter-ests - which became the cornerstone of foreign policy (Ihonvbere 1991c, 1994). The critique by Shehu Othman (1986:35) may be rather harsh but is reflective of widespread skepticism and reevaluation:

> Nigerian foreign policy is in a grave crisis. The once influential African power has suffered re-verses in its African policy aspirations, and also experienced a drastic deflation in its capacity to

moderate its terms of incorporation in the international political economy. A casualty of economic bungling and the international recession, and no longer wooed by the East or West, Nigeria is today unable to assert forcefully its claims in the international political arena, nor even act as the African power broker it recently was.

While reflective of growing frustrations with the maintenance of Nigeria's foreign policy momentum as was evident in the 1970s, such criticisms as above, do not do justice to the continuing, even increasing, influence of Nigeria in ECOWAS, the OAU, the UN, OPEC and the Commonwealth. Even if Nigeria is being criticized within these bodies for its domestic transgression-killings in Ogoniland, detention of human rights activists, harassment of prodemocracy leaders, remilitarization of politics, the execution of Ogoni activists and so on-, the criticisms are done with the realization that Nigeria remains one of the continent's top five nations that cannot be ignored on any issue. Ironically, this is in spite of economic contractions and internal political pressures.

Nigeria was, then, unquestionably *primus inter pares* among African states during its initial three decades of classic Cold War (strategic, political and diplomatic) and Bretton Woods (economic) structures, from 1960 to the end of the 1980s. Furthermore, given its essentially pro-Western and -market orientation, it is unlikely to loose its preeminence in the new international divisions of power and labor in the 1990s and beyond. After all, it is still a major oil producing country, the most populous nation in Africa, a vibrant capitalist society, and its middle and upper classes continue to nurse an insatiable appetite for goods and services produced in the West. Nevertheless, both praxis and analysis will have to be quite revisionist to account for these transitions, especially as in the African case they mark the transformation of South Africa from apartheid towards multi-racial rule. Indeed, post-independence Nigeria under Balewa initially had some difficulty in becoming Non-Aligned because of its overly close association with Britain, a period characterized by Ibrahim Gambari (1991: 6) as "one of uncertainty and timidity." At the height of the Cold War and OPEC affluence and influence in the late 1970s, Nigeria appeared to have become more assertive against Western interests, especially the UK and US, BP and Barclays Bank. But the recognition of the MPLA regime in Angola was really a nationalist, PanAfrican aberration, not reflective of a transformed political economy or culture, notwithstanding the apparent gains of indigenization at that time. Indeed, in both pre- and post-OPEC periods, Nigeria was rather preoccupied with its own internal difficulties: civil war and economic crisis respectively.

Although formally associated with both NIEO and Lagos Plan of Action (LPA) initiatives in the 1970s and 1980s, respectively, Nigeria has always in fact been well-integrated into the global capitalist economy. Thus the difficulties for it than most other African states, in part because of continued cushioning of (albeit diminished) oil (and soon gas) export incomes. Moreover, because of its relative distance from the old Second World- i.e. other than the very fraught connection with the former USSR over the Ajaokuta iron and steel complex- Nigeria has been minimally affected by the disintegration of the Soviet Empire. Indeed, because of the number of Nigerian immigrants in the US and UK in particular, close transnational cultural ties with the West have been a constant no matter what regime type, economic situation, leadership ideology or personality, or interstate relation.

Nigeria in the new post-cold war international division of power, characterized by one super-power and several regional powers, may be able to reexert its influence in West Africa, symbolized by its dominance in ECOMOG in Liberia. In terms of both formal and informal economic and communications structures, now incorporating civil society, it has been central in ECOWAS, even if degree of dynamic varied; but extra-African states did sometimes constrain its activities, notably France and the US. Given the current "new" world order, such powers have less interest in regional conflicts outside the North Atlantic and North Pacific "trilateral" nexuses. Thus regional powers may reestablish themselves in the 1990s even in ways not anticipated by the Lagos middle power "concert" conference of over a decade ago. In the South, regional cooperation may be crucial as the global economy becomes more regionalized as in EC, 1992 and NAFTA. And in Africa in particular, the post-bipolar vacuum may come to be filled by a "concert" of regional powers, especially Nigeria, Egypt and post-apartheid South Africa (and possibly Kenya and post-Mobutu Zaire).

Though serious constraints currently mediate relations between Nigeria and South Africa, the effective construction of a Nigeria-South Africa axis with a focus on development and democracy could have far-reaching implications for the continent. This would of course require the existence of democratic regimes in both countries and some shared views and values on growth, development, and the primacy of Africa in global calculations. Such a strategic and diplomatic link is a "natural" given each state's own self-image and role conceptions. However, it is also a logical economic connection as both are essentially state capitalist economies in which the most major MNCs have branches, notwithstanding the passing discomforts of post-apartheid reforms and "indigenization" and sanctions on Nigeria, respectively. Indeed, these two regional cores of ECOWAS and PTA could together help to revive the stalled continental economy, especially given the oil/gas for manufactures fit. They might also give substance to plans for the African Economic Community (AEC) in the twenty-first century to parallel regionalization elsewhere in the new international division of labor. Nevertheless, both do remain subject to de facto conditionalities given their private as well as public debts externally, so their freedom of màneuver in regional and continental affairs will remain constrained, notwithstanding national, international and informal capitals' advocacy. Moreover, both will have to deal with the realities of new expanded and strengthened EC, and changing technologies in terms of their exports of oil/gas, gold/diamonds and other essential "colonial" commodities. Whether both can remain regional military-industrial complexes in the new order is more problematic, especially given the proliferating SAP conditionalities, now including reduced military expenditure and employment. South Africa remains a major arms exporter and continues to develop new technologies in this area.

This chapter has been conceived to advance a Nigerian view on foreign policy which has evolved from ebullience to caution as political and then economic dreams faded after independence. In the 1980s it became preoccupied with debt and adjustment, following an active role in Zimbabwe's independence. In the 1990s Nigeria will likewise be preoccupied with economic and political conditionalities, following its marginal place in Namibia's decolonization and in the negotiations and reform processes that culminated in the transition in South Africa. Its roles are more problematic than ever given the nature, demands, and challenges of the new globalization: more or less opportunity for Nigerian growth and grandeur in a multipolar global economy and unipolar global security system?

CHAPTER EIGHT

Traumas, Tensions and Transitions?
Abacha and Civil Society
1993-1997

It is part of the tragedy of Nigeria that when the
military decided to intervene finally, it did not do
so on the side of the electorate. Instead, it sided
with those who voided the June 12 verdict. It sided
with the anti-democratic cabal who had been holding the nation hostage for more than three decades
(Babarinsa 1993).

The return of the generals to power in Nigeria with the General Sani Abacha coup of November 1993 has posed fundamental challenges to the survival of the country as a nation.
On the one hand, it has brought out the worst in Nigerian
politics: repression, intimidation, violence, corruption, be-
trayals, manipulation of primordial loyalties, and the suffocation of popular communities and constituencies. On the
other hand, the return of the generals, and the character of
politics since then has exposed the under belly of the Nigerian political rot, and provided added strength and legitimacy to the still fractionalized, weak, and fledgling civil society. Could anyone have predicted the return of the military? Could anyone have anticipated the emergence of Sani
Abacha at the top of the power configuration? Was it possible to anticipate the bloody confrontations between popular communities and constituencies which culminated in the
execution by hanging of nine environmentalists in November 1995? What is the way forward for the contending po-

litical communities in the country (*TEMPO* November 1993)? In this chapter, we wish to explain the implications of the military's return for state-society relations and make some projections for the future of politics in Nigeria.

EXPLAINING THE RETURN OF THE MILITARY

Military coups have been part of Nigeria's political equation since the very first intervention in January 1966 led by Major Chukwuma Kaduna Nzeogwu. We have, elsewhere, already examined the causes of coups in Nigeria and made some theoretical postulations (Falola and Ihonvbere 1985; Ihonvbere and Shaw 1988). Suffice it to note, that all the successful coups, and most of the failed coups, have taken place at the highest points of political, social, and economic decay and unrest in the country. This has made it easy for the military, largely because it legally monopolizes the means of coercion, to intervene, usually on behalf of the dominant classes, to contain popular pressures and stabilize the system. To be sure, the fractionalization and factionalization of the ruling elites, the weakness of civil society, and the fragility of the state have made it easy for the military to seize power again and again. It is for the reasons above that the military has emerged as the most powerful contender in the struggle for power in contemporary Nigeria (*TELL* February 14, 1994). However, two novel developments occurred in Nigeria's coup history in 1993: an open invitation to conservative military officers to seize power from sections of the political class; and consultations with prodemocracy forces by military officers before the actual coup event.

It was an irony, perhaps because Nigerians had grown so used to military coups, and in frustration over the imposition of an Interim National Government (ING) by General Babangida (see below), members of the Nigerian political class, including some prodemocracy activists like Chief Gani Fawehinmi, Lateef Jakande, and Bolaji Akinyemi actually called on the military, and no General Abacha in particular, to intervene. Fawehinmi had called on "all progressives, in and out of the military to defend this country against the ING...the military must intervene to stop this rot, to stop this war of Shonekan's government against the people" (Fawehinmi 1993). Akinyemi, a professor of political science and one-time minister for foreign affairs, actually addressed a letter to Abacha urging him to dissolve the ING and "all democratic structures, readoption of the 1960 constitution, and the formation of a transitional national government based on the June 12 election" because, in his view, the country was "fast running out of options" (*Newswatch* November 29, 1993). Admittedly, they had assumed that such an intervention would be on the side of prodemocracy forces and in support of the struggle to reverse the annulment of the results of the June 12 elections.

Such a naive position could only have been informed by a very poor reading of the character of the Nigerian military, a poor appreciation of the nature of previous interventions which were for "restoration" rather than transformation or revolution, and the fact that it is impossible to get the military to act on behalf of the people when there has been no tradition of collective work, shared experiences, and visions. More importantly, those who were strategically placed to carry out the intervention, especially General Abacha, had been part of the inglorious Babangida regime that precipitated the political impasse in the country. General Abacha, to whom these appeals were made had always nursed an ambition to seize power on his own terms. He had been involved in several coups including Babangida's coup of 1985. He was not on record as having made a single statement in support of moral probity, the subordination of the military to civil order, or an acknowledgement of the importance of a strengthened civil society. He was generally perceived to be corrupt, ruthless, and narrow in his world view.

It must be remembered that years of military rule, and a tradition of toying around with the political class without repercussions, had convinced the military in Nigeria that there are two political parties in the country: the military and the people. Because the military commands the bombs, tanks, guns, and bullets, at least, legally and in larger quantities, it regards itself as the superior political party.

It is also interesting to note that Generals Abacha and his second in command, Oladipo Diya actually held consultations with the Campaign for Democracy (CD), traditional rulers, and other prominent political figures before the coup. Since none of those consulted openly opposed the intervention before it was announced, it could well be assumed that they directly and/or indirectly approved of, and supported the coup. This tacit approval of the coup, was later to constrain the ability of these constituencies to oppose the military. Many were of course misled by promises of a national conference (as against a sovereign national conference), a brief military rule, and commitment to restoring democracy, even if not the de-annulment of the June 12 presidential election.

In terms of specifics, the immediate background to the November 1993 putsch can be located at two levels. First, the terrible economic situation of the country; and second, the normless politics and politicking of the politicians of the defunct third republic which had over stretched popular groups, divided the political class, and precipitated a very dangerous impasse. When General Ibrahim Babangida seized power from Generals Muhammadu Buhari and Tunde Idiagbon in August 1985, the Nigerian economy was in shambles. Three years of civilian rule in the second republic had bled the nation dry, mismanaged huge oil rents, more than doubled the foreign debt profile, destroyed the manufacturing and productive base, and accentuated social tensions and conflicts to unprecedented proportions (Ake ed. 1985; Ekekwe 1986; Ihonvbere 1994). Unfortunately, the Babangida regime made things worse through gross incompetence, unbridled corruption, waste, mismanagement, the privatization of public office and public resources, neglect of non oil sectors, and misplaced priorities. The adoption of a World Bank supervised structural adjustment program in 1986 did not solve the problem. Rather, it made the situation worse as Nigeria's brand of adjustment was pathologically fixated on the exchange rate of the naira rather than on the specific issues of adjusting the structures of the economy, building investor confidence, strengthening the local bourgeoisie, integrating the sectors of the economy, and promoting growth and development (Forest 1986; Olukoshi ed. 1993).

The pain, poverty, uncertainty, frustrations, and hunger which accompanied Nigeria's economic decline, and the implementation of an adjustment program without any protection for vulnerable groups, created an environment which directly challenged possibilities for stability and sustainable democracy (*National Concord* December 9, 1993; *Washington Post* December 31, 1991). With over 45 percent of foreign exchange earning going into debt servicing, with a run away inflationary situation, and with increasing bankruptcies among indigenous investors, the economy sank deeper and deeper into crisis, and the social fabric of the society deteriorated to unprecedented levels. Crime, child abuse, marital violence, disease, institutional decay, urban dislocation, and frustration came to characterize the society (Ihonvbere 1994). Such conditions of economic and social decay created an anarchic environment which political adventurists in the military have traditionally appealed to in the search for legitimacy following every take over *(National Concord* December 9, 1993).

The economic crisis was made worse by the political stalemate which accompanied the June 12, 1993 presidential election. The transition to democracy was the major project to which the Babangida government had committed itself in 1986. It had set up a Political Bureau to consult with Nigerians and make recommendations on the country's political future; and a Constitution Review Committee had reviewed the 1979 Constitution which had guided the defunct second republic. The government also set up the Directorate for Food, Roads and Rural Infrastructure (DIFRRI), the Directorate for Mass Mobilization, Social Justice and Economic Recovery (MAMSER), and the Centre for Democratic Studies (CDS) to work towards promoting rural development and the mobilization and education of Nigerians for democracy. A population census was carried out in 1992, a National Orientation Movement (NOM) was initiated, and other structures aimed at ensuring a lasting democracy were established. In addition, the government scuttled independent efforts at party formation following the lifting of the ban on politics. It banned a category of politicians from politics and constantly blamed the rich for the country's political crisis. In place of independent efforts at party formation, the military created its own two parties-the National Republican Convention (NRC) described as a "little to the right," and the Social Democratic Party (SDP) which was a "little to the left." The government then proceeded to build party offices at the federal capital, state and local governments across the country, and to fund all their activities including deciding and imposing ideological platforms. It intimidated the political class, tinkled with the transition program, banned and unbanned political actors at will, postponed the hand over date three different times, threatened social activists, branded prodemocracy leaders as "extremists," and poured billions of naira in promoting the emergence of a so-called "new breed" political class that would lead the transition to a third republic (Ihonvbere 1994; Gana 1990; Agbese 1991).

Under normal conditions, some or most of these programs should contribute to the process of genuine political liberalization with possibilities for democratization through the empowerment of the people and their communities. Of course, all these and more were mere shadow chasing by General Babangida and the military elite. He had no intention of quitting the political scene. While blaming the politicians and the so called "moneybags" for the country's political problems, he poured more money into the system, increased the political stakes, promised each candidate something in order to strengthen their resolve to capture state power by hook or crook, and continued to make the transition program as uncertain as possible by introducing new rules, reinterpreting existing legislation, and manipulating the transition institutions (*Liberty* January-April 1993; *The Guardian on Sunday* June 20, 1993). For one thing, General Babangida was very confident that, no matter how much, and how frequently he intervened in the transition program, and no matter how often he toyed around with the politicians and the electoral rules, the situation would not degenerate to a level where his control of the political system would be effectively challenged (*The Guardian* July 21, 1993). As Paul Adams (1993: 26) has noted, "(t)ight control of the elections, death threats against dissidents, and press closures ... reinforced the transition to elected civilian rule, ignoring public opposition to the flawed electoral system, the institutions of government, and the federal structure of Nigeria." Adams (1993: 26) also noted that the transition program, "negated any attempt at national consensus or popular involvement in the evolution of government and society in Nigeria."

The successful conduct of elections to gubernatorial positions, state houses of assembly, local government councils, the federal senate, and to the house of representatives gave some observers the impression that a transition was indeed taking place and a third republic was forthcoming. Unfortunately, such optimistic evaluations of the Nigerian reality were misplaced. The focus on superficial dimensions of liberalization overshadowed a more sinister program for dismantling institutions of civil society, entrenching military rule, and totally militarizing the political landscape. A major strategy for achieving this was the exhaustion of the political class; discrediting it through complex divide-and-rule tactics and by exploiting its irresponsibility, division, and greed; and by co-opting those individuals and organizations that were vulnerable enough for the military project.

The political class was completely unprepared for a transition to democracy. Because its agenda for the third republic had virtually nothing to do with service, public education, mobilization, and the restructuring of the nation's political landscape to promote democratization, the political class remained divided, antagonistic, opportunistic, irresponsible, and completely unable to map out an agenda to see the military out of power (*TELL* September 13, 1993). In fact, when General Babangida cancelled the results of the party primaries in late 1992, the political class, in typical fashion, accepted his actions and strove to meet his new demands and regulations. As Femi Falana (*TELL* September 13, 1993) has noted, the Campaign for Democracy (CD) (an umbrella organization of about 35 popular organizations) "was actually prepared to chase out Babangida on January 2 (1993) but our dilemma was that the politicians that were disqualified were not prepared to champion any cause."

With the conduct of the presidential election on June 12, 1993, it was generally expected that given the subservient attitude of the politicians who had obeyed all rules imposed on them, avoided critical and thorny political issues, and promised not to probe the Babangida regime on any issue, that a transition to democracy would take place. Such expectations had not counted on the "hidden agenda" of Babangida, and the weaknesses of the political elite. As Gbenga Tanimowo (*The African Guardian* August 9, 1993) has noted, not only had the political class "shown itself to be apart from the people," but it has succumbed to every move Babangida has made against it: "Ibrahim Badamasi Babangida...(was) the nemesis of the country's political class, indeed of its elite. In the eight years of his rule he ... moved them around his little finger, exploited their greed and showed them to be one thing: lacking in principle or in commitment to higher ideals."

The election was adjudged to be the most free and fair in the country's history. The National Electoral Commission (NEC) pronounced it the very best election it had conducted thus far. The International Observer Team (IOT) had praises for the NEC, the parties, candidates, security forces, and noted in particular, the "maturity and decency" of the campaigns (*Point* July 12, 1993). The Presidential Election Monitoring Group (PEMG) which had been set up by the government to oversee the elections also declared that it was "administered... with meticulous precision." It commended the NEC for its "diligent, dutiful, and in the main, patriotic" handling of the exercise. To the PEMG, the June 12 election was devoid of the failings of previous exercises and this was a positive sign "for the future of elections in Nigeria" (*Point* July 12, 1993). The director general of the government supported Centre for Democratic Studies (CDS), Omo Omoruyi also declared that the "election was the best the nation ever had and should be accepted" (*TELL* July 19, 1993). The Chairman of the CD, Beko Ransome-Kuti noted that "the elections were very orderly. It was a vote for the presidential candidates as well as a clear demonstration of the resolve of Nigerians that they would not give Babangida the excuse he needed to derail the transition to democracy" (interview, Lagos, December 1993). However, on June 26, 1993, General Babangida, in a nationwide broadcast announced that he had annulled the June 12 election. He banned the two candidates from contesting in future elections, and imposed new rules to guide future exercises (*TELL* July 26, 1993).

We would not concern ourselves here with why the election was annulled. Suffice it to note that the explanations provided by the military did not satisfy the majority of Nigerians and the international community which roundly condemned the government. More importantly, since the annulment, things have practically fallen apart in Nigeria with the center clearly unable to mediate conflicts, provide leadership, and put in place an agenda for national unity, political liberalization, and military disengagement from politics. In fact, the constituent units of Nigeria, determined on the basis of religion, region, or ethnicity, have gone farther apart since the annulment than at any other time in Nigeria's political history. There was however, a very positive, certainly unintended consequence of the annulment: it woke up a dormant civil society, encouraged the formation of scores of prodemocracy and civil liberty organizations, compelled Nigerians abroad, to, for the first time, organize along political lines, and exposed the emptiness of Nigeria's so-called transition to the international community.

THE MILITARY VERSUS CIVIL SOCIETY

One reason why the military has always found it easy to hijack popular contestations for political power, aside from its legal control over the means of coercion, is the weakness and fragmentation of civil society (Ihonvbere and Vaughn 1995). The numerous self-help and community-based associations were largely individualistic and narrow in focus. There were hardly points of convergence at which to articulate a *national* project. Though many did sponsor political candidates for office, the vast majority had no political agenda whatsoever. In fact, many were set up in the context of state failure to meet the basic needs of the people and their communities. Until the late 1980s, there was not a single human rights group in Nigeria. The labor and students' unions were the only outlets for articulating and pursuing popular agendas. The Civil Liberties Organization (CLO) was the first such group founded in October 1987 by a group of young lawyers led by Olisa Agbakoba. Nigerians abroad were more concerned with their ethnic and regional organizations than with a pan-Nigerian movement as had been the case in the 1950s. The political miscalculation of the Babangida regime in annulling the presidential election results in 1993 changed all this.

Popular groups led by the Campaign for Democracy (CD), an umbrella organization which had been founded in May 1992 with the principal goal of ensuring the restoration of democracy in Nigeria, immediately made it clear that they were opposed to the annulment, new elections, the new rules for political competition, and to the continuation of military rule. The CD vowed to see the military out of power by August 27, 1993. The CD went ahead and compiled the election results based on data from NEC, the various voting and counting centers, and showed that Abiola of the SDP won an overwhelming victory over Bashir Tofa of the NRC. It put in place a machinery to mobilize all Nigerians through its numerous affiliate organizations to make the country ungovernable, and to force the regime out of power. Massive protests were organized across the country especially in the southwestern portion where the support for Abiola was greatest and the CD had more active activists (*TELL* July 19, 1993; *Newswatch* July 19, 1993). Hundreds of thousands of leaflets against the military, exposing corruption, lawlessness, and abuse of power by the regime, and urging Nigerians to take a final stand against military dictatorship and against the subversion of the popular will were printed by the CD, the Civil Liberties Organization (CLO), the National Association of Democratic Lawyers (NADL), the Committee for the Defence of Human Rights (CDHR), and the Constitutional Rights Project (CRP). Organizations like Women in Nigeria (WIN), the National Association of Nigerian Students (NANS), the Nigerian Bar Association (NBA), the Nigerian Union of Journalists (NUJ), and the powerful Nigeria Labour Congress (NLC) all came out in opposition to Babangida and his new agenda. The very strategic National Union of Petroleum and Natural Gas Workers (NUPENG) called out its members on strike to protest the annulment of the election. SDP state governors announced their support for the popular action, traditional leaders in the southwestern part of the country condemned the military and the annulment of the election and declared their support for Abiola and the SDP. Several prominent politicians in the East and North like Abubakar Rimi, Balarabe Musa, Mallam Lawan Dambazau, and Sam Mbakwe came out in open support for the popular action and the need to uphold the June 12 mandate given by the people to the SDP.

The CD capitalized on the presence of over 80,000 soccer fans at the World Cup qualifying match at the National Stadium, Surulere, on July 3, 1993 to distribute leaflets calling on all Nigerians, to embark on "one week of national protest to force Babangida to go and to enforce the result of the June 12 election" (Campaign for Democracy, July 1993). The leaflet urged Nigerians to take part in "rallies, demonstrations and other actions," it urged workers to stay away from work and come out in support of the protests, market women were asked to close their shops, and cab drivers were advised to keep their vehicles off the roads. Participants were instructed to "block roads with barricades and burn tires on the roads and streets." The CD noted clearly in the leaflet that the protest was not for Abiola as an individual, though at that moment, he represented the democratic desires of Nigerians who gave him a popular mandate. People were warned not to loot or burn public or private properties and to note that the struggle was "not between 'North or south' or between ethnic or religious groups or political parties. Nigerians should not attack fellow Nigerians from other parts of the country." The CD also urged Nigerians to shun plans by the military to organize a new presidential election. The CLO and other constituent members of the CD also issued statements, leaflets and organized demonstrations across the country (Civil Liberties Organization, 1993).

For the first time in Nigeria's post-civil war history, organizations in civil society shook the political foundations of the nation, openly challenged the military dictators, and succeeded in mobilizing millions of Nigerians in urban and rural settings, across ethnic, regional, religious, class, and gender lines to defy the military and take a stand for democracy. The five-day nonviolent protest organized between July 5 and 9, 1993 was a huge success. The CD had done its homework by having meetings with several organizations and special interest groups-meat sellers, market women, shop keepers, students, trade unions, and road transport workers and enlisted their cooperation and support. The protest paralyzed the country as banks, markets, schools, government offices and the streets in the major cities were deserted and taken over by the protesters. Of course, given the high rate of unemployment, thugs and other criminals infiltrated the protests and unleashed a range of crimes on their victims (*Newswatch* July 19, 1993; *TELL* July 19, 1993). Professional associations like the Bar Association in Lagos and Ikeja, Ibadan, Ijebu Ode, Ondo, and Edo State boycotted the courts to protest the annulment. This led to a serious pile up of cases as these were the centers of legal adjudication in the country. Even the National Association of Sea Dogs (Pyrates Confraternity) called on Nigerians to resort to "civil disobedience if the decision is not reversed" (*TELL* July 19, 1993).

The CD action received unprecedented support and encouragement from abroad. Hundreds of organizations representing Nigerians in Europe and the Americas issued statements condemning the annulment, supporting the CD, and calling for more sanctions on Nigeria by the international community. The Organization of Nigerian Nationals (ONN) Dallas-Forth Worth, and the Organization of Nigerians in the Americas (ONA) both in Texas are examples of such activist organizations which worked hard to mobilize support for the CD. Protests were organized in the United States and UK at Nigerian missions against the annulment. Non-Nigerian organizations also joined in the protest. For instance, the New York-based Campaign for Peace and Democracy issued a statement in which it called on the US government to recall its ambassador to Nigeria, ask Nigeria to recall its ambassador to the United States, cancel all previously issued visas to military and political leaders, impose trade sanctions on the government, stop the importation of Nigerian oil, cancel all foreign (not just military) aid to Nigeria, call for the release of detained activists and the reopening of closed media houses and academic institutions, and for "the United Nations and governments around the world to support the prodemocracy struggles in Nigeria through adopting steps along the lines listed above" (*New York Review of Books* October 7, 1993; *Peace and Democracy News* 1993-94).

In response to this new awakening of civil society, the military junta arrested the leaders of the prodemocracy movements, shut down universities and media houses, tightened security around the country, and expand its co-optation network. It also tried to bribe factions of the two political parties, the national assembly, journalists, and social critics (*The Guardian* August 27, 1993). These measures failed to stem the tide of opposition.

The strength of the protests and the resoluteness of the CD and its member organizations forced General Babangida to finally accept that he could no longer hold the political interests together. He held negotiations with the NRC, and the more conservative faction of the SDP on the possibility of setting up an Interim National Government (ING) with some participation from both parties. The SDP at this time had become split into two factions: The pro-June 12 group which believed in upholding the popular mandate and in Abiola as Nigeria's president elect; and those who had been "settled" (bribed), or who belonged to the Yar Adua group who were against Abiola and the June 12 mandate. The latter faction agreed with Babangida's idea because it would terminate the June 12 struggle and provide an opportunity to make another bid for the presidency. In his valedictory address to the nation on August 26 in which he made several claims as to his contributions to peace, stability, democracy, development, and progress in Nigeria, General Babangida also announced the inauguration of a 32-member Interim National Government headed by Chief Ernest Shonekan the former head of the Transitional Council. For the first time since the January 1966 military coup, popular organizations had challenged the military and forced it to make far-reaching concessions. Though it failed to achieve its ultimate goal of a full restoration of democracy, organizations in civil society had succeeded in altering the political landscape, checking the hitherto unabridged power of the military, opened up political spaces for deeper political organization and mobilization, and put issues of democracy, democratization, empowerment, and social justice firmly on the political agenda.

FROM THE ING TO ABACHA: THE CONTAINMENT OF CIVIL SOCIETY

The ING was doomed from the beginning. Not only was it illegal (the decree establishing it was signed by Babangida after he had ceased to be president of Nigeria) but it was also not recognized internally and externally. It simply could not function as it was largely seen as an attempt to divert attention from the June 12 issue, create an opportunity to continue military rule in the name of an interim arrangement, and allow conservative political interests to regroup. The economy continued to deteriorate, several state governments refused to work with the ING, protests and strikes continued as oil workers and members of the CD openly defied appeals from Chief Ernest Shonekan, the head of the interim arrangement, and the military was, as usual, becoming restless in the face of deepening socio-economic and political deterioration.

Abacha had no problems with unseating Shonekan as he had apparently schemed to become head of state several months earlier. He also had no problems with consolidating his regime as the opportunistic political elite found it comfortable to work with a corrupt military elite to continue the system of graft with no accountability, and checks or balances. Military officers who were against disengagement of any sort, contractors and "419" (scam) specialists, political hangers-on of the Babangida era, and those who had been marginalized in the transition to a Third Republic rallied to the side of Abacha. Some leading prodemocracy activists and members of Chief Abiola political machine joined Abacha to dismantle democratic processes and institutions, and to fully remilitarize the political terrain: Baba Gana Kingibe, (Abiola's running mate), Iyorchia Ayu (president of the senate and SDP stalwart), Olu Onagoruwa (leading CD member and human rights activist), Lateef Jakande (seen as heir apparent to Chief Obafemi Awolowo and leading "June 12" activist), Abubakar Rimi (a strong SDP member), and Ebenezer Babatope (a top official of the SDP and leading "June 12" advocate), to name a few.

This development shocked the Nigerian public and eroded the credibility of the CD and prodemocracy community: "It was the biggest shock of life. We took risks in the name of democracy. Hundreds were killed by the National Guards. Hundreds were detained by the SSS and police. Then, our so-called prodemocracy leaders joined the military to terminate democracy. I still cannot believe it" (interview, CD Secretariat, Lagos, December 1993). Till date, the prodemocracy community has not recovered from the support which the Abacha government enjoyed from those who had mobilized Nigerians to oppose military rule and stand for democracy and the popular will.

Abacha, realizing that his coup was not popular in the international community, which was then still threatening sanctions and other punitive measures, announced that a national conference would be called and a swift transition agenda would be placed before the Nigerian people. As it turned out, this was designed largely to buy time, and make it possible to effectively dismantle the prodemocracy movements in the interests of conservative constituencies. Evidence of this was in the appointment of politicians of the past republics and ex-military officers who had been disgraced, even dismissed for corruption by previous regimes as ministers. The government also appointed 97 conservative individuals to defend its interests at the Conference. As well, by drawing ministers, board members, and the like from the Conference, the government sent the message that "good behavior," in support of the government, was a key to plum political appointments. Within a short time, the Abacha junta had waged a war against the universities-closing down several-, students, workers, especially the oil workers and the Nigeria Labour Congress (NLC), the bar association, the human rights groups, especially the CLO, and the prodemocracy movement. The media was not left out. Scores of journalists remain in jail while several, including the influential Guardian newspapers were closed down. When in 1994, Chief Abiola declared himself president of Nigeria during the first anniversary of the June 12, election, he was promptly arrested and clamped into detention. When in July 1994, the National Union of Petroleum and Natural Gas Workers (NUPENG) with widespread support called a strike which crippled the oil industry and the oil dependent economy, its secretary, Frank Kokori and president, Wariebi Agamene were arrested and detained. The leaders of the CD and other prodemocracy and human rights groups were also harassed, arrested, and detained for long periods without charge or trial. The assassination of Chief Alfred Rewane, a prominent NADECO leader and prodemocracy activist in October 1995 was also designed to send signals to the public that criticizing the government was certainly not a wise thing to do. Though the government has not been directly implicated in the assassination, the fact that it took place only after Chief Rewane had published several critical articles against the government, and sinister organization, the so-called Committee of Friends had warned him to back-off, has aroused public suspicions (*The News* 23 October 1995).

The Abacha strategy was quite clear: divide civil society by playing organizations against each other, bribery, misinformation and co-optation; intimidate the leaders and organizations into silence; contain restless communities especially the minorities across the country; rehabilitate discredited politicians and retired military leaders; continue the system of graft, waste and mismanagement; consolidate the power of the military and postpone the transition to civil rule for as long as possible. These objectives have run into very serious obstacles. First, let us look at a general picture of why Abacha has had problems.

WHY ABACHA CANNOT CONSOLIDATE MILITARY RULE IN NIGERIA

First, Abacha has very little credibility with the public. His first foray into national politics was when he announced the Buhari/Idiagbon coup of December 31, 1983 in which he articulated the scores of problems confronting the average Nigerian (*TELL* December 6, 1994). Twenty months later, the same Abacha announced the overthrow of Generals Buhari and Idiagbon in the coup which saw the ascendancy of Ibrahim Babangida. He became the Chief of Staff Army, a very powerful position. During the failed Majors Mukoro/Orka Coup of April 22, 1990, at a time when the whereabouts of Babangida was unknown, it was Abacha again, who came on air, to announce that the coup had been foiled and that General Babangida was alive. Thus under Buhari, Abacha was a member of the Supreme Military Council (SMC), the nation's most powerful political platform. Under Babangida, Abacha was for eight years a member of the Armed Forces Ruling Council (AFRC), was chief of army staff, and later minister for defence. Under the Shonekan ING, Abacha was secretary for defence. Nigerians therefore feel that Abacha had been part of the 8-year Babangida brutal dictatorship, part of the confused and ineffective Shokenan interim arrangement, and had been part of the Nigerian disaster. Hence, critics like Gani Fawehinmi have contended that given Abacha's influence under Babangida, the era should be properly labelled the "Babangida-Abacha era."

Secondly, many Nigerians feel that Abacha's coup was an opportunistic one. He had remained in the ING and did not give Shonekan the required political advice and support to survive the storm. Rather he schemed his way into power capitalizing on the political impasse which had followed the annulment of the June 12 election and the declaration by the Federal High Court on November 10, 1993 that the ING was illegal. The intervention was not to save Nigeria or the promote democracy but a mere fulfillment of his personal ambitions to become president, an ambition which had in previous years generated distrust between him and Babangida. As well, it was widely known that Abacha had plans to become president long before his coup and at a point Colonel Fred Chijuka, director of defence information had to publicly deny that Abacha did not nurse such an ambition. *TELL* (December 6, 1994) had reported in an earlier issue before the coup that "Abacha schemed to head the ING and failing that, to be its only military member, which eventually, was what happened." This placed him in a vantage position to monitor the deterioration of the ING and to move when it was apparent that he would face no resistance.

Thirdly, on coming to power, Abacha surrounded himself with a band of strange bed fellows as ministers-Gowon era ministers, Shehu Shagari politicians, discredited and disgraced ex-military officers, ex-convicts, human rights activists, radical scholars and trade unionists, and intellectuals as well as businessmen. The only thread holding them together is that they are Nigerians. He effectively used ethnic warlords, people who are supposedly popular in their regions and communities, to stabilize and legitimize his regime. When he sacked his cabinet early 1995, he not only got rid of the "radical" and prodemocracy sympathizers in his government but proceeded to appoint more conservative elements, mostly from the Constitutional Conference which had served him very well. As Ayodele Akinkuotu (*TELL* February 14, 1994) has noted, Abacha's "cabinet is loaded with all shades of politicians, the same group that had been pilloried by successive military governments." Olusegun Obasanjo (1994) in a recent evaluation of the Abacha regime also noted that, Abacha lacks the moral authority to rule Nigeria, and that surrounding himself with the criminals of yesterday was no solution to the regime's crisis of legitimacy:

> Those who forget the past are doomed to repeat it. A situation where you do wrong today, lie low for a while and without remorse, emerge to a red-carpet reception to continue to do greater wrong is bad for justice and bad for progress. This present administration in an attempt to clothe itself with the garb of legitimacy and acceptance brought into its fold politicians of all shades of integrity most of whom were previously condemned and brought to disrepute by the same military men. One wonders whether these politicians have now been cleansed in the sea of Galilee.

Rather than increase its legitimacy therefore, the reliance on political, ethnic, and regional "heavy weights" seems to have created more crisis of acceptability and legitimacy. Of course, it has been easy to incorporate top members of the political class including the former chairmen of the two proscribed political parties-Chief Anthony Anenih (SDP) and Thomas Ikimi (NRC). The ease with which these individuals and more were absorbed into the Abacha regime without apologies has alienated millions of Nigerians from them and whatever they represented, completely ruined the June 12 movement, delegitimized the political class, and showed "the opportunism and shamelessness of these elites who will eat with the devil once power and money are attached to the meal" (interview, Lagos, December 1993). With this move, Abacha has succeeded in dividing the opposition, and in weakening the legitimacy of its leadership.

A fourth reason why Abacha has had a hard time is that he has not provided for Nigerians a sharp departure from the past in terms of actions, policies, programs, alliances, and general conduct. Not only was his coup broadcast very short, but it contained nothing of substance. The reason being that Abacha had no prepared coup broadcast. He had wanted Shonekan to announce his resignation and invite the army to power. Shonekan refused to do this and offered to resign. More importantly, Abacha failed to give Nigerians any date for disengagement from power for a long time. Because he promised a Constitutional Conference (as against a Sovereign National Conference demanded by the prodemocracy groups), he announced that the conference would determine the life span of his regime. Those who did not trust him when he made this promise have been vindicated (interview, Lagos, December 1993). After initially passing a resolution that Abacha should disengage in January 1996, the Constitutional Conference, under heavy pressure from the military, revised itself in mid-1995 to allow Abacha to remain power indefinitely. His October 1, 1995 independence anniversary broadcast which declared a new date of 1998 has not been believed by popular communities or the international community. The transition program is so drawn out and complicated that it looks very much like Babangida's zig-zag transition which took eight years, cost over N50 billion, and ended in fiasco. Of course, the Constitutional Conference kept the opposition busy in the belief that its report would not be thrown aside by Abacha and the military government (*African Concord* December 27, 1993; *National Concord* February 1, 1994).

The Abacha regime has not placed before Nigerians any economic agenda which would show a substantial difference from previous governments including the ones in which he participated. There is a seeming pathological fixation on the Liquified Natural Gas (LNG) project involving the major oil companies as if this will solve all the economic problems of the country *UBA Monthly Business and Economic Digest* June 1994). In fact, his 1994 Budget had practically destroyed the economic base of the nation as it was not based on any serious projection or appreciation of the nation's economic realities and predicaments (*The News* 14 February 1994). Unemployment, inflation, rural-urban drift, environmental abuse, smuggling, currency trafficking, and bankruptcies have reached new proportions. Life in the rural and urban areas remains unbearable and the universities have become practically emptied of qualified professionals.

Thousands of Nigerians are making claims for political asylum in South Africa, Zimbabwe and other parts of Europe and North America. Crime has taken over the major cities as drug trafficking and drug use have reached unprecedented heights. Life in Nigeria has really become "nasty, brutish and short" under the Abacha dispensation as political assassinations, gang-style murders, prostitution, and armed robbery have become familiar to all in society.

Finally, fifth, is the person of Abacha as a leader. Without doubt, leadership is critical in the process of change. In the Nigerian situation, the example set by particular leaders has been very critical to the behavior of the followership. In the case of General Abacha, he is locked into a situation where he cannot afford to throw stones because his own house is completely made of very fragile glass. Abraham Useh (*TELL* December 6, 1993) has been right on the mark in his prediction a few years back:

> Abacha, who, on assuming power, promised to give the nation a new start and get it going once again, may not be better than Babangida and could be worse. (Observers) point at the general's stupendous wealth, presumed to be next to only that of his former master, Babangida. He is known to have a sprawling palace-like mansion in Kano, his home town, that may be worth some N200 million. This is complemented by other real estate possessions in Kaduna, Lagos and elsewhere....Abacha is said to have a vast interest in business, one whose octoipoidal tentacles are believed to reach out to the oil and aviation sectors.

Abacha once made a $3 million cash bid for the US Embassy in Lagos when he thought it was relocating to Abuja, the new Federal Capital. As well, it is said that on the eve of his coup against the ING, "Five peugeot J5 buses...left Abuja for Lagos loaded with cash" to bribe "the boys" for their support (TELL December 6, 1993). Like the Babangida days, Abacha has so much in common with Babangida that Olusegun Obasanjo (1994) has concluded that there is really no difference: both are morally bankrupt; they manipulate and abuse the press; the rely on the "politics of settlement" to get support; and they are inconsistent, "changing statements and policies like the weathercock."

With the contradictions above dogging the military junta, it is faced with the problem of how to effectively respond to the crisis of legitimacy, and the continuing demands by popular groups for upholding the June 12 mandate. The Abacha coup, as things stand in Nigeria, reflects a situation where the issues which made the ING ineffective, illegitimate, and eventually saw to its downfall, have not been addressed: what to do with a popular mandate given to the SDP, how to revive the economy, how to restore law and order, and how to win the full support of popular communities and constituencies. Claiming that the regime did not annul the election and so, could not be expected to de-annul it is merely a puerile effort to avoid the reality of addressing what has become the most vexing political issue in the country. The proscription of the two parties has not proscribed the consciousness of Nigerians who now see the military as the biggest and most formidable obstacle to democracy and development in Nigeria. This reality, which Abacha must deal with is clearly articulated by Nick Damzag (*TELL* February 14, 1994):

> In spite of spirited efforts by an amalgam of Babangida's legion of enforcers, caporegimes and thought-police to bludgeon us into amnesia on account of June 12, what has resulted is the very opposite: June 12 got etched firmly on our consciousness and inspired about the most seminal discussion in our annals. Not only did the octave of discourse rise several notches above the common run, it was a season of literary volubility and outpouring: hitherto reticent citizens came forward, marshalling compelling arguments with the most patrician and parliamentary cadence in favour of June 12. It is a measure of its continued dominance of the upper reaches of discussion that two newsmagazines were prompted to appoint June 12 as their man of the year....Its potency derives from the moral force it commands....

The Abacha government continues to have problems with international acceptability; ethnic and regional positions have become very hardened; the legitimacy and stability of the state remains very questionable; and the economic crisis continues to deepen (*The Guardian* July 22, 1993; *National Concord* January 20, 1994; *The Punch* February 24, 1994).

BEYOND JUNE 12: THE MILITARY, OPPOSITION GROUPS, AND MINORITIES IN NIGERIA

The Abacha junta had no doubts that in order to maintain law and order and effectively consolidate its rule, it had to contain growing popular consciousness and destroy the prodemocracy groups. Aside from the strategies described earlier including the open manipulation of the Constitutional Conference, the military also designed specific strategies to contain the opposition. The formation of a liberal political coalition-The National Democratic Coalition (NADECO)- in May 1994 was seen as a very dangerous threat to the interests of the military. In the ranks of NADECO were highly respected politicians of the early years of independence like Anthony Enahoro and Michael Ajasin, retired military leaders like Dan Suleiman and Admiral (rtd) Ebitu Ukiwe, and intellectuals and new generation politicians like Kofoworola Akerele, Bola Tinubu, Ralph Obiorah, and Bolaji Akinyemi. With its declared goals, which included getting the military out of office and reinstating the June 12 mandate, it marked itself out as being on a direct collision path with the junta. The NADECO initiative also encouraged some politicians of the disbanded national assembly to reconvene. The response of the military was swift: it arrested the politicians and detained them without charge at Kirikiri prisons. It also had trade union leaders arrested and dissolved the executive of the NLC. Journalists who were seen to be sympathetic to the cause of the CD and NADECO were promptly arrested and detained. When students of Edo State University organized a public protest over "ethnic cleansing" in Ogoniland (see below) and other indiscriminate arrests, they were simply massacred by the police (CAFA 1995: 4-6).

In early September 1994, the military government promulgated eight new decrees with ouster clauses to expand its arbitrary powers. The decrees were backdated to enable it cover events which had taken place earlier. Decrees 12 and 14 for instance, eliminated the jurisdiction of the law courts and the use of *habeas corpus*. To demonstrate its absolute intolerance for any dissenting opinion, General Abacha sacked Olu Onagoruwa the attorney general and minister for justice when he distanced himself from the decrees with ouster clauses and threatened to resign unless they were amended. With these draconian decrees, hundreds of innocent Nigerians and activists were detained by the SSS.

In March 1995, as a final strategy to get rid of all opposition, and in order to stem the possibility of any mass action in commemoration of the June 12, 1993 election, the Abacha junta initiated an unprecedented crackdown on civil society (*Newsletter of the National Endowment for Democracy*, Summer 1995). Several journalists including Mrs. Chris Anyawu and Bayo Onanuga of *The Sunday Magazine* and *The News* respectively, prodemocracy activists like the CD Chairman, Beko Ransome-Kuti, retired military officers like Generals Olusegun Obasanjo and Shehu Yar Adua, and serving military Officers like Colonel Lawan Gwadabe, the alleged leader of a coup plot, were among the 29 military officers and civilians who were detained and charged with treason (*The News* March 13, 1995). Following secret trials of about 50 accused persons, 40 were convicted and very stiff sentences ranging from death, through life imprisonment to long prison terms were imposed (*The News* July 24, 1995). As a warm up to the enforcement of the sentences, the government carried out a public execution of 40 armed robbers in July, 1995. This execution demonstrated to the prodemocracy groups and the international community that the government would have no hesitation in carrying out the execution of the so-called coup plotters. It took the intervention of the international community, emissaries from President Nelson Mandela, the Pope, the UN Secretary-General, the ECOWAS Chairman Jerry Rawlings of Ghana, as well as appeals from former Nigerian presidents and traditional rulers to mention but a few, for the sentences to be commuted and the life and long prison terms to be reduced.

This decision did not win any mileage for the military government. The opinion of the public and the international community was that most of the accused had been framed by the junta. Even if there had been a semblance of a coup plot involving Colonel Gwadabe (who had been an inner core actor in the Babangida coup of 1985 and had been implicated only recently in the Gambian coup), the alleged involvement of Obasanjo, Mrs. Chris Anyawu, Ransome-Kuti and other civilians was at best ridiculous and unsubstantiated. It was clear to all that the purpose here was to intimidate these individuals, their organizations, and alternative leadership cadres within the prodemocracy community. Since the commutation and reduction of the sentences did not buy sympathy or support for the junta, it had to find another way to domesticate popular opinion and struggles for democracy. The Ogoni episode provided such an opportunity.

Contrary to popular opinion, minorities have never had an easier time under military rule. Because the top leaders of the armed forces have often come from the major ethnic groups, they have generally succumbed to pressure and manipulation of traditional and political interests. Thus public policies, political appointments, revenue allocation, the location of special projects, distribution of strategic military units and so on, have often reflected this vulnerability to ethnic, religious, and regional considerations. To be sure, this is not an absolute. When Obasanjo was head of state, though he was a Yoruba (from the West), Shehu Yar Adua, from the north was effectively the strongman of the regime. Nonetheless, this in no way undermines the patterns of unity within and among elites from the various ethnic groups even if in their politics they still find it more convenient to manipulate primordial differences (Udogu 1990, 1994).

One of the major consequences of the zig-zag march to political pluralism and the eventual annulment of the June 1993 election was the intensification of struggles for identity, visibility, and political space by the ethnic, minority, and other communities. The struggles of the Ogonis, who number about 500,000 in the present Rivers State was only the highest or most visible manifestation of this struggle. Of course, other minority communities, even in oil producing areas like the Ijaws, were involved in similar struggles (*Daily Champion* October 7, 1993; *The Guardian* December 18, 1993; *Daily Times* 29 June 1993; *Vanguard* November 5, 1993; *New Nigerian* 8 January 1993). But the Ogonis were different for three reasons: first, the Ogonis had carefully studied their problems, of "enemies," evaluated their strengths and weaknesses, and effectively mapped out a strategy for pursuing their goals. The preparation and presentation of the "Ogoni Bill of Rights" in October 1990 and the "Addendum to the Bill of Rights" in August 1991 reflected these preparations. Second, the Ogonis had a very broad-based, grassroot organization (the Movement for the Survival of Ogoni People

211

(MOSOP)) which, in spite of initial leadership problems, fully articulated and represented all Ogoni people in their six kingdoms cutting across gender, class, generational, and sub-ethnic lines. Third, MOSOP joined the CD and had the opportunity to disseminate its agenda and struggles through the channels and resources of other Non-Governmental Organizations (NGOs), prodemocracy movements, and grassroot organizations across the country. Finally, fourth, MOSOP adopted a strategy which no prodemocracy movement has attempted in Nigeria's political history: the internationalization of the Ogoni crisis. The MOSOP took the case of the Ogonis to the Unrepresented Nations and Peoples Organization (UNPO), the United Nations, international NGOs (especially environmental and human rights organizations), and enlisted the support of foreign governments to pressure the Nigerian military and Shell Petroleum Development Company to compensate the Ogonis for decades of exploitation and environmental abuse, lack of basic facilities, the destruction of land and marine life, and increased investment in infrastructure and development in Ogoniland (*The Guardian* September 14, 1994; *Daily Sketch* November 23, 1993; Naanen 1995).

Though the strategy of MOSOP was largely peaceful: letter writing, demonstrations and rallies, press releases, and international campaigns, the Nigerian military under Abacha saw the growing influence of MOSOP president Ken Saro-Wiwa and the publicity surrounding the Ogoni predicament as a threat to its agenda for consolidating military rule and containing existing pockets of opposition (Saro-Wiwa 1994; Naanen 1995; Ihonvbere 1996). The military needed to urgently contain the rising tide of opposition and protests by showing an example. The Ogoni situation provide such ample opportunity. Beside the instigation of violent inter-community clashes between the Ogonis and their neighbors-the Ndokis, the Andonis, and the Okrikas-and the frequent detention of MOSOP leaders, the military also occupied Ogoni villages, terrorized the people, and destroyed lives and property (UNPO 1995; Ihonvbere 1996). The murder of four prominent Ogoni elders by a mob which was instigated into violence by the arrest of Saro-Wiwa by the State Security Service (SSS) provide a good opportunity for a full military expedition and the detention of hundreds of Ogoni people including the leaders of MOSOP. Following a clearly flawed trial by a military tribunal without the right of appeal, nine MOSOP leaders were sentenced to death (*The Economist* November 18th-24th, 1995; *TELL* 13 November 1995). The sentences were hurriedly confirmed by the military government and the nine activists were executed by hanging on November 10, 1995. Since the execution, the Abacha junta has had no sleep or peace. It has been condemned by the entire world, by African leaders, the United Nations, international NGOs, and by Nigerian communities abroad. The country was suspended from the Commonwealth following a motion moved by president Nelson Mandela of South Africa, a country, which ironically, had benefitted from Nigeria's anti-apartheid commitments. The EU and other Western nations reviewed diplomatic relations. Protests and rallies have been organized around the world by Nigerians, human rights organizations and NGOs (including Greenpeace, Friends of the Earth, Amnesty International, and TransAfrica) in front of Nigerian missions to protest the killings and continued detention of political activists (*TELL* December 4, 1995, December 18, 1995). Why did the Abacha regime have to kill the nine activists? How does this development affect the disengagement agenda of the military? What are the implications for the forces of democracy and the future of Nigeria?

CONCLUSION: ABACHA AS A "POSITIVE" FORCE IN NIGERIAN POLITICS

Without doubt, the arrival of General Abacha in Nigerian politics (which is really an extension of the Babangida era, 1985-1993) has witnessed a return to the dark ages: the triumph of irrationality, corruption, mediocrity, and the negation of all norms of dialogue and consensus. This had made it possible for atavistic, sectional, and opportunistic interests to emerge in all sectors of society at the expense of popular and democratic interests. It has also made it possible for disgraced and discredited ethnic, religious and regional warlords to be rehabilitated and for their rather sinister interests to triumph on Nigeria's political landscape. More importantly, it has severely bifurcated the country along ethnic and regional lines: the North against the South; the North and East against the West; Christians against Muslims; and the military against civilians. These divisions have far reaching implications for state-society relations. In fact, the politics of the Abacha junta, in particular, the way in which the regime has treated the Abiola and June 12 issue, the minority question, as well as issues of military disengagement from politics has hardened political positions, and forced many usually liberal and nationalistic politicians to return to their ethnic and regional enclaves to now articulate separatist positions. The emergence of scores of narrowly focused, opportunistic, irredentist, ethnically and regionally-based interest groups like the *Afenifere* and *Egbe Omo Yoruba* in the West, the *Oha'Eze* in the East, the Northern Elements Coalition in the North, the National Unity Club, the Peoples' Consultative Forum, the New Dimension, Club '95, Club 258, the Justice Forum, and the Progressives' Summit, to mention only a few have implications for civil society, the national project, and democratization. All these have implications for the future of politics in post-military Nigeria. Only if they are democratic (and they are mostly not) can they serve as platforms for articulating the interests of the people as part of a larger national movement.

The execution of the Ogoni leaders and detention of prodemocracy leaders which attracted international condemnation and sanctions across the world, has further isolated Nigeria and the military regime. The regime, in its desperation has responded like a caged animal, lashing out at opponents, insisting on its sovereignty, and blaming foreign governments, NGOs and Nigerians abroad for its predicaments. Such positions are clearly not remorseful, and have only hardened international and national opposition while attracting further discussions of stiffer punishments for a regime which is now seen as the most vicious in Nigeria's political history. Given such testy and uncertain conditions, what implications can we draw from the current balance of forces and depth of contradictions, coalitions, and conflicts in Nigeria?

The advent of Abacha has had an unintended positive role in deepening the politicization of civil groups, encouraging the emergence of new prodemocracy associations like the National Democratic Coalition (NADECO), and compelling human rights organizations like the CLO, and trade unions like the National Union of Petroleum and Natural Gas Workers (NUPENG) to adopt clear political programs. While they remain suspect of every move by the junta including its so-called transition program, they can be counted on to continue to adopt overt and covert strategies of resistance and protest against the government. Though weakened by the arrest of their leaders and intimidation, they nonetheless cannot pursue any other agenda aside from those already declared which include the full restoration of democracy, convening a sovereign national conference, and strengthening civil society.

The return of the generals has also helped to crystallize the character and strength of leadership in the prodemocracy community. By exposing several opportunists and "emergency democrats" in the prodemocracy constituency when they joined the military to abolish democracy, most Nigerians have tried to transcend this first generation of prodemocracy leaders. Though unintended, these developments hold out the best hope for increasing challenges to the military and the struggle for democracy. New leaders will clearly distance themselves from those who have been domesticated and incorporated by the military, and the people will have to set higher standards for selecting their leaders and holding them accountable for their actions. The issue also raises the need for deeper levels of internal democracy within the prodemocracy movement to avoid situations where they are set up and operated like personal businesses.

While the remilitarization of Nigerian politics clearly sends out dangerous signals for civil-military relations and the development of civil society, it also demonstrates the continuing interest of the military in power and politics. As the CD noted in a press statement in which it rejected general Abacha's intervention in politics, the return of the generals "only confirms that the military is bent on maintaining an eternal grip on the affairs of the Nigerian nation to the detriment of all genuine efforts at self-determination and democratization." In addition, the CD contended that general Abacha "was part and parcel of the Babangida dictatorship as well as the moving force behind the Interim National Government which he now claims to have ousted." Outlining a clear agenda for containing the military and making it subordinate to civil authority will remain the principal challenge for Nigerian politics. Aside from outright constitutional provisions, including the fact that the constitution is not subject to any form of suspension (even when a military adventurist purports to have done so), there is no alternative to a strengthened and enlightened civil society to check the excesses of politicians and prevent military take-overs.

The NGOs must embark on a massive public education to encourage the populace to reject and resist military coups. The existence of such a popular consciousness is bound to send the right signals to the barracks.

Embarking on a democratic path will be extremely difficult for Nigeria in spite of academic and policy support for the prodemocracy movements. There is not one prodemocracy leader in Nigeria who can really claim widespread national support. The political class has lost all credibility to challenge the military or lead civil society. The extent to which they have identified with and supported the military will make it difficult for the same elements to present themselves as lovers of democracy and believers in the principles and practice of popular politics in the future. The fact that the leaders of the defunct SDP and NRC not only joined to dismantle democracy but also proceeded to rationalize and justify the suffocation of civil society, military occupation of rural communities, the execution of environmentalists and so on, has badly eroded the credibility of the Nigerian political elite. This collaboration has disillusioned Nigerians who feel that the political class is not only useless, but has betrayed the people and taken a stand with the military against democracy in Nigeria.

Another major challenge for the future lies not in rotational presidency or multiple vice presidency, but in altering the national political culture, breeding a set of politicians who respect established political rules, consolidating political institutions and traditions, and instituting powerful checks and balances on the practice of politics. The behavior of politicians in the last three republics is nothing but a disgrace. True, corruption and waste is by no means peculiar to Nigeria or Africa. But Nigerian politicians have a way of making a show of buffoonery, irresponsibility, mediocrity, and disrespect for both the constitution and rules of procedure. This has made them vulnerable to manipulation and to military coups. This culture of "any government goes" provided there is food, wine, and money to be stolen has permeated the entire fabric of the Nigerian society. It is no wonder that military coups are often welcomed with heavy drinking, dancing, and congratulatory messages in the papers rather than designing ways to call politicians to order and checking their excesses. These are certainly not the brand of political actors capable of moving Nigeria onto a genuine path of popular empowerment, transparency, accountability, and democracy. Unfortunately, these politicians, bred in the culture of waste and corruption, still dominate many of the so-called prodemocracy movements and ethnic and regional groupings, and are already joggling for positions in the false start to a fourth republic.

There is now, more than at any other time in Nigeria's history, a hardening of political positions, especially among the Yorubas of the West. True, there are new efforts at building bridges across ethnic and regional, even religious lines such as the East-West Dialogue which is aimed at bringing the Igbos and the Yorubas together. But these are led by persons whose politics in the past created the present suspicions and quarrels. Building bridges without addressing the basis and purpose of power will lead to very little. Yet, sections of the Yoruba community feel very angry over the June 12 issue. In December 1994, the Oodu'a Youth Movement (OYM) passed *The Yoruba People's Charter for Self-Determination* in which, among other resolutions, they declared a lack of "faith in Nigeria as presently constituted." Other minorities have seized on the environment created by the impasse and the limited support which the military enjoys to raise the national question, demand self-determination, and withdraw their loyalties from the nation. Thus, there has been as rapid return to "base," and ethnic, regional, and religious identities have become sharpened. This has implications for building a *national* democratic project in the future. However, these primordial associations and coalitions are countered by the emergence of pan-Nigerian organizations like NADECO, CD, Association for Good Governance and Democracy in Nigeria (AGDN), and the Democratic Alternative (DEAL). These organizations represent "an aroused population" which demonstrated its ability to give and withdraw support (Commonwealth Secretariat 1995: 25). Compare the turnout of 14 million voters in the June 12 presidential election with a mere 300,000 in the elections to the Constitutional Conference. However, this constituency would have to be nurtured to retain its commitment to democracy.

Finally, it is clear that only decisive action by the international community can lead to the withdrawal of the military from power. Failure to act will see either of four options: 1) a very bloody military coup organized by middle ranking officers. This will severely dislocate political balances as most of those on the firing line will be northerners.

If the coup is organized by southern officers, Nigeria will find itself back to the situation of 1966 with all the implications; 2) degeneration into civil war with scores of military and well armed factions, "warlords" and "technicals." This will replay the scenario of Liberia or Somalia. It will be more devastating because of Nigeria's 100 million plus population and the ability of the ethnic groups to mobilize more fire power. Such a conflict will be devastating for the regional economy and will cost the Western powers more in terms of lives and money to eventually restore order; 3) total repression through the further degeneration of the Abacha junta. This will lead to more human rights abuses, the systematic elimination of all, intellectuals, journalists, activists, priests, and all with a social conscience. In short, it will mean the elimination of freedom. The regime is moving in this direction at the moment and the more it is ostracized by the international community, the more it is likely to become more desperate and repressive. This can be avoided through an oil embargo, freezing of national and personal accounts of the political leaders, economic and other sanctions, suspension of foreign aid and new investment, and the isolation of the Abacha regime by international organizations. This is the only way to demonstrate to the regime that there is a new global order and that the days of military regimes are almost over; and 4) total decay and dislocation. This will represent a situation of sporadic violence, hijackings, bombings, kidnappings, assassinations, and harassment of the rich and expatriates. There will be no central coordinating body of the opposition. The prevalence of small and automatic weapons in Nigeria, the porousness of the borders, frustrations over the weaknesses of the prodemocracy movements, and increasing repression are the exact conditions to promote political decay. This will cost lives, set the country back significantly, and be very difficult to contain.

It will require a combined effort of the United Nations, the Commonwealth, the OAU, investors, international NGOs, pan-Nigerian organizations abroad, and most importantly, popular organizations *within* the country to force the military from power, restructure the political landscape, and build relevant institutions for the sustenance of democracy in the 21st century.

CHAPTER NINE

SHELL, THE MILITARY AND THE OGONI CRISIS

The relationship between the Nigerian state and transnational oil corporations is underscored by the importance of oil to the state and its custodians. Given the rentier character of the Nigerian state as evidenced in its near total dependence on the production and sale of oil for revenues, the oil industry has come to occupy the most strategic location in its socio-economic, political, and security calculations. Since transnational capital controls the information, technology, high level skills, and access to the global market; the weak, unsteady, unstable, and non-hegemonic neo-colonial state operates at the mercy of capital. To be sure, since the end of the Nigerian civil war in 1970, the state has done a lot to extend its influence and power in the oil sector (Lolomari 1976; Ihonvbere 1984; Soremekun and Obi 1993; Naanen 1995; Amu n.d.). As oil became more critical to its survival, it initiated ways to strengthen its relationship with capital, and domesticate other forces in the sector. It established the Nigerian National Oil Corporation (NNOC) (later the Nigerian National Petroleum Corporation (NNPC)), created an oil ministry, extended its participation through nationalization and joint venture agreements through Decrees, and joined the Organization of Petroleum Exporting Countries (OPEC) in 1971. In addition, it passed several draconian decrees in the 1970s aimed at controlling oil workers and through rapid responses to the needs of the oil corporations, showed the oil producing communities where its interests were located (Ihonvbere 1984; Omoweh 1994, 1996).

The process of recycling oil rents is controlled by capital and forces at the center of global capitalism with the rentier state playing only a very limited role. Though it is possible to argue that the survival of the neo-colonial state is at the mercy of transnational capital, it is also essential to point out that the state does enjoy some autonomy. The state exercises control over the territory; it sets the labor, environmental, and other regulations; it enforces the regulations; it controls the entry and participation of corporations in the oil industry; and finally it has the power (even if at great political risk) to terminate or take over the operations of the oil corporations. The ability to effectively perform these roles is dependent on the state's degree of efficiency and effectiveness, on the ability to maintain hegemonic control over up and down stream operations, on the level of internal legitimacy and solidity;, and finally on the extent of its vulnerability to external manipulation and pressures (Olukoshi and Agbu 1996). As well, the ability to exercise an appreciable degree of control over oil operations is often affected by the character of the dominant classes who preside over the state and its institutions, and the historically constructed relationship between the state and capital.

Our focus in this study is on how this intricate and unequal relationship between the Nigerian state and oil corporations serve to shortchange oil producing communities. We use the case of the Ogonis in the present Rivers State of Nigeria to demonstrate how such exploitative relationship can force hitherto peaceful communities to organize and resist (even confront) the state and capital. Though in this case the cost has been very high in human lives and community peace and harmony, the lessons are equally intriguing and critical for the overall struggle for democracy in Nigeria.

ETHNICITY, ETHNIC VIOLENCE AND THE STATE IN AFRICA

Recent developments in Europe and parts of Africa have once again drawn attention to the dangers which ethnic violence pose to the projects of democratization, nation-building, global peace and security. For multi-ethnic states, ethnic loyalties continue to pose far-reaching challenges even for the most well-intentioned leader and political arrangements. Yet, the processes of modernization, regime change, economic growth, revolutions in science and technology, even changing ideological systems have not substantially eroded the attachment of people to their ethnic groups (Nnoli 1974; Bates 1974;). To be sure, just like cultural identity, ethnic loyalties are not natural or static. They can change depending on environment, consciousness, the nature of the state and politics, and the general factors and forces which discourage or encourage the individual to call on such loyalties and rely on them as the basis of their social and political relations (Banton 1994). As well, pressures for survival and the search for visibility and identity can necessitate the construction of particular loyalties and affinities. Identities can also change with location: being an African, West African, Nigerian, Yoruba, Egba can depend on location, political pressures and terrain, and the content and context of politics.

In Africa, ethnicity remains, perhaps, the most problematic issue confronting the state and its custodians (Coleman 1958; Kenyatta 1965; Ake 1967; Akinwowo 1964; Anise 1979; Nnoli 1978). Initially, it was convenient to deny the existence or importance of ethnic affinities. The introduction of one-party states and military regimes made this tendency seem possible as minorities and their communities were suppressed and civil society was suffocated (Anikpo 1985; Ekekwe 1985; Amnesty International 1994). As the fragile and unsteady post-colonial state confronted communities which operated outside its hegemony, and as large ethnic constituencies systematically resisted the state and its policies of forced political integration, it became necessary to respond to the problems of ethnicity, ethnic consciousness, and ethnic violence, even if the governments still refused to acknowledge these as critical obstacles to nation-building (Young 1979; Diamond 1988; Osaghae 1990; Ihonvbere 1994a; Udogu 1994). Very ingenuous policies were initiated to contain the problem of ethnic loyalty and ethnic conflict: domestication, threats, education, mobilization, ideological encapsulation, quota system, federal systems of government, the one-party state, elite incorporation, rotational political appointments, zoning of political opportunities, special resource allocation, and even the relocation or expulsion of particular ethnic communities (Coleman and Roseberg 1970; Bradshaw 1985; Ihonvbere 1994a). These have all failed to solve the problem of ethnicity and the various ways it is manifested in African politics.

221

Politics in Africa continues to be influenced and conditioned by ethnicity (Glickman ed. 1995). Public programs continue to fail because some ethnic groups continue to withdraw their support for the "national" project (Madiebo 1980; Mainsara 1982; Nwankwo 1987). Worse still, ethnic conflicts, very bloody ethnic conflicts, continue to challenge national stability and development (Saro-Wiwa 1994; Zartman ed., 1995; UMPO 1995). In Rwanda, Burundi, Somalia, Liberia, Nigeria, Togo, Ghana, and Cameroon, to mention a few "hot spots" in Africa, ethnicity remains the real stuff of politics (Ake 1985; Kukah 1993). What is amazing is that ethnicity has overwhelmed the so-called influence and impact of Western education and enlightenment as very well educated Africans have, more often than not, resorted to ethnic appeals in their competition for state power and public resources (Ihonvbere 1994a and b). Given the primacy of the state in the accumulation process, and the lack of a credible platform for mobilizing the people, the elites have easily resorted to the manipulation of primordial loyalties with ethnicity being the most formidable.

Writing on Africa, Daniel H. Krymkowski and Raymond L. Hall (1990: 315), argue that ethnic diversity "remains one of the continent's most difficult internal problems" and this has retarded the "establishment of national political unity." In their explanation of the causes of ethnic conflicts in Africa, they point out that the "legacy of European colonialism, which tended to combine and thus enlarge indigenous political and social territorial units and to centralize resources, power, status, and privilege in the administrative center" (Krymkowski and Hall 1990: 316). This arrangement compelled many ethnic groups to come together in a single unit, restructured historically cultured traditional patterns and social relations, separated kin and kindred mostly for economic and administrative reasons, and generally restructured traditional patterns of conflict resolution.

Political independence in the 1960s did not improve the situation (Ake 1981; Wallerstein 1993). The post-colonial state, like the colonial state, was exploitative, distant, inefficient, unstable, non-hegemonic, and dominated by a largely urban-based, corrupt, factionalized, unproductive, and subservient elite (Ihonvbere 1994b). The state was used for accumulation rather than legitimation purposes (Ake 1985; Ihonvbere 1994b). It relied on violence, intimidation, manipulation of primordial loyalties, depoliticization, and the strengthening of unequal relations with foreign capital to maintain some form of control. Those who dominated the institutions of the state saw themselves as representatives of their respective ethnic groups, and public policies, politics, and the distribution of power, resources, amenities, and opportunities reflected these dispositions. Because they had only a tenuous relationship to productive activities, their hold on power relied not on their economic strengths but on the manipulation of politics and primordial differences. Within a few years of political freedom, ethnicity became, by and large, the "most expedient means through which groups compete for resources controlled by the state" (Krymkowski and Hall 1990: 317). Those ethnic groups which dominated and controlled the state tried to exclude others. This led to alienation and withdrawal, stimulated the distinctiveness in the respective communities, and generated covert and overt forms of resistance. In many instances, the state instigated conflicts between ethnic groups so as to weaken them, divert attention from other pressing problems, provide justification for some political agenda such as the creation of new local governments, or to strengthen the central government itself. Where the dominant elites (reflecting the interests of dominant ethnic groups) complicate the political balances by claiming some form of superiority or rights over the weaker or smaller minority groups, latent structures of ethnic affinities or consciousness can easily be invoked and mobilized to challenge such claims or to directly challenge the state (Baldwin 1978; Barth 1969; Bates 1974).

Irrespective of ideological forms, as David Brown (1989: 47) notes, "ethnic tensions flourish independently of variations in the character of the state," and the "character of the state is indeed a key determinant of ethnic identities and ethnic relations." Where the state fails to promote an environment of equality of persons, communities, and groups, and where a steady economic deterioration erodes the quality of life with more decisive and glaring impact on minority ethnic groups, the response has always been an increase in feelings of neglect, marginalization, and isolation (Udogu 1994; Ihonvbere 1994b; Adekanye 1995; Osaghae 1996). If traditional patterns of resource and amenity allocation have made these same groups feel neglected, they introduce a steady and dangerous pattern of politicization of ethnicity and ethnic consciousness into the political terrain and political balances. If these take place in a political culture that is authoritarian or generally undemocratic, ethnic groups often take political mechanisms to resolve perceived and real contradictions and fears. To be sure, traditional mechanisms for managing ethnic fears, claims, and relations also have a lot to do with the nature of the state, and the degree of political openness which allows for or mediates a rational articulation of interests, dialogue, and concessions. If a "state's modal use of power in the multi-ethnic democratic state involves influence (real or imagined), persuasion, incentives, rewards, and other factors that deter, hinder, dissuade, discourage, or otherwise prevent the use of physical coercion" (Krymkowski and Hall 1999: 320), undemocratic political formations would be unable to utilize these mechanisms effectively. It follows that there is a strong correlation between the degree of political openness, the nature of civil society, and the character of politics on the one hand, and the political methods or strategies adopted by ethnic groups to resolve grievances on the other. Where a particular ethnic group is consistently marginalized, and the members see themselves to be marginalized, the tendency to resort to a combination of legal and extra-legal methods of grievance resolution will be high. As Krymkowski and Hall (1990: 321) note, "(w)here the state favours particular powerful groups, less powerful groups, depending on the nature of their powerlessness, may engage in conflict with the state itself or with the most powerful group(s) in the state or both." This is exactly what has happened in Ogoniland, Nigeria. Having lost faith in the willingness or ability of the state to respond to their needs or enable them to partake in the sharing of resources derived from their territory, the Ogonis decided to adopt political strategies which not only drew attention to their deplorable conditions, but also to how the state and its custodians preferred to rely on acts of aggression, violence, intimidation, massacres, and domination through occupation (Washington 1996).

The recent cases of failed and collapsed states, the near total collapse of the nation-building projects initiated in the early years of political independence, the deepening economic crisis, and the changing character of the global division of labor and power have made the resort to ethnic locales and ethnic politics more prevalent in Africa (Zartman ed. 1995). Given the decreasing size of available resources, and the implications of this development for politics, production, and power within and between ethnic constituencies, the general result has been an increase in ethnic violence. This takes place between ethnic communities, within ethnic communities, and at times between such communities and capital and/or the state. In some instances, the state and capital forge an open alliance against an ethnic group (Saro-Wiwa 1994; Amnesty International 1994; UMPO 1995). The nature of the alliance and the degree or depth of the struggle, as well as the degree of violence, are at times dictated by the issues or territory at stake, personalities and quality or militancy of leadership, the power or strategic location of the ethnic group; the existing dimension of contradictions, coalitions, and crises, and the *nature* of the state (Ake ed. 1985).

In the context sketched thus far, we can examine the conditions, struggles, demands, and strategies of the Ogonis and their confrontations with the Nigerian state and capital (Shell Petroleum Development Corporation (SPDC)). More than any other confrontation between the state and ethnic groups in Nigeria's political history (and these have been quite many) (Anifowose 1982; Ajayi and Ikara 1985; Udogu 1990 and 1994), the conflicts between the Ogonis on the one hand, and the Federal Government of Nigeria and Shell on the other have been the most bloody, brutal, and scandalous. It has involved organs of the United Nations, several international and local Non-Governmental Organizations (NGOs), the world media, and it has attracted the attention and interest of several nations of the world. The nature of this violent confrontation has implications for future relations between the state and alienated ethnic communities, as well as between the communities and capital (UMPO 1995). It also has implications for the strategies of ethnic groups as the Ogonis were the very first such group to successfully internationalize their struggles for autonomy. More importantly, in an era of planned military disengagement from politics, the conflict, state response, international actions, and the coalitions and alienation generated within the Nigerian polity, have far-reaching implications for the democratization enterprise.

THE OGONIS OF NIGERIA

The Ogoni, who number about 500,000, are a distinct ethnic group in present-day Rivers States of Nigeria. They occupy a land area of about 100,000 square kilometers and have occupied this location for over 500 years. The Government of Nigeria, in one of its counter-propaganda publications referred to Ogoniland as a "small piece of territory" (Federal Government of Nigeria, n. d.: 6). The Ogonis are mostly a fishing and agricultural community. It is acknowledged that they occupy one of the most densely populated areas in Nigeria. There are six kingdoms in Ogoniland: Babbe, Eleme, Gokana, Ken-Khana, Nyo-Khana, and Tai. Bori is regarded as the capital of Ogoniland. There are four main closely related languages and several dialects. In spite of the general adherence to Christianity, there is still a widespread regard for traditional religions.

Ogoni history duly acknowledges their strong resistance to British colonialism, a resistance which eventually succumbed to superior military power in the early 1900s. Since the British ruled Nigeria, especially after the 1914 amalgamation as three separate ethnic regions: the North-Hausa-Fulani, the East-Igbos, and the West-Yorubas, the Ogonis were included in the Eastern region. Like other minority ethnic groups, the fears of the Ogonis and their claims to being a distinct ethnic group were ignored by the British. The consolidation of regionalism following political independence "laid the foundations for minority marginalization in Nigeria," (Unrepresented Peoples and Nations Organization (UNPO) 1995: 8). In the Eastern region, the dominant Igbo ethnic group discriminated against and marginalized the Ogonis. The Ogonis were not only "at the bottom of the social ladder," they also were relegated to the "menial jobs, becoming servants, cleaners and manual labourers" (UNPO 1995: 8). The conditions of the Ogonis did not improve with the creation of states in 1967 which relocated them to the present Rivers State (Saro-Wiwa 1994).

The discovery of oil in Ogoniland by Shell in 1958 only brought more woes to the community. The community accounts for about 3.86% of the total oil production in Rivers State which has now been split into two states. With a 28,000 barrels of oil per day output ratio, this amounts to 1.27% of Nigeria's total oil production. The joint venture between the Nigerian National Petroleum Corporation (NNPC), Shell Petroleum Development Company, Elf and Agip has five major oil fields in Ogoniland: Bomu, Bodo West, Ebubu, Korokoro, and Yorla. From these fields, 95 oil wells hooked up to five flowstations have been established. Shell estimates that about 624 million barrels of oil have been extracted from Ogoniland since it commenced operations in 1959 (UMPO 1995: 20).

Unfortunately, rather than improve the lot of the Ogonis and bring them into the mainstream of politics, the discovery of oil only culminated in further marginalization, environmental degradation, and massive socio-economic dislocations. Agriculture and fishing, their main occupations suffered severely as gas flaring, blow-outs, the construction of tank farms, oil pipelines, and the processes of oil exploration and drilling, led to severe environmental abuse (Osaghae 1995; Naanen 1995). As UMPO (1995: 8) has noted, "Large flares burnt gas from the oil extraction process, illuminating the sky and polluting the air. Most of the flares burnt at ground level and some flares were built close to populated areas such as that at K-Dere." In the context of a very weak and unsteady state, where the elites have only a tenuous relation to production and have come to depend almost exclusively on the collection of oil rents since the early 1970s, there were no policies to protect vulnerable communities like the Ogonis (Ihonvbere 1993-1994). The complaints of the Ogonis against the oil companies were ignored by successive governments which often moved to strengthen working relations with the oil companies through several joint venture agreements (Hutchful 1985; Anikpo 1985; Ihonvbere 1994b; Graf 1988). In some instances where the companies cared to pay compensation, the community was often underpaid or compensation was used to deepen social and class cleavages. This was usually done by paying the money to the traditional chiefs, absentee community representatives, and powerful individuals. Of course, Shell in particular has been unable to grow with the times; the company had failed to realize that alternatives sites and platforms of power and influence had emerged in Ogoniland; and it ignored the fact that chiefs were not often necessarily the absolute representative of all their citizens.

It is these conditions of marginalization, domination, exploitation, abuse, and what the Ogonis regard as "disrespect and robbery" (Saro-Wiwa 1994), that were to precipitate the conflict and violence between the Nigerian state and the Ogonis in the 1990s.

THE STATE VERSUS THE OGONIS: THE BASIS OF THE CONFLICT

The basis of the conflict between the Ogonis and the Nigerian state can be found in the flawed, unequal, and exploitative nature of center-periphery relations in the country, the domination and exploitation of the oil producing community by the state and capital, the neglect and marginalization of minority communities, and in the insecurity, instability, and general weaknesses of the neo-colonial state. The Ogonis have always complained of marginalization, neglect, exploitation, and disrespect. The Nigerian federal and state governments and the oil corporations have taken out much from the community and put very little or nothing back. The various formulas for revenue allocation and state/local government creation in Nigeria have simply disregarded the complaints and claims of the Ogonis though several commissions of enquiry set up since the late 1950s have always given credence to Ogoni claims and complaints. The 1979 constitution of Nigeria simply vested all oil resources on the Federal Government. The Land Use Decree which was also written into the 1979 Constitution transferred ownership of all land to the government. Thus the Ogonis not only lost their land, they also lost control of all oil discovered within their territory. The joint venture agreement between NNPC and Shell following the nationalization of British Petroleum (BP) in 1979, simply strengthened the power and control of Shell over economic activities in the oil producing territory of Ogoni. Given the history of neglect and deepening socioeconomic dislocations and decay, the Ogonis decided to intensify their struggles (Goodall ed. 1994). As Ken Saro-Wiwa noted in 1992:

> I have watched helplessly as they (the Ogoni) have been gradually ground to dust by the combined effort of the multinational oil company, Shell Petroleum Development Company, the murderous ethnic majority in Nigeria and the country's military dictatorships. Not the pleas, not the writing over the years have convinced the Nigerian elite that something special ought to be done to relieve the distress of the Ogoni (Saro-Wiwa 1992: 7).

It was realized by Ogoni leaders that given the insensitivity of the Nigerian state and its custodians to their conditions and pleas, only an internationalization of their claims would force the Nigerian government to take them seriously. But the beginnings were to lay out a strategy for challenging the government and use the response of the state as a basis for international appeals. This led to what Saro-Wiwa (1994: 92-103) calls "The Autonomy Option." The basis of the struggle is outlined by Saro-Wiwa (1994: 92) thus:

> In 1990, the Ogoni took stock of their situation in Nigeria and found that for all the wealth of their land, and in spite of the fact that an estimated 100 billion US dollars had been taken from their land in thirty two years of oil mining, they had no schools, no hospitals and no roads. They found that there was an intense pressure on their land and that they lived in a poisoned environment in which wildlife, etc. could not survive. They found that the few Ogoni men and women who had some education, had no access whatsoever to jobs and that when they had jobs at all, they did not obtain promotion, no matter their competence. They found that from time, their leaders had laid faith in co-operation with the rest of Nigeria but that this faith had been grossly misplaced as each ethnic group has its own agenda quite unrelated to the notion of co-operation in a multi-ethnic nation.

Thus the Chiefs and people of Ogoni prepared and submitted an "Ogoni Bill of Rights" to the Federal Government in October 1990 containing 20 major demands and other subdemands. The document demanded "political autonomy" for the Ogonis "as a distinct and separate unit." This autonomy was to include: political control of Ogoni affairs by Ogoni people; the right to the control and use of their economic resources; adequate and direct representation as of right in all Nigerian institutions; use and development of Ogoni languages; the full development of Ogoni culture; the right to religious freedom; and the right to protect the Ogoni environment and ecology from further degradation. As community mobilization intensified, the demands came to in clude the creation of an Ogoni state with 13 local government areas.

The Nigerian government ignored the Bill of Rights. On August 26, 1991, the Chiefs and people of Ogoni addressed an "Addendum to the Ogoni Bill of Rights" to the Nigerian government and international community. It was at this point that the Ogonis noted that "without the intervention of the international community, the Government of the Federal Republic of Nigeria and the ethnic majority will continue (their) obnoxious policies until the Ogoni people are obliterated from the face of the earth" (reproduced in Wiwa 1994: 99). The "Addendum" was therefore an ample opportunity to introduce a new dimension into the struggle for autonomy and attention to their demands. This was a strategy that had not been tried at such a level by an ethnic group that was not seeking secession in Nigeria's history.

What followed was massive internal mobilization, the creation of relevant organizations including The Movement for the Survival of Ogoni People (MOSOP), National Youth Council of Ogoni People (NYCOP), Conference of Ogoni Traditional Rulers, the Council for Ogoni Rights (COR) and others. These were very militant and active organizations. There were mass demonstrations, press statements and conferences, the mobilization of public opinion in support of the Ogonis in the Nigerian media; and more importantly the education of the community on the nature of the demands. MOSOP constantly restated the commitment of the Ogonis to peaceful strategies of struggle for their demands. But the Nigerian state and Shell had other ideas. The state (encouraged by Shell) relied on intimidation, the arrest of Ogoni leaders, support for conservative politicians and traditional rulers in Ogoniland to create divisions, the trivialization of their demands, and counter-propaganda (Federal Government of Nigeria, n. d.). The government drafted police and army units to protect oil executives and workers in the area and to demonstrate its strong alliance with Shell. Shell on its own part refused to dialogue seriously with the community. In April 1993, violence broke out when an American contracting company, Wilbros, bulldozed crops in Biara as part of a project for laying new pipelines in total defiance of the demands of the community. The police drafted in to protect the company fired and killed an Ogoniman, Mr. Agbarator Otu and wounded 20 others who were defenseless. This development strengthened the belief of the Ogonis that the government and oil companies were ganged up against them.

By July 1993, Ogoni neighbors who had traditionally depended on Ogoni trade routes and markets and who had maintained peaceful relations attacked the Ogonis with automatic weapons, grenades, and very sophisticated equipments. This attack by the Andonis led to the death of over 1000 and displaced 20,000. Neither the state nor the federal government responded to the appeals of MOSOP and the Ogonis to intervene and stop the confrontation. In December 1993, a violent conflict erupted between the Ogonis and the Okrikas: "Sophisticated weapons were used to systematically destroy Ogoni areas of the waterfront" (UNPO 1995: 26). The attack which went on for several days left 95 Ogonis dead and thousands wounded and displaced. As before, the government refused to act though military and police installations were close by. In April 1994, the Ogonis were involved in another violent confrontation with their northern neighbors, the Ndokis. This time the Ndokis were aided by Nigerian soldiers who raided seven Ogoni villages destroying lives and property. Ledor village was completely burnt to the ground and all the inhabitants rendered homeless. These acts of violence, which were clearly orchestrated by more powerful forces beyond the warring communities, sent mixed signals to the Ogonis, prodemocracy groups, international NGOs, and other minority communities.

These communities had lived in peace with the Ogonis; they had intermarried for decades. Some depended on Ogoni markets and trade routes; and they had traditional mechanisms for resolving community conflicts. Suddenly, at the peak of mobilization in Ogoniland under the leadership of Ken Saro-Wiwa and MOSOP, one after the other, they became involved in destructive conflicts with the Ogonis. These conflicts also coincided with significant Ogoni gains at the international level. International environmental movements like Greenpeace and the Sierra Club, human rights organizations like Amnesty International and Human Rights Watch, and UN agencies were beginning to take a keen interest in developments in Ogoniland. MOSOP had also joined the UNPO and was beginning to influence global opinion about Nigeria and its military dictators. State-sponsored violence was thus a strategy to divert attention, redirect the blame towards the Ogonis, and generate local challenges for MOSOP.

In May 1994, four prominent Ogoni leaders were murdered while attending a meeting at Giokoo, Gokhana Kingdom by angry youths. The secret memo from the Commander of the Rivers State Security Task Force (RSSTF) had earlier prescribed the killing of prominent Ogonis by the state as a major strategy for internalizing the Ogoni crisis, dividing the community, diverting attention, and justifying military intervention and the use of unmediated force to contain MOSOP (Okuntimo 1994). The murdered chiefs, Edward Kobani, Samuel Orage, Albert Badey, and Theophilus Orage had been members of MOSOP but had disagreed with the more militant positions of younger members. Their resignation from MOSOP saw the election of Ken Saro-Wiwa as MOSOP president and the intensification of grassroots mobilization and the internationalization of MOSOP's demands. They were regarded as conservative and pro-government not only because they had held very important government positions in the past, and were quite wealthy, but they were also seen as stooges of the oil corporations and the military junta. Of course these allegations were never proven though they were part of the group of prominent Ogonis branded as "vultures." In fact, some of the chiefs were related to the younger leadership of MOSOP and had adopted their own ways of wagging the struggle for compensation. Their brutal murder led to divisions within Ogoni communities between the so-called "conservatives" who were seen as government stooges and opportunists on the one hand, and the younger and militant members on the other. This division was exploited by the military government, which tried to present MOSOP in bad light, as unreasonable, violent, irresponsible, and as not representative of the genuine interests of the Ogonis (Federal Government of Nigeria, n.d.).

With the murder of the four chiefs, the military government, this time, responded immediately. It blamed the murders on MOSOP and NYCOP, arrested Ken Saro-Wiwa the spokesperson for the Ogonis and president of MOSOP, and sent a brutal military expedition to sack Ogoniland and occupy it: "In only the first six days of the operation ... 18 villages were raided by shooting soldiers. They left scores dead, many wounded and then looted and burned" (UNPO 1995: 29). Women were raped, farms were set on fire, whole villages were razed, hundreds were arrested and tortured, schools were burnt, and several elderly persons died of exposure. The military commandant in charge of the operation, Major (later Colonel) Paul Okuntimo saw the operation as an opportunity to "waste" the Ogonis. He treated the operation like the Nigerian involvement in the civil war in Liberia (Okuntimo 1994). Road blocs were mounted at strategic points, entrance to Ogoni villages were sealed off, movement was restricted, and Ogoni communities were occupied by the military.

Following a clearly flawed trial at which evidence was suppressed, witnesses were intimidated or bribed to lie against the accused, defense counsels were physically abused and intimidated, and there appeared to have been a predetermined judgement, nine MOSOP leaders, including Ken Saro-Wiwa were sentenced to death by hanging by the Justice Ibrahim Ndahi Auta Civil Disturbances (Special Tribunal). On November 10, 1995, the nine Ogoni activists were executed by hanging in Port Harcourt while an appeal filed on their behalf by Chief Gani Fawehinmi was still pending. In spite of the hanging which has generated extensive international outrage and condemnation, deepened contradictions and coalitions within the country, and forced many nations to impose sanctions on Nigeria, the conditions of the Ogonis remain worse than before they presented their Bill of Rights. Nigeria, suspended from the Commonwealth as a result of the hanging, is expending a lot of time, money and energy in trying to contain domestic opposition and rehabilitate itself internationally. Where does Nigeria go from here? What are the implications of the Ogoni crisis for the actors: the Nigerian state, Shell, MOSOP, the prodemocracy constituency, and the international community.

THE CHALLENGE OF REHABILITATION AND RECON-STRUCTION

The developments in Ogoniland have significantly affected the character of national politics and redefined Nigeria's global image and relations.

First, they have exposed the Nigerian state to the gaze of the world. Not only have limited sanctions been imposed by the Western nations, the Commonwealth in which Nigeria has been a very influential member also imposed a suspension at its 1995 meeting in Auckland, New Zealand. This is costing Nigeria a lot in terns of economic aid, trade, diplomatic room to manoeuver, and ability to comment on developments in other parts of the world.

Second, the Ogoni issue has forced a reconstruction of the sites of politics and mobilization within Nigeria. Ethnic minorities, oil producing communities, human rights associations, and prodemocracy movements have now come to realize the extent to which the junta can go to defend its interests and relations with capital. This has called for new alliances and strategies of struggle.

Third, international non-governmental organizations, in particular environmental movements and human rights organizations have come to target Nigeria and its military regime for special attention and action. Nigeria is one country today where these organizations have established special task forces or desks to monitor development, provide support for the opposition, and expose the regime's misdeeds. Protests and other forms of campaign against the regime calling for international sanctions and support for the Ogonis and political detainees continue world wide.

Fourth, the Ogoni issue has brought the national question to the forefront of Nigeria's political debate. Of course, this has always been part of the contested aspects of state-society relations since the initial liberalization agenda was announced in 1987 by General Ibrahim Babangida. But the massive destruction in Ogoniland, the execution of the activists, the derivation and revenue allocation issues have once again raised questions about the continued unity of the country and forced people to consider under what political arrangements various ethnic communities can live together. Increasingly, it is becoming clear that no matter what the regime desires, these issues would have to be debated beyond mere constitutional manipulation and engineering.

Fifth, the Ogoni issue has made the campaign of prodemocracy groups for external support against the junta more legitimate. Until November 1995, the prodemocracy groups made very limited in-roads in Western capitals. Even Chief M. K. O. Abiola the presumed winner of the annulled June 1993 presidential elections achieved very little in his trips to various Western capitals following the annulment. Most foreign governments took the position of giving the government in Nigeria the benefit of the doubt and hoping that diplomatic pressure and personal appeals would alter the positions adopted by the regime. Even Nelson Mandela of South Africa had, until the executions in 1995, believed in personal contacts and quiet diplomacy. The execution changed all that and several Western nations and African states (Uganda, Zimbabwe, South Africa, Australia, Denmark, New Zealand, Canada, the United States, Britain, and the European Union), not only began to impose sanctions on Nigeria but also to provide open financial and diplomatic support for Nigerian opposition movements inside and outside the country.

Finally, the responses of the military junta to the Ogoni situation has expanded the threshold of politics and political action for the opposition groups. Most opposition movements received a sort of jolt to their activities and were emboldened by the global responses to deepen their contacts and politics. Many found it much easier to link their agitations to the experiences of the Ogoni people and to use them as a basis for mobilizing and recruiting members. Never in the history of Nigeria have so many opposition movements existed outside the shores of Nigeria with the sole purpose of displacing the military and recreating the platforms of politics and power.

SHELL AND THE OGONI CRISIS

It is easy to blame transnational corporations for all the ills of developing nations like Nigeria. That would be convenient. Such positions are of course based on their arrogant, often insensitive, and crass profit motivations as well as direct and/or indirect interference in and manipulation of domestic politics and interests. Yet, the point must be made that Shell is not the only oil company operating in Nigeria, though it is the most powerful, the largest, the most experienced, and the dominant company operating in Ogoniland. It dominates Nigeria's oil industry and is locked into a powerful alliance with the Nigerian state through its joint venture agreement with the NNPC. Shell has a record of not always responding urgently to incidents of pollution or blowouts and leaks. In spite of its numerous propaganda packages in which is boasts of several contributions to the growth and development of Ogoniland, the overall record of Shell is well below expectation by any standards. It is easy to reel out the number of scholarships awarded, roads constructed, and the like: "spending US$100 million on environment related projects and US$20 million on roads, health clinics, schools, scholarships, water schemes and agricultural support projects..." ("Clear Thinking in Troubled Times," paid advert by Shell, 1995). The company can also point at the over 1000 scholarships it awards each year, its $20 million "community development programme," and its investment in skills training, agriculture, jetty construction, and so on. Shell likes to draw attention to the N2 million 3 kilometer undesigned and poorly constructed road at Baen Kpean which was constructed in 1990, the N77,000 worth of seats provided for secondary schools, classrooms constructed at K-Dere to compliment community self-help efforts, and so on. One needs to see the quality of these projects to know that Shell has not demonstrated its international commitment to quality and efficiency in Ogoniland.

The truth of the matter is that most of these had been forced out of the company, and they hardly represent any reasonable or fair response to the degree of devastation caused in the oil producing communities. More importantly, these facilities have been set up in a typical patron-client relationship and have benefitted the elites in the communities. In terms of quality, some of the facilities and services provided by Shell are sub-standard. If its interventions and contributions had been that significant how come Ogoniland is still a poverty-stricken and terrible marginalized community? As Claude Ake (1996) has concluded:

> Shell Petroleum Development Company of Nigeria shows no sign of remorse for causing the strife in Ogoniland which has thrown Nigeria into one of its deepest crises of its history. It insists defiantly that it will not change its ways and denies any part whatsoever in the environmental degradation of the Niger Delta, which it blames on indigenes conniving at oil spills to collect compensation.

According to Ake (1996), a World Bank study "Defining an Environmental Development Strategy for the Niger Delta 1995" confirmed how the oil corporations led by Shell abuse the environment and the Niger Delta and with far-reaching implications for the quality of life and community relations. The report showed that 76 percent of the natural gas produced in the process of petroleum production is simply flared. This is the highest rate of flaring in the developing world: "The flaring is a serious health hazard. At temperatures of 1,300 to 1,400 degrees centigrade, the multitude of flares in the Delta heat up everything, causing noise pollution, and producing CO_2, VOC, CO, NOx and particulates around the clock. The emission of CO_2 from gas flaring in Nigeria releases 35 million tons of CO_2 a year and 12 million tons of methane, which means that Nigeria's oil fields contribute more to global warming than the rest of the world together" (Ake 1996). It is easy to imagine the impact of 95 oil wells in the "small piece of territory" as the Nigerian government described Ogoniland.

In addition to gas flaring and all its impact on land and marine life which simply renders hundreds of thousands of able-bodied men and women jobless as rivers run dry of fishes and farmlands are scorched, is the problem of oil spills. Shell has spent a lot of time and money arguing that "In the Ogoni area-...over 66% of the oil spills were caused by sabotage, usually linked to claims for compensation." There is some truth is this (Ihonvbere and Shaw, 1988). However, Shell cannot definitively prove that 66% of oil spillages are the direct result of community sabotage. Yet, has Shell ever bothered to find out why the sabotaging of its equipment has become a covert (and frequent?) strategy of struggle and resistance? Why have the communities resorted to this strategy to get compensated for the exploitation of their resources? How many indigenes are employed in the oil industry? To whom has the company paid the "compensations" over the years?

Rivers and Delta states alone experience over 300 oil spills every year. These spills "discharge about 2,300 m3 of oil. This estimate would be much higher if it included minor spills which are far more numerous and invariably unreported. It would be higher still if it took account of the fact that the Nigerian crude oil is very light and evaporates rapidly, an estimated evaporation loss of about 50 percent in 48 hours" (Ake 1996). Shell, the giant in Nigeria's oil fields is just as guilty as the smaller oil companies. A typical example is the case of the Shell oil pipeline at Korokoro flow station No. 5 which began to leak on June 12, 1993. The leak continued unattended to, in spite of community reports to Shell, for at least two months! (Environmental Action Rights Project 1996). It is no wonder that the waters used for industrial and domestic applications in Nigeria contain about 6 percent of petroleum and in some locations, up to 60 percent. In the waste water of Oloma Creek, the figure is about 62.7 percent. At the Bonny Terminal where Shell operates heavily, "the mud at the bottom of the Bonny River has a lethal concentration of 12000 ppm" (Ake 1996). The exploitation of Nigeria's oil resources has imposed unprecedented pain, dislocations, and frustrations among oil producing communities and their residents. The Ogonis were simply one of the more prominent communities to resist openly by making their demands and frustrations public.

However, it is important to make the point that what Shell has been able to do in Nigeria is largely a reflection of the shortcomings and weaknesses of the Nigerian state, its custodians, and its institutions as indicated above. If the Nigerian government were legitimate and democratic, accountable, efficient and effective, and if it had a clear and enforceable environmental program, and was not too dependent on oil rents for revenues, it would have exercised better control/regulation over the activities of Shell and other corporations. If the Nigerian government had programs designed to mobilize, support, and empower local communities, especially in the oil producing communities, and if it had structures and processes for regular monitoring and dialogue with local organizations, the oil companies would have been unable to get away with environmental abuse and the manipulation of the oil industry.

SHELL AND THE POLITICS OF VIOLENCE IN OGONILAND

Shell has tried as much as possible to deny any involvement in the Ogoni crisis. This is like arguing that in 35 or more years of oil exploitation in Ogoniland, it has behaved responsibly and created no cause for community agitation. Yet, it was Shell that precipitated the current violent phase of the crisis when its contractor, the American company Wilbros Limited tried, on April 28, 1993, to install oil pipelines to connect the Bomu oilfields. Wilbros embarked on a large scale destruction of farms and crops without clearance from the community or compensation to the poor owners. This resulted in resistance from a community that was not consulted, felt abused, and marginalized. Shell called for support, as usual, from the army which opened fire on defense less villagers on April 30, 1993- the "bloody Friday" as it is known in Ogoniland.

Shell also demonstrated its involvement by financially supporting the "wasting" campaigns and activities of Major Paul Okuntimo who was also behind the orchestration of the violent clashes between the Ogonis and their neighbors. Evidence is available in Okuntimo's "restricted" memo to the Governor of Rivers state, Lieutenant Colonel Dauda Komo on May 12, 1994 in which he reminded the Governor of the need to continue "pressure on oil companies for prompt regular inputs as discussed" to facilitate the brutal activities of the Rivers State Internal Security Task Force (created by Order No. 4149-Restoration of Law and Order in Ogoniland) which he headed. In the same memo, Okuntimo made it clear that the Task Force was mainly concerned with restoring Shell's operations in Ogoniland, not in finding a solution to the problem, or in advancing the interests of the community: "Shell operations still impossible unless ruthless military operations are undertaken for smooth economic activities to commence" (Paul Okuntimo, "Restricted" Memo July 12, 1994).

It must be recalled that over the years, as part of what Claude Ake, has called the "privatization of the Nigerian state," Shell has been able, at will, and at short notice, to call on the police and army to "deal" with oil producing communities, protect its interests and use violence against workers. This has increased the arrogance of the company. As recent revelations demonstrate, Shell has been importing arms into Nigeria and arming the police and its own security personnel. While it reflects on the state of Nigeria's national security for a private firm to import arms for the use of the national police, it also demonstrates the power and influence of Shell in the country and the control it has over the government. To whom can we expect the police officers, armed and subsidized by Shell to be loyal? We can therefore understand why they have often been brutal in the defence of Shell's interest. Shell's claim that it imports the weapons to assist the Nigerian police who guard its facilities and are not well armed has been refuted by a former Chief of Defence Staff, Lt. General Alani Akinrinade to the effect that the police are well armed and did not require any private organization to arm it. Rather than seeking ways to reach some accommodation with local communities, Shell, according to a recent report, has been busy trying to purchase more sophisticated weapons to "update the firearms of its security forces across the country." Claude Ake (1996) has called this "frightening novelty," "accumulation by terror."

Before the murder of the four Ogoni Chiefs, the leaders of the MOSOP had indicate their desire to dialogue with Shell. In fact, they had never expressed the desire to see Shell out of Ogoniland. Their demand had always been for a fair share of the resources extracted from their land and for the protection of the environment. Shell's response has always been half-hearted and opportunistic. Even when MOSOP was invited by Shell to present a list of demands to Shell, which it complied with, neither the communities nor MOSOP received any replies. This strategy of ignoring the community and its organizations only hardened respective positions, deepened the anger of the people, and convinced MOSOP that only a massive international campaign against Shell and the government would draw attention to their problems.

During the trial of Saro-Wiwa and his colleagues, Shell demonstrated that it had a deep interest in the case and in the fate of the accused persons. It had not been summoned to court. Yet, Shell hired O.C.J. Okocha as its legal counsel and entered its appearance in the case. The questions which many Nigerians asked at that time were: Why was Shell so interested in the case? Why was it in court? Why did it have to hire a prominent lawyer when it was not summoned in relation to the case? Whose interest was it watching out for or protecting? Since Shell did not lose any worker or official in the violence and did not lose any property, what exactly was it in court for?

Two of the "star witnesses" of the prosecution in the case against the "Ogoni Nine" who had, according to the prosecution's "Summary of Evidence" alleged that they heard Saro-Wiwa address a crowd of MOSOP members and supporters in his native language at Giokoo ordering them to kill the "vultures," later recanted their statements in sworn affidavits. They alleged that they had been bribed by the military government and Shell through a relative of one of the murdered chiefs, Alhaji Mohammed Kobani, to lie against the Ogoni activists. According to Charles Danwi and Nanonye Akpa, the military and Shell had used a combination of threats, blackmail, intimidation, promises of houses, and OMPADEC and Shell contracts to secure their support against the "Ogoni Nine." In addition, the "witnesses" were promised new jobs and each paid N30,000.00 to them get them to lie against the accused. Though their confessions were recorded on audio and video tapes, the Tribunal refused to allow defense counsels to tender them as evidence. Though the government and Shell have denied any involvement in this scandal, the stories appeared believable to the Nigerian public (Liberty 1995: 16-17).

Finally, it was reported recently that Shell was planning a purge of "executives in Nigeria following the discovery of a `black hole of corruption' involving the payment of millions of dollars in bribes and kickbacks to tribal chiefs, community leaders, and the military in the troubled Ogoni region." The report also alleged that "a senior army officer, accused of ordering the murder and torture of Ogoni dissidents, was on Shell's payroll." The report further argued that documents that have recently leaked to the public, showed that a "close relationship" existed "between local branches of the oil company and General Sani Abacha's brutal military regime," and that Major Paul Okuntimo was paid by Shell officials in his murderous campaigns in Ogoniland to crush "civil unrest...and opposition to Shell's presence." In an interview with the *Sunday Times* (London) (December 17, 1995) Okuntimo actually agreed that while crushing the Ogoni protests, he was "being paid by Shell." In his own words, "Shell contributed to the logistics through *financial support*. To do this (sic the pacification of Ogoniland), we needed resources and Shell provided these." Though Okuntimo, known for his bold and rather erratic conduct later denied this statement, his track record shows that he was not the kind of officer to sanitize his words or keep secrets, even those that damned him (see *Sunday Times* (London) December 17, 1995).

From the points above, it is clear that Shell was involved in precipitating the Ogoni crisis, in provoking the Ogoni people, in forcing the Ogoni people to set up organizations to mobilize themselves and resist the company and the military government, and in encouraging the brutal attacks on the Ogoni communities. As well, by not taking a critical stand, by not distancing itself from the government, and by not taking a firm stand against the executions after the flawed trial without the right of appeal, Shell is just as guilty as the Abacha junta. By continuing with the $3.6 billion Liquified Natural Gas (LNG) project even in the face of global condemnation and the withdrawal of the International Finance Corporation (IFC), Shell showed that profits and market hegemony mattered more than lives and community harmony. Shell cannot claim that it has no interest in the content and direction of Nigerian politics. It cannot now suddenly realize that issues which arise from its own operations and politics, are now *internal* matters in which it can neither intervene nor comment. As well, by claiming that the global campaigns against it and its products have not affected business and that it hopes to resume operations as usual in Nigeria very soon, shows that it is out of touch with the yearnings of the Nigerian people. The Ogonis recently sent a letter to Shell warning it to stay away from their community "until matters have been resolved." Many communities have learnt from the Ogoni experience and will certainly redesign their strategies for challenging (and confronting) capital and the state in the future. In so far as the demands (which are common to all oil producing communities) have not been addressed, the crisis would continue to deepen.

THE WAY OUT OF THE PRESENT CRISIS?

Without doubt, mistakes have been made on every side: the Ogonis, the military government, Shell, and the international community. In spite of clear evidence of the dangerous direction of the Ogoni crisis, warnings from local NGOs, and clear signs of desperation on the side of the military junta, the international community did not act or put pressure on the Nigerian military to adopt a more rational response. Even president Nelson Mandela, who now advocates severe sanctions against Nigeria, never believed that the situation was that serious or that the military would proceed with the executions. In spite of appeals from the Civil Liberties Organization (CLO) and the Organization of Nigerians in the Americas (ONA) to mention just two of the hundreds of NGOs and prodemocracy groups that sent appeals to the UN and world leaders, no significant response was received. It took the execution of Saro-Wiwa and his eight colleagues for the world to realize that the Abacha junta was just as bad as the organizations had claimed. To this extent, the international community let the Ogonis down. The lesson is to develop and strengthen an early warning mechanism, adopt consistent responses to repressive regimes, and learn to take appeals and warnings from popular organizations more seriously.

Following the executions, international response was swift and decisive. Western nations and some African states like South Africa and Zimbabwe recalled ambassadors, imposed limited sanctions, reviewed foreign aid, and promised to impose harsher sanctions with time. Even Daniel arap Moi of Kenya, not known for his belief in democracy and human rights, expressed his displeasure at the executions. The United States bolstered up its earlier sanctions on the regime by condemning the regime's "unlawful actions" and introduced a resolution in the U.N. Human Rights Committee and the U.N. General Assembl,; downgraded diplomatic relations, imposed travel and visa restrictions on officials of the regime and their families, terminated air flights between Nigeria and the U.S., imposed a complete ban on the "sale and repair of military goods and services," banned all "government-to-government development aid with the exception of humanitarian assistance and democracy programs," ended all U.S. support for Nigeria in international financial institutions, and supported legislation in Congress (S. 1419 and H.R. 2697) to "codify...sanctions already imposed administratively and even impose stricter measures" (Embassy of the United States, Bonn, Germany, January 1996). The Commonwealth suspended Nigeria and gave the military junta two years to restore democracy and disengage from politics. The UN issued a rather weak condemnation of the executions and the human rights situation. There were several open demonstrations against Shell and the military junta across the world. Yet, these have not bothered the Abacha regime in any significant way. It engaged in a war of words with South Africa, threatened counter measures against the West if personal and public assets were seized or frozen, vehemently protested the suspension from the Commonwealth, and embarked on a massive propaganda blitz across the world. Ironically, the West has mellowed down in its attacks against the military junta: ambassadors have been returned, the Nigerian case is no longer topical, visa restrictions are not effectively enforced, trade sanctions are loose, and organizations in civil society are not receiving the anticipated support. While a country like Canada, has, through its Standing Committee on International Trade and Foreign Affairs resolved in December 1995 to impose an oil embargo and to impose trade sanctions, the main trading partners of Nigeria (the United States, Germany, and the UK) have refused to do so on the grounds of "national interest." This has emboldened the Abacha junta, which has continued to detain Chief Abiola, prodemocracy and trade union leaders, ban rallies, and intimidate civil society.

Shell is now the "bad boy" of Nigeria's oil industry. Protests against its operations and service outlets continue worldwide. Several important organizations like Friends of the Earth, UW Greens, and Greenpeace continue to campaign for a boycott of Shell and its products (UW Greens, "Don't Let Shell Oil Get Away With Murder!" 1996). One would have expected a major corporation like Shell to distance itself gradually from the junta, retrace its steps, and try to make amends. As Malcolm T. Williams, Shell's Head of Regional Liaison in London noted recently, this is the time for "all parties" to "refrain from taking positions which may lead to further tragedy. It must be a time for understanding and cooperation" (Letter to Fran Buntman, The University of Texas at Austin, 19 December 1995). Expending millions on public relations just like the Abacha junta which has budgeted an initial $50 million to repair its battered image is a wrong step in the wrong direction. It is hardly the way to promote "understanding and cooperation." If such sums had been invested in Ogoniland in the first place, the formation of MOSOP would have been totally unnecessary. Restating its innocence hardly helps the case because very few believe Shell. The following options are available to Shell:

1. Admit that some mistakes have been made especially in Ogoniland. Such public admissions just like the Chief Executive of Texaco did recently in the United States go a long way to heal wounds;,

2. Openly distance itself from the Abacha regime because the regime is not just bad for business, it is bad for Shell in particular. Since Shell has produced no oil in Ogoniland since 1993, this certainly has an impact on profits, at least, from the Nigerian operations. The campaign to boycott Shell products is spreading and sooner than later, it will begin to have some effect. Today, Shell will be deluding itself to think that it is safe in any part of Nigeria. Abacha's government will fall sooner than later, and Shell should not allow the military to drag it down with it,

3. Open a line of dialogue with the Ogoni people and other oil producing communities. It could begin by calling a major conference, inviting the organizations, and involving credible activists, organizations, and scholars to discuss the way out. MOSOP must play a visible role in this. Irrespective of the executions and the repression in Ogoniland, Shell must dialogue with MOSOP, it remains the most popular and legitimate organization of the Ogoni people;

4. Provide open support for popular organizations in their struggle for democracy. Rather than waste resources on funding military officers like Okuntimo and putting adverts in newspapers around the world at great cost, popular organizations especially at the community level, and prodemocracy movements should be supported. A democratic society is better for business than an insecure, violent, unstable, and crisis-ridden society;

5. In consultation with MOSOP and other relevant organizations, come up with a holistic agenda for rehabilitation, reconstruction, and compensation in Ogoniland. It must take some responsibility for the destroyed lives, homes, farms, crops and livestock which were caused by Okuntimo's Task Force which Shell had funded;

6. Come up with a credible environmental program. The recently announced $4.5 million "independent" Niger Delta Environmental Survey (NDES) under the chairmanship of Gamaniel O. Onosode is too late to make any headway in a badly politicized and fractured society. In the first place, $4.5 million is a very minuscule amount if a serious and comprehensive study of the environmental disaster already caused in the Niger Delta by Shell and other companies is to be studied effectively. As noted earlier, the Niger Delta is the most polluted territory in the world with over 300 major spills every year. Secondly, if the NDES was designed to buy support or sympathy, it has already been doomed to failure: 1) by claiming to be innocent of all that has happened in Ogoniland, how can the NDES do otherwise than exonerate Shell?; 2) the representative of the communities in the NDES has resigned in protest over the company's role in the death of the "Ogoni Nine;" 3) The World Conservation Fund which was supposed to provide the effort with some international credibility is also under pressure from

powerful international NGOs to distance itself from Shell and the NDES. The NGOs are contending that funding for the Foundation will compromise its objectivity and erode its well nurtured credibility; 4) The local NGO representative is drawn from an organization which was established by a "former Nigerian petroleum minister who is now a director of Chevron." As Ake (1996), who also resigned from the Steering Committee of the NDES has concluded, aside from the chairman of the NDES, only the representatives of the government and the oil industry are left in the NDES. Thus, clearly, Shell cannot hope to use the NDES to confirm its innocence or demonstrate its interest in addressing problems which it had ignored for decades.

THE WEST AND THE SANCTIONS DEBATE

The Western powers are reluctant to impose sanctions because it will hurt their own interests. For instance, several refineries in the United States will be affected by an oil embargo on Nigeria. Others worry that unless it is comprehensive, it will have no effect. Furthermore, there are those who contend that sanctions will punish only the underprivileged rather than the wealthy elite. Kim R. Nossal (1995) has argued very forcefully against sanctions. According to him, "sanctions enthusiasts" are unrealistic, ignore "several successes and a lengthy string of failures," and tend to overlook the fact that it is the poor, especially women who suffer most when sanctions are imposed on a nation. Beyond making the "sanctioner feel good that a wrong-doer has been punished," Nossal argues that they are a "poor choice of tactics," do an "excellent job of hurting people," and "rarely hurt the right people."

Unfortunately, though academically sound, Nossal's postulations fail to capture the reality on the ground in Nigeria. It seems to trivialize the severity of the Nigerian crisis and its implications for Africa. It over exaggerates the strengths of the Nigerian state, and underrates the power of the international community and the resolve of Nigeria's opposition movements. He compares Nigeria with nations like Libya (3 million people with a lot of money and a more popular leadership), South Africa (then ruled by a white minority with money, technology, and strong support from Western nations), and even Cuba, Vietnam, and North Korea, nations with clear ideological platforms which facilitated a national project, identity, and ability to mediate the effect of sanctions. As well, Nossal is wrong in asserting that sanctions hurt only the poor. In comparative terms, yes, but overall, they embarrass the government and the elite; they restrict the movement and ability to enjoy the perquisites of power; they strengthen opposition groups; they deprive the government of resources required to repress the society; and they further delegitimize dictatorships which, otherwise, would not have considered disengagement from power. True, if a regime is relatively popular, has resources, enjoys policy effectiveness and the support of powerful nations in the global system, it might resist or withstand the impact of sanctions. If it is comparatively self-reliant, does not depend almost exclusively on a single export for foreign exchange, and has a strong industrial/technological base, it might withstand the impact of sanctions. **This is not the case with Nigeria.**

To rely on secondary level responses to the current Nigerian situation is actually to tolerate (even encourage) the Abacha dictatorship. If we understand the inner thinking of Abacha, his track record, and the sort of people he surrounds himself with, and the junta's constant worry over its ability to survive through endless co-optation, intimidation, and diversions, we might appreciate its vulnerability to sanctions. *The Economist* (November 18th, 1995) has referred to Abacha as "an unimaginative man who rarely leaves the presidential bunker in the capital, Abuja." According to Nelson Mandela, Abacha's regime is "barbaric, corrupt, irresponsible and arrogant" (*The Sunday Independent* November 26, 1995). As of December 1996, the Abacha regime has continued to detain prodemocracy activists, ban rallies, harass popular organizations, and 19 Ogonis remain on trial. Ogoniland is still under military occupation. Nigeria's Civil Liberties Organization (ERAP 1996) reports that "over 3,000 policemen and over 1,000 security operatives" now occupy the communities. Roadblocks have been set up at strategic points, movement is controlled, and the villagers are harassed often for no reasons. Chief M.K.O. Abiola, who won the 1993 presidential election has remained in jail, and the government is still as corrupt, insensitive, and repressive as ever. If nothing else, these conditions, and the clear flaws in the regime's 3-year transition program call for more resolute and decisive actions against Nigeria.

Even on mere selfish grounds, the West, especially the United States and the United Kingdom should seriously consider sanctions. If not comprehensive sanctions, then fully enforceable targeted sanctions aimed at weakening the junta and strengthening the opposition. The continued influx of thousands of Nigerian refugees who put a lot of pressure on social and immigration services and add insecurity to the lives and property of Westerners in Nigeria, and the potentially high cost of dealing with the breakdown of law and order as we have seen in Somalia, should encourage stiffer responses. The West African states, and France should be concerned here, will be overwhelmed by the influx of millions of Nigerians should the country implode or explode. Since Abacha is unwilling to dialogue with the opposition and has continued to disregard pleas from the West and international organizations, short of a Haiti-like operation, the most feasible option is at least, a targeted sanction regime: freeze assets, stop trade, embargo the oil, support the prodemocracy movements with resources.

There are several reasons to expect sanctions to work in the Nigerian case especially if it is comprehensive: the regime lacks any appreciable level of internal support; it is up against very powerful African nations like Zimbabwe, Uganda, and South Africa; sanctions and an oil embargo will only be adding teeth to the limited sanctions imposed thus far; they will strengthen local prodemocracy groups and opposition elements; and sanctions will fulfil the yearnings of international NGOs and Nigeria opposition groups abroad who have unanimously called for them.

Oil is the lifeline of the Abacha junta. It is oil money that enables it to buy support, bribe and divide the elites, and engage in a massive propaganda blitz abroad. Oil money enables it to import weapons and to retain the support of the military, especially its senior ranks. Oil money enables it to remain arrogant and to disparage the effects of limited sanctions. Any comprehensive action against the oil industry will deal an immediate blow to Abacha's ability to continue along the lines above. After all, as indicated earlier, oil accounts for more than 90 percent of Nigeria's exports, 25 percent of its Gross Domestic Product (GDP), and a little over 80 percent of public revenues. Within OPEC, Nigeria is the sixth largest oil producer. It is the fourth largest supplier of oil to the United States. The country produces about 2 million barrels of oil per day. While a **unilateral** action might not necessarily work, action by the United States, Canada, and the European powers would be sufficient to lead to changes in Nigeria. In fact, the regime is so fractionalized and factionalized, and so heavily reliant on the use of bribes that an oil embargo which deprives it of revenues **immediately** will be most effective.

The government makes about $45 million daily from the sale of oil. An embargo, coupled with the ban on arms sales will weaken the military junta's repressive ability and save lives. I do not agree with Nossal (1996) that such actions will make the sanctioners "feel good": there is nothing to feel good about-lives have been lost, people are in detention, and millions are living in fear, hunger, and disease. But given that the benefits of oil wealth had never trickled down to the populace before now, there is no amount of suffering that sanctions can generate. More importantly, hundreds of popular groups within and outside the country have called for sanctions to be imposed. This is the only way to weaken the regime and level the playing field somewhat. It is equally the only way to, at the very minimum, compel the regime to stick to a serious disengagement program. This is the more important in view of recent moves to emulate the military civilianization projects in other West African states (Hoffman 1995-96).

It is difficult to take Abacha seriously on his transition agenda. Aside from his personal lust for power, corruption, intolerant attitude, and disregard for popular opinion, the transition agenda is structured in such a way as to exhaust the opposition. As well, beside the establishment of several committees stacked with discredited politicians, a genuine transition cannot take place in a closed political terrain with millions living in fear and uncertainty. Only a major sanction regime will demonstrate to Abacha and his supporters that the world has changed, that lives are precious, and that a long-drawn out transition program which would culminate in further intimidation of civil society will not be tolerated. The transition to democracy in Nigeria is the primary responsibility of Nigerians. To do this however, they need the support of the world in their challenge to a clearly ruthless dictatorship. Oiling the dictator's repressive machine by doing business as usual, and allowing him to collect millions of dollars on a daily basis, would be tantamount to encouraging him in his repressive ways.

If nothing urgent and serious is done, there are four possible consequences:

1. Abacha plays around with his 3-year "transition" and plays a redesigned Babangida strategy and remains in power. In the current context of symbolic and weak global responses, this is a possibility. The establishment of countless committees is designed to incorporate and domesticate as many local elites as possible; the established parties are weak and their leaders have been busy "inviting" Abacha to be their presidential candidate in the coming elections;

2. An all out resort to violence-uncoordinated and very destructive. The emergence of groups such as the Movement for the Advancement of Democracy (MAD), the Revolutionary Movement for Hausa-Fulani Interest (RMHFI), and the United Front for the Liberation of Nigeria (UFLN) points in this direction. MAD hijacked a Nigeria Airways plane to protest the annulment of the June 12 election during the Babangida era, and the UFLN has claimed responsibility for blowing up the presidential jet in which Abacha's first son and eleven others perished on January 17, 1996. The RHFHFI has claimed responsibility for shooting Alex Ibru the publisher of the influential *Guardian* newspaper. There have been bomb explosions in Lagos, Ilorin, Kano, Zaria, and Kaduna. The assassination attempts against Abubakar Umar, Wole Soyinka, and Alex Ibru, as well as the assassination of Chief Alfred Rewane and Alhaja Kudirat Abiola, are pointers in the direction of increasing resort to violence. Persons attempting to smuggle large quantities of arms into Nigeria have been accosted at the Nigeria-Benin border. Small arms proliferate all over the country, thanks to returning ECOMOG soldiers and corruption within the police. The road to violence has never been more open;

3. A military coup led by senior officers, southerners, or militant middle-level officers. Given Abacha's security arrangements, and the badly delegitimized nature of the military, such a coup will be very bloody. If it fails, it will lead to mass executions; and

4. Efforts by foreign-based opposition groups such as the National Liberation Council of Nigeria (NALICON) or the recently formed United Democratic Front of Nigeria (UDFN)

to oust the Abacha junta through military means. This can only culminate in a long drawn out guerilla struggle and the implications will be large scale loss of lives and property.

To be sure, unions like NUPENG continue to resist the junta as are academics, human rights and prodemocracy organizations, and students. Yet, the way in which the Nigerian quagmire is worked out in the very near future will be a major lesson in political calculations and organization, the alignment and realignment of political forces, and the calculated (even if reluctant) intervention of external interests.

CHAPTER TEN

NIGERIA AND THE FUTURE:
EARLY 1990s TO 2000 AND BEYOND

If the mode of analysis — political economy — applied in this book has validity then its conclusions should provide a guide to future relations and directions. Not that either particular events or long-term changes can be predicted with great accuracy; but at least some scenarios can be plotted with a degree of confidence. The cycle of political and economic expansions and contractions has produced a more modest and moderate Nigeria; the experiences of civil war and oil cycles have left their marks and memories. Structural adjustment has created new opportunities as well as challenges, and the growing power of civil society has emboldened popular groups. Unprecedented in Nigeria's political history is the emergence of hundreds of grassroots based movements which together now constitute a formidable, though frequently harassed prodemocracy movement. Responses to "domestic" developments have created a more "alert" Nigeria as an aroused population attempts to mobilize global opinion in support of local struggles for democracy. The challenge of present and future regimes and generations is how to apply these lessons given internal demands and international conditions and pressures.

The futures of Nigeria, as for any political economy, will be a function of past, present and future considerations, coalitions and constraints. Any particular scenario or sequence (e.g. the coincidence or character of coups d'etat) is the result of specific conditions and choices yet broader sets of social relations are identifiable and distinguishable. Alternative futures are inseparable from the factors already abstracted within the political economy so that this concluding overview and preview will consist merely of extrapolations informed by history, theory and policy. In passing, we should also note that future studies are not unknown in Nigeria. Indeed, both a fatalistic culture and an optimistic spirit have encouraged Nigerians to be both irresponsible and irrepressible; hence the extravagant and fanciful claims of being Africa's great, industrial and/or nuclear power.

Both the missionary era — salvation will lead to a bright future — and the nationalist period — independence will result in general prosperity — generated their own false hopes only to be followed by myths of unity — keep Nigeria one and development will ensue — and oil boom — petro-naira will "spray" down on all Nigerians. The hard realities of post-independence, civil war, petroleum recessions and structural adjustments have yet to induce widespread skepticism or alienation, at least until spreading cynicism and apprehension following the failed 1990 coup attempt, the repressive nature of the Babangida regime, the scuttled march to the third republic, and the remilitarization of the political landscape under General Sani Abacha (Ihonvbere 1991e, 1996). Even under the Abacha junta which has turned out to be the most repressive regime the country has ever experienced, there remains a lot of hope, buoyance, and Nigerian arrogance anchored on the country's wealth, size, greatness, oil, and influence in the global system, pressures and sanctions from abroad notwithstanding. The belief remains that in the next boom, if not the next life, popular demands will be satisfied. The vibrant, optimistic mood stands in contrast to unattractive pessimistic projections -- the latter now reinforced by the harshness of structural adjustment conditions and the steady rehabilitation of previously disgraced and discredited politicians and military officers. A large number of Nigerians, especially those resident abroad for a variety of reasons appear to be steadily giving up on the country: Nigeria cannot be rescued, leadership and/or regime changes notwithstanding. The five-year ritual of national "planning" reinforces such unrealistic expectations, for each "plan" anticipates growth rather than decline, while making outlandish claims of "successes" and "achievements." Yet annual budgets, occasional interim plans, economic emergencies, and actual expenditures and results, let alone regular policy framework papers in accord with World Bank policies, usually point in a contrary direction: toward contraction rather than expansion. Nevertheless, the expectations of new constitutions and dispensations continue to fuel optimism rather than pessimism; Nigeria simply needs to design the right political economy. Both "national" planning and adjustment reforms are increasingly a function of World Bank preferences and conditionalities, however.

Nigeria has also adopted fashionable futurist studies for its own purposes, establishing a short-lived "Futures Institute" during the height of the oil boom, and then a Centre for Democratic Studies (CDS) in anticipation of a transition to democratic rule. Each national debate, such as the mid-1970s CDC and mid-1980s Political Bureau palavers, has also treated political, economic and social alternatives as did the WIN and other documents. The current debate on military disengagement or diarchy (joint rule by military and civilians) is also reflective on an increasing concession to the military in the face of a highly fragmented political class and fragmented civil society. However, the degree of rigor and reliability of data in such informal previews are limited. Even the mid-1980s devaluation and reform discourses were diverted and diluted by nationalistic machismo images and illusions. Only in recent struggles against the military and the practical decimation of the prodemocracy constituency by the Abacha junta, did this nationalistic arrogance evaporate as Nigerians within and outside the country began to vigorously seek and enlist the support of western governments, corporations, non-governmental organizations, and individuals in the struggle against the military (Soyinka 1996; Ihonvbere 1996).

Yet, over time, and related to established alternative modes of analysis, a set of issues has emerged as dominant elements in Nigeria's series of discourses. These include political process, economic structure, regional arrangement and social policy - regular features of "official" debates - but these could be expanded to embrace "unofficial" questions such as religion, gender, population and environment, elements of civil society. Positions on the former are quite well-rehearsed; those on the latter more tentative and hesitant. Nevertheless, because of the tendency towards radicalization of academe as well as the insistence of particular interests (e.g. women) the two sets of parallel debates are beginning to intersect in interesting ways: gender cannot be excluded from politics nor population from economics. In short, although on-going items remain on the national agenda, their context has changed and so their treatment is in flux. "Official" debates cannot be completely separated from those in the "informal" milieu, nor vice-versa. They span the spectrum of "national interests" and have evolved along with the political economy and culture, situated in a changing global context.

Happily, with characteristic Nigerian timeliness, a series of debates about the future were joined during the first year of Babangida's presidency in the mid-1980s as already noted: major "official" national debates on economic strategies, political structures and foreign policies, with minor "unofficial" discussions about religion, gender, population and environment. In short, despite military rule, the national agenda begun to reflect major issues in the political economy intensified by the incidence of debt, devaluation and destabilisation. This concluding chapter examines on-going debates as responses to both military rule and economic recession, and then abstracts four plausible alternative scenarios over the mid-term future, to the end of the present century.

a) Official Debates: Economic, Political And Foreign Policies

First, the intense "IMF debate" during the second half of 1985 was in reality a national palaver about overall economic policy. Although the immediate issue was the acceptability of IMF conditions for a short-term loan, the underlying question was that of development direction. A consensus soon emerged to reject IMF conditions - the normal package of devaluation, privatization, deregulation and desubsidization of commodities and services — but this was based on disparate interests: economic nationalists, workers, intellectuals, students, technocrats and socialists. Their opponents - comprador elements and smugglers — could hardly express their reluctance openly given their rather unpatriotic economic roles. The business classes vacillated in the debate unsure as to where to pitch their tents: they needed foreign capital to survive, yet, they needed state support and patronage from the lower classes. However, although the IMF structural adjustment loan was formally rejected by the Babangida regime in its first six months, many of its terms have since become policy: devaluation, termination of petroleum and other subsidies, increased prices for commodity production, abandonment of marketing boards, reductions in state-supported services, and preparation for the privatization of assorted parastatals. Moreover, in mid-1986 the government announced a short-term "Second-Tier" Foreign Exchange Market (FEM) in which demand and supply would determine the "real" value of the naira- i.e. IMF terms without the short-term benefits of foreign aid. The naira has since been devalued beyond all expected levels; by the beginning of 1996, it was exchanging officially at US$1 to N85. A combination of internal and external conditions and declarations favor local production and distribution, even if external inputs are expensive and scarce. Thus, in spite of resistance from the "popular" constituencies, the state used its power to direct the nation's economy towards privatization, deregulation, and desubsidization. Of course, poor implementation, corruption, inefficiency, and the uneven distribution of the costs and pains of adjustment have continued to vindicate the positions of the opposition and intensify challenges to state policy: this is likely to continue in the future.

Second, the intense "political debate" waged throughout the mid- to late-1980s in response to the government's announced intention to transfer power to a "Third Republic" first in 1990, then in 1992, and later in 1993 led to a distinct if orthodox dichotomy of preferences: "capitalism" or "socialism." Although both these forms of production and distribution are based on the assumption of democratic politics, in fact their implications for popular participation are considerable. There was also a set of second-order issues related to "federalism" on the one hand and to "praetorianism" on the other (i.e. how to divide power between center and states and between civilians and soldiers, respectively). The orthodox "superstructural" perspective has continued to focus on constitutional arrangements, particularly how to ensure democracy, accountability, propriety and discipline: federalism, confederalism, consociationalism (i.e. how to deal with regionalisms), military, diarchy, triarchy (ie. how to deal with modern officers and traditional rulers), and/or multi-, two-, one-, or no-party states (i.e. how to deal with the "politicians"). By contrast, the radical "substructural" viewpoint concentrated on economic positions, particularly control over the heights of the economy and the position of proletariat and peasantry, if not women. The assumption was that without a high degree of national control over the economy and relative autonomy from external influences, political and economic programs would always run into problems.

If retired generals, traditional scholars, and established entrepreneurs favored the former perspective, the latter was advocated by progressive intellectuals and a tacit coalition of interest groups in civil society: NLC, NEST, CRP, ASUU, CLO, CDHR, WIN, NANS, CD, DEAL, etc. And distinct interests favor different constitutional arrangements: regionalists prefer confederation, pluralists some form of consociationalism, centralists a unitary structure, officers a civilian-military diarchy, and traditional rulers a triarchy which would reinstate their role. This debate was orchestrated in 1986-87 by the Political Bureau, which included just one woman (Hilda Adefarasin) who was then National President of the conservative National Council of Womens' Societies (NCWS) and one radical (Edwin Madunagu), and in 1987-88 by the Constitution Review Commission, and was staged by a set of national institutions, such as the NIIA, NISER, NIPSS etc. In mid-1988 the 563-person Constituent Assembly was elected, by local authorities, and appointed, by the regime. By mid-1990 the plethora of political structures intended to advance the transition to a state designed and guided two-party democracy included the Directorate for Food, Roads and Rural Infrastructure (DFRRI), Directorate for Mass Mobilization, Social Justice and Economic Recovery (MAMSER), Centre for Democratic Studies (CDS), National Electoral Commission (NEC) and the Transition to Civil Rule Tribunal (TCRT). In short, the insecure state, however diminished and discredited, remained determined to contain and direct civil society. Again, as on the economic front, the state, under military control succeeded in superimposing a bourgeois political structure over other demands. This way, the political structure allowed for the strengthening of traditional political interests and coalitions which in turn carried within them traditional contradictions, suspicions, and conflicts. It is doubtful, recent efforts at whitewashing this structure under General Abacha notwithstanding, that Nigeria will find stability, harmony, and democracy in this arrangement in the future.

And third, related to, but not as widespread as, the other two parallel debates, that on "foreign policy" tended to transcend the artificial, orthodox distinctions between economics and politics and between domestic capacity and external capability. Concentrated at an invitational conference at NIPSS in Kuru, in early-1986, the international relations discussion pitched "radicals" against "pragmatists," notably the critical "Northern" perspective of Yusuf Bala Usman against the nationalist "Southern" viewpoint of Bolaji Akinyemi. Interestingly, this dichotomy was also ideological with Usman representing the militant radical perspective, and Akinyemi the conservative or orthodox perspective. The primary political issue was whether foreign policy could or should be separated from political economy; is good diplomacy enough or must it be supported by a well-oiled economy? Does a "nationalist" external stance require a "socialist" internal structure or not? "Realists" of the established NIIA "school" deny such a connection between economy and diplomacy whereas "radicals" of the alternative critical persuasion insist that progressive positions abroad (e.g. over MPLA in Angola) necessitate internal reorientation and redistribution. Thus intellectual and political debates have once again been joined, with the majoritarian if less assertive position being supportive of orthodox perspectives and policies while the minority of self-proclaimed "socialists" insist that external radicalism is unsupportable or unacceptable without internal reformism. These "official" discussions have been paralleled, as well as affected, by "unofficial" debates about several related yet unrecognized issues.

b) Unofficial Debates: Religion, Gender, Population And Environment

The conjuncture of military rule and economic austerity has concentrated minds. While the Shagari era was preoccupied by petro-naira issues of expansion and accumulation the subsequent Buhari and Babangida periods have revealed a greater willingness to look at more fundamental difficulties. The Abacha era on the other hand has been plagued with conflicts and crises and the mediation of economic opportunities (save in the enclave oil sector) by political developments and pressures. The easy assumptions which prevailed at the end of the heady decade of the 1970s - Nigerian pride and power — have been superseded by a healthy skepticism centering on what to do with minimal resources and opportunities. The swing of the pendulum has resulted in a new readiness to recognize some fundamental issues largely located in civil society. Amongst the most salient of these are religion, gender, population and environment. Since the initial effort at political liberalization, issues of constituency, identity, ethnicity, minority rights, and revenue allocation have become not just topical in national discourses, but also the bases of major conflicts and violence between the state and its custodians on the one hand, and particular communities on the other.

Religion has for long been a controversial issue in Nigeria: one indication of the clash of cultures across the Sahara. Islam spread South from the Mediterranean and the Sudan along trans-Sahara trade routes while Christianity spread north up river basins from the coast. Despite associations with alternative world views and powers and despite tensions within themselves — Shiite versus Suni and Protestant versus Catholic, respectively — Nigerians have incorporated and modified exogenous values and practices, melding indigenous forms into them. Moreover, established traditional religions have survived and prospered along with indigenous churches like Cherubim & Seraphim of the Lagos beaches and shanties. Religious devotion and fanaticism are also a function of class and time with more bourgeois forms being more restrained and secular. As Nigeria's problems have increased with the decrease in oil revenues so religious fundamentalism has grown - "Jesus people" in the South and Moslem "radicals," like the Maitaitsine, in the North. And religion becomes politicized whenever governments seem to become partisan, such as the Babangida regime's unanticipated decision to join the Organization of Islamic Conference (OIC) in 1985 which led to the inconclusive Shagaya Commission on religion, state and foreign policy. In short, religious tension and intolerance are symptomatic of difficult times and require sensitive treatment, especially as Nigeria has been ruled by "Northern" (i.e. "Moslem") regimes for over a decade. In fact, Christians argue that they have never had a chance at ruling the country as they easily point out that under the Obasanjo regime, the real power behind the throne was Major-General Shehu Yar Adua. This tradition of modern moderate Moslem political dominance is unlikely to change in the medium-term without considerable pressure and resistance, although the shadowy "Kaduna mafia" may be more influential in some (e.g. Buhari) than others (e.g. Babangida) (Takaya & Tyoden eds. 1987). Yet, considering the numerous "religious" riots-Kafanchan, Kano, Zaria, Ilorin, Bauchi, Bulumkutu, Jos, etc-and the increasing violence accompanying the clashes, there are enough grounds to expect religion to remain a rather testy and explosive issue in the future. The state has remained incapable of providing an acceptable basis for religious harmony, and not just its politicization, but also its deliberate manipulation by power elites, will continue to place religion within the most critical challenges the Nigerian state will continue to face.

Related in part to religion, particularly Islam, but also to other issues such as household, education, capital and accumulation is that of gender. Nigeria, like every other society, is a patriarchy. But, unlike some African countries, it has produced, tolerated and accepted, albeit to a limited degree, women's perspectives, interests and demands. There is, of course, a conservative, chauvinist reaction to women's pressure, however feminist, often disguised in traditionalist idioms: African women have always been subordinate, maternal, domestic and polygamous! Such chauvinistic positions are to be found at all levels of society, the universities inclusive. Nevertheless, the modern political culture of the state is sufficiently cosmopolitan that the place of women is now on the agenda. But whether orthodox women's or more radical "Women in Nigeria" positions are recognized and adopted remains problematic. Yet, the centrality of female labor, networks and roles is ever more apparent as Nigeria comes to rediscover and rely on the ubiquitous informal sector: the real privatization associated with structural adjustment. A more self-reliant political economy of necessity must recognize the agricultural, domestic, entrepreneurial and rural roles as well as educational, household, professional and welfare contributions of Nigerian women. Furthermore, Nigerians like other women are coming to demand their rightful say in issues of sexual as well as social reproduction. In short, in the mid-term future, Nigerian women are likely to become more vocal, insistent and visible whether men, in or out of power and property, appreciate, acknowledge and accept their claims or not. It is interesting to note that even political debates are beginning to take on specific gender dimensions as men are increasingly being blamed for messing up the economy and politics, organizing coups, squandering the nation's resources, and remaining incapable of reaching accommodation with each other. While suggestions which advocate the handing over of power to women might be simplistic, even opportunistic, as there are contradictions even within women's constituencies, such positions demonstrate that gender issues are coming to the fore and will become critical in future political and other discourses and coalitions.

The size and distribution of Nigeria's population has long been a controversial and contentious issue leading to census riots in the 1960s and even to the first coup. Whilst lack of reliable demographic data is one obstacle to effective planning - one crucial element in the run-up to civilian rule in 1992 (before it was abruptly postponed) was the national census conducted in November 1991 - a more immediate issue is the rapidity and desirability of population expansion. Whilst "overpopulation" is always a relative and sensitive issue, new land decrees along with land alienation and privatization as well as exponential desertification have produced the specter of land hunger. Moreover, the land-people equation has changed as the former has been alienated by cities, roads and other modern infrastructures while the latter has been expanded by improved welfare facilities. In the short-term the population explosion is leading to exponential inequalities in land tenure and hence agricultural production, now exacerbated by the renewed attractiveness of peasant production. In the medium-term it may produce radical social movements along with pro-control (pro-choice) policies. And in the longer-term, if unchecked because of indigenous pro-life values, it will exacerbate economic difficulties and ecological decay. Interestingly, the pains of adjustment and pressures arising from inflation, poverty, unemployment and general insecurity under structural adjustment seems to be influencing population control in a "natural" way, now reinforced by the emerging specter of the AIDS virus in West Africa. The struggle is now mainly on how to survive rather than on how to have more children!

Finally, although the least recognized of the unofficial debates, is the issue of the environment. Nigeria, like most African, especially Sahelian, states is situated in a delicate ecological area, from Saharan to rain forest zones. Population pressures, agricultural policies, lumber extraction, oil production, marine degradation, industrial pollution, garbage disposal and sewage systems all contribute to an ecological crisis. Despite impressive policies, Nigeria's record of on- and off-shore environmental protection is poor; the garbage-strewn cities, creeping desert, gas-flares and oil-spills are the most notorious cases of continuing pollution but the land-people equation is getting out of whack, as symbolized by the physical tenuousness of both new states created in 1987 - Katsina along the Sahel and Akwa-Ibom in the Delta. Social, especially economic, issues may constitute the short-term national agenda particularly in an intense period of structural adjustment but, in the longer-term, ecological problems loom. The dumping of more than 1,000 crates and sacks containing toxic wastes imported by "unknown persons" from Italy in 1988 demonstrates not only the corruption of the security forces and the local bourgeoisie but also the vulnerability of Nigeria to externally-generated environmental degradation (*The African Guardian* June 20, 1988; *Newswatch* June 11, 1990; Ihonvbere 1994b). Despite the imperatives of economic development, then, disregard of ecological difficulties, from desertification to lateriteisation, will pose predictable and profound sociopolitical crises unless recognized and treated urgently. In short, structural adjustment may yet be superseded by a mixture of self-reliance and state intervention to protect an endangered environment, cross-conditionalities notwithstanding.

c) Alternative Scenarios: Political Economy, Culture And Fortune

The trio of current official debates identified above can be divided into deliberations about political economy, political culture and political fortune, respectively. These three features of Nigeria's future are clearly inter-related - economic direction, political situation and international conditions are in reality inseparable - yet they are treated in different ways by distinct coalitions inside and outside Nigeria; and they also reflect rather diverse views of the world: materialism, modernization and dependence, respectively. Although analytic and prescriptive positions are intertwined here we concentrate on the latter because of their implicit projections of the future. And we attempt to reflect the Nigerian flavor of these debates given the country's ability to internalize and revise general concepts and stances, reorganizing the impact of post-Cold War global contexts and moods on Nigerian as other discourses..

The two intersecting economic alternatives facing Nigeria are between more or less capitalism and socialism on the one hand and between more or less indigenous production and accumulation on the other. For both analytic and prescriptive purposes these need to be separated, as the internal versus international orientation or direction of either capitalism or socialism cannot be assumed, despite rhetoric to the contrary. The national mixed economy which emerged out of the colonial, civil war and petroleum periods has been characterized as one of "nurture capitalism"; the state provided *de facto* subsidies in the form of infrastructures and contracts (Schatz 1977). Yet the effectiveness and efficiency of this state role are quite debatable as personal corruption and accumulation apparently took precedence over collective development and self-sustainment (Adamolekun 1985; Joseph 1983). Nevertheless, the 1975-85 decade of policies did produce a Nigerian capital-owning fraction even if it is dependent still on external technology, management and inputs (Biersteker 1978, 1987).

The socialist critique of Nigerian capitalism is, in some sense, rather crude and structuralist, refusing to recognize either that capital has been partially indigenized or that organization under socialism would be just as difficult as under capitalism, if not more so: no bourgeoisie is above corruption and all avoid accountability. To be fair, the socialist camp is divided into two: the super-nationalists who see the "enemy" as solely foreign and not indigenous capitalism. This group is also in a sense super-optimistic in seeing proletarian and peasant forces as almost automatic supporters of structural changes. This group of socialists, remaining orthodox or dogmatic, refuse to seek pragmatic accommodations in their politics, praxis, and debates. To be sure, this mode of analysis has changed over the years, giving birth to "radical' scholars have come to focus on the internal relations of power, politics, production and exchange (Ake (ed), 1985; Ihonvbere and Falola (eds), 1991). This latter school continues to acknowledge the place and impact of history, imperialism, neocolonialism, and transnational domination and exploitation of the Nigerian social formation. Yet, their conclusions, prescriptions, and projections take off from social and class balances at the substructure, the alignment and realignment of class forces and constituencies, and are quite open to necessary strategic alliances to further the processes of structural change and accumulation. Nonetheless the economic choices facing Nigeria are neither easy or speedy: Nigerian socialism as well as capitalism would take considerable efforts to effect if it was to survive. And greater self-reliance in food, manufacturing and technology cannot be realized overnight under any political dispensation. Contemporary structural adjustment is just the beginning, not the end, of change towards a viable, sustainable political economy. And the demise of state socialism in much of the Second and Third Worlds, Africa in particular, cannot but affect socialist demands in Nigeria requiring strategic and realistic repackaging of discourses and praxis.

If the nuanced materialist mode of analysis adopted in this text is correct then future scenarios based on it should be reasonably reliable: the dialectics of economics, politics and culture. We will postpone any ranking of the four alternative political economies abstracted from debates and histories until identifying and introducing them, although our predispositions may show through in the discussion itself. The four scenarios reflect alternative positions articulated in the parallel national debates of the mid-1980s. They constitute mixtures of social forces, economic factors and political choices. They also represent plausible extrapolations from salient conditions and relations and may be ranked on a scale from continuity/conservative to change/radical, respectively, as well as from more to less likely. All must now be situated in the context of intensive national structural adjustment in the beginning of the 1990s- devaluation, debt, negotiations, deregulation and privatizations- as extensive global changes with the end of the Bretton Woods as well as Cold war systems.

The first, "official" alternative is that of revived growth with renewed civilian rule: 1998 onwards? This future is reflected in the continuing political debate as well as in successive national plans. In particular, the continuing commitment of the military to handing power over to elected civilians. While several doubts continue to surround this promise and process (based on past experiences), civil society remains adamant in its demand for democracy and total demilitarization. This scenario assumes a stable higher price for petroleum as well as the extension and rehabilitation of national infrastructures and industries, particularly agriculture, along with an orderly and sustained return to non-military government. A mixed economy, possibly with a higher degree of private ownership than at present because of structural adjustment conditionalities, would co-exist with responsible democratic government in a federal framework. And class, regional, religious and gender differences would be minimized rather than exacerbated: Babangida's dream of the early-1990s, reminiscent of that of Obasanjo in the late-1970s, but different from Abacha's constraints in the later 1990s.

Such a pragmatic projection is based on the assumption of regional, continental and global continuities: regional manufactured exports for labor imports, continental redevelopment, and global revival. Although such a cluster of assumptions is rather fanciful for most "Fourth" world African states, given Nigeria's relatively privileged position as a potential semi-periphery with a large and diversified resource base it may yet benefit from a New International Division of Labor, especially if it can find an appropriate niche in it. However, to capture any gains from such an advantaged position would require considerable effort to restructure and sustain the central "triple alliance" among state, transnational and national capitals (Evans, 1979); i.e. for a mixed economic strategy to be effective it must be organized and efficient. If the current condition of disorganization continues then any aspirations towards semi-peripheral let alone NIC status would be dashed. And such an opportunity may not return soon. Nigeria already squandered the 1970's petro-naira windfall through indulgence and corruption. If it fails to industrialize, revive agriculture, diversify and achieve a degree of self-reliance before the mid-1990s it may never become a NIC, let alone the Brazil of Africa. The emerging global economy, dominated by the Pacific Rim, is unlikely to be beneficent towards disorganized and corruption-ridden states. Some strong and sustainable corporatist arrangement among capitals, regimes and labor might be necessary for Nigeria to become a developmental state in the twenty-first century.

The primary alternative advanced to Nigerian capitalism is Nigerian socialism: a democratic, popular redistribution of power and property so that Basic Human Needs and rights obtain throughout the political economy. Although advanced by several parties and interest groups, notably the

Action Group, UPN, PRP and SDP in earlier democratic spaces and now NLC, ASUU, WIN, NADECO, CD, and CDHR among others, such a future has not been thoroughly articulated; it remains a largely rhetorical response to the contradictions of the established mixed economy. When the ban on party politics was lifted by the Babangida regime in 1989, the Peoples' Solidarity Party (PSP) carried on the tradition established by the AG and UPN. With the failure to register any of the associations and the creation of two political parties by the military regime, the Social Democratic Party (SDP) continued to advocate leftist options. In reality, given the actors, its programs, contradictions, and opportunistic gestures, the now defunct SDP was no different from its populist predecessors, the AG and UPN. Under Abacha, the five registered political parties are yet to demonstrate that they are not part of the junta's political game plan, and they have not distinguished themselves ideologically (Ihonvbere 1996).

Unfortunately, though not unexpectedly, the "left" in Nigeria, although vocal and eloquent, is hardly homogeneous for reasons of personality and ideology, region and gender. Furthermore, its prospects of assuming power are quite minimal despite intensifying inequalities and impoverishment. Alternative explanations are advanced for any regression such as ethnicity, recession, austerity and imperialism: "false consciousness" perhaps, but powerful and persuasive nonetheless. The left has not been helped either by the rapid decline of socialist governments all over the world, a situation which has seriously split the traditional constituency of leftists - labor and students - but it may benefit from *de facto* political conditionalities - pluralism and participation, based on elements of civil society as well as political economy not just a formal two-party constitutional structure. The participation of several "leftists" and "activists" drawn largely from the universities in the various openly repressive and corrupt juntas of Babangida and now Abacha has also done a lot to delegitimize that constituency as many openly engaged in activities they had once virulently attacked!

Thus given the underdeveloped political economy, "revolutionary pressures" are not yet ripe in Nigeria: neither peasantry nor proletariat nor the unemployed are mobilized or organized enough and socialist parties and platforms are not yet sufficiently defined. There certainly exist a lot of anger, disillusionment, frustrations, hopelessness, and alienation from the state and its institutions, but these have not coalesced into a "revolutionary" situation. Even the repressive and corrupt military still has its supporters. Palliative and cosmetic initiatives like failed contracts, failed parastatals, war on corruption, etc. by the Abacha junta in 1995-96 was enough to buy some support for military rule from sections of the public. Attempts by the labor congress to form a Labor Party in 1989 did not meet with the expected mass support and the military refused to register the association as a political party. Moreover, the so-called "newbreed" politicians and two-party format of the Babangida era as well as political initiatives under the Abacha dispensation have tended to exclude the real left. In fact, the Babangida regime describe the left as "extremists," "noise makers," "trouble makers" and "confusionists." Abacha has adopted a similar posture towards the left and intellectuals. This means that they are given little or no space to penetrate the political process and so influence the content of debates and direction of politics. However, a medium-term extension of the current crisis might yet lead to such a conjuncture if the left is persistent and coherent, receiving judicious external support from reformist social democratic as well as remaining communist parties in both North and South; this would be a truly contradictory result of protracted structural adjustment! The recent emergence of scores of civil liberty organizations, the rapid proletarianization of the middle-class, the reconceptualization of old ideological postures and methods and the increasing linkages between liberal, nationalist, democratic and socialist forces in the struggle to strengthen civil society and ensure that the military leaves office, are positive pointers in the direction of this post-1998 (?) scenario.

A third possible alternative, particularly if both the previous pair prove to be elusive, is the advent of authoritarianism of either aristocratic or fascist inclinations. Such a repressive response would be most likely if either the economy continued to falter and/or the polity fails to sustain democracy (Shaw & Ihonvbere, 1989; Ihonvbere 1994a). Thus, if the political economy remains in chaos by the end of the 1990s and NIC status proves elusive then centralized repressive military rule may be inevitable. This would become more of an alternative if the political class remains irresponsible, weak, opportunistic, and factionalized along regional, ethnic, and religious lines. Such a neo-fascist or corporatist scenario could of course be an interim stage in the establishment of a self-sustaining regional military-industrial complex but it is more likely to consist of a non-directed bourgeois holding operation merely to defend a shaky status quo. Nigeria's military and security agencies have to date been as disorganized as the rest of the political economy, when it is convenient to be so. However, over the years the military has come a long way. It has, sent hundreds of its officers to higher institutions. It has in addition to the Nigerian Defence Academy, established a military university as well as the Command and Staff College at Jaji, an elitist institution. It has established a War College and its top officers have continued to emphasize the need for "professionalism." Furthermore, the military has imposed its "superiority" over other fractions of the bourgeois classes, established a tradition of subordination of the police, security services and budgetary institutions to it and reorganized the patterns of accumulation around itself (Ihonvbere 1991d). It would not be an exaggeration to claim that nothing goes on in contemporary Nigeria, from the selection of vice-chancellors for the universities to the installation of traditional rulers without the involvement of the military! Moreover, despite disclaimers to the contrary an authoritarian regime might be compatible with the adjustment project's economic imperatives. Unlike the Babangida and Abacha regimes, such a regime must place before the people a clear program for reconstruction and recovery and thus buy support for both emergency and unorthodox policies and programs.

If such characteristics continue, the possibility of another return to military rule after October 1998, if it ever comes to pass, will be quite high. The human rights rhetoric under which the Babangida regime came to power has been difficult to maintain under the Abacha junta which has waged a more vigorous battle against popular constituencies and organizations. In the case of Babangida, he had benefited from the general hostility to the repressive and intolerant tactics of the Buhari-Idiagbon junta. However, by mid-1991, it had become obvious, even to the most ardent supporter of that clique, that a military regime cannot be relied upon to protect human rights and democracy in an expanded sense no matter how explicit SAP's political contradictions have become. Very few had expected Abacha to commit his junta to a human rights policy. His record in the Babangida dispensation was a clear pointer to the future direction of his regime. He has not disappointed observers with his mixture of guided transition to democracy, emphasis on stability and economic recovery, and the asphyxiation of civil society. Alternatively, a northern, Islamic and aristocratic revival could provide another locus for authoritarian control of a fundamentalist variety: a Kano (religious) rather than Kaduna (entrepreneurial) mafia? This would be far-fetched given the increasing interplay of class forces, the alignment of political interests, and efforts by fractions of the bourgeois class to construct a national project.

If all three previous projections fail to materialize, a fourth prospect is for a descent into anarchy. Given Nigeria's somewhat anarchic culture and condition, such a scenario is not implausible; the failure of central and/or regional governments to maintain institutions and infrastructures along with local survival strategies and appropriate technologies could lead *de facto* to a series of regional "states" not unlike the precolonial conditions outlined in the first chapter. Recent situations in Chad, Mali, Somalia, Ghana, Liberia, Uganda or Zaire are indicative of such situations in which central regimes become dissociated from the national political economy and local warlords or communities establish regional structures; a latter-day "savior" for disaffected regional-cum-religious communities is not implausible. The degree of disorder, dislocation and "decentralization" is unpredictable, but once Nigeria's centripetal tendencies, which have already resulted in civil war and 32 states, were released, reintegration would surely prove problematic if not impossible; several years of structural adjustment, and expanding informal sector, of a shrinking state, may retard prospects for the reexertion of centralization.

Such a scenario may be favored, of course, by internal secessionists and subregional detractors, such as neighboring francophone states. The recent spate of bombings and acts of sabotage suggest that several underground interests are beginning to emerge and are willing to challenge even the military. While still in its infancy, such movements can be expected to draw support from exiles, alienated communities, politicians, and demobilized and retired military officers. Already the generation of retired military officers and the scores of millionaires dotted all over the country live and operate above the law. They get away with unbelievable violations of laid-down laws and with human rights abuses. Many have tried to carve out an alternative, even parallel state, thus relying less on the regime except for primitive accumulation. They operate their own personal electricity, security services, water supply and airlines. They rely on foreign schools for their children, foreign hospitals, courier services in place of public postal services, spend their vacations in Europe and North America, carry out their banking activities abroad and install private satellite dishes to enable them to watch foreign television stations. Their actions since the ban on politics was lifted and their unrepentant belief in ethnic, regional, religious and money politics mean that they have learnt little from the mistakes of the past. By the early 1990s, corruption had reached such an unprecedented level that news about missing millions of naira hardly attracted any reaction from Nigerians, it is now the natural or normal thing to do. The April 1990 Majors Saliba Mukoro/Gideon Orka led coup which, if it had succeeded would have precipitated a major ethnic and religious debacle, is a clear pointer to the fact that possibilities for break-down are certainly not implausible (Agbese and Ihonvbere 1997; Ihonvbere 1991a; Okoye in *African Guardian* September 24, 1991). But this remains an unattractive possibility, implying long-term decline for most peoples and relations, and excluding other futures including that of national renaissance and self-reliance; an informal economy on a "national" scale.

Amongst the major variables or issues in each of these scenarios are, then, at the level of substructure, political economy (notably petroleum production and distribution, non-oil importation, consumption and production, the value and price of money, environmental constraints and opportunities, state sector activities, finance and share-holding, labor and capital, rural and informal sectors, and the elusiveness of Basic Human Needs) and, at the level of superstructure, the political culture (military or civilian rule, parliamentary or presidential system, regions, ethnicity, religions, gender, generation, laws, customs and ideology). These two are, of course, inter-related and inseparable - economic changes affect political relations and vice versa - and constitute the internal determinants of foreign policy, whose impact is also affected by external conditions and perceptions.

In the Nigerian, as other, Third World formations, it would be dogmatic and unrealistic to argue that either political economy or culture is more important than the other. Rather, sub- and super-structure exist in a continuous "dialectical" relationship. However, there are differences between peripheral and other social formations. So to assert, dogmatically, as do some Nigerian "socialists," that proletarian control is inevitable, without a clear understanding of the nature of systemic coalitions, contradictions and conflicts as well as a clear alternative agenda, is naive. Thus, in futures as in historical studies, Marxist methodology may be more reliable guide than Marxist theory, even disregarding the challenges posed by the disintegration and redirection of much of the old Second World. For, in a period of economic contraction, social adjustment, and political repression, to anticipate the success of progressive social organization is both idealistic and simplistic; the likely political and economic transitions towards 1998 (?) involve profound change for all social forces, not just capital and labor.

In any social analysis and prediction it is imperative to recognize class coalitions as well as contradictions; sections of the indigenous bourgeoisie are more cohesive than ever because the challenges to and constraints on it are so intense. The middle class, meanwhile, is being marginalized politically and economically as inflation and repression continue. And the working class is being demobilized as deindustrialization intensifies; while the peasantry is being resuscitated as producer prices improve in some sectors in response to the oil glut and deregulation. Thus to expect non-bourgeois cohesion in a fluid situation when proletariat and peasantry are in flux and in some conflict is equally naive. Finally, even if the political economy of Nigeria is capitalist, displaying increasing degrees of inequity, the political culture is neo-democratic, resistant to any homogeneous, centralized solution. Thus socio-economic contradictions do not inevitably lead to political pressures as "intervening" variables such as ethnicity, region, religion and gender may moderate or divert tensions: hence the irrepressible impacts to date of the structural adjustment "project."

d) Conclusions: Alternative Futures

Given the ambiguity between Nigeria as model (of modernization a la OPEC) or muddle (of underdevelopment), it is hazardous to predict one future rather than another. However, if the analysis of this volume is at all accurate and reliable then certain options can at least be excluded over the rest of the 1990s -- a form of prediction by elimination- notwithstanding the unpredictabilities of the changing global economic and political contexts.

First, on the optimistic side, we expect that Nigeria will not slip into the real periphery of the Fourth World: its population, environment, energy and resourcefulness would militate against any lasting loss of semi-peripheral status. If, at the international level, Nigeria remains something of a leader or magnet in West Africa, at the political level it is unlikely to remain perpetually undemocratic; its people are too irrepressible. If, in environmental terms, Nigeria can control its population and desertification then it should be able to feed itself, despite the limits of so-called Green Revolution or river basin development. At the level of the economy, notwithstanding changes in the price and production of oil and gas, Nigeria could become more self-reliant as a "national" capitalist system; certainly the conditions of structural adjustment are intended to revive agriculture and accumulation for the whole political economy once debt has been restructured and reduced. None of these optimistic conditions are inevitable, however, nor will they necessarily occur in sequence. On the other hand, it is a tribute to Nigeria's considerable resources and resilience that such a mid-term future is still conceivable after civil war, then oil boom, and now "new" world order. To be sure, national political upsets or global economic shocks would undo such a scenario rapidly. But Nigeria's potential - for growth as well as greed - is superior to that of most African political economies; and its potential linkages and compatibilities with post-apartheid South Africa may reinforce such a trend.

On the other hand, however, such a optimistic view may be quite mistaken. If the new international division of labor continues to shift away from commodity, even oil, producers in the Third World towards high-tech manufacturers around the Pacific Rim, then Nigeria's petroleum and gas oversupply and underprice may be generalized to its remaining primary colonial commodities, such as cocoa, tin, cotton, palm oil and groundnut, despite their post-reform renaissance in the private sector. In which case, from a mixed mood, some degree of self-reliance will become an imperative rather than a preference. To be sure, Nigeria has a diverse resource base through which to become more inwardlooking. But whether its peoples will accept relative deprivation and concentration remains to be seen; adjustment is not always with a human face, although the welfare state was never comprehensive in Nigeria. Such an economic condition might lead towards either bourgeois fascism or proletarian dictatorship; it is unlikely to result in either petty bourgeois democracy or proletarian power. National or state capitalism or socialism would be the order of the day, with declining levels of tolerance of either dissent or affluence; i.e. if contradictions outpace coalitions then tensions will ensue. In anticipated hard times with limited choices, the most likely scenario is more state roles but less state resources; i.e. intervention with liberalization as anticipated in the structural adjustment direction. This contradiction will become central rather than labor struggles or peasant protests. For most Nigerians, survival (let alone surplus), will be a preoccupation based on personal resourcefulness rather than collective responses: the ubiquitous informal sector.

Thus it would appear that the choice for Nigeria is not between orthodox forms of either capitalism or socialism but rather between (semi-) peripheral state capitalism or peripheral state socialism. Given the historical problems of state structures in Nigeria - institutions without authority - effective central control will be eroded by federalist and anarchist elements. On the other hand, it is apparent that neither "industrial" capitalism nor "scientific" socialism are likely in the medium- or even longer-term given Nigeria's distinctive history, society and status, as well as the post - industrial and - socialist global order. The challenge for analysis as well as for policy is, then, to identify middle-order "hybrids" that can be reasonably expected to work in the Nigerian context over the medium-term. Neither the neoclassical nor socialist orthodoxies are appropriate as revealed by Nigerians' consistent rejection of both and in the context of a changing global order. Ongoing global reconceptualization and recomposition of political and economic ideologies call for an abandonment of old orthodoxies without abandoning social commitment and the organization of society in the interest of the vast majority. Will some mix of structural adjustment and controlled participation be both designed and effective? This question becomes more salient in a post-Cold War period: the place of an aspiring middle power in the New International Divisions of Labor and Power, given economic and political contradictions due to debt negotiations and reforms.

Seen in historical perspective, then, the palm oil and fuel oil political economies have both been quite brief and transitional with pre-capitalist peasant modes of production remaining vibrant and resistant, and with neo-capitalist forms being grafted onto these as colonial and post-colonial regimes and conditions demand. In short, the peasantry, (particularly the female formations and coalitions) attempt to deal with changeable colonial, post-neocolonial and neo-colonial opportunities and constraints. They, rather than the new bourgeoisie, have been the foundation of modern Nigeria. Given the elusiveness of development, it is unlikely that this peasantry will either be proletarianized or repressed in the medium-term. Other classes, fractions and regimes may come and go but the Nigerian peasantry will go on, well beyond both 1998 (if it is not postponed or declared "unrealistic") and 2000. This confident prediction is one definite comment on the perpetuation of uneven development in Nigeria; it is hardly a risky proposition given the country's distinctive history and contemporary political economy. So given its roots and relevance, the masquerade is likely to continue, policies and plans notwithstanding.

BIBLIOGRAPHY

Achebe, Chinua. (1960). *No Longer at Ease*. London: Heinemann.

_____. (1966). *A Man of the People*. London: Heinemann.

_____. (1982). *The Trouble with Nigeria*. Enugu: Fourth Dimension.

_____. (1985). *Things Fall Apart*. London: Heinemann.

Adam, Mohammed (1987). "Nigeria: the busted boom," *International Perspectives* January-February.

Adamolekun, Lapido. (1985). *The Fall of the Second Republic*. Ibadan: Spectrum

_____. (1986) "Sense and Nonsense," *West Africa* 3584, 12 May: 1992- 1994.

Adamu, Haroun & Alaba Ogunsanwo. (1983). *Nigeria: The Making of the Presidential System - 1979 general elections* Kano: Triumph.

Adedeji, Adabayo. (ed.) (1981). *Indigenization of African Economies*. London: Hutchinson.

_____. & Timothy M. Shaw. (eds) (1985). *Economic Crisis in Africa:African Perspectives on Development Problems and Potentials*. Boulder: Lynne Reinner.

Adekanye, Bayo J.(ed.) (1989). "The Military, Social Classes and revolution," *Studies in Politics and Society* (5) Special issue.

_____. (1995). "Structural Adjustment, Democratization and Rising Ethnic Tensions in Africa," *Development and Change* Vol. 26 (2).

Adeotun, Phillips. (1987). "Structural Adjustment of What? By Whom? For Whom?" *Centre for Management Development* Lagos.

_____. (1990). *Economic impact of Nigeria's structural Adjustment Programme*. Ibadan: NISER.

_____. & E.C. Ndekwu (eds.) (1987). *Structural Programme in a Developing Economy: The Case of Nigeria*. Ibadan: NISER.

Afonja, Simi & Tola Pearce. (eds) (1986) *Social Change in Nigeria* Lagos: Longman.

Agbese, Pita. (1989). "State, Media and the Imperatives of Repression: An Analysis of the ban on *Newswatch*," *International Third World Studies Journal and Review*. Vol. 1, 2, 235-334.

_____. (1991). "Technology Transfer or Automobile

Imperialism: some evidence from Nigeria" in M. D. Vajpeyi, and R. Natarajan(eds.). *Technology and Development: Public Policy and Managerial Issues.* Jaipur: Rawat Publications, 311-334.

_____. and Julius O. Ihonvbere (1991). *The State, Structural Adjustment and Crisis in Contemporary Nigeria.* Washington, D.C.: Howard University Press.

Ajayi, Ade & Ade & B. Ikara. (1985). *Evolution of Political Culture in Nigeria.* Ibadan: Ibadan University Press.

Ajayi, J. F. A. & Michael Crowther. (eds.) (1971 and 1974). *History of Nigeria* (Two Volumes) London: Longman.

Ake, Claude. (1978). *Revolutionary Pressures in Africa.* London: Zed.

_____. (1981a). "Off to a good start but dangers await..." *West Africa* 3330, 25 May: 1163

_____. (1981b). *A Political Economy of Africa.* London: Longman.

_____. (ed) (1985). *Political Economy of Nigeria.* London: Longman.

_____. (1996). *Democratization and Development in Africa.* Washington, D.C.: The Brookings Institution.

Akeredolu-Ale, E. O. (1975). *The Underdevelopment of Indigenous Entrepreneurship in Nigeria.* Ibadan: Ibadan University Press.

_____. (ed) (1975). *Social Development in Nigeria: A Survey of Policy and Research.* Ibadan: University Press Limited for NISER.

Akindele, R.A. & Bassey E. Ate (1986). "Nigeria's Foreign Policy, 1986-2000 AD," *Afrika Spectrum* 86(3): 363-370.

_____. & Oye Oyediran (1986). "Federalism and foreign policy in Nigeria." *International Journal* 41 (3), Summer: 600-625

Akinwomo, A. A. (1964). "The Sociology of Nigerian Tribalism," *Phylon* Vol. 23, (Summer).

Akinyemi, Bolajia A. (ed) (1978). *Nigeria and the World: readings in Nigerian foreign policy.* Ibadan: OUP for NIIA.

_____. (1979). "Mohammed/Obasanjo foreign policy," In Oyeleye Oyediran (ed) *Nigerian Government and Politics under Military Rule, 1966-1979.* London: Macmillan. 150-168

Akpan, N. U. (1982). *Public Administration in Nigeria.*

London: Longman.

Albert, I. O. (1993). *Inter-Ethnic Relations in a Nigerian City: A Historical Perspective of the Hausa-Igbo Conflicts in Kano 1953-1991.* IFRA Occasional Publications, No. 2.

Aluko, Olajide (1981a). "Necessity and freedom in Nigerian foreign policy." *Inaugural Lecture, University of Ife* 17 March.

_____. (1981b). *Essays in Nigerian Foreign Policy.* London: George Allen & Unwin.

_____. (1987). "The Study of International Relations in Nigeria," *Millenium* 16(2), Summer:

Aluko, Sam. (1987). *The Burden of Economic Structural Adjustment: The Nigerian Scenario.* Ile-Ife: Convocation Ceremony Lecture

Amadiume, Ifi (1987). *Male Daughters, Female Husbands.* London: Zed.

Amnesty International (1994). *Nigeria: Military Government Clampdown on Opposition.* London: Amnesty.

Amu, Lawrence (n.d.) *Oil Glut and the Nigerian Economy.* Lagos: Nigerian National Petroleum Corporation.

Andrae, Gunilla & Bjorn Beckmkan (1985). *The Wheat Trap: Bread and Under-development in Nigeria.* London: Zed.

_____. (1987). *Industry Goes Farming: The Nigerian Raw Material Crisis and the Case of Textiles and Cotton.* Uppsala: Scandinavian Institute of African Studies. Research Report No. 80.

Anene, J. C. (1960). *Southern Nigeria in Transition 1885-1906.* Cambridge: CUP.

Anifowose, Remi. (1982). *Violence and Politics in Nigeria: The Tiv and Yoruba Experience.* New York: NOK.

Anikpo, Mark. (1985). "Nigria's Evolving Class Structure," in Claude Ake ed., *Political Economy of Nigeria.* London: Longman.

Anise, Ladun. (1979). "Ethnicity and National Integration in West Africa: Some Theoretical Considerations," in Ramond L. Hall ed., *Ethnic Autonomy-Comparative Dynamics: North America, Europe, and the Developing World.* New York: Pergamon.

Arikpo, Okoi (1968). *The Development of Modern Nigeria.* Harmondsworth: Penguin.

Arnold, Guy (1977). *Modern Nigeria.* London: Longman.

Atanda, J.A.. & A.Y. Aliyu (eds) (1985). *Political Development:Proceedings of National Conference on*

Nigeria Since Independence. Volume 1. Zaria: Panel on Nigeria since Independence History Project.

Ate. Basseu. (1987). *Decolonization and Dependence: The Development of Nigerian-U.S. Relations, 1960- 1984.* Boulder: Westview.

Awolowo, Obafemi (1970). "The Financing of the Nigerian Civil War and its Implications for the Future Economy of the Nation," *Geographical Society and Federalist Society of Nigeria.* University of Ibadan, 16 May.

Ayandele, E.A. (1966). *The Missionary Impact on Modern Nigeria, 1842-1914.* London: Longman.

Ayida, Allison A. (1990). *The Rise and Fall of Nigeria* Lagos: Malthouse

Ayu, Iyorchia, D. (1966). *Essays in Popular Struggle: Fela, Students' Patriotism and the Nicaraguan Revolution.* Oguta: Zim Pan-African.

Bach, Daniel (1986). *Le Nigeria Contemporain.* Paris: Editions du CNRS.

Baker, Pauline H. (1984). "A Giant Staggers: Nigeria as an emerging regional power," in Bruce E. Arlinghaus (ed) *African Security Issues: Sovereignty, Stability and Solidarity.* Boulder: Westview, 76-97.

Baldwin, David (1978). "Power and Social Exchange," *American Political Science Review* Vol. 72, (4).

Bangura, Yusuf (1987). "IMF/World Bank Conditionality and Nigeria's Structural Adjustment Programme," in Kjell J. Havenik (ed) *The IMF and the World Bank in Africa.* Uppsala: Scandinavian Institute of African Studies, 95-116.

_____. (1991a). "Steyr-Nigeria: The Recession and Workers' Struggles in the Vehicle Assembly Plant," in Inga Brandell (ed), *Workers in Third-World Industrialization.* London: Macmillan, 177-196.

_____. (1994). *The Search for Identity: Ethnicity, Religion and Political Violence.* Geneva: UNRISD, Occassional Paper No. 6.

_____. and Bjorn Beckman (1991). "African Workers and Structural Adjustment With a Nigerian Case-Study," in D. Ghai (ed.). *IMF and the South: Social Impact of Crisis and Adjustment.* London: Zed Books.

Barber, Karin (1982). "Popular Reactions to the Petro-naira," *Journal of Modern African Studies* 20(3),September: 431-450.

Barbour, K. Micahel *et al* (1982). *Nigeria in Maps*. London:
    Hodder & Stoughton.
Banton, Michael (1994). "Modeling Ethnic and National
    Relations," *Ethnic and Racial Studies* Vol. 17, (1).
_____. and Mohd Manson (1992). "The Study of
    Ethnic Alignment: A New Technique and an
    Application in Malaysia," *Ethnic and Racial Studies*
    Vol. 15, (4).
Barth, Fredrik. ed. (1969). *Ethnic Groups and Boundaries*.
    Boston: Little Brown.
Bates, R. H. (1974). "Ethnic Competition and Moderniza-
    tion in Contemporary Africa," *Comparative Political
    Studies* Vol. 6, (4).
Beckman, Bjorn (1981a). "Imperialism and the 'National
    Bourgeoisie,'" *Review of African Political Economy* 22,
    October-December: 5-19.
_____. (1981b). "Oil, State Expenditure and Class Formation
    in Nigeria," *Nordic Association of Political Scientists*,
    Turku, August.
_____. (1982). "Whose State: state and capitalist
    development in Nigeria," *Review of African Political
    Economy* 23, January-April.
_____. (1985). "Neo-Colonialism, Capitalism, and the
    State in Nigeria" in Henry Bernstein and Bonnie K.
    Campbell (eds) *Contradictions of Accumulation in
    Africa: Studies in Economy and State*. Beverly Hills:
    Sage: 71-113.
Berry, Saras. (1984). "Oil and the Disappearing Peasantry:
    Accumulation, Differentiation and Underdevelope-
    ment in Western Nigeria," *African Economic History*
    13: 1-22.
_____. (1985). *Fathers Work for Their Sons: Accumulation,
    Mobility and Class Formation in an Extended Yoruba
    Community*. Berkeley: University of California
    Press.
Bhambiri, R. S. (1971). "Second National Development
    Plan: a selective appraisal," *Nigerian Journal of
    Economics and Social Studies* Vol. 13, 2, July.
Bienen, Henry & V.P. Diejomaoh (eds) (1981). *The
    Political Economy of Income Distribution in Nigeria*.
    New York: Holmes & Meier.
Biesteker, Thomas J. (1978). *Distortion or Development?
    Contending Perspectives on the Multinational
    Corporation*. Cambridge: MIT Press.

_____. (1987). *Multinationals, the State, and Control of the Nigerian Economy.* Princeton: Princeton University Press

Bradshaw, York (1985). "Dependent Development in Black Africa: A Crosss-national Study," *American Sociological Review* Vol. 50, (2)

Brown, David. (1989). "The State of Ethnicity and the Ethnicity of the State: Ethnic Politics in Southeast Asia," *Ethnic and Racial Studies* Vol. 12, (1).

Burns, Allan (1955). *History of Nigeria.* London: Allen and Unwin.

Caccia, Goffredo. (1983). "Nigeria: oil plot or oil glut?" *Journal of African Marxists* 3: 78-92.

Campbell, B. and Loxley, J. (eds.) (1989). *Structural Adjustment in Africa.* London: Macmillan

Campbell, Ian (194). "Nigeria: The Election that Never Was!" *Democratization* Vol. 1 (2).

Carlsson, Jerker & Timothy M. Shaw.(eds) (1988). *Newly Industrializing Countries and the Political Economy of South-South Relations.* London: Macmillan.

Central Bank of Nigeria. *Annual Reports.* Lagos, annually.

Chikelu, G.P.O. *et al* (1985). "Implementation of the Lagos Plan of Action: Africa, Nigeria and Sierra Leone," *Dalhousie African Working Papers* Number 6, May.

Clarke, John D. (1986). *Yakubu Gowon - Faith in the Future.* London: Frank Cass.

Clarke, Peter. (1988). "Islamic Reform in Contemporary Nigeria: Methods and Aims," *Third World Quarterly* 10(2), April: 519-538.

Cohen, Robin,Index. (1984). *Labour and Politics in Nigeria.* London: Heinemann.

Coleman, James S. (1958). *Nigeria: Background to National-ism.* Berkeley: University of California Press.

_____. (1963). "The Foreign Policy of Nigeria," in Joseph E. Black & Kenneth W. Thompson (eds) *Foreign Policies in a World of Change.* New York: Harper & Row: 379-506

_____. and Carl Roseberg eds., *Political Parties and National Integration in Tropical Africa.* Berkeley: University of California Press.

Collins, Paul. (ed.) (1980). *Administration for Development in Nigeria.* Lagos: African Education Press.

_____. (1987). "Microeconomic effects of oil on poverty in Nigeria," *IDS Bulletin* 18(1), January: 55-60.

Crocker, W.R. (1936). *Nigeria: A Critique of British Colonial Administration*, London: Allen and Unwin.

Crowther, Michael. (1978). *The Story of Nigeria.* London: Faber

_____. (1981). *West Africa Under Colonial Rule* London: Hutchinson.

Daddieh, Cyril Kofie & Timothy M. Shaw (1984). "The Political Economy of Decision-making in Africa: The Cases of Recognition of Biafra and MPLA," *International Political Science Review* 5(2), January 1984: 21-46.

Derrick, Jonathan (1986). "Nigeria Marketing Boards-Decline and Fall," *West Africa* 3584, 12 May: 989-990 and 3585, 19 May: 1040-1043.

Diamond, Larry (1984). "Nigeria in Search of Democracy," *Foreign Affairs* 62(4), Spring: 905-927.

_____.(1985/6). "Nigeria Update," *Foreign Affairs* 64(2), Winter: 326-336.

_____. (1987a). "Issues in the Constitutional Design of a Third Nigerian Republic," *African Affairs*. April: 209-226.

_____. (1987b). "Nigeria between Dictatorship and Democracy," *Current History* May: 201-204 and 222-224.

_____. (1988a). *Nigeria in Search of Democracy*. Boulder: Lynne Rienner.

_____. (1988b). *Class, Ethnicity and Democracy in Nigeria: the Failure of the First Republic*. London: Macmillan.

_____. (1991a). "Nigeria's Search for a New Political Order," *Journal of Democracy* 2 (2) Spring: 54-69.

_____. (1991b). "Nigeria's Third Quest for Democracy," *Current History* May: 201-204 & 229-231.

_____.et. al.(1992). *Democracy, Transition and Structural Adjustment in Nigeria* (forthcoming).

Diejomaoh, Viemudia P. (1972). *Rural Development in Nigeria*. Ibadan: Ibadan University Press.

_____. (1982). "Nigerian social science research priorities for development," *Afrika Spectrum* 17(2): 151-161.

Dike, K. O. (1956). "John Beecroft 1790-1854: Her Britannic Majesty's Consul to the Bights of Benin and Biafra 1849-54" *Journal of the Historical Society of Nigeria* December.

Dudley, Billy J. (1968). *Parties and Politics in Northern Nigeria.* London: Frank Cass.

_____. (1973). *Instability and Political Order: Politics and Crisis in Nigeria.* Ibadan: Ibadan University Press.

_____. (1982). *An Introduction to Nigerian Government and Politics.* London: Macmillan

Economist. (1984). *The Political Economy of Nigeria.* London.

Economist Intelligence Unit (1982). *Nigeria: Economic Prospects to 1985. After the Oil Glut.* London: EIU Special Report Number 123.

Egboh, Edmund O. (1985) *Forestry Policy in Nigeria 1897-1960.* Nsukka: University of Nigeria Press

Egharevba, J.U. (1973). *A Short History of Benin* Benin-City: Ethiope.

Ekekwe, Eme (1985) "State and Economic Development in Nigeria," in Claude Ake ed., *Political Economy of Nigeria.* London: Longman.

_____. (1986). *Class and State in Nigeria.* London: Longman.

Ekoko, A. E. & M. A. Vogt (eds.) (1990). *Nigerian Defence Policy: Issues and Problems.* Lagos: Malthouse.

Ekuerhare, Bright U. (1996). *Studies in Pattern and Problems of Industrial Accumulation in Nigeria.* Lagos: Van Hurst.

Ekundare, R.O. (1973). *Economic History of Nigeria 1860-1960.* London: Methuen.

Ekwe-Ewe, Herbert (1985). "The Nigerian Plight: Shagari to Buhari," *Third World Quarterly* 7(3), July: 610-625.

Elaigwau, J. Isawa (1986). *Gowon.* Ibadan: West Books.

Eleazu, Uma (1986). "Privatization of Parastatals and Companies." *First Bank Quarterly Review.* June: 21-26.

English, M. C. (1959). *An Outline of Nigerian History .* London: Longman.

Environmental Rights Action Project (1996). *Ogoniland: A Plaundered Environment.* Lagos: Civil Liberties Organization.

Evans, Peter (1979). *Dependent Development: The Alliance of Multinational, State and Local Capital in Brazil.* Princeton: Princeton University Press.

Eyo, Ekpo & Frank Willett (eds) (1980). *Treasures of Ancient Nigeria.* New York: Knopf.

Ezebgobelu, E.E. (1986). *Developmental Impact of Technology Transfer. Theory and Practice: A Case of Nigeria, 1970-1982.* Frankfurt: Peter Lang.

Fadahunsi, Akin. (1979). "A review of the political economy of the industrialisation strategy of the Nigerian state, 1960-1980." *African Development* 4(2/3), April-September.

_____. and B. U. N. IGWE(eds.) (1989). *Capital Goods and Technological Change and Accumulation in Nigeria* Dakar: CODESRIA.

Falola, Toyin (ed) (1986). *Britain and Nigeria: Exploitation or Development?* London: Zed.

_____. & Julius O. Ihonvbere (1985). *The Rise and Fall of Nigeria's Second Republic, 1979-1963.* London: Zed.

_____. (eds) (1988). *Nigeria and the International Capitalist System.* Boulder: Lynne Reinner.

Fashoyin, Tayo (1981). *Industrial Relations in Nigeria.* London: Longman.

_____. (1986). *Income and Inflation in Nigeria.* London: Longman

Fasipe, Akintayo(ed.) (1990). *Nigeria's External Debt.* Ile-Ife: Obafemi Awolowo University Press.

Federal Government of Nigeria (n.d.) *Ogoni Crisis: The Untold Story.* Lagos: External Publicity Department, Federal Ministry of Information.

Feinstein, Alan (1987). *African Revolutionary: The Life and Times of Nigeria's Aminu Kano.* Boulder: Lynne Reinner. Second edition.

Feyide, M. O. (1987). *Oil in World Politics.* Lagos: University of Lagos Press.

Flint, John (1960). *Sir George Goldie and the Making of Nigeria.* London: OUP.

Forrest, Tom (1982). "Recent Developments in Nigerian Industrialisation," in Martin Fransman (ed) *Industry and Accumulation in Africa.* London: Heinemann.

_____. (1986). "The Political Economy of Civil Rule and the Economic Crisis in Nigeria, 1979-84." *Review of African Political Economy* 35, May: 4-26.

Freud, Bill (1978). "Oil Boom and Crisis in contemporary Nigeria." *Review of African Political Economy* 13, May-August: 91-100.

_____. (1981). *Capital and Labour in the Nigerian Tin Mines.* London: Longman.

Gambari, Ibrahim (1980). *Party Politics and Foreign Policy: Nigeria under the First Republic*. Zaria: Amadu Bello University Press.

Garba, Joe (1980). *Diplomatic Soldiering: Nigerian foreign policy, 1975-1979*. Ibadan: Spectrum.

Geary, Willialm (1965). *Nigeria Under British Rule* London: Frank Cass.

Glickman, Harvey ed., (1995). *Ethnic Conflict and Democratiation*. Atlanta: African Studies Association Press.

Goodall, Andrea. ed. (1994). *Shell Shocked: The Environmental and Social Costs of Living: Shell in Nigeria*. Amsterdam: Greenpeace.

Gowon, Yakubu. (1970). "Independence Day Broadcast to the Nation, October 1," Lagos: Federal Ministry of Information

Graf, William. (1989). *The Nigerian State: Political Economy, State, Class and the Political System in the Post-Colonial Era*. London: James Currey.

Hatch, John. (1974). *Africa Emergent: Africa's Problems Since Independence*. Chicago: Henry Regenery.

Helleiner, Gerald K. (1986). *Peasant Agriculture, Government and Economic Growth in Nigeria*. Homewood, IL: Irwin.

Herskovits, Jean (1975). "Africa's New Power." *Foreign Affairs* 53(2).

Hoffman, Adonis (1995-196). "Nigria: The Policy Conundrum," *Foreign Policy* (101) (Winter).

Hutchful, Eboe (1985). "Oil Companies and Environmental Pollution in Nigeria," in Claude Ake ed., *Politicl Economy of Nigeria*. London: Longman.

Ihonvbere, Julius O. (1982a). "Resource Availability and Foreign Policy Change: The Impact of Oil on Nigerian Foreign Policy Since Independence," *Afrika Spectrum* 2, pp. 163-181.

_____. (1982b). "Oil Revenues, Underdevelopment and Class Struggles in Nigeria," *Scandinavian Journal of Development Alternatives* Vol. II, 2, June, pp.45-63.

_____. (1982/83). "Social Aspects of Economic Integration: The Case of the Economic Community of West African States," *Korean Journal of International Studies* Vol. XIV, I, Winter, pp.3-22.

_____. (1983a). *The Oil Industry in Nigeria: An Annotated Bibliography*. Montreal: Centre for Developing-Area Studies, McGill University.

_____. (1983b). "Internal Dimensions of Nigeria's Foreign Policy Towards the West African Sub-Region," *ODU- A Journal of West African Studies* 24, July, pp. 10-29.

_____. (1984). "Foreign Policy of Dependent States: The Impact of Oil on Nigeria's Foreign Policy, 1960-1982," *Indian Journal of Political Science* Vol. XIII, I, January, pp.81-106.

_____. (1985). *The 1983 Elections and the Buhari Coup in Nigeria: Contradictions in a (semi) peripheral political Economy*. Halifax: Center for African Studies.

_____. and Kola Olufemi (1986). "Towards a Radical Study of Foreign Policies of Peripheral Societies," in A. O. Sanda and Olusola Ojo(eds.), *Issues in the Administration of Nigeria's Public Sector*. Ile-Ife: Ife University Press, pp.124-140.

_____. (1988) "Contradictions of Multi-Party Democracy in Peripheral formations: The Rise and Demise of Nigeria's Second Republic, 1979-1983," in Meyns, Peter and Dani Wadada Nabudere (eds), *Democracy and the One Party State in Africa*. Hamburg: Institute for African Studies, pp.257-281.

_____. and Eme N. Ekekwe (1988) "Dependent Capitalism, Structural Adjustment and Democratic Possibilities in Nigeria's Third Republic," *Afrika Spectrum* 3, pp. 273-292.

_____. &Timothy M. Shaw (1988a). "Nigerian Oil Workers in Contextual and Comparative Perspective," in Roger Southall (ed) *Labour and Unions in Asia and Africa: Contemporary Issues*. London: Macmillan.

_____. (1988b). *Towards a Political Economy of Nigeria: Petroleum and Politics at the (Semi) Periphery*. Aldershot: Gower.

_____.(ed.)(1990a). *The Political Economy of Crisis and Under Development in Africa: Selected Works of Claude Ake*. Lagos: JAD.

_____.(1990b). "The African Debt Crisis: Responses and Options," in G. O. Olusanya and A. Olukoshi (eds.), *The African Debt Crisis*. Lagos: NIIA, pp. 81-115.

_____.(1990c) "Structural Adjustment, the April 1990 Coup and Democratization in Nigeria," *Africa Quarterly* Vol. 29 (3-4): 17-39.

_____. and Toyin Falola (eds.) (1991a). *Oil and Nigeria's Political Economy*. Lagos: Longman

_____. (1991b) "Nigeria as Africa's Great Power: Constraints and Prospects for the 1990s," *International Journal* Vol. XLVI (3): 510-535.

_____. (1991c). "Structural Adjustment and Socio-Economic Crisis in Nigeria," *Plural Societies* Vol. 23, 3.

_____. (1991d). "Structural Adjustment, the April 1990 Coup and Democratization in Nigeria," *Africa Quarterly* Vol. 29, 3/4.

_____. (1991e). "Coups and Counter-Coups in Nigeria: A Critical Evaluation of the April 1990 Major Gideon Orka Coup," *Journal of Modern African Studies* Vol. 29, 4, December.

_____. (1991f). "Africa and the New World Order: Implications for the 1990s" *Iranian Journal of International Affairs*. Summer.

_____. (1991g). "The Dynamics of Change in Eastern Europe and Their Implications for Africa," *Coexistence: A Journal of East-West Relations* December.

_____. (1991f) "The Economic Crisis in Sub-saharan Africa: Depth, Dimensions and Prospects for Recovery," *The Journal of International Studies* (27): 41-69.

_____. (1991g) "A Critical Evaluation of the Failed 1990 Coup in Nigeria," *The Journal of Modern African Studies* Vol. 29 (4): 601-626.

_____. (1991h) "Structural Adjustment and Nigeria's Democratic Transition," *TransAfrica Forum* Vol.8 (3) (Fall 1991): 61-83.

_____. (1991i) "The Military and Political Engineering Under Structural Adjustment: The Nigerian Experience Since 1985," *Journal of Political and Military Sociology* Vol. 29 : 107-131.

_____. (1991j) "The Political Economy of Mental Health in Nigeria: A Case Study of Port Harcourt," (With Darlington Iwarimie-Jaja) *Man and Life* Vol. 17 (1-2): 41-64.

_____. (1991k) "Adjustment, Political Transition and the

Organization of Military Power in Nigeria,"
UFAHAMU Vol. XIX (1): 22-42.

_____. (1992a) "The Crisis of Structural Adjustment
Programs in Africa: Issues and Explanations,"
Philosophy and Social Action Vol. 18 (3): 49-63.

_____. (1992b) "Is Democracy Possible in Africa?: The
Elites, The People and Civil Society," *QUEST:
Philosophical Discussions* Vol. VI, (2): 84-108.

_____. (1993a) "Economic Crisis, Structural Adjustment
and Social Crisis in Nigeria," *World Development* Vol.
21, (1): 141-153.

_____. (1993b) "The State and Academic Freedom in Africa:
How African Academics Subvert Academic
Freedom," *Journal of Third World Studies* Vol. X, (2):
36-73.

_____. (1993c) "Prospects for Democracy in Nigeria,"
Peace and Democracy News Vol. VII, (2): 25-27.

_____. (1994a), *Nigeria: The Politics of Adjustment and
Democracy*. New Brunswick, NJ: Tranaction.

_____. (1994b)"The 'Irrelevant' State, Ethnicity and the
Quest for Nationhood in Africa," *Ethnic and Racial
Studies* Vol. 17, (1): 42-60. Republished in Manis
Kumar Raha (ed.), *Dimensions of Human Society and
Culture* (New Delhi: Gyan Publishing House, 1996):
56-73.

_____. (1994c) "The State and Environmental Degradation
in Nigeria: A Study of the 1988 Toxic Waste Dump
in Koko," *Journal of Environmental Systems* Vol. 23,
(3): 1-21.

_____. and Ola Rotimi Ajayi (1994d) "Democratic Impasse:
Remilitarization in Nigeria," *Third World Quarterly*
Vol. 15, (4): 657-677.

_____. (1994e) "Political Decay in Nigeria: Prospects for
Democracy in the 1990s," *COMPO REVIEW- A
Journal of Interdisciplinary Analysis of Nigerian
Issues* (Now *Journal of Nigerian Affairs*) Vol. 3, (1):
22-36.

_____. (1996a) "Are Things Falling Apart? The Military
and the Crisis of Democratisation in Nigeria," *The
Journal of Modern African Studies* Vol. 34, (2): 1-33.

_____. (1996b) "On the Threshold of Another False Start?:
A Critical Evaluation of Prodemocracy Movements
in Africa," *Journal of Asian and African Studies* Vol.
XXI, (1-2): 125-142.

Ikejiani, Okechukwu & M. Odinchezo (1986). *Nigeria: Political Imperative*. Enugu: Fourth Dimension.

Ikoku, S.G. (1985). *Nigeria's Fourth Coup d'Etat: Options for Modern Statehood*. Enugu: Fourth Dimension.

International Labour Office (1981). *First Things first: Meeting the Basic Needs of the People of Nigeria*. Addis Ababa: Jobs and Skills Programme for Africa.

Inwang, Edet (1982). "Nigeria-Foreign Policy: Seeking the Break-even Point," *South* 58.

Isichei, Elizabeth (1983). *A History of Nigeria*. London: Longman.

Iyayi, Festus (1986). "The Primitive Accumulation of Capital in Neo-Colony: the Nigerian Case," *Review of African Political Economy* 35, May: 27-39.

Joseph, Richard (1978). "Affluence and Underdevelopment: the Nigerian Experience," *Journal of Modern African Studies* 16(2): 221-239.

_____. (1983). "Class, State and Prebendal Politics in Nigeria," *Journal of Commonwealth & Comparative Politics* 21(3), November: 21-38.

_____. (1984). "The Overthrow of Nigeria's Second Republic," *Current History* 83, March: 121-124 and 138.

_____. (1988). *Democracy and Prebendal Politics in Nigeria: The Rise and Fall of the Second Republic*. Cambridge: Cambridge University Press.

Kayode, M.O. & Y.B. Usman(eds) (1985). *Economic and Social Development of Nigeria: Proceedings of National Conference on Nigeria Since Independence*. Volume 2. Zaria: Panel on Nigeria since Independence History Project.

Kemi, Tony Kebe (1982). *Isaac Boro: The Twelve Day Revolution*. Benin City: Idodo Umeh Publishers.

Kenyatta, Jomo (1965). *Facing Mount Kenya: Tribal Life of the Kikuyu*. New York: Vintage Press.

Kilby, Peter (1969). *Industrialization in an Open Economy: Nigeria, 1945-1966* London: Cambridge.

Kinney, Esi S(ed.) (1970). African Urban Studies Special issue on African urban music.

Kirk-Greene, Anthony & Douglas Rimmer (1981). *Nigeria Since 1970: A Political and Economic Outline*. London: Hodder & Stoughton.

Koehn, Peter (1989). "Competitive Transition to Civilian

Rule: Nigeria's First and Second Experiments," *The Journal of Modern African Studies* Vol. 27, (3).

Kraus, Jon (1982). "Nigeria under Shagari," *Current History* 81 (473).

Krymkowski, David & Raymond Hall (1990). "The African Development Dilemma Revisited: Theoretical and Empirical Explorations," *Ethnic and Racial Studies* Vol. 13, (3).

Kukah, Matthew Hassan (1993). *Religion, Politics and Power in Northern Nigeria*. Ibadan: Spectrum.

Lolomari, Odoliyi (1976). "The Evolution of Nigerian Oil Policy," in the Proceedings of the 1976 Annual Conference of the Nigeria Economic Society, University of Ibadan, Nigeria.

_____. (1995). "Oil Companies and Oil Communities as Partners in Development," in Kayode Soremkun (d.), *Perspectives on the Nigerian Oil Industry*. Lagos: Amkra Books.

Lubeck, Paul M. (1980). "Labour in Kano since the Petroleum Boom," *Review of African Political Economy* 13, September-December: 37-46.

_____. (ed) (1986). *The African Bourgeoisie: Capitalist Development in Nigeria, Kenya and the Ivory Coast*. Boulder: Lynne Rienner.

_____. (1987). *Islam and Urban Labour in Northern Nigeria: The Making of a Muslim Working Class*. Cambridge: Cambridge University Press.

Mackintosh, J.P. (ed), (1985). *Nigerian Government and Politics*. London: Longman.

Madiebo, A (1980). *The Nigerian Revolution and the Biafran Civil War*. Enugu: Fourth Dimension.

Madunagu, Edwin (1982). *Problems of Socialism: The Nigerian Challenge*. London: Zed.

_____. (1984). *Nigeria: The Economy and the People*. London: New Beacon.

Mainsara, A. M. (1982). *The Five Majors: Why They Struck*. Zaria: Hudahuda.

Marenin, Otwin (1988). "The Nigerian State as Process and Manager: A Conceptualization," *Comparative Politics*. January: 215-232.

Martin, Matthew, (1991), *The Crumbling Facade of African Debt Negotiations: No Winners* London: Macmillan.

Mazrui, Ali A. (1982). "Nigeria and the United States: The Need for Civility, the Dangers of Intimacy," *Orbis* 25 (Winter): 858-864.

_____. (1986). *The Africans: A Triple Heritage*. London: BBC.

_____. (1988). "African Islam and Competitive Religion: between revivalism and expansion," *Third World Quarterly* 10(2), April: 499-518.

Miles, Williams F.S. (1988). *Elections in Nigeria: A Grass Roots Perspective*. Boulder: Lynne Rienner.

Mohammed, Siddique & Tony Edoh& Tony Edoh (eds.) *Nigeria: A Republic in Ruins*. Zaria: Gaskiya.

Morel, E.D. (1968). *Nigeria: Its Peoples and Its Problems* London: Frank Cass.

Musa, Shehu, (1979). "Declining Government Revenue and Measures for Mobilization of Internal Resources for Economic Development and Self-Reliance," in *Self-Reliance and Self-Sufficiency: An Appraisal of the Nigerian Case*. Ibadan: NISER.

Mustapha, A.R. (1986). "The National Question and Radical Politics in Nigeria," *Review of African Political Economy* (37).

_____. (1992a). "Nigeria: The Challenge of Nationhood," *Nigerian Forum* (September-December).

_____.(1992b). "Structural Adjustment and Multiple Modes of Livelihood in Nigeria," in Peter Gbbon et. al. eds. *Authoritarianism, Democracy and Adjustment*. Uppsala: Nordiska: Afrikainstitutet.

Naanen, Ben (1995). "Oil Producing Minorities and the Restructuring of Nigerian Federalism: The Case of the Ogoni People," *Journal of Commonwealth and Comparative Politics* Vol. 33, 1.

Nicolson, I.F., (1969). *The Administration of Nigeria, 1900-1960*. Oxford: Clarendon.

Nigeria: A Country Study (1982). Washington: American University for US Government. *Nigeria Economic Review, Volume 1, 1986*. Lagos: John West.

Nigerian Economic Society (1986). *The Nigerian Economy: A Political Economy Approach*. London: Longman.

Nigeria, (1968). *First National Development Plan*. Lagos: Government Printer.

_____, (1970). *Second National Development Plan*. Lagos: Government Printer.

_____, (1975). *Third National Development Plan*. Lagos: Government Printer.

_____, (1981). *Fourth National Development Plan* Lagos: Government Printer.

Nigeria: The Effects of Population Factors on Social and Economic Development (1985). Lagos: Federal Ministry of Health and National Population Bureau, April. *Nigeria Year Book, 1987*. Lagos: Daily Times.

Nigeria: Yesterday and Today (1985) Lagos: National Commission for Museums and Monuments. "The Nigerian Economy: critical issues."(1986). *Africa Today* 33(4), Fourth Quarter: 3-69.

Nnoli, Okwudiba (1974). "Socio-Economic Insecurity and Ethnic Politics in Nigeria," *The African Review* Vol. IV, (1).

_____, (1978). *Ethnic Politics in Nigeria*. Enugu: Fourth Dimension.

_____, (ed) (1981). *Path to Nigerian Development*. Dakar: Codesria.

Nolutshungu, Sam C. (1983). "Islam and Nigerian Foreign Policy: Tradition and Social Criticism," in Adeed Dawisha (ed*) Islam and Foreign Policy*. Cambridge: Cambridge University Press for RIIA: 129-143.

Nossal, Kim R. (1996). "Canadian Sanctions Against Nigeria?" Brief to House of Commons Standing Committee on Foreign Affairs and International Trade, Ottawa, Ontario, Canada, (14 December).

Nwankwo, Arthur (1981). *Can Nigeria Survive?*Enugu: Fourth Dimension.

_____. (1987). *The Military Option for Democracy: Class, Power and Violence in Nigerian Politics*. Enugu: Fourth Dimension.

Nwokedi, Emeka (1994). "Nigeria's Democratic Transition: Explaining the Annulled 1993 Presidential Election," *Afrika Diskussionpapiere* (5).

_____.(1995). *Politics of Democratization: Changing Authoritarian Regimes in Sub-Saharan Africa*. Munster and Hamburg: LIT Verlag.

Nwosu, E.J. (ed) (1985). *Achieving Even Development in Nigeria: problems and prospects*. Enugu: Fourth Dimension for EDI, University of Nigeria.

Nzimiro, Ikenna (1975). "The Political and Social Implications of Multinational Corporations in Nigeria" in Carl Widstrand (ed) *Multinational Firms in Africa*.

Uppsala: Scandinavian Institute of African Studies: 210-243.

Obasanjo, Olusegun (1976). "Text of 1976/77 Budget Speech." Lagos: Federal Ministry of Information.

_____. (1977). "Text of 1977/78 Budget Speech." Lagos: Federal Ministry of Information.

_____. (1978). "Text of Nation-wide Broadcast, 21 September." Lagos: Federal Ministry of Information.

Odama, J. S. (1985). "SFEM in the Context of a Developing Economy" in J. Attah et. al. (eds.). *The Nigerian Economy Under (S)FEM* Zaria: Department of Economics, ABU.

Oculli, Okelo (1979). "Dependent Food Policy in Nigeria, 1975-1979," *Review of African Political Economy* 15/16, May-December: 63-74.

Odetola, T.O. (1975). "Economic Development and the Structure and Process of Economic Decision-Making," *Nigerian Journal of Economics and Social Studies* 17(1), March.

Ofeimun, Odia (1989). *The Poet Lied.* Lagos: Update Communications.

Ofoegbu, Maziray (1978). "Towards a new Philosophy of Foreign Policy for Nigeria," in A. Bolaji Akinyemi (ed) *Nigeria and and World: Readings in Nigerian Foreign Policy.* 116-135.

Ogunbadejo, Oye (1980). "Nigeria's Foreign Policy Under Military Rule, 1966-79," *International Journal,* 35(4) Autumn: 748-765.

_____. (1988). "Nigerian-Soviet Relations, 1960-87," *African Affairs* 87(346), January: 83:104.

Ogunbambi, R.O. (1985). "The Dilemmas of Nigeria's African Policy," *Journal of African Studies.* 12, 1, Spring: 10-13.

Ogunsanqo, Alaba (1986). *Our Friends; Their Friends: Nigeria's External Relations, 1960-1985.* Yaba:Alfa Communications.

_____. (1989). *Japanese Companies, Labour & Society: Lessons for Nigeria.* Lagos: NIIA.

Ogwu, U. JOY (1986). *Nigerian Foreign Policy: Alternative Futures.* Lagos: NIIA with Macmillan.

_____. and R. Omotayo Olaniyan(eds.) (1990). *Nigeria's International Economic Relations: Dimensions of Dependence and Change.* Lagos: NIIA.

Ohiorhenuan, John,F.E. (1984). " The Political Economy of
    Military Rule in Nigeria," *Review of Radical Political
    Economics* 16(2/3), Summer and Fall: 1-27.
_____."Oil, Debts and Democracy: Nigeria." (1986) *Review
    of African Political Economy* 37, December: 6-118.
Ojo, Olatunde J.B. (1980). "Nigeria and the Formation
    of ECOWAS," *International Organization* 34(4)
    Autumn: 571-604.
_____. (1984). "Nigeria" in Timothy M. Shaw & Olajide
    Aluko (eds) *Political Economy of African Foreign
    Policy: Comparative Analyses*. Aldershot: Gower:190-
    220.
Okereke, Okoro(ed.) (1986). *Co-operatives and the Nigerian
    Economy.* Nsukka: University of Nigeria Press.
Okigbo, P.N.C. (1982). *Nigeria's Financial System*. London:
    Longman.
Okolo, Amechi (1987). *Foreign Capital in Nigeria: Roots of
    Underdevelopment.* Lagos: Heartland.
Okorma, N.S. (ed) *A Guide to WAI.* Port Harcourt: Green
    International.
Okuntimo, Paul Major, (1994). "Restricted Memo RSIS/
    MILAD/LOO/94004 to the Military Administrator
    of Rivers State, Port Harcourt, July 12.
Olagunju, Tunji & Sam Oyovbaire eds. (1991). *For Their
    Tomorrow Gave Our Today: Selected Speeches of IBB
    Volume II.* Ibadan: Spectrum Books.
_____, Adele Jinadu & Sam Oyovbaire (1993). *Transition to
    Democracy in Nigeria 1985-1993.* Ibadan: Safari
    Books and Spectrum Books.
Olaniyan, Richard (ed) (1985). *Nigerian History and
    Culture.* London: Longman.
Olaniyan, Omotayo and Nwoke, Chibuzo(eds.) (1990).
    *Structural Adjustment in Nigeria: The Impact of SFEM
    on the Economy.* Lagos: Nigerian Institute of Inter-
    national Affairs(NIIA).
Olatunbosun, Dupe (1975). *Nigeria's Neglected Rural
    Majority.*Ibadan: OUP for NIIA.
Ologin, S.O. *et al. 1985 Modelling Nigeria's Economic Develop-
    ment.* Ibadan: Ibadan University Press, Centre for
    Econometric and Applied Research.
Olojede, Dele & Onukaba Adinnoyi-Ojo (1987). *Born to Run:
    The Story of Dele Giwa.* Ibadan: Spectrum.
Olowu, Dele (1991). "The Literature on Nigerian Federal-

ism: A Critical Appraisal," *Publius: The Journal of Federalism* Vol. 21, (4).

Olugbode, Kola, (1992). "The Nigerian State and the Quest for a Stable Polity" *Comparative Politics* 24 (3) April, 293-316.

Olukoshi, Adebayo O. (ed). (1990). *Crisis and Adjustment in the Nigerian Economy.* Lagos: JD Press.

_____. (ed.) (1991). *Nigeria's External Debt Crisis: Its Management.* Lagos: Malthouse.

_____. (ed.) (1993a). *The Politics of Structural Adjustment in Nigeria.* London: James Currey.

_____. (1993b). "The Current Transition From Military Rule in Nigeria," Mimeo.

_____. & Osita Agbu (1996). "The Deepening Crisis of Nigerian Federalism and the Future of the Nation-State," in Adebayo O. Olukoshi and Liisa Laakso (eds.), *Challenges to the Nation-State in Africa.* Uppsala: Nordiska Afrikainstitutet.

Olusanya, G.O. & R.A. Akindele (eds) (1986). "Nigeria's External Relations: Agenda for the Future," *Nigerian Journal of International Affairs* 12 (1 & 2).

_____. and Adebayo Olukoshi(eds.) (1989). *The African Debt Crisis.* Lagos: NIIA

Omoweh, Daniel A. (1994). *The Role of Shell Petroleum Development Company and the State in the Underdevelopment of the Niger Delta of Nigeria, 1937-1987.* Ph.D. Dissertation, Obafemi Wolowo University, Il-Ife.

_____. (1996a). "The Crisis of State Capitalism and Adjustment in the Nigerian Petroleum Industry," *21st Century Afro Review* Vol. 2, (1).

_____. (1996b) "Environment and Rural Poverty in the Oil-Producing Areas of Nigeria." Paper presented at the 1996 Annual Meeting of the Association of Third World Studies, Troy State University, Montgomery, Alabama.

Oni, Ola and Bade Onimode (1975). *Economic Development in Nigeria: A Marxist Alternative.* Ibadan: Nigerian Academy of Arts, Sciences and Technology.

Onimode, Bade (1977). "A Critique of Planning Concepts and Methodology in Nigeria," *Review of Black Political Economy* 7(3), Spring.

_____. (1982). *Imperialism and Underdevelopment in Nigeria.* London: Zed.

Onoge, O. (1993). *Nigeria: The Way Forward*. Ibadan: Spectrum Books.

Onokerhoraye, Andrew G. (1984). *Social Services in Nigeria*. London: Kegan Paul International.

Orr, Charles (1965). *The Making of Northern Nigeria*. London: Frank Cass.

Osaghae, Eghosa (1990). "Social Mobilization as a Political Myth in Africa," *Africa Quarterly* Vol. 30 (3-4).

_____. (1995a). *Structural Adjustment and Ethnicity in Nigeria*. Uppsala: Nordiska Afrkainstitutet, Research Report No. 98.

_____. (1995b). "The Ogoni Uprising: Oil Politics, Minority Agitation and the Future of the Nigerian State," *African Affairs* (94).

_____. (1996). "Human Rights and Ethnic Conflict Management: The Case of Nigeria," *Journal of Peace Research* Vol. 33, (2) (1996).

Osoba, Segun (1972). "Ideology and Planning for National Economic Development, 1946-72," in Mahmad Tukur & Tunji Olangunju (eds) *Nigeria: In Search of a Viable Polity*. Zaria: ABU Press.

_____. (1977). "The Nigerian Power Elite, 1952-1965," in Peter C.W. Gutkind & Peter Watermann (eds) *African Social Studies - A Radical Reader*, New York: Monthly Review, 368-382.

_____. (1978). "The Deepening Crisis of the Nigerian National Bourgeoisie," *Review of African Political Economy* 13, May-August: 63-77.

_____. (1980). "The Economic Foundations of Nigeria's Foreign Policy During the First Republic, 1960-1965," in I.A. Akinjogbin and S.O. Osoba (eds) *Topics on Nigerian Economic and Social History*. Ife: University of Ife Press: 208-233.

Ostheimer, John M., (1973). *Nigerian Politics*. New York: Harper & Row.

Osundare, Niyi (1987). *Songs of the Market Place*. Ibadan: New Horn Press.

Othman, Shehu (1986). "Reflections on Nigeria Super Power Relations," *Nigerian Journal of International Affairs* 12(1 & 2): 35-45.

_____. (1984). "Classes, Crises and Coups: the Demise of Shagari's Regime," *African Affairs* 83, 333, October: 446-456.

Otite, Onigu (1990). *Ethnic Pluralism and Ethnicity in Nigeria*. Ibadan: Shoneson.

Owoade, M.A. (1990). *Law of Homicide in Nigeria*. Ile-Ife: Obafemi Awolowo University Press.

Oyavbaire, S. Egite (1985). *Federalism in Nigeria*. London: Macmillan.

Oyediran, Oyeleye, (ed) (1978). *Survey of Nigerian Affairs, 1975*. Ibadan: OUP for NIIA.

_____. (1979). *Nigerian Government and Politics Under Military Rule, 1966-79*. London: Macmillan.

_____. (ed) (1981). *Survey of Nigerian Affairs, 1976-77*. Lagos: Macmillan for NIIA.

_____. and Adigun Agbaje (1991). "Two-Partyism and Democratic Transition in Nigeria,"*The Journal of Modern African Studies* Vol. 29, (2).

Oyejide, T.A. *et al* (1985). *Nigeria and the IMF*. Ibadan: Heinemann.

Panter-Brick S.K. (ed) (1970). *Nigerian Politics and Military Rule*. London: Athlone.

_____. (1978). *Soldiers and Oil: The Political Transformation of Nigeria*. London: Frank Cass.

Parfitt, Trevor & Stephen Riley (1989). *The African Debt Crisis*. London: Routeledge.

Rimmer, Douglas (1986). "The Overvalued Currency and Over- Administered Economy of Nigeria". *African Affairs* 84(336), July: 435-446.

Sanda, Akinade (1986). "Minimum Government and the Sociology of Public Administration in Nigeria," *University of Ife*, June.

Sano, Hans-Otto (1983). *The Political Economy of Food in Nigeria, 1960-1982*. Uppsala: Scandinavian Institute of African Studies. Research Report Number 65.

Saro-Wiwa, Ken (1994). *Genocide in Nigeria: The Ogoni Story*. Port Harcourt and London: Saros Star Series.

Schatz, Sayre P. (1977). *Nigerian Capitalism*. Berkeley: University of California Press.

_____. (1981). "Nigeria's Petro-Political Fluctuation," *Issue* 11 (Spring and Summer): 35-40.

_____. (1982). "The Nigerian Economy since the Great Oil-Price Increases of 1973-74," *Africa Today* 29, Third Quarter: 33-42.

Shagari, President Alhaji Shehu (1981). "Annual Foreign Policy Address," *Nigerian Forum* 1 August: 46-50.

Shaw, Timothy M. (1983). "Nigeria in the International System," In *The Political Economy of Nigeria,* edited by I. William Zartman. New York: Praeger: 207-236.

_____. (1985). "Nigerian Coups and Foreign Policy," *International Perspectives,* November/December: 17-19.

_____. (1987). "Nigeria Restrained: Foreign Policy Under Changing Political and Petroleum Regimes," *The Annals* 489, January: 40-50.

_____. & Julius Ihonvbere (1989). "Nigeria," in Julius Nyang'oro & Timothy M. Shaw (eds) *Corporatism in Africa.* Boulder: Westview, pp.83-103.

_____. & Olajide Alukoi (eds) (1983). *Nigerian Foreign Policy: Alternative Perceptions and Projections.* London: Macmillan.

_____. (eds) (1984). *Africa Projected: From Recession to Renaissance by the year 2000?* London: Macmillan.

_____. & Orobola Fasehun (1980). "Nigeria in the World System: Alternatives Approaches, Explanations and Projections," *Journal of Modern African Studies* 18(4), December: 551-573.

Shenton, Robert W. (1986). *The Development of Capitalism in Northern Nigeria.* London: James Currey.

Sklar, Richard S. Klar, Richards. (1963). *Nigerian Political Parties.* Princeton: Princeton University Press.

Smith, Patrick (1986). "The Entrepreneurs," *New African* 226, July: 65:66.

Smock, D. (1969). *Conflict and Control in an African Trade Union a study of the Nigerian Coal Miners Union.* Stanford: Stanford University Press.

Solodovnikov, V. G.(ed.) (1969). *Africa Today* Moscow: Progress.

Soremekun, Kayode (ed.) (1995). *Perspectives on the Nigerian Petroleum Industry.* Lagos: Amkra Books.

_____. and Cyril Obi (1993). "The Changing Pattern of Private Foreign Investments in the Nigerian Oil Industry," *Africa Development* Vol. XVIII, (3).

_____. and Folake Okediran (1995). "The Response of the Oil Sector to Nigeria's Economic Recession (1983-1985)," in Kayode Soremekun (ed.) *Perspectives on the Nigerian Petroleum Industry.* Lagos: Amkra Books.

Soyinka, Wole (1965). *The Interpreters.* London: Andre Deutsch.

_____. (1996) *The Open Sore of a Continent: A Personal Narrative of the Nigerian Crisis.* Oxford: Oxford University Press.

Stremlau, Johns S. (1977). *The International Politics of the Nigerian Civil War.* Princeton: Princeton University Press.

_____. (1981). "The Fundamentals of Nigeria Foreign Policy," *Issue* 11 (Spring/Summer): 46-50

Suberu, Rotimi (1992). "Federalism and the Transition to Democratic Governance in Nigeria," in B. Caron, A. Gboyega, and E. Osaghae (eds.), *Democratic Transition in Africa.* Ibadan: CREDU.

_____. (1993). "The Travails of Federalism in Nigeria," *Journal of Democracy* Vol. 4, (4).

Takaya, Bala J. & Sonnie Gwale Tyoden (eds) (1987). *The Kaduna Mafia: A Study of the Rise, Development and Consolidation of a Nigerian Power Elite.* Jos: Jos University Press.

Tijjani, Aminu & David Williams (eds) (1981). *Shehu Shagari: My Vision of Nigeria.* London: Frank Cass.

"Towards 1992" (1987) (5-part series). *West Africa* 3651-3655, 3-31 August: 1482-3, 1530-3, 1578-80.

Toyo, Eskor, (1967). *The Working Class and the Nigerian Crisis.* Ibadan: Sketch Publishing Company

Tukur, Mahmud & Tunji Olagunju(eds.) (1972). *Nigeria: in Search of a Viable Polity.* Zaria: ABU Press.

Turner, Terisa (1976a). "Multinational Corporations and the Instability of the Nigerian State," *Review of African Political Economy* 5, January-April: 39-45.

_____, (1976b). "The Transfer of Technology and the Nigerian State," *Development and Change* 7:353-390.

Udogu, Ike (1990). "National Integration Attempts in Nigerian Politics 1979-1984," *Canadian Review of Studies in Nationalism.* Vol. XVII, (1-2).

_____. (1994). "The Allurement of Ethninalionalism in Nigerian Politics: The Contemporary Debate," *Journal of Asian and African Studies* Vol. XXIX, (3-4)

Unrepresented Nations and Peoples Organization (1995). *Ogoni-Report of the UNPO Mission to Investigate the Situation of the Ogoni of Nigeria, February 17-26 1995.* The Hague: UNPO.

Usman, Yusufu Bala (1979). *For the Liberation of Nigeria.* London: New Beacon.

_____. (1986). _Nigeria Against the IMF: The Home Market Strategy._ Kaduna: Vanguard.

_____. (1987) *The Manipulation of Religion in Nigeria, 1977-1987.* Kaduna: Vanguard.

Uvieghara, E.E.(1975). *Trade Union Law in Nigeria* Benin-City: Ethiope.

Uwazurike, Chudi, (1990). "Confronting Potential Break-down: The Nigerian Redemocratization Process in Critical Perspective," *The Journal of Modern African Studies* Vol. 28, (1).

Wallerstein, I. (1993). "Ethnicity and National Integration in West Africa," in Gregory Maddox and Timothy Welliver, eds., *Colonialism and Nationalism in Africa.* New York: Garland Press.

Washington, Deborah (1996). *OGONI-The Struggle Continues.* Geneva and Nairobi: World Council of Churches and All African Conference of Churches.

Waterman, Christopher Alan (1990). *JUJU- A Social History and Ethnography of An African Popular Music.* Chicago: University of Chicago Press

Waterman, Peter (1983). *Aristocrats and Plebeians in African Unions? Lagos Port and Dock Workers Organisation and Struggle.* The Hague: Institute for Social Studies.

Watts, Micahel J. (ed) (1987). *State, Oil and Agriculture in Nigeria.* Berkeley: University of California, Institute of International Studies.

Williams, David (1982). *President and Power in Nigeria: the life of Shehu Shagari.* London: Frank Cass.

Willliams, Gavin (1976a). "Taking the Part of Peasants: Rural Development in Nigeria and Tanzania," in P.C.W. Gutkind & I. Wallerstein (eds) *The Political Economy of Contemporary Africa.* Beverly Hills: Sage, 131-154.

_____. (ed) (1976b). *Nigeria: Economy and Society.* London: Rex Collings.

_____. (1980). *State and Society in Nigeria.* Idandre: Afrografika.

WIN Document: Conditions of Women in Nigeria and Policy Recommendations to 2000 AD (1985). Zaria: WIN. *Women in Nigeria* (1986). London: Zed.

Wright, Stephen1981). "Limits of Nigeria's Power Overseas,"*West Africa* 3339 (27 July): 1685-1686.

_____. (1986a). *Nigeria: The Dilemmas Head. A Political Risk Analysis.* London: EIU, November. Special Report # 1072.

_____. (1986b). "Nigeria: Rising Hopes but Declining Fortunes," in Colin Legum (ed) *Africa Contemporary Record Volume 18, 1985-86.* New York: Africana.

Young, Andrew (1981). "The United States and Africa: Victory For Diplomacy," *Foreign Affairs* 59(3): 648-666.

Young, Crawford (1979). *The Politics of Cultural Pluralism.* Madison: University of Wisconsin Press.

Zartman, I. William (ed) (1983). *The Political Economy of Nigeria.* New York: Preager.

_____. (1995). *Collapsed States: The Disintegration and Restoration of Legitimate Authority.* Boulder: Lynne Rienner.

MAGAZINES

Newswatch
TELL
THE NEWS
TEMPO
The African Guardian
The Analyst
THISWEEK
African Concord
Quality
West Africa(London)
Probe
Newbreed
The President
Times International
Development Outlook
The Nigerian Economist
Labour Militant

NEWSPAPERS

New Nigerian
Nigerian Observer
Nigerian Tide
Daily Times
National Concord
The Guardian
Daily Champion
The Nigerian Standard
The Nigerian Observer
The Democrat
The Nigerian Herald
Satellite
The Nigerian Tribune
The Triumph
The Punch
Daily Star
The Standard

INDEX